Books should be returned or renewed by the
last date stamped above

940·5421

BENNETT, Gill

The end of the war in Europe

The End
of the War
in Europe
1945

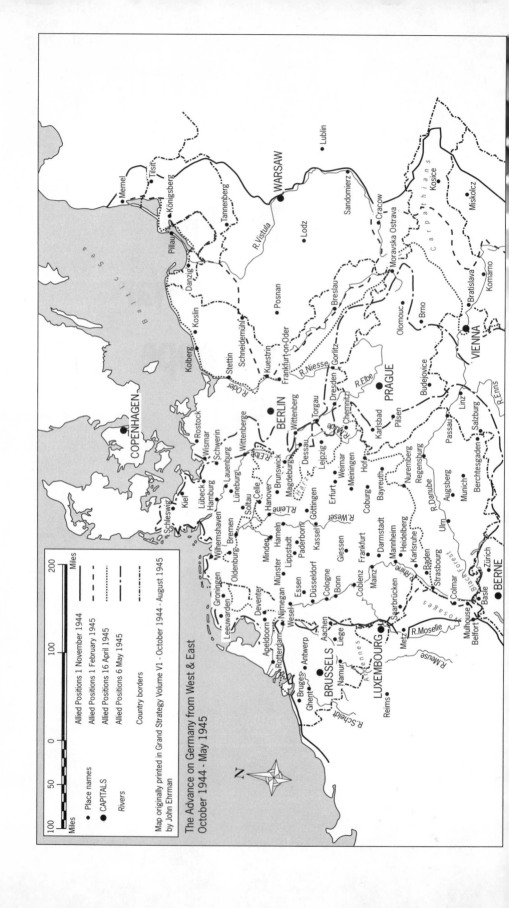

The Advance on Germany from West & East
October 1944 - May 1945

Map originally printed in Grand Strategy Volume VI - October 1944 - August 1945
by John Ehrman

Place names
CAPITALS
Rivers

Allied Positions 1 November 1944
Allied Positions 1 February 1945
Allied Positions 16 April 1945
Allied Positions 6 May 1945

Country borders

Miles
100   50   0   100   200

Miles

The End
of the War
in Europe
1945

Edited by Gill Bennett

London:HMSO

© Crown Copyright 1996

Applications for reproduction should be made to
HMSO Copyright Unit, St Clements House, 2-16 Colegate, Norwich NR3 1BQ

ISBN 0 11 702035 4

British Library Cataloguing in Publication Data
A CIP catalogue record for this book is available from the British Library

Already published in the series:
Britain and Norway in the Second World War EDITED BY PATRICK SALMON

Published by HMSO and available from:

HMSO Publications Centre
(Mail, fax and telephone orders only)
PO Box 276, London SW8 5DT
Telephone orders 0171 873 9090
General enquiries 0171 873 0011
(queuing system in operation for both numbers)
Fax orders 0171 873 8200

HMSO Bookshops
49 High Holborn, London WC1V 6HB
(counter service only)
0171 873 0011 Fax 0171 831 1326
68–69 Bull Street, Birmingham B4 6AD
0121 236 9696   Fax 0121 236 9699
33 Wine Street, Bristol BS1 2BQ
0117 9264306 Fax 0117 9294515
9–21 Princess Street, Manchester M60 8AS
0161 834 7201 Fax 0161 833 0634
16 Arthur Street, Belfast BT1 4GD
01232 238451 Fax 01232 235401
71 Lothian Road, Edinburgh EH3 9AZ
0131 228 4181 Fax 0131 229 2734
The HMSO Oriel Bookshop
The Friary, Cardiff CF1 4AA
01222 395548 Fax 01222 384347

HMSO's Accredited Agents
(see Yellow Pages)

and through good booksellers

Contents

Preface

SIR WILLIAM DEAKIN

The International Committee for the History of the Second World War was formed in Paris in 1967 following a series of international conferences on the history of the Resistance in Occupied Europe. I was invited to form a British Section, in which I brought together a small group of leading historians and heads of the relevant official archives. The Imperial War Museum provided an administrative base and secretariat. With grants from the Wolfson and Astor Foundations I initiated an experimental programme. Besides inviting individual historians to participate in conferences held abroad, the British Section has held a series of bilateral meetings with foreign counterparts (so far, from Belgium, France, the former German Federal Republic, Japan, the USA, Italy, Norway and former Yugoslavia), and a number of international conferences, the latest of which is the subject of this book.

The Committee would like to thank Sir Michael Howard, who wrote the synopsis upon which the programme for the conference was constructed. The Committee thanks all who took part, whether as paper-writers or as invited observers and participants in the discussions.

The Committee also wishes to record its thanks to the Warden and Fellows of St Antony's College, Oxford, for permission to hold the conference in the College during the period 4-6 April 1995, and to those who contributed to the costs of the event, namely the Gerry Holdsworth Charitable Trust, the Cabinet Office, and through the Imperial War Museum Trust, Sir Alexander Glen and the Dulverton Trust. Thanks are also due to the organisers, Jonathan Chadwick (Imperial War Museum) and Dr Ann Lane (Queen's University, Belfast) and to the editor, Gill Bennett (Head of Historians, Foreign and Commonwealth Office).

Extracts from documents in the Public Record Office and from HMSO publications are published by permission of the Controller of HM Stationery Office. The chapter by Sir Frank Roberts was first published in the *NATO Review*, October 1985, and is reprinted by permission of the Editor.

Notes on the contributors

Correlli Barnett is the author of such distinguished books as *The Desert Generals, The Swordbearers, Britain and Her Army* (Royal Society of Literature's Heinemann Award 1970), *Marlborough, Bonaparte* and *Engage the Enemy More Closely: the Royal Navy in the Second World War* (Yorkshire Post Book of the Year Award 1991). His challenging study of Britain's poor performance as an industrial country during the Second World War, *The Audit of War: the Illusion and Reality of Britain as a Great Nation* (1986) has had major impact in the fields of industry, education, Westminster and Whitehall. *The Lost Victory: British Dreams, British Realities 1945-1950* was published in 1995. From 1977 until March 1995 he was Keeper of the Churchill Archives Centre, Cambridge, and he continues to be a Fellow of Churchill College. From 1973-85 he was also a Member of the Council of the Royal United Services Institute for Defence Studies, and in 1991 was awarded the Institute's Chesney Gold Medal for his contribution to military history. In 1993 he was awarded the degree of Doctor of Science (Honoris Causa) by Cranfield University.

Dr Martin Conway is Fellow and Tutor in Modern History at Balliol College in the University of Oxford. He is the author of *Collaboration in Belgium: Léon Degrelle and the Rexist Movement 1940-1944* (1993) and of a number of articles on the history of Belgium during the war years. He is currently working on a study of the Liberation of Belgium.

Norman Davies is Professor, History Department, School of Slavonic and East European Studies, University of London, and author of numerous books on Polish history. These include *God's Playground: a History of Poland* (2 vols, 1981) and *Heart of Europe: a Short History of Poland* (1984). He has lectured at many places round the world, having served as visiting professor at Columbia, McGill (Canada), Hokkaido (Japan), Stanford and Harvard. Although all his works were banned by the communist censorship in Poland prior to 1989, they are now widely translated. In recent years, he has been decorated with the Commander's Cross of Poland's Order of Merit, and has been awarded an honorary doctorate at the Marie-Curie Sklodowska University in Lublin and the Medal of the University of Warsaw. His *Europe: a history* will shortly be published by Oxford University Press.

Dr Dennis Deletant is Reader in Romanian Studies at the School of Slavonic and East European Studies, University of London. He is the author of a number of studies on aspects of Romanian history, his most recent volume being *Studies in Romanian History* (1991).

David Dilks taught at the London School of Economics from 1962 to 1970, when he became Professor of International History at the University of Leeds. In the autumn of 1991 he moved to Hull as Vice-Chancellor. He was previously Research Assistant to the Earl of Avon (formerly Mr Anthony Eden), Marshal of the Air Force Lord Tedder, and Mr Harold Macmillan (later Earl of Stockton). He was a contributor to *The Conservatives* edited by Lord Butler; editor of and a contributor to *Retreat from Power* (2 vols) and *The Missing Dimension: Governments and Intelligence Communities in the Twentieth Century* (with Christopher Andrew); editor of *The Diaries of Sir Alexander Cadogan*; author of *Curzon in India* (2 vols) and *Neville Chamberlain: Pioneering and Reform*; editor (with Professor John Erickson) of *Barbarossa: The Axis and the Allies*; editor of (with Professor Klaus-Jürgen Müller) and a contributor to *Grossbritannien und der deutsche Widerstand*. He is author of numerous articles and has been President of the International Committee for the History of the Second World War since 1992.

John Erickson is Professor of Defence Studies, University of Edinburgh. He is the author of *The Soviet High Command 1918-1941; The Road to Stalingrad; The Road to Berlin; Soviet Military Power;* joint author of *Soviet Ground Forces: An Operational Assessment*; and joint editor of and a contributor to *Barbarossa: The Axis and the Allies*. He is currently completing *Tsars, Generals, Commissars: The Russian General Staff 1716-1964.*

M R D Foot was a British army officer from 1939 to 1945, mostly working on intelligence duties; served as a parachutist in Brittany; taught at Oxford; was briefly Professor of Modern History at Manchester. He has written several books on SOE and on Resistance, including the official history of SOE in France.

Sir David Hunt was, before the war, a Fellow of Magdalen College, Oxford, specialising in Greek archaeology. He served with the First Battalion of the Welch regiment in Egypt and Greece from 1940, and from 1943 to 1945 as GSO1 and Colonel GS (Intelligence) to Field Marshal Alexander, whose war despatches he subsequently composed. Now retired from HM Diplomatic Service, he was formerly High Commissioner in Uganda, Cyprus and Nigeria, and Ambassador to Brazil. He is author of *A Don at War; On the Spot: An Ambassador Remembers* and *Footprints in Cyprus*. He has been Chairman of the Commonwealth Institute and of the Classical Association and President of the Society for the Promotion of Hellenic Studies.

Malcolm Mackintosh was Assistant Secretary in the Cabinet Office dealing with Soviet and East European affairs. He has been Hon Senior Research Fellow, Kings College, London, since 1987, and was a Senior Fellow in Soviet Studies at the International Institute for

Strategic Studies in London from 1989 to 1991. Since 1991 he has been Hon Lecturer in International Relations at the University of St Andrews. He served in the army from 1941 to 1946 in the Middle East, Italy and the Balkans, and was a member of the British Military Mission in the Allied Control Commission in Bulgaria from 1944 to 1946. He is the author of *Strategy and Tactics of Soviet Foreign Policy; Juggernaut: A History of the Soviet Armed Forces*, and chapters on Soviet and Warsaw Pact affairs.

Dr Klaus-Jürgen Müller is Professor Emeritus of Modern and Contemporary History at the University of the Bundeswehr, Hamburg, Germany, and Professor in the Department of History at the University of Hamburg. For several years he was President of the (West) German Committee for the History of the Second World War and President of the *Comité Franco-Allemand de Recherches sur l'Histoire de la France et de l'Allemagne*. He is author of *Das Heer und Hitler* (1969, 2nd edn 1989), *General Ludwig Beck* (1981), *The Army, Politics and Society in Germany* (1987); editor of *The Military in Politics and Society in France and Germany in the Twentieth Century* (1995), and, with David Dilks, of *Grossbritannien und der deutsche Widerstand* (1994). He was Visiting Professor at the Universities of Tel Aviv, Paris IV Sorbonne and Montpellier, and Visiting Fellow of St Antony's College, Oxford.

Dr Maurice Pearton is Honorary Fellow, School of Slavonic and East European Studies, University of London, and was formerly Reader in Political Science, Richmond College, London. He is a member of the International Institute for Strategic Studies and the Royal Institute for International Affairs. He is author of *Oil and the Romanian State* and *The Knowledgeable State: Diplomacy, War and Technology since 1830,* and of articles on Anglo-Romanian relations.

Dr Olav Riste is Director of Research at the Norwegian Institute for Defence Studies, Adjunct Professor of History at Bergen University, and Fellow of the Norwegian Academy of Science and Letters. He was Senior Scholar, St Antony's College, 1959-62 and obtained his DPhil at Oxford in 1963. His published works include a two-volume work on Norway in the wartime alliance.

Sir Frank Roberts, during his long diplomatic career (1930-1968), was British Chargé d'Affaires in Moscow at the end of the war, while serving there as Minister from 1945 to 1947. He was later Ambassador in Belgrade, at NATO and in Moscow and Bonn, retiring in 1968, when he became a member of the Foreign Secretary's Committee to advise on British Overseas Representation. During his career he was Private Secretary to Ernest Bevin. Since his retirement he has held and still holds many senior appointments with major international companies, and in international business organisations. He is also or has been President or Chairman of many voluntary international organisations, most of them concerned with NATO, Anglo-Russian and Anglo-German relations, and has been active in the media, including Radio Free Europe, Radio Liberty and the European Media Institute.

Dr Peter Romijn has been a Research Fellow of *Rijksinstituut voor Oorlogsdocumentatie*, the Netherlands State Institute for War Documentation, since 1985, and its Deputy Director since 1991. He is the Treasurer of the International Committee for the History of the Second World War. He studied history in Gröningen University and in 1989 defended his doctoral dissertation in the same University on the Problem of Collaboration and Collaborators in Post-War Dutch Politics (1945-1955). He has published on this theme, as well as on historiographical subjects, on the persecution of Dutch Jews and on the Second World War in the Pacific. His current research deals with the role of local government in the German-occupied Netherlands as an instrument of the politics of nazification.

Oleg Rzheshevsky is Professor at the Institute of World History in Moscow. Born in Leningrad in 1924, he was educated at the Air Force School, Military Institute. He is a Colonel (Retd) and is Chairman of the Russian Association of Second World War Historians. He is author and editor of several books including *War and History* (1976, 1984), Russian editions of *B Liddell Hart: History of the Second World War* (1976) and *Michael Howard: Grand Strategy* (1980). His forthcoming work in English is *War and Diplomacy: Documents from Stalin's personal archive*, to be published in 1995 by Harwood Academic Publishers.

Christopher Seton-Watson served in the Royal Horse Artillery from 1939 to 1945, ending up as a major commanding a battery throughout the advance up Italy from Cassino to Bologna in 1944-45. Immediately after demobilisation he was elected to a Fellowship and Lectureship in Politics at Oriel College, Oxford, where he taught from 1946 until his retirement in 1983. He has made contemporary Italian history and politics his main interest. His major publications have been *Italy From Liberalism to Fascism 1870-1925;* jointly with his brother Hugh, *The Making of a New Europe: R W Seton-Watson and the Last Years of Austria-Hungary 1906-20;* and most recently, *Dunkirk-Alamein-Bologna: Letters and Diaries of an Artilleryman 1939-45*. In 1982 he founded the Association for the Study of Modern Italy (ASMI).

Dr Peter Sipos is a senior research adviser at the Institute for History of the Hungarian Academy of Sciences, and Professor at the Faculty of Humanities of the Eötvös Loránd University in Budapest. He is a Doctor of Philosophy and Academic Doctor of Historical Studies. He is author of several books and studies on Hungarian political and social history in the 20th century. He takes part regularly in international conferences and seminars. He is a member of the Board for History of the Hungarian Academy of Sciences and Chairman of the Hungarian National Committee for the History of the Second World War.

*

Dr Vilém Precan, Director of the Institute of Contemporary History in Prague, was also a Contributor to the Conference and delivered a paper on *The End of the Second World War in Czechoslovakia*. Unfortunately, however, it has not been possible to include his paper in this printed collection.

*

The spelling of proper names specified by individual authors has been retained.

*

Participants in the Conference

In addition to the paperwriters, among those who accepted invitations to attend part or all of the Conference on the End of the War in Europe, 1945, held in the Nissan Institute of St Antony's College, Oxford, and to take part in the debates and oral presentations were:

François Bédarida, Gill Bennett, Ralph Bennett, Dr Geoffrey Best, Dr Dusan Biber, David Brown, The Lord Bullock, Dr Lucio Ceva, Jonathan Chadwick, Christopher Cviic, Sir William and Lady Deakin, Dr Anne Deighton, Sir Douglas Dodds-Parker, Sir Alexander Glen, Dr Viktor Gobarev, Professor John Gooch, Harry Hanak, Dr Alistair Horne, Professor Sir Michael Howard, Dr Magdalena Hulas, Professor Domokos Kosáry, Dr Ann Lane, Ambassador Jean Marie Le Breton, Group Captain Ian Madelin, Dr Aglika Markova, Sir Carol Mather, Professor Williamson Murray, Dr Anthony Nicholls, Sir Brooks Richards, Dr Patrick Salmon, George Schöpflin, John Whitney Shephardson, Dr Harry Shuckman, Sir Peter Thorne, Sarah Tyacke, Dr Jera Vodusek Staric, Alexandra Ward, Sir Peter Wilkinson and Christopher Woods.

Abbreviations

ACC	Allied Control Commission
AHFQ	Allied Force Headquarters
AMGOT	Allied Military Government of Occupied Territory
CAB	Cabinet Office
CCS	Combined Chiefs of Staff
CIGS	Chief of the Imperial General Staff
CinC	Commander-in-Chief
ERP	European Recovery Proggramme
FO	Foreign Office
GFSG	Group of Soviet Forces in Germany
JIC	Joint Intelligence Committee
MMLA	*Missions Militaires de Liaison Administrative*
NKVD	*Narodny Kommissariat Vnutrennikh Del* (Soviet People's Commissariat of Internal Affairs)
OB	*Oberbefehlshaber* (Commander-in-Chief)
OKW	*Oberkommando de Wehrmacht* (German Supreme Command)
OSS	US Office of Strategic Services
POL	Petrol, Oil, Lubricants
PRO	Public Record Office
SACMED	Supreme Allied Commander, Mediterranean
SD	*Sicherheit Dienst* (German Security Service)
SHAEF	Supreme Headquarters Allied Expeditionary Force
Sigint	Signal Intelligence
SOE	Special Operations Executive
UNRRA	United Nations Relief and Rehabilitation Administration

Abbreviations for printed sources

DBFP	*Documents on British Foreign Policy 1919-1939* (HMSO, London, 1946-86)
DBPO	*Documents on British Policy Overseas*, Series I (1945-50) and Series II (1950-60) (HMSO, 1984f)
FRUS	*Foreign Relations of the United States: Diplomatic Papers* (Washington, 1861f)
Hinsley	*British Intelligence in the Second World War*, vols 1-5 (HMSO, 1979-90)
Woodward	Sir L Woodward, *British Foreign Policy in the Second World War* (HMSO, 1962 and 1970f)

Abbreviations

Introduction

GILL BENNETT

Summing up the Conference on *The End of the War in Europe, 1945* during the closing session on 6 April 1995, Sir Michael Howard described it as 'climactic'. The Conference had, in a sense, been anticipated by the formation of the International Committee on the Second World War and of its British section: despite many successful meetings no subject was yet remotely exhausted, but this Conference represented the natural climax of all previous discussion, bringing together and synthesising a number of dominant themes. It also brought together a unique combination of participants which may never be repeated: Resistance leaders, military heroes, key figures in wartime and post-war planning; eminent historians, academic experts on the wartime and post-war history of a range of countries; and a considerable number who fell into both categories. This produced an often thrilling mixture of academic analysis and personal reminiscence, and some very lively discussion sessions.

Fifty years after the end of the Second World War, with a wealth of intervening scholarship available in published form, it is difficult to avoid the pitfall of hindsight. It is only too easy to impute to the Allied victors, meeting to decide the shape of the post-war world, motives and policies which are based on the knowledge of what has happened since 1945. The context is important: 1945 was, as described by Sir Michael Howard, a year of 'total chaos and confusion'. Everyone, from both civil and military leaders to the millions of desperate refugees and Displaced Persons, was tired, shocked and bewildered. A number of speakers stressed the need to try and understand the position and priorities not only of the Big Three, but of all European countries at the end of the war. Nevertheless, it was noticeable how often discussion was informed and to some extent directed by the knowledge of the extension of Soviet control over Eastern Europe after 1945: although in 1945, for the mass of people in Western Europe, the enemy was still Germany, not the Soviet Union, and only those 'in the know' were worrying about the dominant Soviet position in Europe.

Taking the Conference as a whole, a number of key themes emerged. The first is the parallel between 1945 and 1918-19, drawn by a number of speakers. The question of how far an analogy can be drawn in matters of military tactics and developments may be open to debate, but there is no doubt that a number of the main protagonists at the end of the war in Europe—Hitler and Stalin in particular—had clear memories of the end of the First World War and, even more tellingly, of events in the early 1920s, and had learned lessons from them which informed their actions in 1945. Professor Erickson, for example, saw Stalin's treatment of Koniev and Zhukov over the race to Berlin as firmly rooted in Stalin's own experiences in Poland in 1920. On a more personal level, Christopher Seton-Watson traced Churchill's dislike of Sforza—noted by Sir Frank Roberts—to events in 1920-21, when Sforza did a deal with Mustafa Kemal behind the backs of the British.

The parallel hinges, however, on the peace-making process. Professor Dilks felt that a truer parallel with 1945 would be the Vienna settlement in 1814-15 (a view supported by Sir Michael Howard in the 1995 Foreign & Commonwealth Office Annual Lecture, delivered on 4 May 1995[1]). It is true that there was no real peace settlement in 1945, in the sense that there was no peace treaty. The Potsdam Conference did not represent a clear end to the war: the atomic bomb had not been dropped, nor war in the Far East ended; some decisions had been preempted at Yalta or before; some were deferred in anticipation of a future peace treaty, and in a desperate desire to give the new World Organisation, the United Nations, a chance. While it seems possible to draw an analogy between the Great Powers in 1918 and in 1945, deciding the shape and form of post-war Europe, the realities of military power and strategic interest were quite different. In 1918 the victorious powers—dominated by Britain, France and the United States—felt secure in their right to re-order the affairs of Central and South Eastern Europe on the basis of principles previously enunciated by Woodrow Wilson. In 1945, any 'ordering' had to take account of the Soviet Union, not just as an Ally but as a dominant military presence in Europe and a potential threat. This affected the balance of Allied relations, and in particular the Anglo-American relationship, as Britain was squeezed into the role of third party by the military might of the United States and Soviet Union.

The strategic facts of life in 1945 made it inevitable that the interests of smaller powers would be subordinated to the cause of harmonious Great Power relations—another clear theme of the Conference. Much discussion was devoted in particular to Poland, whose territorial and political integrity was sacrificed in the end because Churchill and Roosevelt (and later Truman) needed to secure Stalin's cooperation and agreement on issues more important to them. The famous 'percentage agreement', of which Professor Rzheshevsky presented to the Conference the translation of a Soviet text, can be seen as another stark example of Great Power politics determining the future of small countries. Christopher Seton-Watson's description of 'massive' CIA intervention to influence the outcome of Italian post-war elections, and of American readiness to intervene militarily if the Popular Front won, added another dimension to the 'spheres of influence' argument. The dominant interests of the Great Powers, however, even when exercised in an apparently malign fashion, could have some positive result: a number of speakers agreed that post-war tribulations and upheaval had contributed to the development of a tougher, stronger and more stable society, for example in Poland.

The different ways in which the various European countries emerged politically and socially from the war proved one of the most fascinating strands of the Conference. It was clear that in each case a decisive factor in post-war political development was the way in which the wartime Resistance movements were or were not integrated into peacetime government. This was linked to the role played by pre-war and wartime governments during Occupation, whether in exile or in a form of working partnership with the Occupying Power, and to the popular perception of those governments. As Professor Bédarida pointed out, in some countries, such as France and Belgium, the government was held responsible by the populace for wartime developments: in others, such as the Netherlands or Norway, it was not. In addition, Resistance leaders, accustomed to a degree of radical autonomy and social freedom during the war, often favoured a deeper change in post-war government and society than did the political élite abd made their views known forcefully (for example, in several countries the enfranchisement of women was a direct result of Resistance influence). Not all Resistance fighters, however, were capable of bearing the responsibilities of political power in a peacetime situation. All this made the absorption of Resistance into government problematical, but where it was achieved, at least partially—for example, in Norway—the resulting mix could be dynamic and beneficial. Where the situation remained fragmented and unresolved, such as in Belgium—where Liberation, according to Dr Conway, represented a 'passive moment in Belgian history'—the power of existing élites and the traditional social fabric was reinforced, until underlying tensions re-emerged, for example with the ethnic conflicts of the 1960s.

Though discussion in the Conference centred on the politics and policies of governments, the psychological profile of key players— Churchill, Roosevelt, Truman, Hitler, Stalin, Attlee, de Gaulle—was accepted as an important issue and subjected to examination. In particular, the character and motives of Stalin were debated extensively, since his monolithic authority meant that his decisions were Soviet policy. In this context Sir Frank Roberts's personal memories of negotiating with Stalin added, as always, a valuable dimension to the discussion. Other personal reminiscences, retailed during the Conference, added brushstrokes to the overall picture: Sir Douglas Dodds Parker, describing how he bugged the bedroom in which the Italian armistice negotiations were proceeding; Sir Alexander Glen, marching 18 miles behind the coffin of a senior Soviet general shot down by Allied aircraft over Macedonia; Christopher Seton-Watson describing the painful intellectual process undergone by him and his contemporaries in making the transition to suspicion of the Soviet Union. An unforgettable mental picture was also created by Professor Erickson's description, taken from Soviet military radio transcripts, of Soviet tank troops seeking the *Reichstag* in Berlin but finding instead tigers and lions in the *Tiergarten*.

*

The proceedings of the Conference were divided into five sessions: terminal campaigns in 1945; Yalta decisions and their implementation; the Potsdam Conference and high politics to December 1945; the Liberation of Western Europe and restoration of democratic government; and the Soviet Occupation of Eastern Europe. Within those sessions, however, the papers sometimes dealt with varied subjects—though common themes and threads are apparent—and for this reason the main points of discussion have been summarised at the end of each paper, rather than at the end of a section. Editorial additions, whether in Discussion or in footnotes, are indicated by italics.

In the first session, *Dr Barnett, Professor Erickson and Sir David Hunt* concentrated on the military detail of the campaigns they described. Their approaches differed, and indeed in some cases they differed on matters of both fact and interpretation, but nevertheless this session underlined the interdependence of the different battle fronts, and the importance of timing in determining the overall military position in Europe at the end of hostilities. Session 2 focused on the Yalta Conference. *Sir Frank Roberts*, in the unique position of having attended the conference, gave an authoritative and thought-provoking presentation on what Yalta 'was and was not', arguing that it was not the agreements reached there, but the way they were carried out—or, in case of the Soviet Union, by-passed—which had far-reaching implications for the future of Europe. *Professor Müller* dealt in particular with Yalta's implications for Germany, where the results of the transfer of populations triggered by decisions at Yalta and Potsdam are still discernible today. This session flowed naturally into *Professor Dilks's* atmospheric overview of the Potsdam Conference, stressing the importance of the personalities of Churchill, Stalin and Truman in determining the course of events at the conference, both in formal session and in significant personal encounters in the margins.

The papers presented in the third session showed how widely the experience of Liberation differed in Western Europe. Occupation had in each case interrupted the flow of political life, and the direction that flow had been taking was crucial in determining the extent to which Liberation marked a move towards a revitalised and reformed democratic system, or a descent towards stagnation or confusion while the elements of political authority sought to restore some form of order. In each country, the role of the Resistance movements was a significant influence on this process. The final session, on the Soviet occupation of Eastern Europe, provided a forceful contrast to the experiences of Western European countries, although in the Eastern European countries, too, the form, method and extent of Soviet Occupation differed. *Professor Rzheshevsky* underlined the blurred distinction between Liberation and Occupation in countries whose chief reaction at the end of the war was relief at the removal of German Occupation, rather than apprehension at the possible future extent of Soviet influence. *Malcolm Mackintosh*, describing Bulgaria's efforts during the war to keep all sides happy, encapsulated the ambiguity of the situation in 1945. This lack of a clear-cut picture—a common European experience, with many common themes, complicated by an infinite range of national, regional and political diversity, shaded by the personalities and motives of the leading statesmen of the time—remains the strongest impression of this interesting and important Conference.

Notes and References

[1] FCO Historians Occasional Papers No. 11, October 1995: *The 1995 FCO Annual Lecture, 1945-1995: Fifty Years of European Peace.*

1 The Terminal Campaign in Western Europe 1945

CORRELLI BARNETT

For the United States of America and the British Commonwealth the final battles with the German Army in the West, and the subsequent pursuit beyond the Rhine until the enemy's disintegration and unconditional surrender, constitute the triumphant finale of a war waged by maritime powers against a continental enemy. Without the hard-won victory over the U-boat in the Battle of the Atlantic in the spring of 1943 it would have been impossible to build up a great American army in the United Kingdom for Operation 'Overlord' in June 1944. It would also have been impossible to ship into Britain the aviation fuel without which the Allied bomber forces would have been grounded and so unable decisively to disrupt German communications in France, crippling the enemy's freedom of manoeuvre and reinforcement during the Battle of Normandy.

Moreover, it was the subsequent sea-nourished Allied advance to the German frontier which transformed the parameters of the strategic air offensive by pushing the German air-defence radars and fighters back from the Channel to within the German frontier, and *pari passu* advancing the ground stations of Allied target-finding devices like Oboe. This opened the way for the destruction of German road, rail and canal communications as well as petrol-from-coal plants, so bringing about the final collapse of the enemy's war economy behind his armies. Even by the end of December 1944 all but one of the main petrol-from-coal plants had been put out of production, along with a fifth of the smaller ones.[1] As early as January 1945 damage to the motor-vehicle industry led to a reduction of a quarter in the truck strengths authorised for panzer and panzer-grenadier divisions.[2]

It must equally be borne in mind that in 1945 the Allied land campaign in the West itself continued to remain totally dependent on maritime supply. In April, when the Allied armies burst over the Rhine in the climactic offensive of the war, no fewer than 1,341,610 tons of stores were discharged through Antwerp (some two-thirds for the American armies) and 288,809 tons of 'POL' (petrol, oil, lubricants); 91,505 tons of stores for 21st Army Group through Ostend, and 4,893 through Calais and Boulogne. Through Le Havre and Rouen for the American armies came 406,146 tons of stores and 144,721 tons of 'POL'; through Cherbourg and minor Normandy ports 228,585 tons of stores and 161,045 tons of 'POL'; and through Mediterranean French ports (above all, Marseilles) 484,631 tons of stores and 153,871 tons of 'POL'.[3]

In terms of strategic return on investment of maritime and military resources, the re-constituted Western Front of 1944-45 vindicated those like General G C Marshall, Chief of Staff of the US Army, who had urged since 1942 that the *Schwerpunkt* of Allied strategy should lie on the direct route from Britain to the heart of Germany via the English Channel. For whereas an average total of one million tons of shipping supported a maximum of 90 divisions on the Western Front, nearly *seven million* deadweight tons of shipping allotted to the Mediterranean supported a maximum of only 27 Allied divisions on the Italian Front (which in any case finished up in a cul-de-sac before the barrier of the Alps).[4] Even when the Allied forces in Italy were reduced to some 20 divisions by early 1945[5] they still numbered some 536,000 men to Field-Marshal A Kesselring's 491,000, with double Kesselring's strength in artillery pieces and treble his strength in armoured fighting vehicles.[6] The latest historians of the Italian campaign, Shelford Bidwell and Dominick Graham, go so far as to comment: 'It could be said, therefore, that it was not Alexander who was drawing forces that would otherwise be employed against the Allies in north-west Europe, but Kesselring who was containing Alexander.[7]

Indeed, the cost-effectiveness (and strategically decisive nature) of the renewed Western Front in 1944-45 as compared to the cost-ineffectiveness of the Mediterranean theatre (especially when the latter was the Western allies' sole theatre against Germany in 1940-43) serves to vindicate the arguments of 'Westerners' like Haig and Robertson during the Great War, and discredit those of 'Easterners' like Lloyd George in that war and Churchill in both wars (the latter being, remarkably enough, the victim, to adapt Dr Johnson on second marriages, of the triumph of strategic hope over strategic experience).

There are also comparisons, historically illuminating as well as fascinating in themselves, to be made between the Western Front of 1918 during Haig's and Foch's final series of offensives from July onwards, and that of 1945 during the advance to the Rhine and beyond of Supreme Commander General Dwight D Eisenhower. In both cases the Allied triumphs followed the repulse of the enemy's last grand offensive effort in the West: Operation 'Michael' and its successors in March-July 1918; Operation 'Herbstnebel', the Ardennes Offensive, in December 1944. In each case the heavy human and material losses sustained by the enemy while on the offensive decisively damaged his fighting power in the subsequent defensive. Yet the contrast in scale between the two German final strokes is no less interesting. In the greatest of the German 1918 offensives, 'Michael', Ludendorff fielded a mass of 47 superbly trained 'attack' divisions[8] in the Battle of the Ardennes, Hitler could only muster 26 divisions;[9] not all of them first-class formations. While 'Michael' had been long and carefully planned and organised, 'Herbstnebel' was a Hitlerian improvisation.

The grand-strategic picture of the war as a whole was immensely more favourable to the Allies on the Western Front in 1944-5 than in 1918. Ludendorff had been able to concentrate his 47 'attack' divisions opposite Haig because the Eastern front had been largely closed down since the October 1917 Revolution in Russia (formal armistice signed at Brest-Litovsk on 16 December; the Treaty of Brest-Litovsk finally taking Russia out of the War signed on 10 February 1918). Thus in 1918 the Allies on the Western Front, having themselves endured four years of heavy loss in attrition battles, had to contend with the main bulk of the German Army's fighting strength.

In striking contrast, the year 1944 had witnessed the Red Army on the Eastern Front reach the apogee of its offensive power, totally destroying the German Army Group Centre in the summer battles, and by the end of the year advancing to the border of East Prussia, to the Vistula and deep into Hungary. Between June and November 1944 irreplaceable German losses on the Eastern Front amounted to 903,000, as against 553,000 on the Western Front.[10] Moreover, in contrast to Haig, Pétain and Foch at the beginning of 1918, the fortunate Eisenhower in planning his 1945 campaign knew that he could count on further gigantic strokes being launched on the Eastern Front against a German army now desperately short of manpower. On 9 January Churchill reported to him Stalin's signal of the previous day that the Soviet Supreme Command had decided 'regardless of the weather, to commence large-scale operations against the Germans along the whole Central Front not later than the second half of January.'[11] In fact, the Red Army struck on 12 January in an offensive which by the beginning of February had taken them from the Vistula to the Oder, within 40 miles of Berlin. This emergency led to a switch of *panzer* divisions from the West to the East, a fact revealed to the Anglo-American command by Sigint decrypts in the course of February. Throughout the coming Rhineland battles Sigint was also to provide continual and highly valuable insights into enemy readings of Allied intentions as well as of proposed German movements.[12]

With regard to the design of Allied strategy for the 1945 campaign, the British, in the form of the abrasive personalities of Field-Marshal Sir B L Montgomery (C-in-C 21st Army Group) and Field-Marshal Sir Alan Brooke (Chief of the Imperial General Staff), had continued to urge (as they had done since September 1944) that there should be a single grand offensive across the Rhine and north of the Ruhr by 21st Army Group swelled by American formations, while the rest of the Western Front was reduced to a defensive. This grand onslaught would be conducted by Montgomery, the loser of Arnhem, as Allied 'ground force commander', thus restoring him to his former glory. Eisenhower himself agreed, as he wrote to Marshall on 10 January, that the main thrust should be on the allied left flank north of the Ruhr, and that on the right flank south of the Moselle 'the whole task is defensive...'.[13] But he believed that to stand on the defensive in the centre would not adequately secure the flank of the main thrust. He therefore decided that in the first phase of the campaign (an advance to the Rhine) not only 21st Army Group but also the all-American 12th Army Group (General Omar Bradley) would take the offensive, in the latter case on the axis Prum-Bonn. At the same time Eisenhower finally put paid to Montgomery's obsessive ambition to become ground-force commander, on the grounds that a separate commander for ground operations would be redundant and lead to 'great duplication in personnel and communications...'[14]

Nor did Eisenhower agree with Montgomery that once across the Rhine the Allies should confine themselves to a single thrustline north of the Ruhr. As he wrote to Marshall on 15 January, the fact that this constituted 'an invasion route of the first importance' was 'equally obvious to the German, and if he concentrates in its immediate defense, I may not have the necessary overwhelming superiority to force a satisfactory breakthrough'. He therefore wished to enjoy 'the ability to maneuver': meaning, for example, 'the ability to advance also on Frankfurt and Kassel, rather than to rely on a single thrust in the north.'[15] On 20 January the Supreme Commander fleshed out his preliminary thinking into 'an appreciation and plan of operations for the winter and spring of 1945' submitted to the Combined Chiefs of Staff:[16]

> *These operations fall into three phases:*
>
> *Phase 1—The destruction of the enemy forces west of the Rhine and the closing of the Rhine.*
> *Phase 2—The seizing of bridgeheads over the Rhine from which to develop operations into Germany.*
> *Phase 3—The destruction of enemy forces east of the Rhine and advance into Germany.*

In Eisenhower's judgement, if the bulk of the enemy west of the Rhine could be destroyed, 'the remaining phases will be immeasurably simplified'. In regard to Phase 3,

> *operations across the Rhine north of the Ruhr offer the greatest strategic rewards within a short distance, but this area will be most strongly held by the enemy. An advance in the Frankfurt area offers less favourable terrain and a longer route to vital strategic objectives. Depending on the degree of enemy resistance it may be necessary to use either or both of these two avenues.[17]*

This broad scenario was to be fulfilled in the event. Yet the sequence of the phases offers a striking contrast with the pattern of the Red

Army offensives first established in the counter-stroke at Stalingrad in November 1942, whereby a sudden smashing blow with massed divisions and firepower burst the enemy front asunder, to be followed by a phase of exploitation and pursuit. Instead there was to be an opening phase of attrition to write down the enemy's reserves—what Haig called 'the wearing-out battle'—only then followed by a breakthrough to 'the green fields beyond.' In other words, the proposed phases of the campaign of 1945 took the form of foreshortened replays of the campaigns of 1915-1918.

The nature of the battlefield itself during 'Phase 1' would have been familiar enough to veterans of the First World War. Operation 'Veritable', the offensive by Crerar's First Canadian Army (2nd Canadian Corps and 30th British Corps) to advance to the Rhine between Xanten and the Dutch frontier, opened on 8 February with a bombardment by more than 1,000 guns, followed by a barrage lifting ahead of the infantry and tanks. Thereafter the attackers, 450,000 strong, fought their way week by week south-eastwards between the Maas and the Rhine against General Schlemm's First Parachute Army: a battle, often in drenching rain, from one natural feature to another, one village or farm to another, through mud sometimes so waterlogged that all vehicles were bogged down except for the wide-tracked Churchill tanks.

The German defences too would have been familiar enough to veterans of Third Ypres, consisting of three defensive belts each of two or three lines of trenches and fortified villages or farms, the whole covered by minefields and barbed-wire. Given too a fresh display of the German talent in both wars for vicious local counter-attacks, it was no wonder that Operation 'Veritable' became, in Eisenhower's words, 'a bitter slugging match'.[18] The historian of the British 11th Armoured Division described its experience in Operation 'Blockbuster' (a later phase of 'Veritable') on 26 February as 'a slow, miserable and costly operation... confronted by impenetrable forests, impassable bogs, numerous craters, roadblocks, mines and every form of demolition...'[19] Only on 8 March was the objective of the Rhine between Xanten and the Dutch frontier finally reached, Schlemm completing his withdrawal across the river in good order. It was all a far cry from the visions of instant breakthroughs and mobile manoeuvre entertained by pre-war tank-warfare prophets like Liddell Hart and Fuller, and briefly realised by the German *Blitzkrieg* victory in the West in 1940.

On 23 February the American Ninth Army (General William H Simpson, under command of Montgomery's 21st Army Group) on the right flank of the Canadians had launched a parallel offensive aimed at the Rhine between Xanten and Dusseldorf, Operation 'Grenade'. Here the principal obstacle lay in the flooded River Roer. Nonetheless the Americans quickly won bridgeheads up to four miles deep against a weaker defence than opposite the Canadians and British. With the American First Army (of Bradley's 12th Army Group) protecting its right flank, the Ninth Army began an accelerating drive which brought it to the Rhine opposite Dusseldorf on 1 March and to all its objectives by the 5th. Nevertheless the Germans succeeded in blowing all the Rhine bridges opposite the American front as well as opposite the Canadian and British before withdrawing across the river.

The attrition battles of 'Veritable' and 'Grenade' had cost the allies dear enough—15,500 Canadian and British casualties, just under 7,300 American.[20] But it had cost the enemy much more, and his losses at this stage of the war were virtually irreplaceable—51,000 prisoners and an estimated 38,000 killed or seriously wounded.[21]

For Adolf Hitler (in practice Eisenhower's opposite number rather than Field-Marshal von Rundstedt, the titular OB West) had played exactly into Eisenhower's hands by refusing the request of Field-Marshal Model (Army Group 'B') to organise a main defence behind the Rhine, and by instructing him and General Blaskowitz (Army Group 'H', opposite the British and Canadians) instead to fight for the Rhineland. He thus condemned to a murderous battle of attrition their tired, discouraged and heavily outnumbered troops, short of armour and without air cover. Hitler had indeed no strategy for the campaign in the West in 1945 other than to order his commanders to fight for every inch of ground.

Meanwhile, the US First and Third Armies (General Omar Bradley's 12th Army Group) between the US Ninth Army's right flank and the Moselle had been carrying out Operation 'Lumberjack', with the objective of closing up to the Rhine between Dusseldorf and Mainz. Once the First Army had crossed the flooded River Roer the enemy's resistance took on the character of a fighting retreat except for a brief stand by *panzers* on the Erft Canal. American advanced guards entered Cologne on 5 March and by the 7th the entire city was in American hands. On the same day the right-flank corps of First Army, having swung south-eastwards according to plan, reached the Rhine at Remagen—and seized the Ludendorff bridge, the one Rhine bridge that the Germans had failed to blow in time. Without hesitation Eisenhower decided to exploit this opportunity by ordering Bradley to put at least five divisions on the far bank to secure a bridgehead. In the meantime the Third Army (Patton) had reached the Rhine between Remagen and Coblenz.

On 8 March Eisenhower issued a fresh directive which definitively altered the balance of his strategy away from a single thrust by 21st Army Group to the north of the Ruhr, and towards greater effort along the front south of the Moselle. While D-Day for 21st Army Group's assault crossing of the Rhine at Wesel was confirmed as 24 March, the US 6th Army Group (General Jacob L Devers), on what had been (except for the clearance of the Colmar pocket) a purely defensive front, was now ordered to 'initiate offensive operations in the Saar' with the object of keeping 'all possible German forces away from the main effort in the north, by defeating the enemy west of the Rhine, closing on the Rhine from the Moselle southward and establishing bridgeheads over the Rhine in the Mainz-Mannheim sector'.[22]

The hardest task in these operations fell to the 6th Army Group's Seventh Army (General Alexander M Patch), which had to break through the West Wall between Saarbrucken and Lauterburg on the Rhine and then fight its way through the hilly and thickly wooded Palatinate to its final objective Mainz-Mannheim. In a pincer movement, General George S Patton's Third Army (on the right flank of the 12th Army Group) was at the same time to attack south-east across the Moselle towards the Rhine between Coblenz and Bingen. Both armies at first encountered tough resistance, but within a fortnight had cleared the entire Palatinate up the line of the Rhine, surrounding much of the German Seventh Army, taking 107,000 prisoners, and seizing a second bridge over the Rhine, at Oppenheim.[23] By 25 March German resistance everywhere west of the Rhine had ceased.

The historian of the Western Front in the Great War cannot fail to be struck by the similarity of Eisenhower's strategy of successive blows along a broad front against an overstretched enemy to that of Haig and Foch between August and November 1918. In Eisenhower's case he and his subordinate commanders had brilliantly fulfilled his objective of gutting the German army west of the Rhine (the number of prisoners alone amounted to 280,000[24]) in order decisively to weaken it for the defence of the river and the German heartland. Moreover, this success on the grand scale serves completely to vindicate Eisenhower's broad-front strategy as against the strategy of the single thrust urged so persistently by Montgomery and Brooke.

To the success of these attrition battles the Allied tactical air forces, although hampered by appalling weather, greatly contributed, attacking enemy road and rail communications, defensive positions, and troops and vehicles on the move—with accompanying moral impact on soldiers increasingly convinced of the hopelessness of their fight. In a single week during operations in the Saar, the American 1st Tactical Air Force flew over 8,000 sorties.[25] On 22 February over 9,000 aircraft (strategic bombers as well as tactical air) from bases in England, France, Holland, Belgium and Italy took part in Operation 'Clarion', involving targets across an area of 250,000 square miles, from Emden to Berlin, Dresden, Vienna and Mulhouse, and aimed at dislocating enemy communications by destroying such key points as railway bridges and viaducts, signalling and canal locks.[26] Meanwhile the strategic bomber forces were finally smashing the German war economy to a standstill, with steel plants, oil-from-coal plants, gas works and power stations reduced to wrecks. By March oil production had ceased, and German air and ground forces were limited to stocks remaining in underground storage depots. Even these were soon to be the targets of attack. In any case the economy as a whole had been brought to the point of paralysis by the cumulative destruction of communications—breached and emptied canals, dropped viaducts, cratered marshalling yards. Coal still being mined could not be moved from the pitheads, nor munitions from underground factories still in production.[27]

On 11 March Hitler replaced von Rundstedt as OB West with Kesselring, who had conducted such a brilliant and dogged defence of Italy against the odds since 1943. In defending the Rhine against some 85 allied divisions he could only field 51, most of them down to a strength of about 5,500 soldiers, and those increasingly dispirited and prone to desert. He was desperately short of armour.[28] Here was a situation beyond the recuperative powers even of 'Smiling Albert'.

On 13 March Eisenhower confirmed in a directive that as well as the planned crossing of the Rhine at Wesel on 24 March by Montgomery's 21st Army Group (Operation 'Plunder'), Bradley's 12th Army Group was to break out from the Remagen bridgehead and thrust therefrom on Frankfurt.[29] In preparing 'Plunder', 21st Army Group again benefited from the clear picture revealed by Sigint and Army Y of the enemy's dispositions, strengths and intentions, as well as his appreciation of Allied plans; in particular, that the enemy had correctly guessed the most likely sector for the main assault. According to Sigint intercepts, the enemy's defence consisted of a thin crust of understrength formations—even thinner on secondary sectors, with 2nd Parachute Division, for example, holding a front of 33 kilometres.[30]

Montgomery organised his assault crossing with his usual meticulous thoroughness, building up a maximum preponderance of men and firepower. For three days beforehand the Second Tactical Air Force attacked German army and Luftwaffe installations in the neighbourhood of Wesel. The assault crossing on the night of the 23rd was covered by the fire of some 3,500 guns. After the first waves had obtained a lodgement, Bomber Command dropped 1,100 tons of high explosive on the town of Wesel. With divisions of the British Second Army and the American Ninth firmly ashore, there followed the landing of parachute and gliderborne troops of the British 6th Airborne and the American 17th Airborne Divisions behind the enemy front north of Wesel (Operation 'Varsity'). Despite a skilled and determined fight by the heavily outweighted German 1st Parachute Army against this massive combined assault, 21st Army

Group had won a bridgehead some 35 miles wide and 20 miles deep by 27 March.

Montgomery now issued orders for the break-out and a pursuit to the Elbe: on the left, Second Army (with its left thrusting for Hamburg); on the right, Ninth Army (its right directed on Magdeburg, with a swing south round the Ruhr). Meanwhile, on 24 March Eisenhower had signalled the Combined Chiefs of Staff that the victories west of the Rhine had 'resulted as planned in the destruction of a large proportion of available enemy forces on the Western Front'.

> *While not desiring to appear overoptimistic, it is my conviction that the situation today presents opportunities for which we have struggled and which we must seize boldly. The dash and daring in First and Third Army sectors have gotten us two bridgeheads very cheaply which can be consolidated and expanded rapidly to support a major thrust which will assist the northern operation and make our exploitation effective.*[31]

In fact:

> *While we are continuing to plan for and to be ready to meet stern resistance, it is my personal belief that the enemy strength on the Western Front is becoming so stretched that penetrations and advances will soon be limited only by our own maintenance.*

In a directive to army-group and army commanders next day Eisenhower confirmed that the final offensive into the German heartland was to consist of two main thrusts—Montgomery's north of the Ruhr as always intended, and a second one south of the Ruhr by Bradley, the two army groups encircling the industrial region and effecting a junction to its rear in the area Paderborn-Kassel.[32] The 6th Army Group would protect the right flank of the 12th Army Group.

Yet the Supreme Commander was already looking ahead to the operational problems involved in effecting a tidy junction with the Red Army advancing from the east, signalling Stalin personally on 28 March to suggest that 'the best axis on which to effect this junction would be Erfurt-Leipzig-Dresden'—meaning that the main thrustline for Eisenhower's own forces after the encircling of the Ruhr would lie in the centre (on the axis Kassel-Leipzig), not in the north in the 21st Army Group sector, as Montgomery and Churchill were still urging. In fact, to their indignant protests, he proposed to remove Simpson's US 9th Army from Montgomery's command in time to strengthen this central thrust.

There now blew up the last great Anglo-American row over strategy. While Montgomery's motivation in contending for the pre-eminence of his thrust for the Elbe may only be guessed at, Churchill's intervention was prompted by political considerations. In the first place he wanted Simpson to remain under Montgomery to 'avoid the relegation of His Majesty's Forces to an unexpected restricted sphere'.[33] But more importantly

> *If the enemy's resistance should weaken, as you evidently expect... why should we not cross the Elbe and advance as far eastward as possible? This has important political bearing, as the Russian Army of the south seems certain to enter Vienna and overrun Austria. If we deliberately leave Berlin to them, even if it should be within our grasp, the double event may strengthen their conviction, already apparent, that they have done everything.*[34]

Churchill put this view even more strongly to Roosevelt on 1 April:

> *If they also take Berlin, will not their impression that they have been the overwhelming contributor to our common victory be unduly imprinted in their minds and may this not lead them into a mood which will raise grave and formidable difficulties in the future?*[35]

Roosevelt, however, refused to overrule the military judgement of the Supreme Commander for such political reasons.[36] And Eisenhower remained convinced that Berlin was no longer a prime military objective, and that the important thing was a tidy junction with the Red Army rather than an untidy encounter. In any case, he was very conscious (as Churchill did not seem to be) that the Red Army already lay within 40-50 miles of Berlin, while his own armies were still some 250 miles from the city, which did not offer good odds on the Western Allies winning the race. So, after a flurry of argument running on into the middle of April, Eisenhower's strategy stood.

But was Churchill's proposal well judged even on the political plane? The boundaries of the three occupation zones into which Germany was to be partitioned after her defeat had been formally agreed in a Protocol signed at the Yalta summit conference in February 1945, with Berlin designated as a tripartite enclave deep inside the Soviet zone. As it was, the end of the war found Anglo-American forces occupying almost half that part of the Soviet zone lying west of the Oder-Neisse line, from which they then had to withdraw.[37] Churchill proved reluctant to do so, wishing to retain a political bargaining chip in settling outstanding European problems with the Soviet Union. However, frigid though relations with Stalin were becoming, it must be asked in retrospect whether the immediate aftermath of the war was the right moment thus to bring about an open confrontation.

Meanwhile, by the time the 21st Army Group broke out from its bridgehead over the Rhine at Wesel on 28 March, the 12th Army Group's First Army, breaking out from the Remagen bridgehead on

25 March, had already advanced far enough to begin its swing north to encircle the Ruhr. Further south the Third Army had broken out of the Oppenheim bridgehead, while the Seventh Army (6th Army Group) had won a new bridgehead astride Worms on 26 March and broken out towards Aschaffenburg on the 28th. Further south still the First French Army crossed the river at Speyer on the 31st. With the defence of the Rhine swiftly disintegrating, so began to disintegrate with it a coherent and controlled German resistance. In this phase of the campaign too Sigint had made a key contribution by revealing in detail the dire straits to which the enemy Army Groups 'B' and 'H' were reduced, and so encouraging the Allied command to risk bold offensive action.[38]

On 1 April the US Ninth and First Armies completed the encirclement of the Ruhr, now a wilderness of wrecked and paralysed industries, by linking up at Lippstadt. The whole of Army Group 'B' and two corps of Army Group 'H' were trapped. For over a fortnight Model fought on, attempting two break-outs in conjunction with efforts at relief by other German forces. On 18 April the Ruhr pocket was finally eliminated along with 21 enemy divisions. No fewer than 325,000 prisoners fell into allied hands. Model himself committed suicide.

The campaign of 1945 was now well into its final phase, with the German Army suffering the kind of rout and collapse which it had inflicted on the Polish Army in 1939, the French Army in 1940, and the Yugoslav and Greek Armies in 1941. The racing Allied advances were only briefly checked by uncoordinated local German actions on a river or canal, in a village or wood—the last guttering flames of the soldierly virtues of the best army of the twentieth century. By 18 April, when the Ruhr pocket surrendered, 21st Army Group, on its thrustlines north and north-east, had reached the Elbe at Lauenburg, had freed the north and east of the Netherlands, and lay some 40-50 miles from the German North-Sea and Baltic coasts; the 12th Army Group, on Eisenhower's principal thrustline to the east, was on the Elbe and Mulde between Wittenberg and Plauen, and had taken Bayreuth; and the Sixth Army Group, wheeling south-eastwards, was nearing Nuremberg and Stuttgart.

Meanwhile, Eisenhower and his staff had accepted intelligence reports (not confirmed by Sigint) that the Nazi régime was preparing for a last stand in a 'national redoubt' based on the mountainous region running from the Black Forest to the Austro-Hungarian frontier, and southwards to include the Alpine areas of Northern Italy. This mistaken belief in the existence of a 'national redoubt' induced the Supreme Commander to hasten the advances of 6th Army Group southwards into Bavaria.[39]

On 16 April the Red Army launched its final offensive, smashing through German defences on the Oder and surrounding Berlin on 25 April—the day that Soviet and American advanced guards met at Torgau on the Elbe, splitting the Reich and its armed forces into two. Yet even now some German formations rallied and offered a hard fight, such as the last stand of First Parachute Army in defence of the Bremen-Oldenburg area against Montgomery in the second half of April. But the last days of April and the first days of May saw the Anglo-American armies complete the last furlong of their race. On 2 May the 11th Armoured Division (British Second Army) reached Lubeck on the Baltic; next day the garrison of Hamburg surrendered; and on 4 May General-Admiral von Friedeburg unconditionally surrendered to Montgomery all German forces in Holland, north-west Germany (including the Friesian Islands and Heligoland), and Denmark. For Montgomery personally, this marked the crowning moment of his long march from Alamein. In the south the US Seventh Army took Augsburg and Munich on 30 April, and pressed on to the Brenner Pass (making contact with the US Fifth Army in Italy) and Salzburg by 4 May. Meanwhile the US Third Army captured Linz in Austria and Pilsen in Czechoslovakia, and was nearing Prague.

On 7 May in Reims General Jodl, Chief of Operations, *Oberkommando der Wehrmacht*, signed the unconditional surrender of the German armed forces on all fronts. General Eisenhower, Supreme Commander Allied Expeditionary Force, then made a signal to the Combined Chiefs of Staff:

> *The mission of this Allied force was fulfilled at 0241, local time, May 7th, 1945.*[40]

Discussion

Discussion between *Dr Correlli Barnett* and *Sir David Hunt* regarding the relative importance of the Italian campaign, the strength of the Allied and German forces and the method used to calculate it, was heated but inconclusive.

Sir Douglas Dodds Parker stressed the important role played by both the US Navy and the French Resistance in keeping the ports of Marseilles and Toulon open. *Dr Alistair Horne* considered that Montgomery's failure to open Antwerp in 1944 was an 'all-important mistake', and that Eisenhower should have ordered Montgomery to capture the port.

With regard to the disagreement between Eisenhower and Montgomery over the route to be taken by the Allies after crossing the Rhine, *Sir Carol Mather* defended Montgomery's strategy, which might have shortened the war and allowed the Allies to reach Berlin first. *Dr Barnett*, however, argued that Eisenhower realized that a Northern thrust was logistically impossible, the Allies possessing neither the transport nor supplies to accomplish it. *Sir Michael*

12

Howard asked why, if the Ultra information was so good, Eisenhower had been taken in by the German bluff about an Alpine redoubt. *Dr Barnett* admitted that there had been no definite Sigint information on this, and a multiplicity of Ultra signals had confused the picture.

Notes and References

1 Earl F Ziemke, *Stalingrad to Berlin; The German Defeat in the East* (New York, Military Heritage Press, 1986), pp 411-12.

2 Ibid, p 412.

3 L F Ellis, with A E Warhurst, *Victory in the West*, Vol. II, *The Defeat of Germany* (London, HMSO, 1968), Appendix VII, p 408.

4 Even the 'lock-up' element in the Mediterranean total came to nearly 1 million tons. See C B A Behrens, *Merchant Shipping and the Demands of War* (London, HMSO and Longmans, Green, 1955), p 391, notes 1 and 2.

5 Cf Nigel Nicolson's biography of Field-Marshal Alexander, *Alex* (London, Weidenfeld and Nicolson, 1973), p 274.

6 1225 tubes to 665; 1320 AFVs to 400: cf Nicolson, ibid, and Sir Harry Hinsley, *British Intelligence in the Second World War: Its Influence on Strategy and Operations*, Volume III, Part II (London, HMSO, 1988), pp 697-702.

7 D Graham and S Bidwell, *Tug of War: the Battle for Italy, 1943-1945* (London, Hodder and Stoughton, 1986), p 382.

8 C Barnett, *The Swordbearers; Studies in Supreme Command in World War One* (London, Eyre and Spottiswoode, 1963), p 292.

9 Ellis and Warhurst, op cit, p 178.

10 Ziemke, op cit, p 412.

11 Alfred D Chandler (ed), *The Papers of Dwight David Eisenhower; The War Years: IV* (Baltimore and London, The Johns Hopkins Press, 1970), p 2231, note 1.

12 Hinsley, op cit, pp 670-84.

13 Eisenhower to Marshall, 10 January 1945, cited in Chandler, op cit, p 2419.

14 Ibid.

15 Ibid, p 2431.

16 Ibid, p 2450.

17 Ibid, p 2451.

18 Ellis, op cit, p 264.

19 *Taurus Pursuant: History of 11th Armoured Division* (BAOR Publication, 1945), p 85, quoted in Ellis, op cit, p 273, note 2.

20 Ellis, op cit, p 277.

21 Ibid.

22 Quoted ibid, p 282.

23 Ibid, p 283.

24 Ibid, p 284.

25 Report by the Supreme Commander to the Combined Chiefs of Staff on the Operations in Europe of the Allied Expeditionary Force, 6 June 1944 to 8 May 1945 (London, HMSO, 1946), p 114. No account of the operations of the British tactical air forces in 1945 is given in John Terraine, The Right of the Line: the Royal Air Force in the European War, 1939-1945 (London, Hodder and Stoughton, 1985).

26 Supreme Commander's Report, p 116.

27 C Webster and N Frankland, The Strategic Air Offensive Against Germany 1939-1945, Volume III: Victory, Part 5 (London, HMSO, 1961), pp 183-205 and Chapter XIV. Albert Speer, Inside the Third Reich (London, Sphere Books, 1970), Chapter 28.
28 S Bidwell, 'Kesselring', in C Barnett (ed), Hitler's Generals (London, Weidenfeld and Nicolson, 1989), p 286.
29 Chandler, op cit, pp 2536-7.
30 Hinsley, op cit, pp 686-7.
31 Chandler, op cit, p 2539.
32 Ibid, p 2542.
33 Signal of 31 March 1945, cited ibid, p 2563, note 2.
34 Ibid.
35 Ibid.
36 See E L Woodward, British Foreign Policy in the Second World War (London, HMSO, 1962), pp 516-18, and note 2 on p 518.
37 See T Sharp, The Wartime Alliance and the Zonal Division of Germany (Oxford, the Clarendon Press, 1975), Chapter V for an analysis of this whole question in its political and military aspects.
38 Hinsley, op cit, pp 688-90.
39 Ibid, pp 712-18.
40 Chandler, op cit, p 2696.

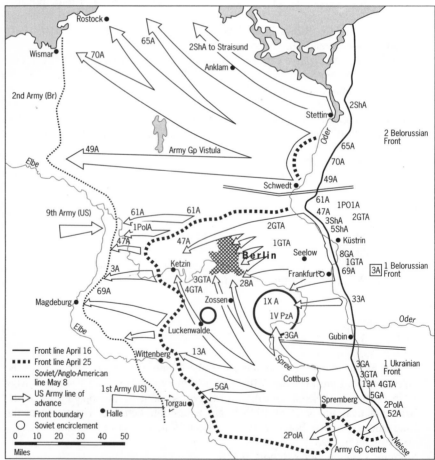

The Berlin operation, 16 April - 8 May 1945

2 *Poslednii Shturm*: The Soviet Drive to Berlin, 1945

JOHN ERICKSON

'Each Marshal thinks that he fulfilled this plan or that plan, that his place is most important.'
(Boris Polevoi in conversation, Moscow 18 April 1963)

Although the fighting in Berlin ceased half a century ago and the capitulation of Germany followed very swiftly, the 'battle for Berlin' and the attendant final Soviet campaign in 1945 has been fiercely re-fought many times in Soviet memoirs, narratives and documentary publication. In April 1946, amidst the rubble to which much of Berlin had been reduced and fresh from the carnage, a 'military-scientific conference to study the Berlin operation'[1] was convened by the Staff of the Group of Soviet Forces in Germany (GSFG), one of three such conferences. A collection of first-hand accounts, diary notes and personal letters was published in 1948 by Voenizdat in a handsome volume *Shturm Berlina*, edited by V S Veselov.[2] The first serious study of the Berlin operation must nevertheless be attributed to Major-General N A Talenskii, *Berlinskaya operatsiya 1945 goda*, published by Voenizdat in 1950 (with a high security classification), a volume of 651 pages divided into two parts, the first dealing with the organisation of all arms for the Soviet offensive, the second covering the operations of three fronts (1st and 2nd Belorussian, 1st Ukrainian) complete with a dossier of operational documents.[3]

In 1964 Marshal Chuikov ignited a furious controversy with his assertion, first published in *Octyabr*,[4] to the effect that in February 1945, with Soviet armies on the Oder, Berlin could have been taken by a daring *coup de main*. Much of this was in stark contrast to the view Marshal Chuikov had expressed to me in a lengthy discussion in Moscow on 27 April 1963. On that occasion he asserted: 'My opinion is that *if* our communications had not been so spread out, in February we *could* have struck out for Berlin.[5] But, he continued, ammunition and fuel were in short supply, pontoon bridging was needed for the Oder and also for the numerous canals. Furthermore, German troop transfers from the Ardennes of Sixth *Panzer* and *Grossdeutschland* to 'the Oder area' meant that 'a more thorough preparation lay ahead of us [the Red Army]', while the *Wehrmacht* had more than two months in which to organise German defences.

In 1965, at long last, Marshal Zhukov was unmuzzled and, in his first published account of the Berlin operation, tore into Chuikov's 'version', pointing out that this notion of a dash for Berlin had first been advanced by Major-General Enyukov from the General Staff at the post-war study conference, eliciting no response from Chuikov.[6] There was also the problem of Marshal Chuikov's recounting meetings, conversations and conferences which never took place, though Zhukov saw in this not merely improbable fiction but, more seriously, defamation of his person and assault on his reputation.[7] On the occasion of the conference of military historians in August 1966 Zhukov himself was closely questioned on his handling of the Berlin battle, in particular the manner in which he employed his tank armies.[8] Also in 1965 Army General Shtemenko published his account of the planning for the Red Army's final campaign in Europe, part of the material which appeared in 1968 in the first version of his *General'nyi shtab v gody voiny*,[9] re-worked and re-published in several editions throughout the 1970s and 1980s. It was not an account which met with Zhukov's entire approval.

In 1970, twenty years after General Talenskii's study, an unclassified attempt at a definitive study appeared, *Poslednii shturm (Berlinskaya operatsiya 1945 g)*, compiled by F D Vorob'ev, I V Parotkin and A N Shimanskii. A second edition in 1975 coincided with the 30th anniversary of 1945, conveniently exploited this time to include the name of none other than Brezhnev by way of his formal salute to the final outcome in Berlin.[10] Since then the multiple editions of Marshal Zhukov's memoirs have appeared, each cut and shaped to suit the prevailing political climate, though with the 10th edition of *Vospominaniya i rasmyshleniya* his tale of Berlin might be regarded as well and truly concluded.

*

Towards the end of October 1944 the Soviet General Staff studied deployment maps and calculations of relative strengths while planning nothing less than a giant strategic operation. In the looming 'race for Berlin' the strategic balance sheet looked most promising. All four German Army Groups had suffered drastic losses: over one and a half million men, 96 divisions, eliminated together with 6,700 tanks, 28,000 guns, 12,000 aircraft. At this point the Red Army in the east and the Allied armies in the west stood roughly equidistant from Berlin. Seventy German divisions in the west faced 87 Allied divisions and 6,000 tanks, while in the east the *Wehrmacht* retained 3 million men and some 4,000 tanks. Given this 'balance sheet', Soviet planners drew certain immediate conclusions. For the Red Army the 'central sector' was decisive, affording a direct route into Germany but one where resistance would be the fiercest. To weaken German concentration here at the centre meant maximising the Soviet effort on the flanks, with the main task of smashing the German strategic front assigned to 1st Belorussian and 1st Ukrainian Fronts heavily reinforced with armour. The entire strategic balance of the Eastern

Front had to be reviewed once more, since the correlation of forces had changed appreciably.

The General Staff plan drafted in November 1944 advised that the German war machine could be destroyed within 45 days, with Soviet offensive operations reaching to a depth of 373-440 miles in a two-stage operation mounted *uninterruptedly, without any 'operational pauses'*. The first stage would require 15 days, the second 30. Rates of advance were not fixed too extravagantly since heavy German resistance was anticipated as Soviet armies closed on Germany, but General Staff planners were confident that Soviet forces on the lower reaches of the Vistula could reach Bromberg and capture Poznan, bringing them to a line running from Breslau to Pardbitse on the Elbe, while to the south the Red Army would be closing on Vienna.

The Soviet plan envisaged 'stretching' German concentrations at the centre by heavy Soviet attacks on the flanks, involving Hungary, Austria and notably East Prussia. The configuration of the Soviet-German front tended to confirm this approach, showing stronger German concentrations on the flanks and 'a relatively weak centre with few reserves'. For the offensive in East Prussia at least two Fronts would be required, one to strike at Königsberg, a second to isolate German forces from Army Group A holding the 'Berlin sector'.[11] In the summer of 1944, after the defeat of Army Group Centre in Belorussia, Zhukov had proposed transferring forces from Koniev's massive command northwards to Vasilevskii to complete the isolation of Army Group North and strike into East Prussia. Stalin disagreed, arguing that an inevitably tenacious defence of East Prussia would only tie Vasilevskii down, the more profitable course being to drive into eastern Poland. A further attempt at the beginning of November by Marshal Zhukov and General Antonov of the General Staff to strengthen 2nd Belorussian Front 'to knock out the East Prussian grouping' failed to impress Stalin. The East Prussian time-bomb was left ticking away.

In late November 1944 Stalin and the *Stavka* approved the overall operational plan. Zhukov had earlier been removed as '*Stavka* representative' and assigned command of the 1st Belorussian Front 'operating in the Berlin strategic zone', though remaining First Deputy to Stalin as Supreme Commander. Zhukov's appointment displaced Marshal Rokossovskii who was transferred to the 2nd Belorussian Front, though assured by Stalin that his was no 'secondary' assignment.[12] To emphasise the point and possibly to mollify an aggrieved Rokossovskii, Stalin personally detailed Rokossovskii's operational tasks involving an advance in a north-westerly direction, yet taking no account of the 'East Prussian grouping' which was the responsibility of Chernyakhovskii commanding 3rd Belorussian Front. Using a specially marked map, Stalin emphasised the importance of Rokossovskii's co-ordination with Zhukov's right flank, particularly in the event of 1st Belorussian Front's being slowed down. However, the *Stavka* directive of 28 November formally committed Rokossovskii to two objectives on divergent axes, a flaw which was all too speedily to generate serious complications. The *Stavka*'s assumption of 'no complications' on Rokossovskii's northern flank proved to be seriously wide of the mark.[13]

Marshal Zhukov had insisted that this was no immediate dash for Berlin. Stalin had only agreed to the first phase of the offensive, involving operations directed against East Prussia, Zhukov's thrust towards Poznan and Koniev's drive to the Oder.[14] In his instruction to Koniev, Stalin laid great emphasis on the importance of the Silesian industrial region, a priceless asset, '*zoloto*'...'pure gold'...not to be carelessly imperilled.[15]

In December 1944 Stalin invoked weather conditions before fixing an exact date for the Soviet offensive (nominally timed for 20 January) but unfavourable weather did not prevent his launching the Red Army in response to the appeal from Prime Minister Churchill for relief from the German offensive in the Ardennes. So Stalin would duly 'accommodate' his allies '*regardless of the weather*' but also chose to unleash a massive offensive along the Warsaw-Berlin axis with intemperate haste, even with aircraft grounded, targets shrouded by mist, submissions for postponement ignored.[16] For the four major break-through operations aimed at Königsberg (Chernyakhovskii), Danzig (Rokossovskii), south of Warsaw (Zhukov) and from the Sandomierz bridgehead (Koniev), the Red Army deployed: 30 field armies, five tank armies and four air armies plus mobile formations and special artillery 'breakthrough divisions' with heavy guns. Reinhardt's Army Group Centre and Harpe's Army Group A lay directly in the path of this mass of men and machines.

Following a personal order from Stalin, Koniev opened his offensive on 12 January 1945, relying on artillery alone with aircraft fogged in. Chernyakhovskii followed on the 13th, Zhukov and Rokossovskii on the 14th. Such was the power of the Soviet blow that the rate of advance proved to be twice that prescribed in the original operational plan, causing the *Stavka* on 17 January to issue revised orders. Zhukov was instructed to reach the Bromberg-Poznan line no later than 2-4 February, Koniev to break through to the Oder by 30 January.

After one week of Soviet offensive operations the German defensive system had been staved in, overrun or bypassed, a drifting mass of men and smashed machines left far to the rear, falling back to the Oder and homewards. On 18 January Zhukov reported an enemy broken and unable to offer serious resistance, simultaneously ordering his tank armies to speed up to a daily rate of advance of 75-100 kilometres a day, the rifle formations 20-25 kilometres. He informed formation commanders of the extensive fixed fortifications on Germany's eastern frontiers: 'Forestalling the enemy in taking up these positions will secure the rapid and successful execution of the Berlin operation. If enemy reserves succeed in taking up the positions I have indicated the Berlin operation will be dragged out'.[17] With both tank armies (1st and 2nd Guards) 80-100 kilometres ahead of the main body of his Front, Zhukov ruthlessly demanded even greater speed, conveniently forgetting his undertaking to allow the armour to refurbish and refuel.

Late in January, as both Zhukov and Koniev pushed towards the Oder, the problem of coordinating this advance, within the Fronts and between the Fronts, became increasingly urgent. On 25 January Stalin telephoned Zhukov to interrogate him on his intentions. Zhukov intimated that he would strike with all speed for Küstrin on the Oder, with his right flank forces swinging north and north-west to check any threat from East Pomerania, though as yet there was no immediate danger. Stalin appeared unconvinced, reminding Zhukov that his Front would be separated by 150 kilometres from Rokossovskii. Zhukov was to wait until Rokossovskii had completed the 'East Prussian operation' and had his forces 'out beyond the Vistula'. That, Stalin added, would take ten days, while at the same time Koniev could not cover Zhukov's left flank due to the involvement of 1st Ukrainian Front in investing the Silesian industrial region. Stalin would neither give Zhukov the additional reinforcement he sought nor a definite decision about continuing the offensive. Zhukov calculated that German forces could not organise a counter-stroke before Soviet units reached the Oder and even if a threat developed, there would be time to regroup from the Oder and contain the situation. Stalin grudgingly agreed but added a further warning about Zhukov's right flank, still refusing to provide further reinforcement.

Though *Festung* Poznan could not be reduced off the march, the Miedzyrzec 'fortified line', largely unmanned, was taken and on the morning of 31 January forward elements of 5th Shock Army reached the Oder, seizing a bridgehead. Five days earlier Zhukov had evidently decided to go for Berlin at top speed, submitting what he called 'a tentative plan' for a non-stop offensive opening on the morning of 1-2 February. With ammunition replenished and armour at full readiness, 3rd Shock Army and 1st Polish Army moved into the first echelon. The plan was to strike along 'the Berlin axis', with 2nd Guards and 1st Guards Tank Army converging on Berlin from the north-west and north-east respectively.[18]

Marshal Koniev's plan followed within 24 hours. The first stage of his operations involved the elimination of German forces in Breslau with an attack launched from two bridgeheads north and south of the city, followed by an advance to the Elbe (reached by 25-26 February), with the right flank armies of 1st Ukrainian Front co-operating with

Zhukov's Front to capture Berlin.[19] Koniev's left flank would strike for Dresden, relying on support from 4th Ukrainian Front.

Stalin approved these plans without apparent demur. Zhukov's Front 'orientation order' did not anticipate strong German counter-attacks. It advised the absence of a firm enemy front, required immediate consolidation of positions, replenishment of fuel and ammunition, and with bridgeheads taken on the western bank of the Oder the seizure of Berlin on 15-16 February in a 'lightning thrust' (*strtemitel'nym broskom*).[20]

The 'lightning thrust' never materialised. Soviet armies had already outrun not only *Stavka* directives but also supplies of fuel and ammunition.[21] Fuel might be scraped up but not ammunition. Zhukov was increasingly concerned with both flanks: to the north and south. On 31 January he informed Stalin that his frontage now extended for 500 kilometres and that on his left Rokossovskii was lagging behind, needing urgently to advance his 70th Army, while Koniev was not yet on the Oder. The General Staff had also to resolve the problem that while Stalin had earlier designated Zhukov the sole 'victor of Berlin', Marshal Koniev was now apparently to participate in the assault on the German capital. Losses and shortages increasingly denuded Zhukov's forces, which he had to assemble for the coming assault but also re-deploy to buttress his right flank, where 'a huge and almost unprotected gap' was opening up with 2nd Belorussian Front.[22] Air reconnaissance now reported a German build-up in East Pomerania.

As early as 25 January Stalin had appeared to waver in his assessment of the situation. The *Stavka*, in effect Stalin, pondered German reinforcement and the problem of the two flanks. If Stalin had at the end of January approved the 'dash for Berlin', in a matter of days he rapidly rescinded that decision. Priority was directed to fending off the threat of 'converging attacks' from East Pomerania and Silesia and as the original *Stavka* plan unravelled Stalin plumped for what amounted to a 'no risks' policy.

The flaws in the original *Stavka* plan now began to show up, bringing confusion to both the Front commands and the centre. Additionally Stalin had to reckon on the imminence of the Yalta Conference, where he took his stand on implementing *joint* plans for the defeat of Germany and in so doing gained the support of the United States for his designs for post-war Germany. Strict though his terms proved to be, in the context of 'Big Three' unity at Yalta, Stalin held out at least the prospect of collaboration, which a unilateral Soviet seizure of Berlin would have contradicted, if not completely sundered. Throughout the Yalta conference Stalin harried both Zhukov and Koniev over the problem with their flanks, Zhukov's right to the north, Koniev's forces facing a possible German counter-blow to the south, with the German command unreconciled to the loss of the

Silesian industrial basin, the 'second Ruhr'. 'You had better watch out' Stalin cautioned Koniev at a time when it seemed possible that Sixth *SS Panzer* Army might be deployed against 1st Ukrainian Front.[23] Stalin now demanded plans for an operation to reduce Upper Silesia.

While this period of 'co-operative policy' on the part of Stalin persisted, in late February the *Stavka* issued orders for a joint operation involving 1st and 2nd Belorussian Fronts to eliminate the threat from East Pomerania, an offensive running from the south in a northerly direction aimed at Kolberg (Kolobrzeg) designed to split German forces in two. Zhukov was ordered to complete his preparations by the end of February and to attack no later than 1 March.[24]

*

At the first symptoms of the Allies' having designs on Berlin Stalin speedily abandoned his show of a 'co-operative policy'. Early in March 1945, during the East Pomeranian operation, he summoned Zhukov to Moscow and ordered him to look over the calculations for the Berlin operation with General Antonov at the General Staff. This meant amending the original November 1944 plan, which had envisaged a 'non-stop' strike on Berlin, but which now needed readjustment in the light of the East Pomeranian and Upper Silesian operations.

The General Staff planning was augmented by submissions from the chiefs of staff of the three Fronts, Bogolyubov (2nd Belorussian), Malinin (1st Belorussian) and Sokolovskii, subsequently replaced by Petrov (1st Ukrainian). The staff of 1st Belorussian on 28 March submitted two 'variants' for the Berlin operation:

Plan A which proposed an offensive from those positions and bridgeheads already in Soviet hands, mounting the main attack from the Küstrin bridgehead with three all-arms armies and two tank armies;

Plan B which suggested a number of limited attacks to improve the operational position, seizing a new bridgehead south of Schwedt from which three all-arms armies would attack, as well as enlarging the Frankfurt bridgehead in which the main striking force would be concentrated, three all-arms armies and two tank armies committed to the main assault.[25]

The three-Front 'Berlin operation' envisaged by the *Stavka* drew in: 21 all-arms armies, four tank armies, 3 'air armies', 10 independent tank and mechanised corps, plus four cavalry corps. Additionally, units of the Baltic Fleet were to be committed with aircraft of the 18th Air Army of Long-Range Aviation (*ADD*) also assigned to the operation. Air defence elements (*PVO strany*) and the Dnieper River Flotilla were subordinated to the command of 1st Belorussian Front. Two Polish armies (1st and 2nd) were attached to this force, 185,000 men with a tank and aviation corps, two artillery 'breakthrough' divisions, independent 'mortar brigades' ('*Katyusha*' MRLs), 508 tanks and self-propelled guns and 320 aircraft.[26]

The overall strategic concept called for powerful attacks by three Fronts supported by Long-Range Aviation across a front running from Stettin to Prenzlau (Pensk), encircling defending enemy forces, splitting up the 'Berlin group' into isolated pockets prior to eliminating them and seizing Berlin. By the 12th-15th days of operations Soviet forces should have reached the Elbe on a broad front, linking up with the Allied armies.

1st Belorussian Front was committed to three simultaneous thrusts to overcome enemy defences on a 90-kilometre sector between the Hohenzollern Canal and the Oder-Spree. The task was to destroy the German Ninth Army at the approaches to Berlin, storm the German capital and drive westwards to the Elbe within 12 to 15 days of the operation. The main assault was to be mounted by four all-arms and two tank armies breaking out of the bridgehead on the Oder west of Küstrin, with the tank armies exploiting the breakthrough to outflank Berlin from the north and north-east. This main assault force was to be reinforced by an additional all-arms army drawn from the second echelon, a reinforcement promised by Stalin. To secure the main assault force two supporting attacks each with two armies were aimed north-westwards to Eberswalde and in the general direction of Furstenwalde-Potsdam-Brandenburg, the latter designed to outflank Berlin from the south. Artillery density was fixed at 250 pieces per kilometre of front.

Koniev's 1st Ukrainian Front was charged with the destruction of Fourth *Panzer* Army in the Cottbus area and south of Berlin, attaining the Beelitz-Wittenberg line and the river Elbe in the area of Dresden no later than the 10th-12th day of operations. The main attack was aimed in the direction of Spremberg, a supporting blow towards Dresden using two all-arms armies. The left flank was to go over to a firm defensive, covering the 'Breslau axis'. Reinforcement, even if late in arriving, was expected to come from 3rd Belorussian Front (28th and 31st Army). Both tank armies (3rd and 4th Guards) were to be committed to the main attack once enemy defences had been overrun. Artillery density was fixed at 250 pieces 'of 76-mm and upwards calibre' per kilometre of front.

Rokossovskii's 2nd Belorussian Front was assigned to an offensive towards Stettin-Rostock. His task was to force the Oder north of

Schwedt, destroy Third *Panzer* Army and prevent it falling back on Berlin. At the same time he was to cover 1st Belorussian Front operations from the north, striking westwards and north-westwards. The main assault was to be launched from north of Schwedt towards Neustrelitz with three all-arms armies, three tank and one mechanised corps.

The whole grand design of the 'Berlin operation' encompassed the co-ordination of three Fronts mounting six powerful offensives designed to smash in enemy defences on a broad front, first encircling and then destroying the defenders piecemeal. The encirclement of the main defensive force (Ninth Army and Fourth *Panzer* Army) would be effected by right-flank elements of 1st Belorussian Front, outflanking Berlin from the north and north-west, and right-flank forces of 1st Ukrainian Front outflanking the city from the south and south-west.

Splitting the encircled enemy units into two parts was assigned to the left flank of the 1st Belorussian Front to the south of Berlin and Brandenburg. Success here would seal off the German Ninth Army from the fighting for the city. North of Berlin the destruction of Third *Panzer* Army by 2nd Belorussian Front and blocking any retreat to the west would prevent this force lending any aid to the German capital. The Baltic Fleet was assigned to cover 2nd Belorussian's coastal flank and sustain the blockade of German forces in Kurland.[27]

The General Staff, however, faced what appeared to be an intractable problem. In November 1944 Stalin had stipulated that Zhukov with 1st Belorussian Front was designated the sole 'victor of Berlin', a ruling which seemed to shut off Koniev's 1st Ukrainian Front from any part in the capture of the capital. It was a 'somewhat heated' Marshal Koniev who brought up the awkward question of the demarcation line between his 1st Ukrainian Front and Zhukov's 1st Belorussian. General Antonov 'drew the Supreme Commander's attention' to this problem, the frontal boundaries which ran from Gross Gastrose on the Oder to Gross Michendorf south of the capital and further to Brandenburg. Such a demarcation prevented Koniev from aiming his right flank, above all the tank armies, at the south-western suburbs of Berlin and thus possibly prejudiced the whole operation which provided for the 'co-operation' of Koniev's right flank forces with 1st Belorussian in the capture of Berlin.

Koniev's plans, fully developed in his submission of 28 January 1945, made sense to the General Staff but ran foul of Stalin's diktat. Without a word of explanation, a not unusual circumstance, Stalin produced his own cunning solution, one which literally set Zhukov and Koniev at each other's throats. On the operational map he struck out the section which excluded 1st Ukrainian Front from Berlin, allowing it to run as far as Lübben, some 60 kilometres south-east of the capital. He also gave *verbal* orders to Koniev to make provision in his operational plans for the possibility of turning his tank armies *northwards* to strike towards Berlin once the German defences on the Neisse had been overrun. Aware that he was deliberately starting a race, Stalin commented: *'Kto pervyi vorvetsya—tot pust' i beret Berlin'*, 'Whoever breaks in first takes Berlin'.[28] It was also a signal that the Berlin operation would be run on virtually an hour-to-hour basis with control exercised by Moscow and Stalin acting as his own *'Stavka* co-ordinator', the Front commands reacting to a rapidly changing situation.

Rokossovskii, earlier robbed of his prize command of 1st Belorussian Front, arrived in Moscow on 6 April. Unlike Zhukov and Koniev, Rokossovskii had no prior Front plan on which the subsequent *Stavka* directive could be based and moreover his forces were as yet more than 300 kilometres distant, driving on Gdynia and Danzig. His Front had to re-deploy to the lower Oder, taking over the positions held by one army on Zhukov's right flank. Given the extent of the movement involved, Rokossovskii asked for his offensive to be postponed for four days, to 20 April, a concession which had to be dragged out of Stalin, though he had previously recognised that delay would be inevitable—*'nie beda'*, 'no great loss'.[29] Rokossovskii received the formal *Stavka* directive, No 11062, on 6 April 1945.

As more than two million Red Army men, 6,250 tanks and 7,500 aircraft were moved into their assault positions, in Moscow Stalin carefully parried Ambassador Harriman's query about the imminence of a Soviet attack on Berlin. Studiously offhand, Stalin admitted that an offensive was indeed in the offing but it might or might not be successful and in any event the main axis was directed at Dresden rather than Berlin, a state of affairs well known to General Eisenhower. But at the appointed hour, 5 am on the morning of 16 April, thousands of Soviet guns aided by bombers rained down half a million shells, rockets and bombs from Zhukov's Küstrin bridgehead, with 143 searchlights to illuminate the ground in front of the infantry. To the south Koniev's guns opened fire at 0615 hours, laying down both fire and smoke-screens across the length of the Front.

*

On the Neisse the first 60-ton bridge was opened on the stroke of noon and Lelyushenko's lead tanks from 4th Guards Tank Army moved off for the western bank precisely at 1300 hours, much to Koniev's satisfaction. No such precision attended Zhukov's assault to the north, where a mighty traffic jam added to the confusion on the approaches to the Seelow heights. Against the protests of the infantry commanders Zhukov decided to call on his tanks, six armoured corps, intent on loosing 1,700 tanks and self-propelled guns to smash his way forward. The tanks jammed the few roads available for movement, hampering the artillery which the infantry desperately needed.[30]

The failure of the first day was accompanied by an uncomfortable exchange with Moscow. In his telephone report to Stalin, Zhukov learned of Koniev's successes, achieved 'without difficulty', and had to suffer Stalin's increasing aggravation at his recital of failure. Stalin rounded angrily on Zhukov for having committed 1st Guards Tank Army on Chuikov's 8th Guards sector, contravening the *Stavka*'s original instructions. Brushing aside Zhukov's explanations, though noting the promise of success on 17 April, Stalin intimated that 'we', namely, the *Stavka* and himself, were thinking of instructing Koniev to swing his tank armies on to Berlin from the south, at the same time ordering Rokossovskii to speed up his attack on the Oder and outflank Berlin from the north. All that Zhukov got was a curt 'Good-bye' from Stalin.[31] Koniev meanwhile issued orders for the 17th: penetration of the second line of German defences, forcing the Spree and an advance to north-west of Cottbus. Luchinskii's 28th Army was to move in the wake of Rybalko's 3rd Guards Tank Army, and strike along the 'Berlin axis' without waiting for the full concentration of the army.[32]

Zhukov regrouped the formations scattered in the abortive fighting on 16 April, launched 800 bombers on night attacks on the German positions and began the day with a massed artillery barrage. At the close of 17 April the village of Seelow fell to 8th Guards, German lines began to crack but the flanks still held. To the south Rybalko's tanks raced for the Spree where one Soviet tank found shallow water for a crossing. Lead brigades were over the Spree, all promptly reported to Stalin, and inspiring him to consider a fresh manoeuvre, encircling the entire enemy force defending Berlin with powerful tank forces driving on the capital from the south, simultaneously outflanking the city from the south-west. This also depended on speeding up the movements of 1st Belorussian Front. Zhukov's delay caused Stalin growing concern, prompting him to instruct Koniev to aim his right flank to approach Berlin from the south, with 3rd Guards Tank Army striking through Zossen, 4th Guards Tank Army aiming at Potsdam.

Koniev issued the requisite Front directive at 0247 hours on 18 April, ordering Rybalko to 'break into Berlin from the south on the night of 20-21 April', with Lelyushenko instructed by the same date to seize Potsdam and the south-western suburb of Berlin.[33] From Zhukov Stalin demanded 'requisite measures' to speed up his attack and, rubbing salt in the wound, offered the *Stavka*'s assistance. Zhukov's ferocious dictum was now 'advance or face the consequences'. 1st Belorussian Front commanders were given until 1200 hours to put their units in order, issue precise operational orders, replenish ammunition and then advance *according to plan*. Fully two days late,

Zhukov could only hope that on the fourth day of his offensive he would attain the objectives originally set for the second day.

At 11 am on 20 April Zhukov's artillery opened fire directly on Berlin. Third Shock Army was through the third belt of German defence and Bogdanov's 2nd Guards tanks reached open country to strike for the outskirts of Berlin, with two corps (9th Tank and 1st Mechanised) driving to outflank the city from the north. Koniev's tank armies sliced north-westwards, isolating Fourth *Panzer* Army, cutting Busse's lines of communication, driving to Zossen and Potsdam, but Koniev wanted more. On 20 April he radioed the tank armies: 'Order you categorically to break into Berlin tonight. Report execution. 1940 hours 20.4.45 Koniev.' One hour later Zhukov issued his own special orders to Katukov with 1st Guards Tank Army, emphasising the 'historic mission' of being the first to break into Berlin. Katukov was personally charged with this mission: 'no later than 0400 hours morning 21 April at any cost to break into the outskirts of Berlin and report at once for transmission to Comrade Stalin and for press announcement'.[34]

During the course of 22 April, with five rifle armies and four tank armies fully engaged, the noose tightened round the German capital. Zhukov committed 1st and 2nd Guards Tank Army, 8th Guards, 5th Shock, 3rd Shock and 47th Army to the inner battle for Berlin. Rybalko's 3rd Guards Tank Army, operating with 1st Ukrainian Front, was simultaneously deploying at the approaches to the city and about to break in, supported by the infantry of Luchinskii's 28th Army, while Lelyushenko's 4th Guards Tank Army was driving at speed to the south-west.

But any idea that the city might be taken in a rush, off the march, vanished abruptly once both infantry and armour were consumed in bitter street battles. Fighting within prescribed sectors, formations deployed assault squads and assault companies supported by tanks, sappers, flame-throwers and artillery used to blast away strong-points and buildings, with each corps holding a division in reserve.[35] Meanwhile, Lelyushenko's tanks sweeping south-westwards were now less than 50 kilometres from Perkhorovich's 47th Army advancing from the north, thus on the verge of clamping a huge encirclement ring round the city to the west. The trap was almost sprung, with Rybalko about to make contact with Katukov's tanks and Chuikov's infantry in the southern suburbs of Berlin.

Further to the south the German 'Frankfurt-Guben group' was trapped, while to the west the German escape route to the Elbe had been cut. At this juncture, with Soviet armies about to become enmeshed with each other, Stalin acted. At 0045 hours on 23 April he issued *Stavka* directive No 11074, classified secret, setting the boundary between 1st Belorussian and 1st Ukrainian Front. The cut was deep and decisive, slicing through Berlin and placing Koniev's demarcation a matter of some 100 metres *west of the Reichstag,* leaving the outstanding prize—the very symbol of the defeat of the Reich—to Zhukov. The new boundary line took effect as from 0600 hours, 23 April.

Directive 11074 also demanded the elimination of the German 'Frankfurt-Guben group' by 24 April, blocking any attempt by the German Ninth Army and elements of Fourth *Panzer* to break through to Berlin 'on western or south-western axes'. The German force, some 200,000 strong with 300 tanks and assault guns, was hemmed in by Soviet forces numbering 277,000 men with 280 tanks. Soviet armies had closed on Berlin from three sides, leaving only three roads open to the west. Within the city a great link-up was about to take place with the junction of Chuikov's 8th Guards and Katukov's tanks with Luchinskii's 28th Army and Rybalko's tanks in the south-eastern sector of Berlin, but Russian losses were beginning to tell.[36]

With the inner ring closed, at noon on 25 April the outer encirclement wings of 1st Belorussian and 1st Ukrainian Front finally met at Ketzin. The encirclement line was now manned by no less than nine armies. In the wooded country south-east of Berlin the Frankfurt-Guben group was blockaded by a further five armies. The encirclement of Berlin was completed by 25 April and the splitting of the *Reich* itself accomplished on the afternoon of that day with the junction of Soviet and American troops on the Elbe. Marshal Koniev reported details of that contact in most precise terms to Stalin: '1330 hours, 25 April, in the area of Strela'.[37]

On 23 April Stalin cancelled his 18 April orders to Rokossovskii to outflank Berlin from the north and reinstated the original directive of 6 April: a drive to the west and the destruction of German forces at Stettin. Having battered Third *Panzer* almost to destruction, Rokossovskii intended to envelop it from the south and south-west, isolate it from Berlin and cut the escape route to the west. Far to the south Zhukov issued orders on 25 April for attacks from the north and north-west to split the Frankfurt-Guben group and effect a junction with 69th and 33rd Army from 1st Ukrainian Front, units quickly engulfed in holding desperate German attempts to break out. Inside blazing, shell-shattered Berlin on 26 April 464,000 Soviet troops supported by 12,000 guns and mortars, *Katyusha* rocket-launchers, 1,500 tanks and hundreds of aircraft from 16th and 18th Air Armies swarmed for the final assault.[38]

Zeroing in on the *Reichstag*, Chuikov's 8th Guards advanced on the *Tiergarten* from the south, 5th Shock moved from the east, 3rd Shock from the north-east. Not only did the range close but the confusion increased as Rybalko's tanks and Luchinskii's infantry tangled with Chuikov's deployments, much to the fury of Zhukov who sought from Stalin one further, final demarcation line for his forces and those of Koniev. Not to be outdone in the contest for the real prize, the *Reichstag*, Koniev ordered Rybalko to clear all the south-eastern districts of Berlin, determined to have him on the western edge of the *Tiergarten*. But Zhukov won the day on the demarcation at Stalin's behest. Much to Rybalko's disgust and despite his passionate, even insubordinate protest, Koniev ordered him to shift the axis of his attack to the north-west, effectively sealing him off from the centre.[39]

German battle groups trying to break the Soviet outer encirclement inflicted heavy losses on both sides. Inside Berlin on 28 April Rybalko pushed his attack into Charlottenburg and Lelyushenko launched his assault on Wannsee island late in the evening. In the heart of the city General Perevertkin's 79th Rifle Corps prepared to attack the *Reichstag*, the orders specifying that the first to raise the 'Victory banner' over the building would be decorated Hero of the Soviet Union. Shortly after midnight on 30 April Hitler learned that no relief for Berlin would be forthcoming from outside, though he forbade a general surrender.

Towards midday Soviet regiments prepared for the final assault on the *Reichstag*. At 1300 hours 89 Soviet guns opened fire on the building: Captain Neustroyev's 1st Battalion from Colonel Zinchenko's 765th Rifle Regiment prepared an assault, though surprised to learn that Zhukov had already issued an Order of the Day announcing that the *Reichstag* had been seized and the 'Victory Banner' hoisted. Colonel Zinchenko shrugged and issued his final orders: 'Off you go, lads, and stick the Banner up there'.[40] At 3 pm on the afternoon of 2 May 1945, after General Weidling, signing himself 'former Commandant of the Berlin Defence Zone', had issued orders to end resistance, Soviet guns ceased firing and a general surrender ensued.[41]

*

Addressing the question of a possible assault on Berlin, General Omar N Bradley, commander of the United States 12th Army Group, warned General Eisenhower that the cost in casualties, killed, missing and wounded, could well be in the order of 100,000. The 'Berlin strategic offensive operation' conducted by the Red Army cost almost four times that number: 352,475, of whom 78,291 were killed or missing in action, and 274,184 wounded, to which should be added the casualties sustained by 1st and 2nd Polish Army, 8,892 (2,825 killed or missing in action). The heaviest losses were borne by Zhukov's 1st Belorussian Front (179,490, of which 37,610 were killed or missing), followed by Koniev's 1st Ukrainian (113,825 of which 27,580 were killed or missing). On closer inspection, Zhukov's casualty figures might appear less dreadful, since his Front mustered 908,500 men while Koniev's command had only half that number, 550,900. Marshal Rokossovskii's 2nd Belorussian Front,

441,600 strong, suffered losses of 59,110 (13,070 killed or missing). The Baltic Fleet escaped with losses of 23 (15 killed).[42] The total Soviet force committed to the Berlin operation consisted of 161 rifle divisions, 20 corps, 15 brigades and 2 'fortified areas' (*UR*s), with Zhukov's Front deploying the bulk of the rifle divisions, 72 as opposed to 33 for Rokossovskii and 44 for Koniev.

With a smaller force but incurring proportionately heavier casualties, Koniev enjoyed striking success in the Berlin operation. With hindsight Zhukov considered that the capture of Berlin could have been conducted 'in a somewhat different way'. From the outset it should have been a two-Front operation with a specific line of demarcation between them, thus enabling 1st Belorussian to strike on a narrower sector, outflanking Berlin from the north-east, north and north-west, 1st Ukrainian taking the shortest route to Berlin to outflank the city from the south, south-west and west. Alternatively, the operation could have been mounted by one Front only, 1st Belorussian, the left flank reinforced with two rifle and two tank armies, one air army, artillery and engineers. The deployment of 2nd Belorussian Front could have been altered and simplified.

The 'Berlin strategic offensive operation' had been conceived, organised, timed and executed almost exclusively in accordance with Stalin's will and whim. But even his satisfaction was qualified. It may be, as Marshal Rokossovskii observed, that the idea of Stalin's demanding that Berlin be taken by 1 May was 'imagination', but the city was indeed in Soviet hands by that date and Marshal Zhukov had made sure that Stalin knew of it. Stalin could congratulate himself on having played the 'Supreme Commander' to the end, but this was seemingly not enough, whatever the plaudits. On being saluted for the capture of the city by Ambassador Harriman, Stalin reportedly replied: 'Yes, but Tsar Alexander I reached Paris.'[43]

Discussion

Presenting his paper, *Professor Erickson* (introduced by *Sir Michael Howard* as the man who knows more about the Soviet army than they did themselves) stressed the importance of trying to understand what was in Stalin's mind. He wanted a no-risk military strategy, and to achieve his ends diplomatically if possible. He may well have thought that the Allies were playing a double-bluff, and that he had time to play with. Professor Erickson described the Russian style of war as 'grand opera': on a huge scale, but with elements of farce. In reply to *Sir Frank Roberts's* request for his opinion on Stalin as a commander, *Professor Erickson* replied that Stalin was not a great strategic commander: his great strength was his ability to relate military to political strategy; 'clear-cut, cold and calculating', as a political strategist he was a great war leader, but his military strategies based on war-shortening tactics could be reckless. *Professor Rzheshevsky* agreed that Stalin's word was always final.

With regard to the Koniev/Zhukov race, Marshall Rokossovki had told *Professor Erickson* in 1963 that the real aim was to seal off Berlin from the Western armies: if Zhukov failed, he would join Koniev in finishing the job. But Koniev was a more efficient commander, and if the race had been treated rationally, the Berlin operation would have been over more quickly with fewer casualties. *Professor Rzheshevsky* stressed how much it meant to the Soviet forces to get to Berlin first: 'the highest moment of Communist ideology coming from the soul'. *Professor Erickson* agreed with *Sir Frank Roberts* that the Zhukov/Koniev issue was a throwback to Stalin's experiences in Poland in 1920.

Notes and References

In April-May 1963 in Moscow I had the opportunity to discuss the Berlin operation with several Marshals of the Soviet Union, senior formation commanders and Soviet soldiers from the units involved. In addition, with the assistance of Lieutenant-General Platonov of the General Staff, I was given access to the planning documents, including the *Stavka* directives and operational orders from Front commanders. I was given the originals on condition that they could not be photocopied but I was free to copy all documents by hand, material which I have kept over the years. One aspect of this process was the possibility of discussing particular directives or orders with the commanders involved, hence an extensive verbatim record of these exchanges. The material on the German surrender in Berlin was at that time classified but I was given access to it on the condition that it was not immediately published nor shown to 'any third party'. All this is many years ago but it has given me the opportunity to compare what was shown to me at first-hand, or discussed across the table and in subsequent exchanges.

1   This conference, held from 9-12 April 1946, was attended by 349 generals, senior officers, representatives of the General Staff and General Staff Academy under the chairmanship of Army General V D Sokolovskii, C-in-C GSFG who had replaced Marshal Zhukov, by then in disfavour with Stalin. 1st Belorussian Front was represented by Colonel-General M S Malinin, Chief of Staff GSFG, an experienced staff and operations officer, chief of staff 1st Belorussian Front in 1944. That conference had been preceded in February by the study conference, held by the C-in-C of Central Group of Forces (CGF) Marshal Koniev, discussing both the Berlin and Prague operation (see *Voenno-istoricheskii Zhurnal*, henceforth cited as *ViZh*, 1985 No 4, pp 52-59 for an abbreviated version of Marshal Koniev's lecture); Marshal Rokossovskii had been quickest off the mark, holding his study conference as early as 20-24 August 1945. A list of the participants and their lecture subjects at these three study conferences is supplied in Major-General N A Talenskii (ed), *Berlinskaya operatsiya 1945 goda*, (Moscow, Voenizdat, 1950), pp 544-46.

2   *Shturm Berlina* is a compilation of first-hand accounts under the following headings: The Oder Bridgehead; The break-through; At the approaches to and in

the suburbs of Berlin; The forcing of the Spree; The steel pincers of our troops; In the central districts [of Berlin]; The capture of the Reichstag; The capitulation of Berlin. Much of this first-hand material was also represented in the 1956 20th anniversary publications: see items in *Pravda, Izvestiya, Pravda Vostoka* (Uzbekistan), *Kazakhstanskaya Pravda, Sovetskaya Kirgiziya, Turkmenskaya Iskra, Kommunist Tadzhikistana, Krasnaya Zveda* for the period 30 April-8 May 1965. A bibliography of publications 1947-67 is supplied in *SSSR v Velikoi Otechestvennoi voiny 1941-1945 gg, Ukazatel' sovetskoi libteratury*, (Moscow, Nauka, 1977) Ch III (12) on the Berlin operation, pp 304-12.

3   This volume was produced under the auspices of the Main Military-Scientific Administration of the General Staff of the Soviet Armed Forces, and drew its sources from (i) the *Stavka* directives for the period April-May 1945 plus the Supreme Commander's [Stalin's] orders; (ii) manpower/manning strengths for the Soviet Fronts from the records of the *Glavnoe-organizatsionnoe upravelnie General'nogo shtaba*; (iii) intelligence reports, *Razvedyvatel'nye svodki,*. GRU GS; (iv) war diaries, three Fronts; (v) Front directives, operational reports, intelligence summaries, training schedules; (vi) war diaries all armies (though not 4 Gds Tank Army?). There were 79 tables and a supplement of 122 maps.

4   V I Chuikov, *Oktyabr 1964*, Nos 3-4 and *Novaya i noveishaya istoriya*, 1965, No 2.

5   Verbatim, Marshal V I Chuikov, Moscow, 27 April 1963. Colone! Albert Seaton has the most apt verdict in *Stalin as Warlord*, (London, 1976), p 239, describing Chuikov as 'a retrospective "if only" man'. The logistics problem facing Chuikov and 1st Belorussian Front is discussed in some detail by Lieutenant-General N Antipenko, 'Ot visly do Odera', *ViZh*, 1965 No 3, pp 69-81.

6   Marshal G K Zhukov, 'Na berlinskom napravlenii', *ViZh*, 1965, No 6, here pp 16-18: also Zhukov, *Vospominaniya i razmyshleniya*, (Moscow, APN, 1990), (10th edn), Volume 3, pp 206-7.

7   See Marshal G K Zhukov, *'Pechat porochit moyu deyatel'nost'*, letter to Comrade N S Khrushchev, First Secretary TsK KPSSS, copy to Comrade V Kochetov, editor of *Oktyabr'*, in *Istochnik Prilozhenie k zhurnalu RODINA*, 1993, Nos 5-6, pp 153-5, refuting Chuikov's arguments and restating the problem of Zhukov's right flank, plus Zhukov's exchanges with Stalin. Zhukov also complained about Voronov taking the credit for the planning of the Soviet counter-stroke at Khalkin-Gol in 1939. Zhukov's letter is dated 18 April 1964.

8   See Lieutenant-General N G Pavlenko, *Bykla voina... Razmyshleniya voennogo istorika* (Moscow, 'Rodnik', 1994), pp 413-14. General Pavlenko asked Zhukov to explain why he used tank armies in a 'frontal attack' on Berlin and rifle armies to outflank the city. On the employment of tank armies and related controversies, see Marshal of Tank Troops P A Rotmistrov, April 1946 conference lecture, 'Ispol'zovanie tankovykh voisk v Berlinskoi operatsii', *ViZh*, 1985, No 9, pp 43-50, also Army General A Radzievskii (Chief of Staff, 2nd Guards Tank Army), 'Stremitel'nye deistviya tankovykh armii', *ViZh*, 1965, No 1, pp 8-15. Also Colonel-General Yu M Potapov, 'Primenenie

tankovykh armii v Berlinskoi operatsii', *ViZh* 1985, No 5, pp 27-30: on 1st Guards Tank Army, A Kh Babadzhanyan et al, *Lyuki otkryli v Berline* (Moscow, Voenizdat, 1973); on 3rd Guards Tank Army, Colonel-General A M Zvartsev (ed), *3-ya gvardeiskaya tankovaya* (Moscow, Voenizdat, 1982). On 4th Guards Tank Army operations see General D Lelyushenko, 'Pered nami Berlin!', *ViZh*, 1970, No 6, pp 66-72.

9   A two-volume version, *The Soviet General Staff at War 1941-1945*, was published in English by Progress, Moscow, Books 1-2, 1985-86. For an initial version dealing with 1945 see S Shtemenko, 'Kak planirovalas poslednyaya kampaniya po razgromu gitlerovskoi Germanii', *ViZh*, 1965, No 5, pp 56-72.

10   *Poslednii shturm (Berlinskaya operatsiya 1945)* (Moscow, Voenizdat, 1975), 2nd edn, 455 pp, supplement of 10 maps. (The 1970 edition runs to 464 pp and has a supplement of 15 maps.) On closer inspection this volume (in both its editions) appears to be an unclassified version of Talenskii's 1950 study (see note 3), upon which the colonels Vorob'ev and Parotkin had worked previously, together with Major-General Zamyatin. The 1970/1975 volume follows the main outlines of the 1950 work, but much of the documentary material has been stripped out.

11   Shtemenko, *op cit* (with map of stages of the planned offensive). Though Shtemenko advertises it as such, Zhukov, *Vpospominaniya*, vol 3, pp 183-4, makes it plain that this was not a 'non-stop' drive for Berlin: 'the subsequent advance was not planned' once 1st Belorussian Front reached the Bromberg-Poznan line and made tactical contact with 1st Ukrainian Front to the left. It is possible to argue that much of the later confusion and complication was brought about by the flaws in the original *Stavka* plan.

12   Marshal K Rokossovskii, *A Soldier's Duty*, (Moscow, Progress, 1985), p 267, quotes Rokossovskii saying to Stalin: 'What have I done to be transferred from the main to a secondary sector?' Though these 'Rokossovskii memoirs' were something of a concoction, Rokossovskii had some cause to be aggrieved and also troubled by the *Stavka* assignment: see Marshal K Rokossovskii, 'Na berlinskom i vostochno-prusskom napravleniyakh', *ViZh*, 1965, No 2, pp 25-28.

13   *A Soldier's Duty*, p 270, makes the comment that the *Stavka* 'evidently expected our neighbour [3rd Belorussian Front] to advance abreast of us. But we had not even been informed where the Commander of the Third Belorussian Front, I D Chernyakhovskii, was to deliver his main attack'. The *Stavka* had failed 'to say anything about co-ordination on the right, evidently assuming that *"no complications could be expected on our northern flank"'* (emphasis added).

14   Zhukov, *'Vospominaniya'*, vol 3, p 183.

15   I S Koniev, *Sorok pyatyi*, (Moscow, Voenizdat, 1970), Series *'Voennye memuary'*, p 4: also I S Koniev, 'Ot Visly do Odera', *Novyi Mir*, 1965, No 5, pp 3-60.

16   The genuineness of Stalin's response to Churchill's request for relief from the German offensive in the Ardennes has ignited a recent controversy. V N Kiselev's article, 'Visla-Ardenny, 1944-1945', *ViZh*, 1993, No 6, pp 29-34, argues that the Soviet response by way of advancing the date of the offensive was in reality a piece of Stalinist cunning, a political ploy, and that the date of

the Soviet attack was not deliberately 'advanced' but was a myth deliberately propagated, to which the several marshals also subscribed. E N Kul'kov, 'Kto kogo spasal v Ardennakh?', *ViZh*, 1994, No 3, pp 34-37, was one of several who objected to the 'subjectivism' of Kiselev's earlier article and who seeks to validate Churchill's request and Stalin's response

[17] See V N Kiselev, 'Pocherk dvukh polkovodtsev', *ViZh*, 1995, No 1, p 10, comparing the operational handling by Zhukov and Koniev of tank armies in particular, in January 1945. Kiselev declares Zhukov 'the winner'.

[18] Zhukov, *Vospominaniya*, vol 3, p 199.

[19] Vorob'ev et al, *Poslednii shturm*, 2nd edn, p 40.

[20] Zhukov, *Vospominaniya*, vol 3, p 200 for the text of the order (para 2). What is omitted from this and previous versions of the Zhukov memoirs is the text of his operational plan, timed and dated 15.15 hrs 10 February 1945, submitted to Stalin, outlining an attack on Berlin with 1BF opening on 19 February 1945. Zhukov emphasised the need to preempt the reported transfer of Sixth *S S Panzer Army* to reinforce the Berlin defence. The 10 February plan does partially support Chuikov's arguments favouring a February strike, but does not confirm the possible success or otherwise of a 'high-risk' operation. Chuikov and Zhukov are agreed on the urgent need for substantial supplies of fuel, ammunition, etc. Full text 10 February order, *VizH*, 1995, No 2, pp 4-6, presented by General Yu M Komarov.

[21] In addition to these difficulties, which Marshal Chuikov freely acknowledged and urgently signalled, only 50% of 8th Guards Army would have been available for any drive on Berlin (the remainder held back at Poznan), losses having reduced regiments to two battalions and companies down to 22-45 men. Other armies, 5th Shock, 33rd and 69th reported shortages of ammunition and depleted ranks. Divisional strengths were down to an average of 4-5,000 men on both 1st Belorussian and 1st Ukrainian Fronts. Tank brigades were reduced to 40 machines or even 15-20. Chuikov argued that these two Fronts would have had 8-10 rifle armies and 3-4 tank armies for a thrust on Berlin. Zhukov points out that in fact 1st Belorussian had only 4 under-strength rifle armies available, the remainder of Front strength having been re-deployed northwards to East Pomerania. Marshal Koniev recognised the problem posed by East Pomerania as well as the effect of under-estimating German capacity to regroup and restore formations badly mauled in the Vistula-Oder operation. Over-extended lines of communication and the slowness in restoring rail links, also brought fuel and ammunition shortages to 1st Ukrainian Front. 2nd Guards Tank Army had suffered losses of 50% in tanks and SP guns: on 11 January its tank and SP gun strength amounted to 683 and 238 respectively, a total of 921; on 15 February that total strength had dropped to 418 (*3-ya gvardeiskaya*, pp 199 and 227).

[22] Zhukov, *Vospominaniya*, vol 3, p 197, signal to Stalin on the crisis on 1st Belorussian Front's extended right flank as Rokossovskii 'continues to stand still'. Zhukov also urged that Koniev should close on the Oder.

[23] I S Koniev, *Zapiski komanduyushchego frontom* (Moscow, Voenizdat, 1991), Series '*50 let pobedy. Biblioteka izbrannykh voennykh memuarov*', p 363. General Antonov laid the same stress on the danger to Koniev's left flank. In the event Sixth *SS Panzer* Army was deployed by Hitler in Hungary.

[24] For details see A S Zab'yalov and T E Kalyadin, *Vostochno-Pomeranskaya operatsiya sovetskikh voisk. Fevral'-mart 1945 gg. Voenno-istoricheskii ocherk* (Moscow, Voenizdat, 1960, supplement of 21 maps); for *Stavka* orders and Front decisions, pp 94-105. See also General P Batov, 'K 40-letiyu Vostochno Pomeranskoi operatsii', *ViZh*, 1985, No 2, pp 15-20; and Colonel I Yarosheko, 'Nekotorye dokumenty po Vostochno-Pomeranskoi operatsii, *ViZh*, 1985, No 3, pp 75-80 for *Stavka* directives and Front operational orders.

[25] Vorob'ev *et al*, *Poslednii shturm*, pp 43-4.

[26] On 1st Polish Army see Zdzislaw Stapor, *Bitwa o Berlin, Dzialania 1 Armii WP kwiecien-maj 1945. Seria Wojna wyzwolencza polskiego* (Warsaw, Mon, 1973), Part 1, pp 19-60 and Part 2, Ch VII, pp 109-126, 'Stan bojowy i zadania 1 armii WP'. For detailed material on Polish forces in the Vistula-Oder and Berlin operation see *Polski czyn zbrojny w II wojnie s wiatowej*. Tom VI, *Bibliografia wojny wyzwolenczej narodu polskiego 1939-1945* (Warsaw, Mon, 1973), pp 443-68 (refs 5120-5449).

[27] *Stavka* directives: to commander 1 Belorussian Front, Directive No 11059, dated 2 April, to commander 1 Ukrainian Front, Directive No 11060, dated 3 April, issued 2100 hours (demarcation 1 BF and 1 UF to Lübben as from 15.4.45), commander 2 Belorussian Front, Directive No 11062 issued 6 April 1945. *Stavka* directives for the whole period of the war are available in the recently declassified four volumes of *Sbornik dokumentov Verkhovnogo Glavnokomandovaniya za period Velikoi Otechestvennoi voiny, Sekretno* (Moscow, Voenizdat, 1968-69). vol I 6-12 1941; vol II 1-12 1942; vol III 1-12 1943 and vol IV 1 1944. Also printed in Talenskii, 'Berlinskaya operatsiya' (1950), pp 548-51.

[28] The famous phrase comes from Shtemenko, op cit, p 71. In line with his January operational plan, Koniev maintained that the Berlin operation essentially and inescapably involved both 1BFF and 1UF. Marshal Koniev, speaking on 23 April 1963, said: 'In view of the [*Stavka*] directive, my own order to 1 Ukrainian Front was to bear in mind that part of the forces of the right flank were to help 1BF in taking Berlin'. This was embodied in his orders to Rybalko's 3rd Guards Tank Army (which the Marshal proceeded to read out): 'From the line of the Spree, south of Cottbus, to strike in the general direction of Luckenwalde...on the 5th day of operations...to take Brandenburg with a reinforced tank corps and attack Berlin from the south'. What was of 'outstanding importance' was that 'there was no front boundary between 1UF and 1BF beyond Lübben'. As for the key question of the line of advance of the two tank armies of 1UF, Marshal Koniev said the following: 'This idea came to my mind at the beginning of April, when I was at the *Stavka* in Moscow. To finish the German forces would be difficult. In the actions of the forces of 1BF and 1UF very high skill would be needed and it could be supposed that all forms of operational manoeuvre would be used: (1) breakthrough, (2) manoeuvre in operational depth, especially the tank armies, (3) encirclement, (4) capture of Berlin. This task was impossible with one front, to move only from the centre, for both fronts fulfilled a mutual strategic task'.

[29] See Marshal K Rokossovskii, 'Severnee Berlina', *ViZh*, 1965, No 5, pp 37-41. Rokossovskii's orders (*Stavka* Directive No 11062) specified an offensive with 3 rifle armies, 2 tank and 1 mechanised corps to be mounted from the area north

of Schwedt in the general direction of Strelitz. Transport for regrouping was difficult. Neither the *Stavka* nor the General Staff could give Rokossovskii information about enemy forces along the line of his advance. This necessitated intensive reconnaissance which held up the necessary planning for the new offensive, much of it done by reference to maps. Discussing 2BF operations on 24 April 1963 Marshal Rokossovskii emphasised that the terrain with two rivers (West and Ost Oder), a river, swamp, then a second river greatly assisted the German defence. The task of 2BF was to eliminate any possibility of a counter-stroke by Manteuffel's Third *Panzer* Army against 1BF. 'We could not underestimate or over-estimate Manteuffel's strength'. See also General P I Batov, *Operatisiya 'Oder'* (Moscow, Voenizdat, 1965) 143 pp on operations of 65th Army.

[30] See Marshal of Tank Troops M E Katukov, *Na ostrie glavnogo udara* (Moscow, Voenizdat, 1974) for 1st Guards Tank operations, Seelow heights, pp 393-400. The Front command, namely Zhukov, failed to take account of the effectiveness of the German second line of defences: the first line had been thinned out so that the Soviet 'lightning blow' hit thin air, leaving Soviet units 'snagged' in one enemy defensive position after another. General Yushchuck, whose 11th Tank Corps was attached to 1st Guards Tank for this operation described (29 April 1963 in Moscow) heavy losses due to German tanks dug in: 'We moved forward the first day but we couldn't take the [Seelow] heights and we got stuck on our nose'.

[31] Zhukov, *Vospominaniya*, vol 3, pp 242-3.

[32] General Luchinskii's 28th Army had been transferred from 3 Belorussian Front to Koniev's 1st Ukrainian command. Briefing Luchinskii Koniev pointed to the map and to the centre of Berlin: 'That's where 3rd Guards Tank Army is going. Your army must catch up and together with it [3 Gds TA] break into Berlin'. After a pause Koniev added, 'I will subordinate a Front motor-transport regiment to your army'. See General A Luchinskii, '*Na Berlin!*', *ViZh*, 1965, No 5, pp 81-91.

[33] See Koniev, *Zapiski komanduyushchego frontom*, p 398. Towns and populated centres were to be bypassed, frontal engagements avoided, with the 'tank fist' pressing ahead boldly and decisively. The full text of Koniev's orders, as those of Zhukov, is included in the 'Appendices' (*Prilozhenii*) to Talenskii, *Berlinskaya operatsiya 1945 goda.*

[34] Full text in A Kh Babadzhanyan, *Dorogi pobedy*, Moscow, '*Molodaya gvardiya*', 1975, p 271. Also Talenskii, Zhukov's operational orders.

[35] Vorob'ev, *Poslednii shturm* has a section on German forces and preparations for the defence of Berlin, pp 22-38. Talenskii in the text and appendices (which under No 29 include a captured document, the German defence plan dated 9.3.45) has more detail, much drawn from Soviet intelligence reports on German strengths and deployments facing 1BF and 1UF; see pp 1-40 and appendices. The interrogation of General of Artillery Weidling, conducted by Major-General Trusov, '*Orvety byvshego komanduyushchego goroda Berlina general artillerii G. Veidlinga...*' was published with details of German strength and defences in *ViZh*, 1959, No 5, pp 89-95. On the Berlin defence and the German defenders in particular, see W Willemer, *The German Defense of Berlin*, MS P-136, Historical Division HQ US Army Europe, 1953.

[36] The question of losses, in particular Soviet tank losses, is complicated by the need to determine a base-line figure. *ViZh*, 1956, No 4, pp 79-86 supplies a vast array of figures in 'Berlinskaya operatsiya v tsifrakh' and while it has become a convention to cite 6,250 tanks as the total the Red Army committed to the Berlin operation, close inspection of the Soviet order of battle and tank-strength for all three Fronts reveals a figure of 3,594. Many tank formations had only 50-60% of their full strength, with a number of tank brigades and regiments distributed as infantry support. Total strength in SP/assault guns amounted to 2,519 pieces, deployed between 3 brigades, 61 regiments and 25 batteries. Adding tanks and SP guns gives the 6,000 round total, but concentrating on the tanks, the official figure for Soviet tank losses is 1,997 which does not vary significantly for losses declared in separate formations, namely in the order of 40-65%. General Yushchuk, commanding 11 Tank Corps, estimated the losses in his corps at about 40%. Overall Soviet losses and figures for German losses are discussed in note 42.

[37] Koniev's signal was more than a formality. In responding to criticism of how the tank armies were employed Zhukov pointed out that while on his Front 2nd Guards Tank Army followed in the wake of 47th Army moving round Berlin towards the Elbe, Koniev also raced for the Elbe. Stalin had asked Zhukov 'What if the Americans and English should break into Berlin before us?' Zhukov replied that the plan was to reach the Elbe with all speed, cut off (*otsech*') and isolate the Western armies from Berlin and only then concentrate on reducing the city: Pavlenko, *Byla voina...*, p 414.

[38] A General Staff Academy study on air operations was prepared by N I Veselov in 1948, *Deistviya aviatsii v Berlinskoi operatsii. VAGSh*. See, for example, the Air Operations Plan, 16th Air Army, assets, strikes, timings, targets, first phase of the offensive, Appendix 17, Talenskii, *Berlinskaya operatsiya*, pp 600-06. An excellent summary is provided by Von Hardesty, *Red Phoenix. The Rise of Soviet Air Power 1941-1945*, (Smithsonian Institution Press, Washington DC, 1982), pp 203-11.

[39] *Stavka* Directive 11077, dated 28 April. The demarcation between 1BF and 1UF ran as before though Mariendorf, but was now adjusted to slant north-westwards from the Tempelhof station to Viktoria-Luise-Platz, on to the Savigny station, thence along the railway line to Charlottenburg, Westkreuz and Ruhleben stations. See also I S Koniev, *Zapiski komanduyushchego frontom*, p 462.

[40] Colonel Neustroyev (a captain in 1945), whom I first met in 1963, has recently sent me the manuscript of his part in the storming of the *Reichstag*, a volume of memoirs which he has entitled 'Russian Soldier' and which he would like to see published outside Russia.

[41] Among a considerable volume of documentation, see the transcript of the Krebs-Weidling talks to arrange the Berlin surrender, 'Opisanie peregovorov s nachal'nikom shtaba sukhoputnykh voisk germanskoi armiii generalom pekhoty Ganson Krebsom...', *ViZh*, 1959, No 5, pp 81-89. For transcript of Krebs-Chuikov exchanges (and Sokolovskii), see J Erickson, *The Road to Berlin*, (London, 1983), pp 608-17.

[42] These figures are taken from Colonel-General G F Krivosheyev (ed), *Grif sekretnosti snyat*, (Moscow, Voenizdat, 1993), data pp 219-20. Talenskii (Appendix 26) gives figures classified at that time on German losses, recorded

by Soviet Fronts. For 2BF enemy killed: 49,770, PW: 84,234, total 134,004; 1BF killed: 218,691, PW: 250,534, total: 469,225; 1UF killed: 189,619, PW: 144,530, total: 334,149. The grand total for those killed in action: 458,000. For German losses in tanks and aircraft (destroyed/captured) the figures presented in the Talenskii volume are 4,183 and 4,995 respectively.

APPENDIX I

SOVIET ORDER OF BATTLE:
2ND AND 1ST BELORUSSIAN FRONT, 1ST UKRAINIAN FRONT, APRIL 1945

2nd Belorussian Front

2nd Shock Army
108 Rifle Corps, 116 Rifle Corps
65th Army
18 Rifle Corps, 46 Rifle Corps
70th Army
47 Rifle Corps, 96 Rifle Corps, 114 Rifle Corps
49th Army
70 Rifle Corps, 121 Rifle Corps
19th Army
40 Gds Rifle Corps, 132 Rifle Corps, 134 Rifle Corps
(Only 40 Gds Corps committed to the Berlin operation with three divisions, 100, 101, 102 Gds Divisions)
5th Guards Tank Army
(not part of the Berlin operation)

4th Air Army
4th Ground-attack Corps, 5th Bomber Corps, 8th Fighter Corps

Formations subordinated to 2nd Belorussian Front
98 Rifle Corps (not committed to the Berlin operation), 3 Gds Cavalry Corps, 1 Guards Tank Corps, 8 Gds Tank Corps, 8 Mechanised Corps

1st Belorussian Front

61st Army
9 Gds Rifle Corps, 80 Rifle Corps, 89 Rifle Corps
1st Polish Army
1, 2, 3, 4, 6 Infantry Division

47th Army
77 Rifle Corps, 125 Rifle Corps, 129 Rifle Corps
3rd Shock Army
7 Rifle Corps, 12 Gds Rifle Corps, 79 Rifle Corps, 9 Tank Corps
5th Shock Army
9 Rifle Corps, 26 Gds Rifle Corps, 32 Rifle Corps
8th Guards Army
4 Gds Rifle Corps, 28 Gds Rifle Corps, 29 Gds Rifle Corps, 11 Tank Corps
69th Army
25 Rifle Corps, 61 Rifle Corps, 91 Rifle Corps
33rd Army
16 Rifle Corps, 38 Rifle Corps, 62 Rifle Corps, 2 Gds Cavalry Corps
3rd Army
35 Rifle Corps, 40 Rifle Corps, 41 Rifle Corps
1st Gds Tank Army
8 Gds Mechanised Corps, 11 Gds Tank Corps
2nd Gds Tank Army
1 Mechanised Corps, 9 Gds Tank Corps, 12 Gds Tank Corps
16th Air Army
3rd Bomber Corps, 6th Bomber Corps, 6th, 9th Ground attack Corps
18th Air Army
1st Gds Bomber Corps, 2nd Gds Bomber Corps, 3rd Gds Bomber Corps, 4th Gds
  Bomber Corps

Formations subordinated to 1st Belorussian Front
7 Gds Cavalry Corps, Dnieper Flotilla (1, 2, 3, Brigades).

1st Ukrainian Front

3rd Gds Army
21 Rifle Corps, 76 Rifle Corps, 120 Rifle Corps, 25 Tank Corps
13th Army
24 Rifle Corps, 27 Rifle Corps, 102 Rifle Corps
5th Gds Army
32 Gds Rifle Corps, 33 Gds Rifle Corps, 34 Gds Rifle Corps, 4 Gds Tank Corps
2nd Polish Army
5, 7, 8, 9, 10 Infantry Division, 1 Tank Corps
52nd Army
48 Rifle Corps, 73 Rifle Corps, 78 Rifle Corps
28th Army
3 Gds Rifle Corps, 20 Rifle Corps, 128 Rifle Corps
(on 1UF strength as of 20 April 1945)

<u>3rd Gds Tank Army</u>
6 Gds Tank Corps, 7 Gds Tank Corps, 9 Mechanised Corps
<u>4th Gds Tank Army</u>
5 Gds Mechanised Corps, 10 Gds Tank Corps
<u>2nd Air Army</u>
1st, 2nd, 3rd Gds Ground-attack Corps, 4th Bomber Corps, 6th Bomber Corps
[6th, 21st, 59th Army not committed to the Berlin operation]
<u>Formations subordinated to 1st Ukrainian Front</u>
1 Gds Cavalry Corps, 7 Gds Mechanised Corps

APPENDIX II

German Strength, Deployment 1 April 1945 (Talenskii, *Berlinskaya operatisiya*, pp 9-11).

| I | i | Tukums/Libau 16A 18A |
| | | 19 infantry, 2 Tank Divisions |

| | ii | Königsberg/Danzig Gydnia |

Army Group North (4A, 2A)
13 Infantry Divs., 3 Tank Divs., 10 infantry and 1 motorised Battle Group, remnants one infantry div
Total: 18 ⅓ infantry divs equivalents. 3 Tank divs, 1½ motorised divisions.
German calculation that this force pinned down the equivalent of 50-60 Soviet divisions (2 Baltic Front, 3 and 2 Belorussian)

II   Deployment on approaches to Berlin

i   **Facing 1 BF**: Army Gp. 'Vistula' (3 *Panzer*, 9 Army) 19 Inf. Divs, 4 *Panzer* divs, 6 motorised divs, 1 inf brigade, 1 inf combat group; divisional equivalents equal 20 inf, 4 *Panzer*, 6 motorised divs.
270 km front.

ii   **Facing 1 UF**: Army Group 'Centre' (4 *Panzer*, 17 Army, elements 1 *Panzer* Army), 16 Inf Divs, 6 *Panzer* Divs, 3 motorised divs, 6 infantry battle groups, remnants one inf div; divisional equivalents 19N inf divs, 6 *Panzer* divs, 3 motorised divs.

iii	Breslau: 43,000 men, 540 guns, 120 tanks.
III	21 infantry divisions, 1 infantry brigade in process of being raised in central districts of Germany.

3 The Defeat of the German Southern Armies

SIR DAVID HUNT

Introduction

At the end of March 1945 the situation of the German troops engaged on the southern front was perilously anomalous but still tolerable if taken by itself. While the main masses of the defenders of the Reich were being driven in opposite directions across the northern plains, with formations disordered and central control only fitfully exercised, in Italy a well-organised Army Group whose subordinate formations were kept fully up to strength in men, arms and supplies was defending strong positions far south of the Alps against numerically inferior Allied forces. This result represented the triumph of Allied strategy in the Mediterranean. To contain the maximum enemy forces with the minimum of our own was the line that had been pursued with iron consistency since it was first formulated in May 1943. It was a fitting testimonial to the efficacy of this strategy that in the last battle in Italy twenty-three German divisions faced seventeen Allied divisions.[1]

On the other side of the Adriatic the Germans had been fighting since April 1941. Their invasion of Russia two months later brought into the field against them the Communist-led Yugoslav Partisans. For over a year now they had undertaken several large-scale operations to exterminate them, entirely without success. Since their withdrawal from Greece, and the fall of Belgrade to the Red Army in November 1944, German control had been limited to Slovenia, Croatia, Dalmatia and Bosnia. With the Croat and Bosnian troops under command, they constituted Army Group E, under Colonel-General Löhr, C-in-C Southeast. His opposite number in Italy was Field-Marshal Kesselring, commanding Army Group C and C-in-C Southwest.

Originally there was no doubt which of these two theatres was regarded as the more important by the German Supreme Command (OKW): it was Yugoslavia. 'Domination of the Balkans' it declared in 1943, 'is decisive for winning the war for tactical, military-political and economic reasons'.[2] British deception took advantage of this obsession. The plan codenamed *Barclay* of 1943[3] indicated that the Allies were only in Italy to acquire launching sites for an invasion of Yugoslavia and/or Greece. It was nurtured also by a false order of battle for the Mediterranean codenamed *Wantage*[4] which was accepted even by the normally cautious intelligence branch of OKW as proving that the Allies disposed of thirty 'offensive quality' divisions over and above those engaged in Italy; at the moment that we were about to enter Rome the same branch confidently announced as imminent an invasion of Albania from Bari.[5]

In fact the Allies never seriously considered operations in the Balkans unless the Germans in Italy, by withdrawing to the Alps, refused to let themselves be contained. The Americans vigorously refused to commit any of their troops to such an un-American area.[6] Apart from raids, naval and air co-operation and the provision of supplies and arms, the British also kept clear. The first contact between the Eighth Army and the Yugoslav Army of National Liberation took place on 2 May 1945 in Trieste. That marked the end of the Second World War and the beginning of the Cold War.

Plans for the Final Battle: German

The Germans having for the previous ten months abandoned any idea of seizing the strategic initiative, it will be simpler to start by considering first the strength and dispositions of the German Army Groups. Army Group E was in the weaker position of the two. Largely because of Hitler's determination to defend, first, Budapest and, later, the west Hungarian oilfields, it had been obliged to send large detachments northward. When Field-Marshal von Weichs, who then commanded it, protested that this would make it impossible for him to fulfil his principal task, the defence of Croatia, he was dismissed from his post and succeeded by Colonel-General Löhr on 23 March. At this moment he was already being heavily attacked by the Yugoslav Fourth Army. He had no specific directions other than to hold on. Hitler personally, with the general encouragement of OKW, laid much value on the defence of Croatia. Apart from its economic resources it provided a large part of the troops under Army Group E, for the removal of German divisions for use in Hungary meant that the German component was reduced to the 21st Mountain Corps, of two infantry divisions, until 10 April 1945 when the 97th Corps, also of two divisions, was transferred to it from Army Group C.

On the eve of the Yugoslav offensive the Germans and Croats held a line running from Karlobag on the Dalmatian coast to Gospic on the inland road, thence across the Plejesivica Mountains to Bihac and down the river Una to its confluence with the Sava. This covered Zagreb and Ljubljana. Bihac and Gospic were held by powerful garrisons and surrounded with elaborate defences in order to block the inland routes to Zagreb. The weakness in these dispositions was that the coastal road along the Adriatic was less strongly held. It was this sector that the Yugoslav Fourth Army chose for the *schwerpunkt* of its offensive, which began on 20 March, because it was aimed directly at Trieste. The capitals of Croatia and Slovenia could wait.

The dispositions and intentions of Army Group C call for a more comprehensive exposition than the forlorn-hope rearguard actions of von Löhr's Army Group. The front held by Kesselring had the merit of resting both its flanks on salt water, denying access by land to the main industrialised regions of Italy. Apart from that its irregular and

42

over-extended configuration reflected the influence of two men: President Roosevelt, who insisted on removing seven Allied divisions from Italy for a pointless invasion of southern France, and Hitler, who allowed no withdrawal.

The Allies, even after their numbers were reduced, had come close to breaking through the Apennine barrier south of Bologna; in the eastern sector the fallacy of Oliver Leese's preference for flat ground, however cut up by river lines, had brought his army to a stop at the Senio River with four more rivers still to cross before Bologna. The German line was long, and Kesselring and all his generals considered it should be shortened. As far back as August 1944 a contingency plan, codenamed *Herbstnebel* ('autumn mist'), had been worked out, which envisaged a withdrawal to and across the Po with the main defensive line behind the Adige.[7] The proposal was vetoed by Hitler on 5 October 1944. It was strategically sound not only because it would have enabled forces to be sent from Italy to more vital sectors but also because to force Army Group C to resist to the last south of the Po risked exposing it not merely to defeat but to encirclement.

Even when thus confined to the defence of an irrational front with no freedom of action Kesselring was always famous for a sunny and sanguine outlook. When he was transferred to command the western front on 10 March 1945, handing over to Colonel-General von Vietinghoff, a former commander of Tenth Army, he could feel confident that the armies he had led so long would continue to defend their positions with determination and unaffected morale. Vietinghoff was an experienced commander with good knowledge of Italian conditions. He had under his command three Armies, the Tenth (General Herr), the Fourteenth (General Lemelsen) and 'Army Liguria' (Marshal Graziani). The last-named contained three Italian and two German divisions; it was stationed along the coast from Genoa westwards and on the French-Italian border; it played no part in the final battle. Tenth Army had four corps under command amounting to thirteen divisions. Fourteenth Army had two corps with one Italian and seven German divisions. One German division was in Army Group reserve.[8] A high proportion of the German formations and their commanders had served continuously in Italy for nearly two years.

It is important to note that whereas on the western and eastern fronts many German formations had been reduced to a small fraction of their nominal strength Vietinghoff took over a functioning machine well up to strength. Central control was maintained until the final disintegration on the banks of the Po. Whatever the reason, and it seems irrational, reinforcing drafts had averaged 11,000 over the last nine months. For example, the two Parachute divisions (fighting as infantry) totalled 30,000 men between them. The mobile divisions were similarly above establishment. The average strength of all the

German divisions was 17,500, slightly over the standard war establishment for infantry divisions at that period of the war.[9] The four Italian Fascist divisions were equally strong in manpower though less reliable both in German and Allied judgements. Logistically it was calculated that the German formations held stocks of ammunition sufficient for three to four weeks' full-scale defensive fighting. Fuel was adequate for short moves.

The Germans had the superiority in numbers of troops on the ground. The Allies had the great advantage of air superiority. By now experience had taught Allied air forces in the field to use their powers not only against enemy communications but also, contrary to their original dogma, in direct support of the army. In spite of such tactical assistance, however, the task of making good river crossings in flat country remained a most exacting one for the assailant.

Plans for the Final Battle: Allied

Field Marshal Sir Harold Alexander was Supreme Allied Commander, Mediterranean (SACMED), a designation covering a wide geographical range of responsibilities and all three Services. In Italy was Fifteenth Army Group, commanded by Lieutenant-General Mark Clark, US Army. Under him were Fifth (US) Army (Lieutenant-General Truscott) of two corps totalling nine divisions, of which one was Brazilian and another South African, plus an Italian Combat Group; and Eighth (British) Army (Lieutenant-General Sir Richard McCreery) of four corps totalling eight divisions plus three Italian Combat Groups.[10]

The Allied front line at the start of the final battle reflected the varied fortunes of the previous autumn and winter offensive which had come so close to success. The western coastal sector was not regarded as important by either side. In the centre, where two roads, Nos 64 and 65, converge on Bologna, the Fifth Army (with XIII (British) Corps under command) had broken through the Gothic Line and over the crest of the Apennines to capture commanding positions on the last northern spurs of the mountains. It advanced to within nine miles of Bologna, chosen as an objective because of its key position on the road network south of the Po, and four miles from the Via Emilia, the backbone of that road system. The cost in casualties had been very high and the period of recuperation and re-organisation correspondingly long. Fortunately Fifth Army received just in time the 10th (US) Mountain Division, a fresh, well-trained and full-strength formation which was to distinguish itself in the coming battle.

Eighth Army's front was a dog-leg. Its left wing continued Fifth Army's line along the Apennine ridges from the Monte Grande position held by XIII Corps until it met the Senio River. At this point it turned sharply northeast and ran behind the Senio down to its mouth in Lake Comacchio, a shallow marshy lagoon whose southern edge had been extended by planned inundations. This line across the southeastern corner of the Romagna had only been reached after Eighth Army had fought its way across three major rivers and numerous canals and flood drains. The repeated effort had been great and casualties heavy.

On the Allied side morale in both armies remained sound and the same was true, remarkably enough, on the German side. The Allies had not received the steady reinforcement of large new drafts of men that continued to flow to the German armies but they had made good progress towards replenishing the gaps left in their ranks by the severe losses incurred during the winter offensive. Wounded men returned to duty and men taken from superfluous units, such as anti-aircraft and anti-tank, were retrained as infantry. Fifth Army, by this means, had converted into a reliable formation the 92nd Infantry Division, which had not been employable hitherto in offensive operations, and rebuilt its other infantry divisions. Eighth Army had similarly acquired enough manpower to restore the establishment of its infantry battalions to four companies, reversing the reduction made in the previous autumn. General McCreery was heard to say, not wholly seriously, that his army was a good horse, rather tired, but he thought he could get one more jump out of it.

The intention was still to mount an offensive as soon as the weather had improved sufficiently. This was based on the decision by General Eisenhower that the war in the west must continue in full intensity throughout the winter and into the spring.[11] Mark Clark's plans for Fifteenth Army Group's offensive, codenamed *Grapeshot*, did not differ in essentials from the one favoured by his predecessor, Alexander, but gave it a different emphasis. Alexander had demonstrated in his plans for the *Diadem* offensive of the previous May that in fulfilment of his assignment in Italy he attached little value to the mere gaining of ground, pushing the Germans back from one defensive position to another. He had startled Churchill before *Diadem* by avowing indifference to the capture of Rome. His aim was to pin the enemy down and encircle them. A spectacular manoeuvre of this nature only just escaped him at the end of May 1944 because General Clark, commanding Fifth Army, attached more importance to immediate personal publicity than to strategy and, over Truscott's vehement protests, diverted his troops from the encirclement to march straight on to Rome. The situation in March 1945 offered an equally good chance for a decisive encirclement.

It was certain that if the Allies were successful in breaching the German defence line Army Group C would have to abandon north-western Italy, withdraw across the Po and occupy one or another of the strong defensive lines already prepared on the rivers of the Veneto. This would involve the movement of large bodies diagonally across the Allied front and was bound to take time. The whole manoeuvre would pivot on the eastern flank, which must hold firm to give the western flank time to take up its appointed positions. It would be difficult, but from the German point of view no other strategy was possible. The vital pivot rested on Lake Comacchio, which was thought impassable, on extensive inundations and, even before these could be approached, on two heavily fortified river lines. Alexander, however, whose mind ran always in the direction of outmanoeuvring an enemy rather than attacking him frontally, had noted a possible weak point in this position.[13] The town of Argenta stands on the main road, the Via Adriatica, which runs from Rimini to Ferrara, passing just to the west of Lake Comacchio. The road had been narrowed to a strongly defended defile by the artificial flooding on either side. If this could be forced the whole German deployment would be disrupted and the bulk of their troops to the west could be surrounded.

Mark Clark's plan was designed to give the major role in the offensive to Fifth Army. He enabled Truscott to concentrate his forces by shortening his front, transferring to Eighth Army the sector east of Monte Grande. He even proposed a deception plan which would indicate that formations had been transferred to Eighth Army both from Fifth Army and from the (fictitious) Army Group Reserve, and he wished Eighth Army to open the offensive about a week before Fifth Army in order to draw enemy attention away from the latter. These proposals did not commend themselves to McCreery, except for the last. He had some confidence that if he was given a good start he would be able to dominate the progress of the operation. Truscott for his part was already convinced that Clark's insistence, repeated in the plan, on his putting the weight of his attack on his right, where the enemy defences were strongest, was mistaken; but at this stage he thought it prudent not to raise the question.

The appreciation produced on 26 February by Alexander and his Chief of Staff, Sir John Harding, accepted the plan but insisted that the object should be not just to push the enemy back along three axes leading to the Po, as Clark proposed, but to encircle and destroy them south of the river. This was accepted at a conference held at 15th Army Group on 18 March.[14] Truscott was given freedom of choice of his main axis of attack. McCreery was first to force a crossing of the Senio and Santerno rivers. Thereafter, depending on circumstances, it would be left to him to decide whether he should attack westwards towards Budrio, thus ensuring a small-scale encirclement in the area north of Bologna, or northwards to force his way through the Argenta Gap aiming at Ferrara. In this latter case he would be able to swerve north-westwards to join hands with Truscott, coming up from Fifth Army's breakthrough west of Bologna, and simultaneously to press on to the Po at the crossings north of Ferrara and Bondeno. This would be the manoeuvre by which the grand design would be achieved.

There was no scope for deception in order to force the enemy to take action, rather than just entertain erroneous beliefs, since there was nothing that the Allies either wanted him or expected him to do. They certainly did not want to frighten him into withdrawing to a more rational position. They did try to induce him to weaken his front by moving troops north of the Po to guard against an amphibious landing in the Veneto. When it was learned that the 29th Panzer Grenadier Division, one of Vietinghoff's best, had been ordered to make that very move, starting on 22 March, to take up position between the Piave and the Po, this was naturally regarded as evidence of success. It has been argued, however, by the Official History[15] that this was merely 'a basic military precaution'. It remains a fact that this valuable formation was out of the battle when it began and its nugatory transfer and return was costly in wear and tear and depletion of fuel stocks, not to mention losses sustained in crossing the Po under air attack.

The Offensive in Yugoslavia

The offensive against the German southern front was opened on 20 March by the Fourth Army of the Yugoslav Army of National Liberation commanded by General Drapsin, supported by a strong RAF detachment based on Zadar.[16] The first operation was designed to expel the German and Croat garrison from Bihac. a town again bitterly contested in the 1990s. It lies in the valley of the Una at an important road junction. Drapsin's purpose was to remove a threat from his right flank, not to advance on Zagreb, since his principal thrust-line was north-westward along the Dalmatian coast, aiming at Trieste. Bihac was defended with desperate courage since both Germans and Croats had reason to fear reprisals; it fell on 27 March after a week's fighting which involved an assault crossing of the Una. The main effort was then transferred to the Adriatic coast. Having overrun the first German line of defence based on Karlobag and Gospic in an attack on 4 April, Fourth Army's élan was sufficient to carry them by 8 April to the coastal town of Senj. At this point the Yugoslavs, assisted by the Royal Navy and RAF, began an advance through the off-lying islands. Pag, Rab, Krk and Kres had fallen by 19 April and on the coast road the main army had come into close contact with the defenders of Rijeka. Both on the mainland and on the islands the regular Yugoslav troops had been assisted by the Ninth, Seventh and Eleventh Partisan Corps, semi-irregular formations of varying sizes, operating behind the enemy lines in the fashion that had been standard in the Resistance movement up to the previous year. They were of great value in obstructing, restricting and finally mopping-up the Axis forces remaining in the fertile and well-populated area between the Adriatic and the region of Ogulin and Karlovac. They also assisted Fourth Army in its exploitation into the Istrian peninsula which followed immediately on the occupation of Kres.

The Germans put up a serious resistance in the defence of Rijeka. The troops of Army Group E who had suffered the effects of a protracted retreat out of Montenegro and Bosnia and along the Dalmatian coast were now at last reinforced by the strong and hitherto unengaged XCVII Corps. This consisted of two good German divisions, who came under Löhr's command when on 10 April OKW moved the boundary between Army Groups C and E westwards to the Isonzo river. The reinforcement was used to make good the defence of what was called the *Ingrid* line on the pre-war Italo-Yugoslav frontier running north from Rijeka into the mountainous Karst country east of Trieste. It had been elaborately fortified by the Italians between the wars and the Germans had lately added some hasty modern improvements. But the line was vulnerable to attack both from Yugoslav partisans who had crossed into Istria and from other irregulars operating in the Karst, which was the direction in which General Drapsin was directing his heavier forces. It was a hazardous manoeuvre because it left the *Ingrid* line, intact and manned by fresh, well-supplied troops, in a position to threaten his left flank and exposed his marching right wing to a counter-attack from the direction of Ljubljana, where the Germans were strongly posted. It must nevertheless be attempted because three days of battering at the *Ingrid* line had produced no result beyond a small bridgehead across the narrow Rjecina river. Time was pressing. The Allies in Italy had already crossed the Po in strength and would soon be in a position to stake out claims in Trieste and Venezia Giulia.

Drapsin, like a good communist commander, was prepared to pay a military price for a political gain. He detached one of his divisions and parts of another to the outflanking move, supported by an armoured brigade in Stuart tanks, recently supplied to Tito from British stocks. On 28 April an impetuous infantry attack carried the village of Pivka, at the northern extremity of the Yugoslav outflanking move. The way to Trieste, through Basovizza, its eastern defensive outpost, was clear. The final advance was ordered on 29 April and at dawn next day the (Italian) Committee of National Resistance proclaimed a general uprising. This brought out in arms the Italian Partisans. The Germans withdrew into strongpoints: the medieval castle, the Law Courts, the sports stadium and the remaining eastern defences at Villa Opicina and Basovizza. As German and Yugoslav regular troops, Italian and Yugoslav partisans clashed in convoluted conflict a new element was added: troops of the 2nd New Zealand Division under Lieutenant-General Sir Bernard Freyberg crossed the Piave on 1 May and by next day had secured Monfalcone and central Trieste. The race had ended in a dead heat.

The offensive in Italy

D-Day for *Grapeshot* was 9 April, which was the day on which Eighth Army was to open its main attack by forcing the crossing of the Senio. There were preliminary operations on both flanks. On Fifth Army's extreme left an attempt was made to pin down the enemy forces and, if possible, draw in additional ones by an attack in the coastal theatre directed on Massa. In the difficult terrain not much ground was gained but, surprisingly, the Germans reinforced by sending units from Army Group Reserve to this unimportant sector. On the right the British object was to capture ground on the south shore of Lake Comacchio from which a flanking attack in amphibious vehicles could be launched later against Argenta. The operation was successful though costly; Italian partisans of the 28th Garibaldi Brigade took part.

Eighth Army's attack on the Senio line was designed to initiate the final offensive of the Italian campaign, with Fifth Army to join in about a week later. The Senio crossing was daunting. The 25-foot high flood-banks on both sides were riddled with fire trenches and communications trenches. There was a gap of 200 feet between these banks in the middle of which ran the river, 30-foot wide and 10-foot deep. Mines were scattered lavishly. A defensive programme for 10th Army's numerous artillery, rockets and mortars had been carefully prepared.[17] Against such defences, stronger than many a well-known fortress, a supreme effort was required. The Allied air forces, both tactical and strategic, were concentrated against the sector chosen for the attack. Flame throwers both hand-held and tank-borne were used by the assault troops. The evidence from the German side suggests that the actual casualties were not especially high but the psychological effect was very great. The attack was made by the Polish Corps and the British V Corps. Both were successful in crossing the Senio on the first day and on 11 April reached the next defence line, on the Santerno. Both had established a bridgehead across it, after varying difficulties, by midnight on 12 April.

At this point McCreery decided to put into action the scheme for a wider encirclement. The British 78th Infantry Division turned sharply north and advanced down the corridor between the Santerno and Sillaro rivers, directed on Argenta. The Poles and New Zealanders continued west-north-west, directed on Budrio, which was Eighth Army's objective for the smaller encirclement. In the fighting for the long defile known euphemistically as the Argenta Gap the British 56th Infantry Division came in on the eastern flank, carried in amphibious vehicles across the inundations. Both divisions were engaged in the most determined fighting in the whole battle; the Germans, as fully expected, made their greatest efforts to protect the essential pivot of their withdrawal. The struggle continued for eight days, mainly a soldier's battle between infantry on fronts so narrow that only battalions could be employed on both sides. By the morning of 19 April the British 6th Armoured Division, McCreery's pursuit force, had formed up north of Argenta. Ahead of their tracks lay flat ground with no more river obstacles and the prospect of a clear run to their goal, the appropriately named *Finale nell' Emilia*, where they would join hands with Fifth Army's 6th South African Armoured Division.

The New Zealanders and the 10th Indian Division, now under command of XIII Corps, had an equally violent though shorter struggle on 18 April on the river Gaiana, just east of Budrio. They were opposed by the German 1st Parachute Corps of three divisions, all at full strength or over. General Freyberg called for the support of artillery on a lavish scale (72,500 rounds for the field guns, besides medium and heavy guns) to force the crossing; losses on the German side, especially among parachutists, were very heavy. By dark on 19 April the Polish Corps was also across the Gaiana and moving to the north of Bologna.

D-Day for Fifth Army's attack was originally 12 April but low cloud and fog caused it to be postponed for two days. Truscott, whose eye for country was better than Clark's, had chosen to make his main effort on his left flank rather than follow his predecessor's plan of direct assault down Route 65. The 10th US Mountain Division improved its position on Route 64 but violent air and artillery bombardments were relatively ineffective against German troops well dug-in in mountainous terrain. Nevertheless the South Africans were successful in capturing the imposing Monte Sole in a skilful infantry attack. There followed a period of hard pounding and attrition until IV Corps, the American left-hand formation, was enabled by a deliberate withdrawal on the German side to advance to the last remaining defensive position before Bologna. Truscott took immediate advantage to reinforce his left by extending II Corps' front west of the Reno.

The concentration of strength in the vulnerable sector that this re-organisation produced showed results on 19 April. The stubborn defence of the German troops, now clinging to the last foothills of the Apennines, was broken on a wide front. By 20 April Fifth Army had got down into the plain and crossed the Via Emilia west of Bologna. On the same day Vietinghoff ordered a general withdrawal from the Bologna area as part of a retreat to the Po, which was denounced in the usual threatening terms by OKW. It was already too late to permit of an orderly manoeuvre. The South African Armoured Division was directed to advance north-eastwards between the Reno and the Panaro 'with the utmost speed and boldness'. On 21 April the Americans entered Bologna unopposed; it had already been entered, in similar circumstances, by the Poles about two hours before. This was incidental: the main theme was the race to the Po which the US 10th Mountain Division reached on 22 April, at San Benedetto. On Fifth Army's right flank a junction was made with Eighth Army just south of the river at Finale on 23 April, on which day both armies had closed up to the Po from San Benedetto as far east as Poleselle, and next day both had passed detachments to the north bank. By that time the number of German prisoners taken was 54,000.[18]

The Po bridges had been destroyed by the Allied forces and the preparations made for improvised crossings had been disrupted by the speed of the advance. All the heavy equipment that the Germans had brought so far with such difficulty had to be destroyed and abandoned on the south bank; the men used such few boats as they could find or swam, as did the commander of I Parachute Corps, Lieutenant-General Heidrich. The Po in effect ruled a line across the battlefield and brought an end to the Italian campaign. South of it there had been vigorously-contested actions which called for skill and resolution, with both sides fighting well; north of it there was nothing but rapid pursuit, unhampered by small-scale delaying attempts. Only two days after the Allies began to cross the Po the CLNAI (Committee of National Liberation for Upper Italy) ordered a general insurrection for 25 April. In greatly reinforced numbers the Partisans in the area took up arms and were able to seize most of the big cities of northern Italy from the retreating Germans before Allied columns could arrive. The great exception was Trieste, where the partisans had to fight both the Germans and the Yugoslavs.

Capitulation

While the pursuit proceeded at a more than *blitzkrieg* speed across the Transpadane region into the lower Alps, negotiations were already proceeding for the unconditional capitulation of all enemy forces under command of Army Group C. The first approaches had been in the previous October. The initiative was taken, to the Allies' surprise, by the senior SS Commander in Italy, General Karl Wolff, and even more surprisingly he was able to claim that he had the support of Himmler himself. His proposal was that the Allies should join Germany against the Russians; on hearing this the Allies broke off the contact, which had been conducted by Italian intermediaries. A more realistic line was taken when contact was resumed in January/February 1945. In March arrangements were made for the first Allied negotiators to be sent to Switzerland. This produced no immediate results beyond a violent protest from Moscow, but it became clear that Kesselring was in agreement with Wolff about the need for surrender without conditions. There was no suggestion of a final stand in an Alpine fortress.[19] At this point Kesselring was transferred to become C-in-C West and Wolff had to start again with Vietinghoff. It was not until 24 April that German plenipotentiaries arrived in Switzerland, and it took time before they were brought to Italy on 28 April. The capitulation was signed at Alexander's Headquarters at Caserta at 2 pm on 29 April, specifying that hostilities would cease at noon (GMT) on 2 May. The difficulties about getting acceptance from all concerned on the German side were lengthy, recriminatory, even minatory, and the full details make entertaining reading.[20] In the end the orders were sent out just in time. Close on a million men laid down their arms, including all those in Austria. It was the first official surrender on a large scale.

One piece of unfinished business remained: to settle, even if only temporarily, the fate of Trieste. It was important because it was to be the base for the occupation of Austria. The question was: should it come under Allied Military Government or should it be administered by the Yugoslavs who would allow us its use on their own terms? Alexander believed that he had firm assurances from Tito that he accepted the former solution but from the behaviour of the Yugoslav troops on the ground—both armies were represented in strength—this seemed doubtful. Strong threats were issued by Churchill and Truman, reinforced by a vigorous Order of the Day from Alexander, and on 22 May Alexander, Clark and McCreery assembled in Trieste to supervise a move forward towards the Morgan Line, which Alexander's Chief of Staff had designated as the line of demarcation. In the background Stalin instructed Tito to give way. On 9 June an agreement was signed in Belgrade which brought an end to the crisis. The Yugoslavs conceded Allied administration up to the Morgan Line, including the port of Pula. It was not until 1954, after lengthy and strictly confidential negotiations, that the Yugoslavs agreed to accept the present frontier with Italy.

Epilogue

It has become conventional to conclude a discussion of the Italian campaign with a pronouncement on its measure of success in achieving the object prescribed for it in 1943. Since that object was expressed in purely statistical not geographical terms—the containment of the maximum German by the minimum Allied forces, not the occupation of any particular territory—the proof turns on mathematics. A satisfactory and conclusive answer has been given by a consensus of historians.[21]

Taking a wider view, the value to Allied Grand Strategy of the Mediterranean diversion can be demonstrated by the fact that at the turning-point of the whole war, D-day for *Overlord*, it tied down fifty-five German divisions.[22] Another significant statistic is that casualties on the German side, excluding the surrender on 2 May, exceeded Allied casualties: a strange fact since the latter were always on the offensive, and the Italian terrain favours the defensive.[23]

A parallel from an earlier British victory suggests itself. In the Battle of Blenheim the bulk of the English infantry under General Cutts was engaged in costly attacks on the village which gives it its name. They never captured it; its French garrison capitulated next morning. The vigour of their attack, however, so impressed the French commander, Tallard, that he crammed more and more battalions into Blenheim village at the cost of weakening his centre. It was on this sector that Malborough launched his overwhelming attack. The troops of Cutts' brigades consoled themselves for painful losses that had achieved no obvious end with the thought that by doing their duty and obeying their orders they had made a decisive contribution to victory.

Discussion

Sir Michael Howard referred to the 'amazingly polyglot' nature of the Allied forces in Italy, including Poles, Greeks, Sikhs, Ghurkas, Japanese Americans, Black Americans, Brazilians and Italians, which led to consequent problems with management and uneven peformance. *Sir David Hunt* and *Dr Correlli Barnett* continued their discussion on the relative strength of German and Allied forces in Italy (see Paper 1 in this collection), and *Mr Seton-Watson* and *Sir M Howard* agreed with *Sir David Hunt* that air supremacy was the decisive factor in favour of the Allied forces. There followed a discussion of the role of General Mark Clark, whom *Sir David Hunt* described as looking on war as 'the pursuit of publicity by other means': he was determined to capture Rome before D-Day for Overlord.

Sir Frank Roberts asked about the Russian reaction to the Italian surrender: *Sir David Hunt* replied that Stalin was suspicious because he was not given prior information on the surrender, and consequently regarded it as a betrayal.

Notes and References

1   On the German side there were also four Italian divisions, German-equipped, none of which held front line positions, together with miscellaneous formations such as an Italian SS division, Cossacks, Czechs and Slovaks who were used exclusively against the Italian Partisans. The Allies, at Alexander's instigation, raised four Italian combat groups of about brigade strength. The Allies had also the support of the Italian partisans under the general direction of the Upper Italy Committee of Liberation (CLNAI); numbers, which varied, are hard to quantify.

2   John Ehrman, *History of the Second World War: Grand Strategy,* vol V (London, 1956), p 61. The economic reasons mentioned included Yugoslav mineral resources (bauxite, chrome, copper, manganese) and Romanian oil.

3   For *Barclay* see Michael Howard, *British Intelligence in the Second World War* vol 5 (London, 1990), pp 85-94, 89-92. The ruse of planting false documents on the body of a supposed Royal Marine courier, codenamed *Mincemeat*, was part of the mechanism by which the *Barclay* deception was successfully commended to OKW.

4   For *Wantage* see PRO WO 204/1561, a memorandum by Brigadier Dudley Clark. The results are summarised as follows: there were in truth in the

Mediterranean area thirty-eight Allied divisions; in the *Wantage* order of battle this became sixty-four; in the order of battle accepted by OKW there were seventy-one.

5   C J C Moloney, *The Mediterranean and Middle East,* vol VI, Part 1 (London, 1984), p 341.

6   General Marshall, Chief of Staff of the US Army, was reported to have said in May 1945: 'Where is Trieste? If it's in the Balkans we can't go there'.

7   General Sir William Jackson, *The Mediterranean and Middle East* , vol VI, Part 2 (London, 1987), p 156.

8   For an outline order of battle of Army Group C see Jackson, op cit, pp 234-5.

9   F-M Earl Alexander of Tunis, *Dispatch*; supplement to *London Gazette,* 12 June 1950, p 2958 and *The Italian Campaign 12 December 1944 to 2 May 1945, Report to Combined Chiefs of Staff* (London, 1951), p 8 fn.

10   For order of battle of Fifteenth Army Group see Alexander, *Dispatch,* p 2967, Jackson, op cit, pp 222-3.

11   Alexander, *Dispatch* , p 2953.

13   Ibid, p 2958.

14   Jackson, op cit, p 203.

15   Ibid, p 236.

16   The account of operations in Yugoslavia is an enlarged version of the one given in a paper entitled 'Trieste and Venezia Giulia in Spring 1945' which I presented to an Anglo-Yugoslav conference in Brdo (now Slovenia) in December 1985. The proceedings of the conference were published in Slovene under the title *Konec Druge Svetovne Vojne v Jugoslaviji* (Ljubljana, 1986). See also Sir Geoffrey Cox, *The Race for Trieste* (London, 1977), pp 171-85.

17   Jackson, op cit, p 112 and see Diagram 11. General Herr, commanding 10th Army, had pleaded to be allowed to withdraw to the Santerno, where the defences were equally strong, the day before Eighth Army attacked. This was vetoed by OKW but in frustration he fired off his artillery programme in the night of D-1, much to the alarm of Eighth Army HQ who feared nothing more than a withdrawal.

18   As reported by Alexander to CIGS, 25 April, WO 214/17, F 65841. He added that numerous pockets of resistance had been by-passed.

19   The story about an *Alpenfestung* was put about by Goebbels's Ministry of Information; it had no existence in reality. Eisenhower's Intelligence staff believed it but Alexander's did not. See R Bennett, *Behind the Battle* (London, 1994), pp 274-6, and cf note 39 to paper 1 in this collection.

20   See Appendix E to Alexander, *Report to Combined Chiefs of Staff.*

21   See, for example, Jackson, op cit, pp 351-2.

22   Of which 25 in Italy, 19 in the Balkans and 11 in the south of France; see Alexander, *Dispatch,* p 2960 fn.

4 The Yalta Conference

SIR FRANK ROBERTS

[*Sir Frank Roberts did not present a formal paper at the Conference, but spoke extempore from his extensive knowledge and from personal recollection of the Yalta Conference (he was introduced by the Chairman of the session as the 'super horse's mouth'). He used as reference his article 'Yalta reviewed after forty years', first published in October 1985 in the NATO Review; at his suggestion that article is reproduced here, by permission of the Editor.*]

So many myths have grown up about Yalta that my first task as a participant in that conference of the 'Big Three' in the Crimea in February 1945 is to recall what Yalta was and what it was not. It was not, as Versailles had been after the First World War, the only such meeting to reach decisions on the termination of the Second World War. It was one, and not necessarily the most important, in a series of such Allied conferences, preceded at top level by Teheran in 1943 and Moscow in 1944, and succeeded by Potsdam in 1945, and accompanied by many important meetings at Foreign Minister level between December 1941 and the end of 1947.

How, then did Yalta acquire its notoriety as the meeting where Europe was supposedly divided by Stalin, Roosevelt and Churchill, where Poland and Eastern Europe were said to have been given to Stalin by Roosevelt and Churchill, whom he had outwitted? The place and the timing contributed to establish this myth, the timing because the end of the war in Europe was then in sight and the place because it was so obviously under exclusively Soviet control and so far from Western eyes. But what were the facts, what did the three leaders meet to discuss, what decisions were reached, how far were they carried out or twisted afterwards and what lessons are to be learnt from this particular chapter in Summit diplomacy?

Four main issues

The 'Big Three' had four main issues to discuss: first, the completion of victory as rapidly as possible in the war against Germany, which still had strong forces in the field on the Eastern and Western fronts, and to agree the subsequent arrangements for the occupation and denazification of Hitler's Reich; secondly, the achievement of victory against Japan, far from being vanquished as yet on its own territory; thirdly, the future settlement in Eastern Europe, already almost completely 'liberated' or 'occupied' by the Red Army; and fourthly, looking to the future, the establishment of a peaceful world order based upon a United Nations more effective and representative than the former League of Nations, of which neither the US nor the Soviet

Union had initially been members. Greece and Yugoslavia were also mentioned and Stalin raised certain Soviet claims related to Turkey and the Mediterranean, where the Anglo-American forces were as much in control as the Soviet forces were in Eastern Europe, but little time was spent on these other matters at Yalta.

On Germany, all three leaders were in broad agreement. Old will-of-the-wisps like dismemberment were put aside and they concentrated upon what proved the easy task of approving the plans prepared over the past year by the Three Power Commission in London for the occupation zones in Germany, for the different sectors in Berlin and for the Allied Control Commission and its activities. This agreement was most important in ensuring orderly arrangements for the final victory and so avoiding or at least postponing to a later date dangerous disputes which, given the suspicions of each other held alike by Stalin and the Western leaders about the other's possible readiness to use the defeated Germans as allies, might have led to conflicts among the victorious Allies.

At the time of Yalta (February 1945), this agreement could be held to favour the West, since the Red Army was then advancing more rapidly towards Berlin than the Western allies, who had been held up by the German counter-offensive in the Ardennes and by the barrier of the Rhine. It should be noted that these arrangements for Germany, as also for Austria, were based upon the concept of maintaining national unity under the Allied Control Commission. Yalta did *not* point the way to the subsequent division of Germany in the late 1940s. The other German issue raised by Stalin at Yalta was reparations. A Three-Power Commission was established to meet in Moscow, but other matters of considerable importance for Germany and elsewhere were left to the three Foreign Ministers, who met frequently after Yalta. For Germany, Potsdam in July 1945 was to be the decisive conference.

One other major European question was however settled at Yalta, that of French participation in the Control arrangements for occupied Germany. This was a considerable victory for Churchill over the original opposition of Stalin and Roosevelt. Knowing that Roosevelt had informed Stalin of his intention to withdraw US forces from Europe within two years, realising that Britain alone could not provide a balance in Europe against the Soviet Union and influenced also by his long-standing and genuine affection for France, Churchill already in 1945 felt the need to restore the strength of Western Europe and especially of France.

The second issue, Japan, was one of Roosevelt's two main priorities at Yalta. There was no certainty yet that the atom bomb would work, still less that it would itself force Japan into capitulation. After the fanatical resistance of the Japanese on the smaller islands of the Pacific, it was estimated that an attack on the Japanese mainland would cost at least half a million casualties. Roosevelt therefore obtained Stalin's secret undertaking to enter the war against Japan in Manchuria, for which Stalin was to receive back, without any consultation with America's Chinese allies, what Tsarist Russia had lost in the Far East after the Russo-Japanese war.

Roosevelt's other priority at Yalta was to secure Stalin's agreement to setting up the United Nations. Stalin's price, which Roosevelt and Churchill were ready to pay, was the right of veto and the independent membership of the Ukraine and Belorussia as well as of the Soviet Union itself. Roosevelt was activated by his conviction that a peaceful post-war world required the continuation of the wartime alliance on the basis of cooperation between what would then be the only two Super Powers. He had therefore come to Yalta determined to charm and win Stalin over to this concept and, perhaps rather naively, seems to have considered that in this case, as in that of Japan, he had to pay Stalin a price for doing what was so clearly in Stalin's own interest.

He went out of his way to try to remove from Stalin's mind any idea of a special Anglo-American relationship by treating Churchill as an old 'imperialist' out of touch with the modern world and in any case of lesser account than the two 'Big Boys'. Churchill resented this and also considered it unwise to unveil Western differences to Stalin, who was clever enough to take or create opportunities to pay respect to Churchill as a great war leader and also to respect British interests in Greece and in the Middle East.

Eastern Europe

In my view, these other priorities of Roosevelt and his tactical handling of Stalin unfortunately had some effect upon the remaining issue under discussion, Eastern Europe. The future settlement there, and especially in Poland, was Stalin's first priority at Yalta. Poland was also of great importance to Churchill, because of the debt of honour Britain owed to the ally for whom it had gone to war, and to whom it had been able to give so little help in 1939, but whose significant armed forces had fought so bravely and effectively from the Battle of Britain to the campaigns in Italy, in Normandy and at Arnhem.

Churchill's hand was weakened by the fact that the Red Army had already overrun Poland and was setting up their own Polish administration there, while the Polish government in London had rejected their Prime Minister, Mikolajczyk, who was prepared to join in some arrangement with Moscow. Churchill was also left to save what he could for Poland without strong support from Roosevelt, who did however secure from Stalin in the 'Declaration on Liberated Europe' a commitment to democratic values, including free elections. The final agreement on Poland also provided for free elections there and for the eventual return of Mikolajczyk with other Western Poles to join Stalin's Lublin Poles. Indeed Mikolajczyk's Peasant Party was able to make a good showing in the first such 'free elections'. On frontiers, Britain had herself advocated the Curzon line in the East and Churchill was concerned with obtaining, as he did, compensation for Poland in her new western frontiers. There is little wrong with the terms of the agreement on Poland, or the Declaration, had they been observed by Stalin. But Russian and Western interpretations of such key words as democracy and free elections proved very different and when the Commission composed of Molotov and the US and UK Ambassadors met in Moscow to put the Yalta Agreement on Poland into effect, Soviet actions revealed very soon and very brutally that Stalin's word was to be law in Poland as throughout Eastern Europe, whatever he might have signed at Yalta.

Similar face-saving arrangements were agreed for the ex-enemy countries, Romania, Bulgaria and Hungary, with US and UK representatives on the tripartite Control Commission. But it was not many months before the US and UK Ambassadors in Moscow were sent to Bucharest to protest, in vain, at high-handed and unilateral Soviet conduct. Yugoslavia went its own way, with Tito then in a strongly pro-Soviet and anti-Western frame of mind and Czechoslovakia was allowed until 1948 to keep a foot in East and West alike.

It is, above all, the Polish, and to a lesser extent other East Europe settlements, which took up most time at the conference and which have earned Yalta its unfortunate reputation for having divided Europe and abandoned the East. Stalin's intentions in Eastern Europe had been clear since the Strang mission to Moscow in 1939. They were broadly to recover or control all territories previously within the Russian (Tsarist) Empire. He had then demanded control of the Baltic States and the right of entry into Eastern Poland, with Bukovina and Bessarabia also within his sights. Since he had not been able to get this from the West, who were, in his own words, expecting him to pull their chestnuts out of the fire, he had turned instead to the Ribbentrop-Molotov Pact of August 1939, making inevitable Hitler's attack upon Poland and a war in which he had expected the Germans, French and British to bleed each other white, while he remained at peace, pocketing the gains he at once took in the Baltic States, Eastern Poland, Bukovina and Bessarabia, and later to a lesser extent from Finland.

Even after Hitler had taken all this back from him and with German troops just outside Moscow he still pressed Eden in December 1941 to guarantee these gains in the eventual peace settlement. So there was little doubt of his intentions when the Red Army had already advanced through Poland and most of Eastern Europe and when the end of the war was in sight. The old Western 'Cordon Sanitaire' against the young and weak Soviet Union was to be reversed into a similar but more effective cordon protecting an older and stronger Soviet Union against the West. This was the hard reality, against which Churchill battled, without strong support from Roosevelt, and did indeed obtain a Polish settlement, which on paper at least was not too unsatisfactory.

Soviet implementation of Yalta decisions

So much for the Yalta decisions. On the Soviet side their immediate implementation was uneven. Stalin fulfilled his commitment to Roosevelt on Japan and took his agreed reward from Chiang Kai Shek's China and, in the case of Sakhalin and the Kurile islands, from Japan. Subsequently, at the time of the friendship between the Soviet Union and Mao's China, Soviet gains in Manchuria and Port Arthur were returned to China. But the Soviet Union has hung on to Sakhalin and the Kuriles at the price of continued tension with Japan. Stalin also fulfilled his commitment on the United Nations, and took his rewards in the veto and triple representation, using the veto all too frequently in the early years. Against Litvinov's advice he even agreed to the UN being set up at New York and not in some neutral site. He also fulfilled his commitments at first to the letter, if not always in the spirit, over the occupation of Germany, although only after he had strained Churchill's goodwill almost beyond endurance by his hostility and insulting suspicion over the German surrender in Italy and by his strange behaviour over the arrangements for the final German surrender. So it was probably as well that the Western allies had unexpectedly advanced far beyond the Elbe and so obtained a bargaining counter to ensure their admission to Berlin. Again Stalin took his price above all in reparations.

But for a year or so many in the West, in and outside government, continued to believe in the possibility of continued cooperation between what were now the four occupation powers in Germany. Even so realistic an anti-Communist as Ernest Bevin was still trying to renew the Anglo-Soviet Treaty and adapt it to peacetime requirements as late as the spring of 1946. Soviet performance in Germany, as elsewhere, deteriorated during 1946 and the continued pursuit of common policies was revealed as an impossible dream by the time of the Foreign Ministers' Conference in Moscow early in 1947. But this, as well as the Berlin Blockade, the Communist take-over in Prague and the Russian refusal themselves to join or to allow Poland and Czechoslovakia to join in the Marshall Aid programme, all in 1947 and 1948, takes us too far away from Yalta.

In Eastern Europe and especially in Poland, as I have already indicated, the Soviet Union blatantly evaded its undertakings at Yalta in the letter as well as in the spirit. The arrest only weeks after Yalta and the subsequent show-trial in Moscow of the Polish underground leaders who had been asked to declare themselves to the Soviet forces, were clear warnings about Soviet implementation of the agreements. It required American intervention in the form of some tough talking, for the first time over Poland, from Truman's (and Roosevelt's former) personal representative, Harry Hopkins, to get Stalin finally to admit London Poles into the new government. But it was not long before their role was made impossible. Stalin's interpretation of a 'friendly' Poland was a Poland absolutely under his control and therefore cut off from its traditional links with Western Europe.

The question naturally arises, could this Soviet domination of Poland and Eastern Europe, extended later to Eastern Germany and Czechoslovakia, have been avoided or prevented at Yalta? In my view, unfortunately not, given the overall situation and Roosevelt's other priorities at that time. Even today I doubt whether better results in practice (the diplomatic agreements were satisfactory enough) could have been achieved, even if Roosevelt had supported Churchill more strongly and had pressed harder to the extent even of throwing America's economic preponderance into the balance at the expense of his other objectives.

Control of Poland and Eastern Europe was a vital matter for Stalin, as indeed for most Russians. The Red Army had obtained it for him and he was determined to keep it, as his successors have been ever since. Those who suggest that Roosevelt might have resorted to the threat of using his atom bombs forget, first that they had not yet proved their efficacy and, secondly, that public opinion in America and Western Europe at that time would never have permitted our leaders to threaten in this way an ally which had suffered so much in achieving the common victory. In theory, the Western leaders could have refused to sign the agreements on Eastern Europe but this would have done no good in Eastern Europe, would have released Stalin from the subsequent stigma of having broken them and would clearly have jeopardised agreement on other equally important matters.

Lessons to be learnt

Finally, what lessons are to be learnt in the West from this important chapter in Summit diplomacy and East-West relations, which was incidentally the last such conference held before the use of nuclear power against Japan transformed defence and diplomacy? The first and most important, I would suggest, is that already learnt before Yalta by Churchill, but not yet by Roosevelt, that their hope that by treating Stalin as a member of their club he would eventually behave as such, was illusory, if only because he preferred his own Communist club, which he intended to run on his own and in his own way. The US or the UK were little if any better in his eyes than Hitler's Germany or Japan. There was a lesson here also for Roosevelt who, in the interest of the wartime alliance had rejected reminders of Stalin's ideological priorities and of his ruthless treatment of his own and other peoples. Even Churchill had succumbed to this temptation when he had dismissed Tito's establishment of a Communist régime in Yugoslavia by asking his then interlocutor whether he intended to live in Yugoslavia under Tito after the war. In dealing with Communist régimes it is not realistic to ignore ideological differences and to concentrate only upon national ambitions.

The second lesson to my mind is that it is nevertheless possible to reach agreement over the ideological divide where interests are similar or not too far apart and that such agreements are observed in the letter, if not always in the spirit, by Moscow. This applied at Yalta to three of the main issues discussed, Germany, Japan and the United Nations, as for example, it applies today in the Super Power relationship to crisis management, although not to Third World or 'ideological' issues. It did not apply to Poland, nor to Eastern Europe, deemed by Stalin to be in his sphere of interest and control. But he did make important concessions elsewhere, eg on Greece and on including France in the control arrangements for Germany and Austria.

Perhaps Stalin also should have learnt a lesson from Yalta or rather from the effects of his subsequent refusal to carry out his commitments over Eastern Europe. It was this behaviour, following on Stalin's refusal to support the Poles in the Warsaw rising in the summer of 1944, which destroyed Churchill's remaining illusions and led to the Fulton speech of 1946 warning Western opinion, hitherto sympathetic to the Soviet Union, about the Iron Curtain in Europe. From this, and from the more or less simultaneous disenchantment of Truman in America and of Bevin in Britain over the prospects of continued collaboration with the Soviet Union in Germany, flowed the Marshall Plan, the growing unity of Western Europe and the Atlantic Alliance. The political cartoonist, David Low, illustrated this in one of his best cartoons, showing Stalin on the high Kremlin battlements confronted by a little man building a still low wall called NATO, and saying 'there's not a brick in this wall which you, Stalin, have not thrown'.

Discussion

Dr Correlli Barnett suggested a parallel between Yalta and British approaches to Hitler in 1937-8: the Allies in 1945 trying to treat Stalin—like Hitler—as a member of the club in expectation of reasonable behaviour. *Sir Frank Roberts* expressed a measure of agreement, but pointed out that in 1937-8 there was not a war on. It was true, however, that in both cases diplomats were unhappy about approaches being made at higher levels. (Sir Frank added that the nature of the arrangements at Yalta meant that there were no press, no fraternisation between delegations and no gossip, only high level meetings).

Dr Deighton asked Sir Frank whether his impressions at Yalta had been of Great Britain being 'squeezed' between the US and the Soviet Union. *Sir Frank Roberts* replied that while it was clear that Roosevelt was intent on establishing a close relationship with Stalin, he (Sir Frank) had had a 'funny, illogical feeling' that Britain would in fact remain one of the Big Three, thus leaving him somewhat unprepared for the British role as a world power of the second rank.

Referring to Poland, *Dr Hulas* pointed out that Stalin had been encouraged by Sir Stafford Cripps to tell Eden that he wished to recover all the gains of the Ribbentrop-Molotov Pact. *Dr Hanak* commented that Cripps had no authority to negotiate on Poland, a point *Sir Frank Roberts* agreed with but said he had not wished to make himself.

5 Yalta Decisions and Germany

KLAUS-JURGEN MULLER

'Yalta and Germany' is too large a subject to be dealt with in a single paper. I have, therefore, selected four specific issues which are at the very centre of what may be called the German problem at Yalta:

—some methodological problems connected with Yalta;
—the French problem discussed at Yalta and its implications for
    Germany;
—the Polish question and its consequences for Germany;
—some aspects of the implementation of what one may call the Yalta
    decisions on Germany.

I

Can we actually talk about 'Yalta decisions'? Some historians maintain that no major decisions were taken at Yalta: the Conference only produced rhetorical compromises and vaguely phrased intentions, or postponed major problems. Yalta was a sort of in-between conference, sandwiched between Teheran and Potsdam: the most important and far-reaching decisions had already been taken; the Curzon Line designated Poland's new eastern border; Königsberg, an ice-free port, given to Soviet Russia; Germany's dismemberment; the recognition of Tito as the leader of Yugoslavia—all this had already been discussed or had even been more or less decided upon at Teheran.[1] As a matter of fact, many military and political decisions made earlier in the war were more important in shaping post-war Europe than Yalta.

According to Wilfried Loth in *Die Teilung der Welt 1941-1955*, Yalta is only significant because of the failures, shortcomings and mistakes made, not for any major decisions.[2] Certainly, one may challenge Loth's statement. But, in one point, at least, he is correct: much of what was left undecided at Yalta has nevertheless had the most important consequences, which have determined more than 40 years of European and, by implication, of German history, for what was decided about Poland, or to be more precise, what was vaguely agreed upon by the Big Three, equally affected Germany, and vice versa. Yalta has become a myth, a legendary name,[3] but one thing remains true: Yalta—or more precisely, the interpretation that has been applied to the Conference—has served as a weapon in the Cold War and as an argument in internal conflicts within the Western World as well.

For many years, there were two divergent opinions about what happened at Yalta: one, making the point that the Crimean Conference brought about the partition of Europe and the delimitation of respective spheres of influence. This view was or still is held by, General de Gaulle, Chancellor Helmut Schmidt and President Mitterrand; and many historians, such as Brzezinski,[4] have agreed with this opinion. In contrast, there are others who maintain that it was the Soviet Union which pushed the Yalta agreements aside, disregarding the common 'Declaration on Liberated Europe', a document whose importance has been stressed by many statesmen of the Western world, as well as by numerous historians and political scientists.

Both interpretations aroused bitter controversy up to the very end of the Cold War, for both had highly political implications.[5] But now, since the Cold War has ended—at least for the time being—the issue at stake is no longer of real political importance: as Timothy Garton Ash has put it, '...we no longer live in the Europe of Yalta...Yalta has become history in a way that it was not for 45 years until the end of the Cold War'. He continues by saying that 'the history of the Yalta myths is now probably as interesting, perhaps even more so, than that of the actual conference'.[6]

In a way, the assessment of the Yalta Conference depends on how one defines the character of the conference. This is largely a matter of preconceived opinion, according to the view taken of American or Soviet politics and strategy. Was Yalta simply a single event, a 'normal' example of power politics and traditional diplomacy? Or was it (according to Arthur Schlesinger) a universal experiment with world government which failed, but which had two antecedents: the Holy Alliance and the Versailles Treaty with the League of Nations?[7] Actually Yalta was both: to Roosevelt it was certainly part of a projected system of world government in partnership with Soviet Russia, with the UN as the global mechanism. This approach explains, at least to a certain extent, why he was willing to compromise with Stalin on other important issues. For Churchill it was an episode of classic and pragmatic diplomacy in the context of worldwide power politics. As for Stalin, the answer is difficult and depends how one views Soviet policy: pragmatic Russian imperialism or part of the communist strategy of world revolution.

In any case, it is impossible to deny that whether the Big Three had universalist aspirations or not, and whatever their afterthoughts, Yalta was a fine example of diplomatic power politics. It was, of course, conditioned and determined to a large extent by domestic policy: Roosevelt had to consider the domestic situation in the USA where Senator Vandenberg, the influential Chairman of the Senate Foreign Relations Committee, had already made it clear that as Senator for Michigan, a State with a high percentage of immigrants from Eastern Europe, he would cooperate with the Roosevelt administration on the

UN issue only on condition that Polish sovereignty was protected; Churchill, too, several times stressed the need to take British public opinion into consideration. But in the end, Yalta was a test of the ability of the three leaders to resolve the issues dividing them. In view of the urgency of coming to terms with each other, the shortcomings and mistakes produced by the Conference are appalling. The present map of Central and Eastern Europe—or more precisely, the German-Polish and Polish-Russian borders— are the enduring results of what was decided, or rather what was not really decided at Yalta.

II

With regard to the French problem, it must be stressed that in the final communiqué the informal, although crucial debate during the Yalta conference on France's future role in Europe remained unmentioned. Nevertheless, the Big Three discussed at length France's share in the occupation of Germany and whether France should be granted again the rank of *la Grande Nation* after the humiliating defeat of 1940. Stalin was persuaded to concede to France a seat on the Control Council, a zone of occupation and a sector in Berlin. Thus France gained acknowledgement as one of the big powers.[8]

The consequences for Germany of these decisions regarding France were significant, but one has to distinguish between short-term consequences and far-reaching ones. In the short run, French occupation was regarded by the Germans as extremely unpleasant, to say the least.[9] In contrast to British and American forces the French troops entering Germany committed a series of very nasty acts, such as rape, pillage and wanton destruction. French occupational authorities exploited, without any restraint, the economic resources of their zone; moreover, they displayed an ostentatiously victorious and triumphal attitude as an occupational power. The German population understood, though grudgingly, the vengeful spirit of the French after almost five years of humiliating German Occupation.[10] But they were also well aware that France's role as one of the four occupational powers had only been conceded to her by the Big Three. 'They came to victory on the baggage lorries of the Americans' was a common saying in those days.

On the other hand, the French Occupation had lasting effects as the French, quite in contrast to their political and economic policy, conceived and executed an extremely constructive cultural and educational policy.[11] Although short of financial and material resources the French expended an enormous amount of human and material resource in these fields. They refounded the University of Mayence, reconstructed the system of professional education, promoted literary and artistic life (one of Germany's most prominent authors of the 1920s, the emigré writer Alfred Döblin, was, as a

French colonel, one of the influential members of the cultural branch of the French Military Government), and they laid the foundations of an advanced social welfare system.[12] The dividends of this policy contributed later to what is commonly called the Franco-German reconciliation.[13] To a large extent, the nasty aspects of French occupation have quickly been purged from the collective memory by the lasting cultural effects. I personally also believe that the experience of victory and defeat in slightly more than two decades prepared psychologically the fertile ground from which this reconciliation could spring.[14]

III

Four main issues were dealt with at Yalta, of which two concern us here:
the Polish question, which was twofold: on the one hand, the question of the future social and political structure of Poland, and specifically the democratic character of the Polish Government; and on the other hand, the problem of Poland's future territorial configuration, that is, the definition of her future borders;
the German problem, which was to an extent directly connected with the Polish question, and which had five aspects: Germany's eastern borders; the question of dismemberment; reparations; the zones of occupation, including France's admission to the Control Council which implied her role in post-war Europe; and last, but not least the issue of denazification and demilitarisation.

The decisions taken at Yalta regarding the Polish problem had important consequences, for Poland and Germany in particular, and for Europe in general. At stake was nothing less than Poland's independence and liberty on the one hand, and her territorial configuration on the other. That there were strong divergences on these issues between Soviet Russia and the Western Allies was obvious. The three statesmen stated in paragraph VI of the 'Communiqué Issued at the End of the Conference', released to the press on 12 February 1945: 'We came to the Crimea Conference resolved to settle our differences about Poland'.[15] However, the agreements reached on this issue were far from clear.

The first problem to be solved was that of Poland's future political system. Before the Moscow Conference of October 1944 Stalin had already taken an important initiative in this respect by recognising the communist Lublin Committee as the only Polish political authority (26 July 1944). This initiative put the Western Allies in an awkward position: not only had Polish troops fought gallantly and vigorously for the Allied cause, but Britain and the United States had maintained relations with the strongly anti-communist Polish government-in-exile in London.

Roosevelt, therefore, insisted that the Communist Lublin Government 'be reorganized on a broader democratic basis with the inclusion of democratic leaders from Poland itself and from Poles abroad'.[16] A compromise was reached on this basis but the decision infuriated the exiled Polish Government in London. They had not agreed or even been consulted and foresaw the *de facto* partition of their country or worse, for the contorted formula just quoted was powerless to prevent the abandonment of the legitimate Polish Government-in-exile and the recognition of the Communist provisional government imposed by Moscow. The statement that the new government was to be 'pledged to the holding of free and unfettered elections as soon as possible on the basis of universal suffrage and secret ballot. In these elections all democratic and anti-Nazi parties shall have the right to take part and to put forward candidates' was equally ineffective.

In fact, Stalin soon made it clear that the new government would be dominated by communist elements. Churchill exerted a certain pressure on Roosevelt to remain firm on this issue, and US public opinion kept pressure on the President, so that in his last cable to Stalin at the end of March Roosevelt warned the Soviet leader that 'a thinly disguised continuance of the present Warsaw regime would be unacceptable and would cause the people of the United States to regard the Yalta agreements as having failed'.[17] Churchill's anxiety— as he wrote to the President almost a month later—was that 'it will soon be seen to the world that you and I by putting our signatures to the Crimean settlement have under-written a fraudulent prospectus'.

The other issue which was to be definitely resolved was the border question. From the very beginning of interallied talks on post-war Europe the Soviets had insisted on keeping virtually all those parts of Poland which they had annexed in 1939 under the Hitler-Stalin Pact. Poland would lose more than 11.5 million people (admittedly more Ukrainians and Russians than Polish, as about 40% of the population in this region was Polish) and about 180,000 sq km. This caused some embarrassment and annoyance to the British Government. The Polish Government in exile were not at all willing to accept the Russian-Polish borderline agreed upon by Hitler and Stalin. But Roosevelt, eager to get Stalin's approval for his United Nations scheme, made concessions to the Soviet leader on the Curzon Line: Poland's frontier with Soviet Russia was agreed, though the question of her western borders was left in abeyance.

It was obvious that Poland had to be compensated in the north and the west by German territory. At Teheran in 1943 it had already been agreed in a general way that Poland should be shifted to the west as compensation for her eastern provinces' remaining part of the Soviet Union. But at Yalta the extent of this compensation and where it would be was still left open. The relevant document stated: 'They recognized that Poland must receive substantial accessions of territory in the north and the west. They feel that the opinion of the new Polish Provisional Government of National Unity should be sought in due course on the extent of these accessions and that the final delimitation of the western frontier of Poland should thereafter await the Peace Conference.'[18]

Hidden behind this formula were substantial differences of opinion as to the territories concerned. Agreement seemed to have been reached before Yalta, that the annexations were to go 'up to the line of the Oder', which runs from north to south and then, in Silesia, turns south east. This included half of the province of Silesia. But during the talks at Yalta Stalin proposed that from the point where the Oder turns south east the new Polish border should run directly further to the south along the (western) Neisse up to the Czech border, thus giving the whole province of Silesia to Poland.[19] Both Roosevelt and Churchill protested against this maximalist interpretation of what had been previously if vaguely agreed. Churchill, in his colourful way of speaking, declared that 'it would be a pity to stuff the Polish goose so full of German food that it got indigestion'.[20] The outcome, therefore, was a vague formula postponing the final decision and leaving the controversial issue unresolved.

In fact Stalin had already taken the initiative of entering into an agreement with the Lublin Committee on 27 July 1944, according to which Poland's western borders should run from the Oder directly to the Lausitzer (western) Neisse. Long before the Crimean Conference considered the problem, therefore, Stalin and the Polish communist committee had anticipated the proposed settlement which was deferred at Yalta by the Big Three to the Peace Conference. The fact that Stalin had reached an agreement on the present Oder-Neisse border with the Polish communists on the one hand, and that he signed the Yalta Agreement providing for a final settlement of the borderline by a Peace Conference on the other hand, had two consequences: first, it became a contentious issue between Germany and Poland for a long period; and secondly, it limited to a large extent West Germany's diplomatic freedom of manoeuvre in international politics. Up to 1989 all Governments in Bonn were handicapped by the Yalta formula on the border problem, which prevented them from definitely normalizing relations with Poland. In the Federal Republic the political opposition, refugee organisations and the Constitutional Court always maintained that final agreement on the frontier must be left to a Peace Conference, thus keeping the issue open. What was left in suspense in Yalta became a matter of dispute and mistrust in European politics, and in German domestic and foreign affairs too, for 40 years.

The immediate consequence of the unsettled frontier issue was that Soviet Russia backed the Polish communist Government in a policy of *faits accomplis*: even during the Yalta Conference, on 5 February 1945 the Polish Government declared that they were extending Polish administration to Silesia and most of East Prussia. A month later, on 14 March, in contrast to the terms of the Yalta Communiqué, they established in these territories four new provincial administrations (*woiwodias*): Upper Silesia, Lower Silesia, Pomerania and Masuria, thus anticipating the annexation theoretically reserved to a Peace Conference.

Although the final decision to expel the German population from these territories was only taken at the Potsdam Conference, the Polish authorities had already set their plans in train. When the Big Three began their negotiations in Potsdam about 300,000 people had already been expelled and more than 5 million fled from the four new *woiwodias*. About 1 million returned to their homes after the end of the hostilities only to be expelled soon afterwards. The same happened in Czechoslovakia and Hungary, where Germans were expelled in the period between Yalta and the Potsdam Conference, although this issue had not directly been dealt with at Yalta. The Czechoslovak Government issued several decrees destined to destroy the economic and social basis of the German population and force them to leave the country. Between 600,000 and 700,000 Germans were thus expelled between Yalta and Potsdam.

At Potsdam the Big Three declared the expulsion of Germans from Poland, Czechoslovakia and Hungary should be executed in a humane and orderly way.[21] But this did not prevent the explosion of feelings of revenge and hatred, which often turned the expulsion into a fatal catastrophe for the people concerned.[22] The fact that 2.2 or even 2.5 million people were killed or died of hardship and exhaustion during the expulsion has long been accepted, though the results of new research work have recently brought these numbers into question. But in Germany these events have left a lasting and traumatic impression which remains in the nation's collective memory up to the present day and which has made many people unable or unwilling to recognize the linkage between cause and effect. This in turn has been exploited by interested parties.

In historical perspective, however, these events have to be set in a larger context: what we now call by hypocritical euphemisms 'ethnic cleansing', 'ethnic disengagement' or transfer of population, started in 1913 with the forced transfer of almost 1 million people between Bulgaria and Turkey. Henceforth it became a means of solving minority problems: between Greeks and Turks in 1922-23; with Baltic and Rumanian Germans in the wake of the Hitler-Stalin Agreement; Polish people, Ukrainians and Russians, but also German-Italians from Southern Tyrolia then became victims of Nazi racial doctrines; and in the Soviet Union Stalin transferred to Siberia or elsewhere minorities who were regarded as disloyal; in 1945-46 Communist governments transferred Polish-Ukrainians and Poles from the Vilnius region, mostly against their will, to the new western provinces in East Prussia, Silesia and Pomerania. All in all, some 20 million people were forced to leave their home and country just before and during the Second World War and the phenomenon has continued into our day. The German population, expelled from where they had settled for centuries, fit into this grim picture of European power politics: they had to pay the debts of Hitler's war and racial policy.[23]

There have been two more or less unexpected—in any case unintentional—but nevertheless remarkable results in this context: first of all, contrary to the apprehensions of the western leaders—and certainly to what might have been the calculation behind the Soviet strategy of expulsion—occupied Germany, and later on the Federal Republic, did not descend into chaos and starvation as a result of the avalanche of refugees and expelled people, but succeeded in integrating between 12 and 14 million of these Germans. During a meeting of the War Cabinet at the end of January 1944 Churchill stated that one could perhaps expel 4 to 5 million people, but nine or ten million would be absolutely impossible. He returned to this point during the Yalta Conference.[24] In a way, he anticipated the catastrophic picture Germany presented in 1945: more than two-thirds of the population without a home, literally on the streets; demobilised or escaped soldiers, liberated concentration camp inmates (about 700,000), refugees and expelled people, people who lost their homes during the air raids—not to mention the millions of displaced persons (some 13 million) or Allied prisoners in German captivity (another 2 million).

Two years after the war had ended the number of refugees and expelled persons rose to more than 16 million. According to a census ordered by the Allied military government in October 1945 the percentage of refugees and expelled was 20.8% in the Soviet occupied zone and 13.4% in the western zones.[25] In view of this massive influx it must be taken into account that in 1945 more than 90% of the railway system and 25% of the houses (mostly in the western zones) had been destroyed. Industrial production had sunk to 15% of pre-war output, and coal production to 10%. Churchill's apprehension was not exaggerated. Nevertheless, within ten years the problem was solved in western Germany, where more than 10 million people had been settled. Social unrest never created a problem either for the western occupational authorities nor, later on, for the new Federal Government.

The second result, not generally realised, was that the millions of refugees and expelled Germans deeply affected and moulded the character and the structure of the country in the same way and to almost the same extent as the Huguenots (at one time one-third of Berlin's population!) did in the 18th century to Frederic the Great's Prussia. It was not only their political importance which, for more than two decades, proved a relevant factor in West Germany's political life,[26] but they contributed also to the unique mixture that became the population of the Federal Republic. Never before have so many Germans of different religion, dialects and culture, hitherto unknown to each other, met and been forced to live together; they formed a new population that is, to a large extent, quite different from what the German people had been before the war.

IV

Three other aspects of the implementation of the Yalta decisions with regard to Germany must be considered.

The *reparation problem* had already been discussed before Yalta, and had been postponed due to obvious differences between Soviet Russia and the western Allies. In the US administration, those who supported the future integration of a peaceful Germany into a free world market had succeeded in pushing their point through against the Morgenthau concept of a predominantly agrarian Germany. At Yalta, Roosevelt and Churchill supported the idea of reparations paid in kind, ie to be taken only from current production and the service industry and by using the German labour force, rather than by financial payments. The problem of guaranteed reparation for Soviet Russia remained unsolved.[27] It was only at Potsdam through the compromise put forward by Foreign Secretary Byrnes that the Alliance solved this problem. The Soviet Union was given the exclusive right to take goods, services and financial assets out of her zone of Occupation. The effect of this decision was that the fundamental principle of the economic unity of Germany could no longer be maintained.

This leads to the issue of *dismemberment*. At Teheran the Big Three had agreed on the dismemberment of Germany without going into the details, and this decision was confirmed at Yalta. An amendment of Article 12(a) of the Surrender Terms was agreed which read as follows: The Allied powers 'will take such steps, including the complete disarmament, demilitarisation and the dismemberment of Germany, as they deem requisite for future peace and security'. The exact procedure for dismemberment was referred to a Committee.[28] Stalin, however, renounced the dismemberment project as early as 26 March 1945, and shortly afterwards the British Government also distanced itself from it.[29] At Potsdam, the Big Three renounced definitely, although tacitly, all dismemberment plans, and agreed to treat Germany as an 'economic entity', although the compromise on the reparation issue put forward by Byrnes actually sacrificed the economic unity of Germany at a stroke. The consequences were an economic partition of Germany along the demarcation line to the Soviet zone, as a prelude to the political partition into two states.

The consequences of the *denazification and demilitarisation* decided upon at Yalta[30] are well known. Between the Yalta Conference and 10 May 1945 all German forces had either been destroyed, like the Army Group West in the Ruhr pocket (17 April) or had surrendered unconditionally between 1 May (in Northern Italy) and 10 May (Army Group Kurland). During the war and in consequence of the surrender in 1945 more than 11 million members of the *Wehrmacht* became prisoners of war. They were to be repatriated in different stages: the United States continued to send them back until June 1946; Great Britain and France repatriated German prisoners-of-war until autumn 1948, but the last of the German prisoners in Soviet custody did not return until January 1956. The General Staff were tried as war criminals, but eventually acquitted of the charge. Former professional soldiers did not get any pension (until 1953 when the Federal Government passed a bill to this end).[31] The intensive Allied re-education policy bore fruit later on when in the 1950s the massive wave of the so-called 'Ohne-Mich' movement arose against German remilitarisation, and even today the German reticence towards offering a military contribution to the UN or to NATO actions 'out of area' can be interpreted as long-lasting effects of the Allied demilitarisation policy in the wake of Yalta. Up to the present day the military are not popular in Germany.[32]

Party officials, SD and Gestapo members, civil servants, diplomats and industrialists of a certain rank, and analogous groups were put under automatic arrest. In accordance with what had been decided in Yalta, SHAEF edited a *Handbook for Germany*, which enumerated the categories to be earmarked for internment. In July 1945 in the American occupied zone there were more than 70,000 internees, a number which rose to 1 million by about the end of the year. Most civil servants and other officials were—at least for a while—hounded from office and replaced by politically reliable persons. However, the Allied authorities handled the purge and the internment in different ways. The American occupational authorities were, in a way, the most thorough in executing the decisions destined to eliminate party members even in most junior public positions: but the French were more subtle; apart from party officials, war criminals or very high ranking civil servants those in positions vital for the smooth running of the administration and securing the necessities of life were generally allowed to remain in office provided they were willing to cooperate.[33]

The Soviet Military Administration (SMA) distinguished between active and nominal party members: they eliminated those belonging to the former category from all positions in political and public administration, justice and cultural or economic life. Moreover, they took advantage of denazification to destroy the existing social and economic structures and bring about a new 'anti-fascist society'. Under the pretext of prosecuting war crimes and purging society of 'fascist and militarist tendencies', the SMA expropriated big landowners and industrialists and nationalized large companies and banks. On the other hand, in order to win the sympathy of nominal party members or '*Mitläufer*' they favoured the integration of this category into the 'new order'. In the Soviet Zone denazification thus became a means to prepare for the projected social revolution in Germany.[34] The failure of the Big Three at Yalta to reach an agreement on how they could act in accordance with one another while putting into effect the relevant part II of the trilateral Yalta Communiqué ('...to destroy militarism and Nazism...') contributed to structural separation of the Soviet zone and the three western zones of Occupation.

But all four occupational powers were willing to make use of German officers, soldiers and experts if it served their interests. In this respect all four acted more or less in the same way. In any case, 'destroying militarism' was going to be defined (and limited) according to what they thought to be appropriate. It is well known that all four powers tried to get hold of as many German specialists as they could in advanced weaponry and armament constructions, especially missiles specialists. Also German service units, such as minesweeping services under British and American control, but commanded by German officers, were set up in occupied Germany. A considerable number of officers of the future German Federal Navy continued to serve in those units until they were able to join the new *Bundeswehr*—a strange continuity of German military tradition.[35]

Equally, a considerable number of German general officers and General Staff officers of all three services worked as specialists (first in captivity, later under contract) for American and British authorities preparing historical studies on German warfare experience.[36] General Colonel Halder, Chief of General Staff from 1938 to 1942, became the head of this group in summer 1945 after having been liberated from a Nazi prison by the Americans. Later he received one of the highest American decorations for his services. The Soviets in turn put German generals and high ranking officers who, in Soviet captivity, had joined the 'National Komitee Freies Deutschland' in not unimportant positions in the political and public life of their zone immediately after the occupation.[37] But this goes beyond the scope of this paper. In the final analysis, the Yalta decisions or compromises and even what was left undecided in Yalta affected Germany and the

German people deeply and determined, to a large extent, the central European scenery for about forty years.

Discussion

There was some discussion of the change in attitude towards the dismemberment of Germany between the conferences at Yalta— where, as *Sir Frank Roberts* pointed out, it was not really discussed—and at Potsdam.

Dr Hulas made the point that it was in the interests of the Soviet Union that Poland, which would be a dependant and a communist state should be pushed as far west as possible: on the same reasoning, the British Government did not want the Polish frontier too far west.

Notes and References

1   The question of Poland's borders and the dismemberment of Germany had already been discussed during Eden's visit to Moscow in December 1941.

2   It is important to distinguish between Europe, on which most agreements made or formulae found at Yalta were actually vague and ambivalent, although of far-reaching consequences; and on the other hand, the issues concerning the organisation of the UN and the Far East, where decisions taken were in fact definite and unambiguous. They, therefore, were implemented without any problems: Roosevelt succeeded in getting Stalin's approval on the technical issue of voting in the Security Council; Stalin, on the other hand, succeeded in getting the Ukraine and Byelorussia included in the list of independent states to become original members of the UN; Roosevelt equally succeeded without difficulty in getting Stalin's agreement to entering the war against Japan after Germany's military defeat. It must be added, however, that the decisions on East Asia were to the detriment of Nationalist China, America's ally, who was neither consulted nor advised about them.

3   Cf the fine analysis of the genesis and nature of this myth in Agnes Heller and Ferenc Fehér, *From Yalta to Glasnost* (Oxford, Basil Blackwell, 1990), p 5.

4   Z Brzezinski, 'The Future of Yalta', in *Foreign Affairs*, Winter 1984/85, pp 295 ff.

5   For an Eastern European oral assessment of Yalta, cf Heller and Fehér, op cit.

6   T Garton Ash, *The Times*, 11 February 1995.

7   Cf Heller and Fehér, p 6.

8   *FRUS, The Conferences at Malta and Yalta, 1945* (Washington, 1955), pp 283-309, 617, 629, 660, 970-1, 978ff.

9   Cf Edgar Wolfrum, 'Das Bild der "dusteren Französenzeit", Alltagsnot, Meinungsklima und Demokratisierungspolitik in der französischen Besatzungszone nach 1945', in Stefan Martens (ed), *Vom 'Erbfeind' zum 'Erneuerer'. Aspekta und Motive der französischen Deutschlandpolitik nach dem Zweiten Weltkrieg* (Siegmaringen, 1993), pp 87-114.

10 Martens (ed), op cit: cf also C Scharf and H-J Schroder, *Die Deutschlandpolitik Frankreichs und die französische Zone*; also the interesting comparison by Rainer Hudemann, 'The Army as an occupying power. The German Army in 1940-1944, the French Army in 1944-1949', in Klaus-Jürgen Müller (ed), *The Military in Politics and Society in France and Germany*, German Historical Perspectives, vol ix (Oxford, 1995), pp 139-63.

[11] Cf Jerôme Vaillant (ed), *Französische Kulturpolitik in Deutschland 1945-1949. Berichte und Dokumente* (Konstanz, 1984: first published as *La Dénazification par les Vainqueurs. La Politique culturelle des occupants en Allemagne 1945-1949*, Lille, 1981). See also relevant contributions in Martens, op cit.

[12] Franz Knipping and Jacques Le Rider (eds), *Frankreichs Kulturpolitik in Deutschland 1945-50* (Tübingen, 1987); Rainer Hudemann, *Sozialpolitik im deutschen Südwesten zwischen Tradition und Neuordnung 1945-1953* (Mainz, 1988).

[13] Cf the excellent analysis by Rainer Hudemann, 'Französische Besatzungsmacht und deutsche Bevölkerung nach zwei Weltkriegen' in E W Hansen et al (eds), *Politischer Wandel, organisierte Gewalt und nationale Sicherheit : Beitrage zur neueren Geschichte Deutschlands und Frankreichs* (München 1995), pp 427-62.

[14] Cf Klaus-Jürgen Müller, op cit.

[15] *FRUS*, op cit, p 973.

[16] Ibid, p 974, and see L Aronson & M Kitchen, *The Origins of the Cold War in Comparative Perspective* (London), p 29.

[17] Aronson & Kitchen, op cit, p 29.

[18] *FRUS*, op cit, p 974.

[19] Michael Balfour, *Germany, The Tides of Power* (London/New York, 1992), pp 81-83.

[20] *FRUS*, op cit, p 717.

[21] See *DBPO*, Series I, Volume I, No 603, Section XII; cf Volume V, No. 26.

[22] Cf A M de Zayas, *Nemesis at Potsdam—the Anglo-Americans and the Expulsion of the Germans* (London, 1977, 2nd rev ed, New York 1994); *Vertreibung und Vertreibungsverbrechen 1945-1948, Bericht des Bundesarchivs vom vom 28. Mai 1974* (Bonn 1989); *Dokumentation der Vertreibung der Deutschen aus Ost-Mittel-Europa*, 4 vol, ed Th Schieder & Bundesministerium für Vertriebene, Berlin 1953-1961 (2nd ed, München 1984, 3rd ed, Augsburg 1993/94).

[23] Cf W Benz (ed), *Die Vertreibung der Deutschen aus dem Osten. Ursachen, Ereignisse, Folgen* (Frankfurt aM, 1985); and A Theisen, *Die Verteibung der Deutschen—Ein unbewältigtes Kapital der europäischen Zeitgeschichte*, in *Aus Politik und Zeitgeschichte*, ed Bundeszentrale für Politische Bildung (Bonn B 7-8/1955), p 20-33. The number and fate of German civilians who in 1945 had been deported as slave workers from Soviet occupied German territories are unknown even today. A Russian historian from St Petersburg, Pavel Poljan, presented a paper at an international conference organized by the Evangelische Akademie in Mülhem in March 1995, in which he maintained that more than 160,000 persons of German origin had been deported from Soviet-occupied Germany and Eastern European countries to the Soviet Union, a high percentage of whom died of exertion and starvation during the deportation.

[24] Cf Churchill's remark during the Plenary Session of 7 February: 'He felt that there was a considerable body of British opinion that would be shocked if it were proposed to move large numbers of Germans...He said he felt it it were confined to East Prussia, six million Germans probably could be handled quite aside from moral grounds, but the addition of the line west of the Neisse would create a problem in this respect' (Harriman to the Secretary of State, 19 December 1944, *FRUS*, op cit, p 717; cf also pp 219ff).

[25] In 1950 one in four inhabitants of the GDR was a refugee or an expelled German or born of a refugee or expelled family.

[26] In particular the Germans from Bohemia and Moravia (commonly called *Sudetendeutsche*), who are well known for their discipline (they were once nicknamed 'Austria's Prussians'), intelligence and dynamism, became comparatively influential, especially in Bavaria.

[27] Cf *FRUS*, op cit, p 971: 'We have considered the question of the damage caused by Germany to the Allied Nations in this war and recognized it as just that Germany be obliged to make compensation for this damage in kind to the greatest possible extent.'

[28] *FRUS*, ibid, p 978: Protocol of Proceedings, released to the press 27 March 1947.

[29] Cf *DBPO*, Series I, Volume I, No 74.

[30] Cf Part II of the trilateral Communiqué, *FRUS*, p 970: 'It is our inflexible purpose to destroy militarism and Nazism…We are determined to disarm and to disband all German armed forces; break up for all time the German General Staff…wipe out the Nazi party, Nazi laws, organizations and institutions, remove all Nazi and militarist influences from public office and from cultural and economic life of the German people…'

[31] Cf G Meyer, 'Soldaten ohne Armee. Berufssoldaten im Kampf um Standesehre und Versorgung', in M Broszat et al, *Von Stalingrad zur Wahrungsreform. Zur Sozialgeschichte des Umbruches in Deutschland* (München, 1989), pp 683-750.

[32] In all polls on social reputation army officer ranks among the last five on a given list of careers or jobs.

[33] Cf W Benz, *Potsdam 1945. Besatzungsherrschaft und Neuaufbau im Vier-Zonen-Deutschland* (München 1986); C Schick, 'Die Internierungslager', in: Broszat, op cit, pp 301-26. K-D Henke, *Politische Sauberungen unter französischer Besatzung* (Stuttgart, 1981); Rainer Mohler, *Entnazifizierung in Rheinland-Pfalz und im Saarland unter franzosischen Besatzung von 1945 bis 1952* (Mainz, 1992); J Foschepoth and R Steininger (eds), *Die Britische Deutschland und Besatzungspolitik* (Paderborn, 1985). See also *DBPO*, Series I, Volume V, Nos 48, 49, 95.

[34] Cf Ruth-Kristin Rössler (ed), *Die Entnazifizierungspolitik der KPD/SED 1945-1948. Dokumente und Materialen* (Frankfurt aM, 1995); Hartmut Mehringer (ed), *Von der SBZ zur DDR. Studien zum Herrschaftsystem in der Sowjetischen Besatzungszone Deutschlands* (Szeitgeschichtetuttgart 1995, = Sondernummer der Schriftenreite der Vierteljahrshefte für Zeitgeschichte).

[35] H-L Borgert et al, *Dienstgruppen und westdeutscher Verteidigungsbeitrag* (Boppard, 1982). Cf also *DBPO*, Series I, Volume V, Nos 29, 42, 56.

[36] Cf the relevant article by Georg Meyer in *Von der Kapitulation bis zum Plevenplan (Anfänge deutscher Sicherheitspolitik*, vol I, ed Militär-geschichtliches Forschungsamt, München, 1982); cf generally Alexander Fischer et al, *Entmilitarisierung und Aufrüstung in Mitteleuropa 1945-1956* (Hertford & Bonn, 1983).

[37] Cf Bodo Scheurig, *Freies Deutschland. Das Nationalkomitee und der Bund Deutscher Offiziere in der Sowjetunion 1943-1945* (München, 1960, 2nd edn Köln 1984); Vincenz Müller, *Ich fand das wahre Vaterland* (Berlin, 1963) and Jesco v Putkamer, *Von Stalingrad zur Volkspolizei. Geschichte des 'Nationalkomitees Freies Deutschland'* (Wiesbaden, 1951).

6 The Conference at Potsdam, 1945

DAVID DILKS

We returned to our places, these Kingdoms,
But no longer at ease here, in the old dispensation,
With an alien people clutching their gods.

T S Eliot, *Journey of the Magi*

The sumless tale of sorrow
Is all unrolled in vain

A E Housman

After Yalta, Churchill was wont to say that there he sat, the poor little British lion, between the great American buffalo and the great Russian bear; and in an occasional variation of the metaphor, he would observe that he had represented the British donkey, which was the only one of the animals knowing the way home. The westward-rolling Russian tide and the ever-swelling preponderance of American force in the alliance had transformed the military and political position in a matter of months. Deep forebodings rather than a settled conviction about Russia's intentions ran constantly through the minds of Churchill and Eden. Incredible as it might seem after escapes so perilous and sacrifices so enormous, the result of the second German war might be to substitute one tyranny for another, and the astonishing advance of weaponry might have the effect of enabling powers in the next struggle to inflict upon each other a destruction which would dwarf even that of the struggle then ending.

Mr Harold Macmillan's diary remarks with a twist of grim humour in December 1944, 'We do not wish to start the Third World War against Russia until we have finished the Second World War against Germany—and certainly not to please M. Papandreou.'[1] As a matter of fact, the Greek imbroglio did not for the moment disturb Anglo-Russian relations, though it occasioned a temporary strong difference of opinion with the government of the USA. Stalin's adherence to his promise not to meddle in Greece affected Churchill profoundly at the time; the more profoundly perhaps, because no-one was more conscious than the Prime Minister of Britain's economic and financial exhaustion. The British had disposed of their pre-war overseas assets to the tune of at least £1000m. They knew the inadequacies of their gold and dollar reserves; they had lost most, perhaps all, of their creditor position as it stood in 1939; when the war was over, they would need something resembling an economic miracle, and could not achieve that without the sustained goodwill of the United States.[2]

And how was this act of goodwill to be secured? Partly by acts of submission in order to secure the continuation of the coalition or, that failing, the support of the United States. In that light we should read Churchill's signature of the agreement which had been concocted in secret between Stalin and Roosevelt during the Yalta conference; this was the document covering the Far East which both the Foreign Secretary and the Permanent Under-Secretary of the Foreign Office, Anthony Eden and Sir Alexander Cadogan, said that Britain should not underwrite. For understandable reasons, Churchill felt that he must endorse the bargain. Britain would otherwise forfeit influence in the Far East, where her role was already sufficiently reduced. In this, as in the other agreements made in that pregnant week, we see the ironies of comparison between Yalta and Munich; China and Poland were no more consulted over their fate in 1945 than Czechoslovakia over hers in 1938, and for much the same set of reasons. In each case, an expansive power not afraid to use force demanded to have its way at the expense of a weaker neighbour; and in neither case did those of a different view feel that they had the power, or sufficient at stake, to resist.

There followed what Churchill would have called a loaded pause: the events in Poland and Roumania, to name no other countries; Molotov's initial refusal to go to the conference at San Francisco which was to devise a constitution for the United Nations; Russian pressure upon Turkey; all caused the Foreign Secretary to confide to his diary but a few weeks after Yalta, 'I take the gloomiest view of Russian behaviour everywhere.' He added with commendable candour, 'Altogether our foreign policy seems a sad wreck and we may have to cast about afresh.'[3]

The expression 'a sad wreck' was not far wide of the mark, in the sense that until this stage the leading British ministers thought that the chief danger of the post-war world would lie in a resurgent Germany rather than an expansive Russia. That perception was to change rapidly, but not completely, in the weeks separating Yalta from Potsdam. Eden had even wondered whether there was any point in his attending the conference at San Francisco. 'How can we lay the foundations of any new World Order when Anglo-American relations with Russia are so completely lacking in confidence?'[4] Perhaps because of the rapid assumption of power by the Russians in Eastern and Central Europe, perhaps out of sheer weariness, perhaps from a conviction that San Francisco had not turned out too badly, the British do not seem to have raised any similar questions about attendance at Potsdam, the main themes of which conference were apparent well before it met: the nature of the 'liberation' of those territories in which the Soviet Army was now supreme; the meaning to be given to the promises about free elections; the treatment of Germany; the frontiers to be established for Poland, east and west.

Of them all, the Polish issue loomed largest. There was one sense in which the British, who felt the Polish issue more acutely than either

Roosevelt or Truman, were responsible for the tensions over this issue, though theirs was a negative responsibility; that is, they had repeatedly accepted the Russian claim that there should be a glacis of 'friendly' states around Russia's borders. The magnitude of Russia's sacrifices in the war extorted agreement with that claim. Inevitably it conflicted with the equally valid demand for a free and independent Poland. By definition, if Poland were truly free and independent, she must be at liberty to adopt an attitude of coolness, wariness, even hostility, towards Russia. After the events of the previous three centuries, and especially the events of the second world war itself, it was well-nigh certain that any truly independent Poland would be as hostile to Russia as to Germany. Only by tact and compromise on the Russian side could that dilemma have been resolved; and of those qualities there was precious little sign.

It seemed as unlikely that the developing situation in Europe could be reconciled with the Atlantic Charter as that Russian demands in the Far East could be harmonised with the declarations made after the Cairo Conference of 1943. In the last few days of his life, Roosevelt had been shocked by blatantly hostile messages from Stalin, upon whose telegrams more than one complexion might be put: he might be ill-informed and hasty, which on previous experience of him seemed unlikely; or paranoid, which was not the conclusion to which the British and Americans had hitherto come; or seeking a pretext for a break. Even Roosevelt telegraphed to him, 'Frankly, I cannot avoid a feeling of bitter resentment toward your informers, whoever they are, for such vile misrepresentations of my actions or those of my trusted subordinates.' The War Cabinet in London associated itself explicitly with this message. Stalin replied somewhat unconvincingly that he had never doubted the trustworthiness of Roosevelt or Churchill.[5]

In considering what happened and failed to happen at Potsdam, we ought to think by way of parallel not of Versailles, but of the later stages of the Congress of Vienna. In each case the incentive to unity, fear of an enemy of immense strength and military prowess, had vanished. True, the victors in 1945 did not emulate their predecessors of 130 years before by seeking an accommodation with the defeated colossus; but that was only a matter of time.

The records of the proceedings at Potsdam have been published by all three partners.[6] Here we are concerned less with the detailed exchanges than with the atmospherics of the conference; the nature of the relations between the great powers, the degree to which they still hoped for collaboration, the uncertainties, the diminished position of the British. To what degree would the USA, conscious of its immense strength, unthreatened by invasion, with a domestic standard of consumption well above anything achieved in peace time, be willing to support Britain and, more problematically, Britain's colonial position and special interests? As Churchill once remarked, in countries where there is only one race

> *broad and lofty views are taken of the colour question. Similarly States which have no overseas colonies or possessions are capable of rising to moods of great elevation and detachment about the affairs of those who have.*

In a similar but subtler vein, Eden remarked that Roosevelt did not confine his dislike of colonialism to the British empire alone 'for it was a principle with him, not the less cherished for its possible advantages. He hoped former colonial territories, once free of their masters, would become politically and economically dependent upon the United States, and had no fear that other powers would fill that role.'[7] Mr Adolf Berle, of whom it was mischievously said that he worked night and day to make the world safe for peace and Pan American Airways, advised the State Department that the USA must support Turkey in resisting Soviet demands, even though the effect might be to bolster up the British empire in the near east; a thing which, Mr Berle remarked with candour, 'no American could contemplate in the ordinary way with any pleasure. But at least', he conceded, 'the British and Americans spoke more or less the same language and the British would discuss matters reasonably frankly whereas the Russians would not.'[8]

Immediately after the quarrel between Stalin, Roosevelt and Churchill had been patched up, the President died. Eden, who represented the British government at Roosevelt's funeral, found his successor Harry Truman honest and friendly, conscious of his new responsibilities but not overwhelmed by them.[9] The Foreign Secretary was equally encouraged by the friendly and co-operative temper of the Senate Foreign Relations Committee.[10] Before long, Churchill pressed upon Eden, who needed no convincing, the view that the Polish deadlock could probably only be resolved at a conference between the three heads of government. The Prime Minister believed that terrible things had happened during the Russian advance through Germany to the Elbe. He dwelt upon the tide of Russian domination moving westwards and begged that the Allies should not retreat from their positions until satisfied about Poland and other issues. He feared that if matters could not be settled before the US armies withdrew from Europe and the western world folded up its military machine, there would be no prospects of a satisfactory solution 'and very little of preventing a third world war. It is to this early and speedy showdown and settlement with Russia that we must now turn our hopes. Meanwhile I am against weakening our claim against Russia on behalf of Poland anyway...'.[11]

In a series of telegrams to Truman, the Prime Minister argued on similar lines. At that stage, he did not know when the general election would occur. Truman had already suggested that he could not get away until July. The Prime Minister hoped that at least the new President would pay a visit to Britain, which Roosevelt had promised to do. Then the British and American leaders could move on to a rendezvous with Stalin in Germany.[12] A day or two later, the celebrated 'Iron Curtain' telegram was despatched to Washington. Again and again Churchill expressed his anxiety that the main British and American armies should move as little as possible before the proposed conference. It followed that he did not desire any large movements which would enable French forces to take over their agreed zone, because that might well stimulate the Russian demand to occupy the heart of Germany.[13] The crux of the British dilemma may be simplified thus. Despite the military and political reasons for dismembering Germany, the attractions of that policy diminished as fears about the ambitions of Russia mounted. The zone which the British would occupy, under the elaborate arrangements worked out through the European Advisory Commission in London, could be nowhere near self-sufficient in food, and was heavily industrialised. If the American armies withdrew, might not the British Isles after years of rationing and near-starvation find themselves feeding a good portion of Germany? Would that not be beyond Britain's resources? And would it be politically possible?

The new President had said to Eden in mid May, 'I am here to make decisions, and whether they prove right or wrong I am going to take them.'[14] He was as good as his word, even if not all those decisions were palatable to the British. For example, Truman turned down 'in order to avoid any suspicion of our "ganging up"' the suggestion for a meeting between the British and American leaders in advance of the conference.[15] In his private talks with Eden, the President referred bitterly to the failure of the Russians to keep their word about the agreements reached at Yalta and suggested that it might be possible to come to Europe earlier than 1 July. In a note which Churchill immediately dictated, but then decided not to send to Truman, we find, 'From a military point of view every minute counts... Everything is melting very fast and meanwhile all our questions with Stalin are unsettled... I regard the situation as most grievous and darkening.'[16] Churchill regretted that London had not been chosen as the venue for the Conference but accepted Stalin's suggestion of Berlin. He reacted vigorously against a suggestion conveyed on Truman's behalf by Mr Joseph E Davies that the President and Stalin should meet together first and be joined later by representatives of the British government, and the more so because Truman had already ruled out an Anglo-American meeting in advance of the main conference.[17]

In London, the wartime coalition government now dissolved. Churchill had hoped to the last that it might hold together until the defeat of Japan. Although he had decided to call an early general election and would therefore be occupied for most of June in campaigning, the Prime Minister would have preferred to interrupt the process and attend the conference in that same month. The issue was however settled by a message from Truman to Stalin, delivered by Harry Hopkins, who was in Moscow to negotiate about Poland. The President had decided upon a meeting in mid July, of which Churchill learned from Stalin.[18] In vain did Churchill protest against this late date: 'I have proposed June 15, repeat June, the month before July, and if that is not possible, why not the first, second or third July?'[19]

There was clearly nothing to be done. Perhaps with the experiences of Teheran and Yalta in mind, the British insisted that each side should be responsible at Berlin for its own quarters and security. For the whole of June, Eden was unwell and away from the Foreign Office. During much of that time, Churchill was himself campaigning in every part of the United Kingdom, conducting business from his train or car, physically exhausted, mentally alert and oppressed by the international prospects. At this stage, he had no doubt about the outcome of the election; nor had most others. The Foreign Office had drawn up a list of questions for consideration at Potsdam. They ranged from the broad and general—the procedure for a European settlement, the application of the Yalta Declaration on Liberated Europe, war crimes, permission for representatives of the press to function freely in Eastern Europe—to Poland; Germany, including the transfer of German populations from Poland and Czechoslovakia, and the treatment of Germany as an economic whole; the conclusion of the peace treaty with Italy; the internal situation in the countries of South East Europe and the question of eventual peace treaties with them; Yugoslavia; Turkey; and Persia.[20] This list harmonised closely with topics suggested by the State Department, in which Mr Stettinius after a brief tenure was being replaced as Secretary of State by J F Byrnes.

'We are hoping to prepare for you', Sir Alexander Cadogan wrote to the Prime Minister just before polling day, 'a list of the cards that we and the Americans hold in our hands. They are not many. The most important is American credits. Also our possession of the German fleet, of German industrial plant and resources in the west, and of the German archives, and lastly, of course, any concessions which Stalin may want to extract from us, for instance about the Straits or about Tangier. It seems to me very important that we should not give away at any early stage of the conference any of the few cards which we hold. Even if Stalin's requests are reasonable, we should not grant them except in return for his agreement to reasonable requests on our part.'[21]

The list of cards held in the British hand, as provided by Eden to Churchill, scarcely added to the tally which Cadogan had already sent.[22] In another paper, he commented to the Prime Minister, 'I find the world outlook gloomy and signs of Russian penetration everywhere.' As for the conference itself, the British did not know the views of the new Secretary of State in Washington, and were conscious of divergent opinions within the State Department; there was not an agreed agenda for the meeting. Eden proposed that as at Yalta, the heads of government should decide upon the items which they wished to discuss and remit the preliminary work to the Foreign Ministers, who would meet in the mornings.[23] This was in substance the procedure followed at Terminal, the code name given to the conference, which no doubt signified the end of the war but might equally have referred to the state of health of the alliance.

Correctly, Churchill judged that the view taken in Washington of the European prospects was rosier than that entertained in London: 'They seem to think that, given the settlement of a few outstanding problems, and the enunciation of general political principles and desiderata, Europe can safely be left to look after itself and that it will soon settle down to peaceful and orderly development. Our view, on the contrary, is that unless we all work very hard the situation in Europe will deteriorate rapidly and dangerously.'[24] Halifax's reply proved reassuring in part; and while the Prime Minister remarks in his account that as for the business of Potsdam 'I did not need to prepare myself for the conference, for I carried so much of it in my head...',[25] it was rapidly plain to his senior British colleagues that all was not well.

Immediately after the election, the Prime Minister set off for a week's holiday in the sun, for the first time in the whole war living without the flurry of red boxes, telegrams and despatch riders. He read in the mornings, painted in the afternoons, reminisced in the intervals and confessed to depression and lack of energy. Not realising how long the conference at Potsdam would last, he remarked that nothing would be decided there. 'I shall be only half a man until the result of the poll'; and that result would not be known until 25 July.[26]

While Churchill painted at Hendaye, elaborate papers were drawn up in London for use at Potsdam. The shattered condition of Germany, which had no government, made it impossible to negotiate a treaty like that of Versailles, even if that had been desirable. Yet it was clearly in the interest of Britain, and by extension America, to make a definite settlement as quickly as possible, for both those countries would demobilize and both were at war in the Far East. Generally, the British wished to encourage Austrian independence, reach an early settlement with Italy, retain a say in South East Europe and see the formation of a Council of Foreign Ministers, ideally in London. The Embassy in Moscow reported that many of the darker clouds which had threatened the meeting at Potsdam had been dissipated. The Ambassador detected a relaxation in tension within Russia and a marked improvement in relations with the allies. The new world organisation had been established with full Soviet support; agreement had been reached in

Germany on decisions concerning occupation and control; the problem of Vienna seemed to be on the way to a solution; the Polish question, as the Ambassador imagined, had been 'disposed of on the lines of the Crimea Agreement', although he did admit that this list of happy events did not include a single instance in which the Soviet government had given way substantially on an issue affecting its vital interests. He expected to see the Russians and Americans drawing closer together in the months immediately ahead and described the Soviet Union as a country teeming with vitality and bent upon making her influence felt, even far from her own frontiers. Sir A Clark Kerr believed that the Russians were still uncertain about how far the British were ready to go to back their friends and stand up in good time for their principles and vital interests.[27]

*

General de Gaulle observed that the British and Americans rushed without France to Potsdam, where they hoped to recover in practice what they had conceded at Teheran and Yalta.[28] This is certainly not true of the British, and unlikely to be true of the Americans. President Truman stated that the most urgent reason for his going to Potsdam was to secure a reaffirmation of Russia's intention to enter the war against Japan. Not surprisingly, Stalin promised this promptly. As Truman observed privately after a first encounter with the Russian leader, 'I can deal with Stalin. He is honest—but smart as hell.'[29] The President returned to his temporary home at the aptly-named Babelsberg with some confidence, hoping that Stalin was a man who would keep to his agreements. As Chairman of the conference, Truman tells us, he did not under-estimate the difficulties and realised that he would be faced with problems arising from the conflicts of interest. 'I knew that Stalin and Churchill each would have special interests that might clash and distract us' he recorded long after the event, as if the United States had no such 'special' interests.[30]

Thus in mid July the three delegations to the Potsdam Conference had taken up their separate quarters, the Prime Minister in the home of a Director of the *Deutsche Bank*. The plenary sessions of the conference itself were held in the Cecilienhof, once described as resembling 'a stockbroker's idea of paradise', with pinnacles, spires and stained-glass windows. The British and American armies had some weeks before withdrawn from their forward positions in Eastern and Central Europe, despite all Churchill's pleadings. He paid a visit to the ruins of Berlin, where the scent of limes had been replaced by the stench of death; and then to the business of the conference, with the result of the general election still unknown.

'You mentioned in conversation yesterday', wrote Eden to Churchill on 17 July, 'that the Russian policy was now one of aggrandisement', a phrase which implies that this was previously not so, or not

84

understood. Eden agreed with the diagnosis, and in that context considered the additions which Molotov had said he wished to make to the agenda. Amongst them were Tangier, the Levant, trusteeships, all of them matters in which Russia had no direct interest. 'The truth is that on any and every point, Russia tries to seize all that she can and she uses these meetings to grab as much as she can get.' Here the language makes it plain that the Foreign Secretary was basing himself upon the experience of previous conferences; but on those occasions, the powers had met in the knowledge that Russia was bearing the heaviest burden of the war and her casualties were far worse than any suffered by the British or Americans. All that was now over. As for Russian access to the sea, Eden recommended that the British should not discuss the subject at Potsdam. Russian demands on Turkey might result in Constantinople's being placed under Russian guns and probably mark the first stage of the subjection of Turkey to Russia; and if the Russians were free to move into the Mediterranean from the Black Sea, where would they seek the freedom to leave? Was their interest in the Lebanon a first stage on the way to an interest in Egypt, 'which is quite the last place where we want them, particularly since that country with its rich Pashas and impoverished fellahin would be a ready prey to Communism?'[31] Attlee, attending as a member of the British delegation, thought that this was to choose the wrong ground and feared a situation in which the British and Russians would meet each other as rival great powers at points of strategic importance. 'We ought to confront the Russians with the requirement of a world organisation for peace, not with the needs of the defence of the British empire.' He argued for 'the only realistic policy', which was to place all these strategic areas under the international control of the United Nations.[32]

If Attlee's view assumed a role for the United Nations Organisation which events would soon belie, the attitude of the British ministers towards Stalin does not indicate that they understood what they were dealing with. That Stalin disliked and mistrusted Churchill seems evident.[33] It was one thing to give way under duress to superior military strength; it would have been another to recognise that Britain and America were dealing with a monster of depravity and cynicism, guilty of countless deaths. The strong suspicion or worse that all the Russian denials about Katyn had been false; the memories of Stalin's behaviour during the Warsaw rising of 1944; the fate of many of the promises made at Yalta—even when such memories rose to the surface or fed fears for the future, they were apt to be overlaid by fatigue, relief that defeat at the hands of Hitler had been so narrowly averted, genuine admiration for the unimaginable sacrifices made by Russia during the war, half a hope that Stalin had become less of a communist than a nationalist who had caused the portraits of Marx and Engels in the rooms of the Kremlin to be replaced by those of Kutusov and Suvorov.[34] What hope could there be for the future world organisation, and what expectation of anything but another and still more ruinous war, if some ground of co-operation with Russia could not be reached?

At the first formal session of the conference, on 17 July, Churchill performed well below the standard of his prime, according to Eden and Cadogan. After that session, however, Churchill and Stalin had a cordial private meeting. Stalin told the Prime Minister that a message had been received through the Japanese Ambassador in Moscow stating in the name of the Emperor of Japan that unconditional surrender could not be accepted; if it were not insisted upon, Japan might be prepared to compromise. Churchill said that Stalin should inform Truman at once, whereas the Generalissimo (a title recently conferred, or seized) preferred that Churchill should mention the subject to Truman. We may note the interesting community of interests between Churchill and Stalin on this point; Stalin did not wish Truman to think Russia was acting as an intermediary, and Churchill did not wish Truman to believe Britain was not at one with the United States in the intent to win a complete victory against Japan. People in America, the Prime Minister added, were beginning to doubt the need for 'unconditional surrender' and were saying: was it worthwhile having the pleasure of killing ten million Japanese at the cost of one million Americans and British? Grimly, Stalin rejoined that unconditional surrender in practice could be seen in Berlin and the rest of Germany.

Nevertheless, the conversation went well. Stalin informed Churchill genially that he had taken to smoking cigars; the Generalissimo 'appeared to be touched' when Churchill spoke of the women workers in Stalingrad whom Mrs Churchill had seen on her recent visit. Despite the Foreign Secretary's warnings, Churchill also observed that Britain 'welcomed Russia as a great power and in particular as a naval power. The more ships that sailed the seas the greater chance there was for better relations.'[35]

Cadogan remarked at the time that Stalin knew exactly how to manage Churchill. The Foreign Secretary was of the same view. 'Alec and I and Bob [Dixon, Eden's Private Secretary] have never seen W [Winston] worse. Dined alone with him and again urged him not to give up our few cards without return. But he is again under Stalin's spell. He kept repeating 'I like that man' and I am full of admiration of Stalin's handling of him. I told him I was, hoping that it would move him. It did a little!'[36] Again, it is scarcely conceivable that Churchill would have said 'I like that man' if he had realised the full truth about Stalin or the régime he dominated. The same must be said of Cadogan, whom no-one ever accused of undue partiality towards the Soviets, or Eden, who remarked that after a life-time's experience of international conferences, if he had to pick a team for going into a conference room, Stalin would be his first choice.[37]

It must be added that since the Russians had physical possession of the Baltic States and the larger part of Central and South Eastern Europe, even the fullest appreciation of the nature of the regime would have made little difference. 'I prayed the Americans on my knees not to hand over to the Russians such a great chunk of Germany, at least until after the conference. It would have been a bargaining counter. But they would not listen. The President dug in. I shall ask Stalin, "Does he want the whole world?"' So said Churchill a few days later, when it had become apparent from Russia's attitude about reparations that the notion of Germany as an economic unit had vanished. 'The Russians', Churchill said in the same conversation, 'have stripped their zone and want a rake-off from the British and American sectors as well. They will grind their zone, there will be unimaginable cruelties. It is indefensible, except on one ground: that there is no alternative.'[38]

On the following day, 18 July, Churchill had a long conversation with Truman. Churchill had been impressed by his first contacts with the President, by his precise and sparkling manner and obvious power of decision.[39] Over a lengthy luncheon, Truman showed Churchill the telegrams about the successful experiment with the atomic bomb in New Mexico. The President made it abundantly clear that he was not going to impart any particulars to the Russians. The two of them then discussed how they should handle the Russian request for a division of the German fleet. Churchill again expressed the view that 'We should welcome the Russians on to the broad waters and do it in a manner which was whole-hearted and gracious', but the question of shares of the German fleet could not be handled on its own. Truman seemed to agree. As Churchill recorded their conversation later that day:

> Were all these States which had passed into Russian control to be free and independent or not? Of course they could not pursue a policy hostile to Russia. The President attached great importance to this, and evidently intends to press with severity the need of their true independence in accordance with free, full and unfettered elections. He seemed to agree with my point that everything should be settled as a whole, and not piecemeal. When I mentioned Persia, Turkey and Greece, he seemed to be in full accord.

Over luncheon, Truman also spoke generously of the immense debt which the USA owed to Britain for having held the fort at the beginning of the war. Churchill replied that while the British had no intention of being kept by any country, however close the friendship, the British would have to ask for American help. He spoke of the melancholy financial position of Great Britain, which had freely expended her foreign investments. No doubt tact forbade him to say that many of those investments had been liquidated in the United

States at knock-down prices while the United States was herself neutral. Britain would be emerging from the war with an external debt of some £3,000m in the values of 1945. To arrive at an equivalent figure for 1995, we should have to multiply that by a factor approaching 20; let us say, to be on the safe side, £50,000m. The figure itself, let alone the means of repaying it, seemed beyond imagination. Luckily for the Prime Minister, he did not know how soon and how abruptly lease-lend would be cut off.

In conclusion, Truman said that this had been the most enjoyable luncheon he had had for many years, and how earnestly he hoped to enjoy with Churchill the cordial relations which had flourished between the Prime Minister and Roosevelt. He invited personal friendship and comradeship and seemed to the Prime Minister a man of exceptional character and ability. 'Let us hope that further developments at this Conference and hereafter will vindicate these hopeful notes', Churchill recorded that day.[40] On balance they did, but less at the conference than in the years to come. For the moment, Truman perhaps stood somewhat in awe of Churchill, with all his experience, renown, vivid presence and wonderful command of language. The Prime Minister, whose habit it was to look for the best in his companions at least until the worst was proved, perhaps exaggerated the import of friendly remarks and tributes to British gallantry. At any rate, we find the President writing about the Prime Minister:

> *He is a most charming and very clever person—meaning clever in the English not the Kentucky sense. He gave me a lot of hooey about how great my country is and how he loved Roosevelt and how he intended to love me, etc. Well, I gave him as cordial a reception as I could—being naturally (I hope) a polite and agreeable person. I am sure we can get along if he does not try to give too much soft soap.*[41]

In fact, Churchill and Truman had already reached a level of closer understanding than the Prime Minister and President possessed in the latter stages of Roosevelt's life. Perhaps the very directness of Truman's responses and his willingness not to take offence emboldened the Prime Minister to speak candidly; not that he usually needed much encouragement in that direction. There is little sign in Truman's reactions of the jealousies and veiled mockeries with which Roosevelt would sometimes greet Churchill's interventions, even though the new President disliked staying up late (whereas Churchill and Stalin liked nothing better), and wished to cut out discussion and come to clear conclusions on issues which turned out to be more complicated than he had sometimes realised. Truman was prompter and clearer in decision, and more straightforward by nature, than Roosevelt. Nor did Churchill have occasion to say of his relations with Truman, as he more than once did of those with Roosevelt, that no lover ever studied the whims of his mistress more carefully. This must have come as no mean relief to the Prime Minister, scarcely suited for a sustained role as suppliant and suitor.

In respect of Japan, Churchill was sure from conversations with the Secretary for War, Stimson, with General Marshall and then with Truman, that the Americans were searching their hearts about the 'unconditional surrender' of Japan and that the British would not need to press the case for some softening of the policy. That the conference at Potsdam should fall at a critical moment for this issue was pure coincidence for, as we have seen, Churchill would much have preferred it to take place four or six weeks earlier, in which case the availability of the atomic bomb would have remained uncertain. The need to secure Russia's entry into the war against Japan vanished overnight: which did not prevent Stalin from making a timely declaration of war when the contest was over, and claiming what Russia had been promised at Yalta.

The decision to use the bomb was Truman's, entirely approved by Churchill: the decision not to share the secrets of its manufacture was taken by both of them, again with no hesitation. That the existence of a new weapon, different in kind from any which had gone before, should not have been discussed between the Big Three tells its own story. Neither the President nor the Prime Minster seems to have had any inkling that the Russian government, and presumably Stalin himself, knew a great deal about the processes which had just culminated in New Mexico. On the eve of Churchill's departure from Potsdam, and therefore of his last meeting with Stalin, the Prime Minister watched from a few yards away the brief conversation in which Stalin was told about the testing of the bomb:

> *I can see it all as if it were yesterday. He seemed to be delighted. A new bomb! Of extraordinary power! Probably decisive on the whole Japanese war! What a bit of luck! This was my impression at the moment, and I was sure that he had no idea of the significance of what he was being told... As we were waiting for our cars I found myself near Truman. "How did it go?" I asked. "He never asked a question", he replied. I was certain therefore that at that date Stalin had no special knowledge of the vast process of research upon which the United States and Britain had been engaged for so long, and of the production for which the United States had spent over four hundred million pounds in an heroic gamble.*[42]

On the night of 18 July, however, Churchill and Stalin had enjoyed a genial meal. Marshal Stalin opined that no country needed a monarchy so much as Great Britain because the crown was the unifying force throughout the empire and no-one who was a friend of Britain would do anything to weaken the respect shown to the monarchy. We do not know how seriously Churchill took this: with rather less scepticism, we may surmise, than Eden or Cadogan would have done, for Churchill was not suspicious by nature and always responded at once to friendly gestures. Again the Prime Minister said that it was his policy to welcome Russia as a great power on the seas: 'He wished to see Russian ships sailing across the oceans of the world. Russia had been like a giant with his nostrils pinched....' This was a favourite phrase of Churchill's at the time, and referred to the narrow exits from the Baltic and the Black Sea. When Stalin had the hardihood to speak of Greek aggression on the Bulgarian and Albanian frontiers, the Prime Minister retorted that in place of the 50-50 arrangement in Yugoslavia, it was now 99 to Russia and 1 to Britain; but he merely received the reply that it was 90% British, 10% Yugoslavian and nil per cent Russian. The Soviet government, Stalin added, 'often did not know what Marshal Tito was about to do'. Moreover, 'Marshal Tito had the partisan mentality and had done several things he ought not to have done'. With our knowledge of what happened in the next few years, we can accept these assertions as having at least a grain of truth and probably more.

The two of them agreed, not for the first time, that the Germans were like sheep and once more Stalin recounted his experience in Germany in 1907, when 200 Germans had missed a Communist meeting because there was no-one to take their railway tickets at the station barrier. In a mood of apparent affability, Stalin apologised for not having thanked the British for their help by way of supplies in the war and promised that this would be done. In reply to a question, Stalin 'explained the working of collective and state farms'.[43] Since Churchill tells us that they conversed agreeably for five hours without reaching any crucial topic, we can be confident that Stalin's explanations about the collective farms did not err on the side of candour. Stalin of course gave his word that there would be free elections in the countries 'liberated' by the Red Army. It seems that the Prime Minister was, at least for the moment, half-disposed to believe such assurances. He even said, 'I think Stalin wants me to win the election'.

Estimates from the Conservative Central Office and from political opponents varied somewhat, but concurred in indicating a safe Conservative majority; and not until the last minute was the Prime Minister himself assailed by serious pangs of doubt. All the same, he said on 20 July, 'I shall be glad when this election business is over. It hovers over me like a vulture of uncertainty in the sky.'[44] We readily understand the Prime Minister's dilemma. Confident of victory as he might be, he could not count upon it and it was plain that no early agreement could be reached upon most of the vexed issues. His technique was therefore to move on each time the conference came to a stony patch, letting the unresolved issues accumulate so that he could go home for the declaration of the polls for a day or so and return with a renewed mandate. Of such stony places, indeed boulder-strewn deserts, there was no shortage: the treatment which should be accorded to Italy;[45] anxieties about the financial position, where the President seemed, according to the anxious Chancellor of the Exchequer, not to understand how parlous was Britain's financial position, with net reserves of $1.8 billion and overseas liabilities against them of about $13 billion;[46] the question of the attitude to be adopted to Spain and to General Franco, to whom the British felt no tenderness but of whom they felt they should not make another implacable enemy;[47] Russian behaviour in Roumania, Bulgaria and Persia;[48] and a good deal else. On 24 July, at the Eighth Plenary Meeting of the Conference, Churchill said that in respect of Roumania and Bulgaria an iron curtain had been rung down. Stalin merely retorted that 'these were fairy tales'. The Prime Minister retorted sharply that they were not. President Truman, while remarking that very great difficulties had been imposed upon the United States missions in those two countries, 'did not mean to cast any reflection on the Soviet Government or their representatives at the Conference, and he was sure that Mr Churchill would agree with him'.[49] All the same, Churchill in conversation that evening was full of Truman's praises. 'If only this had happened at Yalta', he said; and then after a long pause, 'It is too late now.'[50]

Two issues, however, mattered more than any others: Germany, especially in respect of reparations; and Poland. The British and Americans had gone to Potsdam hoping to see Germany treated as an economic unit, by which they meant unified control of German economic life and free exchange of goods and services between the four zones of occupation. Even before the conference opened, that policy looked visionary. Russia had already taken much and destroyed much. She was putting forward claims which amounted to the obliteration of a large part of German industry. 'We have no wish to let Germany off lightly or prevent Russia recouping some of her physical losses from German plant and assets,' wrote the Chancellor of the Exchequer from London; 'but for the sake of the sanity and peace of Europe we cannot push the policy of destroying Germany's economy to the point of a complete breakdown.'[51]

Poland mattered even more. Churchill dwelt lengthily upon Britain's obligations to Poland and rightly said that the honour of the British government was involved. He agreed that the new government, though not all the British could wish, marked a great advance. This was perhaps said to lubricate the negotiation. President Truman added that he hoped the Yalta agreement would be carried out as soon as possible, to which Stalin rejoined that the provisional government of Poland had never refused to hold free elections.[52] But that hardly got to the heart of the matter. The Polish government, improved or not, was plainly under Russian domination and had pushed forward. The westward advance of Russia's frontier meant that perhaps three or four million Poles would have to be moved into the new Poland; and the government of Poland had meanwhile occupied the territory to the line of the western Neisse. If that line were accepted as the definitive frontier, several million Germans would be turned out.

Repeatedly tackled on this subject, more often by Churchill than by the American delegation, Stalin would reply that most of the Germans had fled or been killed in the war. But the land thus vacated had been the bread basket of Germany and the western allies would be largely responsible for feeding the displaced population. Churchill's habits of mind being what they were, we need hardly turn to his account to realise that Alsace-Lorraine and the Danzig Corridor entered into his thinking. For the future peace of Europe, he remarks, the wrong of allowing the frontier to advance to the western Neisse was something beside which Alsace and the Corridor were trifles. 'One day the Germans would want their territory back, and the Poles would not be able to stop them.'[53] The fact that this has not happened in a bloody fashion in the fifty years since Potsdam ought to be seen in the balance against Churchill's own gloomy judgement of the results of the war.

More than any other, Poland became a tombstone of goodwill, a yardstick of the capacity or incapacity of the powers to agree. When Churchill said at the Sixth Plenary Session of the conference on 22 July that the British had 'grave moral scruples about vast movements of population', Stalin replied that 'very few Germans had remained, and even these had fled when the Russians approached'. He also said that at Teheran in 1943, he had always stood out for the line of the western Neisse.[54] (At this same plenary session, he added that the Soviet delegation at San Francisco had stated that they were anxious to secure the mandates for certain territories, and had in mind chiefly the former colonies of Italy. Whether such claims were ever meant seriously must be open to some doubt.) These were the circumstances in which, on Stalin's proposal, a Polish delegation was awaited at Potsdam.

The Permanent Under-Secretary of the Foreign Office minuted on 23 July 'If we allow the Poles to go as far as the Western Neisse, we should certainly at least get some quid per quo of this sort [promises about free elections and civic liberties in Poland]. But I am not sure that we should trade that area for simple assurances by the Poles.' The Foreign Secretary, on his last full day at Potsdam, commented 'I am strongly against Western Neisse anyway. But I agree that we should take up these points with the Poles when they come.'[55] To the President of the provisional government of Poland, Bierut, Churchill rehearsed the arguments which he had put already to Truman and Stalin. He was met with the reply that Poland's claims were modest and that the new Poland would be far from Communist; the whole Russian army would leave Poland; and more to the same effect. At the end of their second conversation, just before Churchill left Potsdam for good, he said to the Poles that they were asking too much. Britain and America might pursue one policy and the Russians a different policy; that would have serious consequences.[56]

Underlying many of Churchill's observations at the conference, we sense his fear that the new world organisation might prove impotent or positively harmful and his conviction that either result might readily attend disharmony among the allies. He had also believed throughout that there must be a direct connection between the stake of the powers in a given region and their willingness to commit themselves to its security. In his account of Potsdam, he says openly 'I failed to carry conviction with the Russian Foreign Minister'.[57]

The new Prime Minister and Foreign Secretary arrived in Potsdam on 28 July. Scandalised that Attlee did not have a man to look after his clothes and other arrangements, Churchill insisted on sending his valet back to Potsdam with the new Prime Minister. The latter, a man of genuine modesty, used to remark that this was the first and last time in his life when he enjoyed such a luxury. We cannot say that the arrival of the new administration was greeted, at least in the short term, with any marked enthusiasm by President Truman. We find in his diary towards the end of July, 'The British returned last night... Attlee is an Oxford man and talks like the much-overrated Mr Eden and Bevin is a John L Lewis.'[58] It is fair to add that Truman soon had cause to revise these opinions.

The remaining business at Potsdam was quickly wound up. Byrnes in effect proposed an arrangement which would link reparations and the Polish frontier. The business of that frontier was not a simple one. The paper prepared for the new British ministers allowed that there was considerable substance in Polish arguments to the effect that the area up to the Oder and the Western Neisse must be treated as a whole and that Poland must control the entire river system there if possession of Upper Silesia were to be of the fullest advantage. Even Mikolajczyk, whom the British liked and knew well, contended strongly that an early settlement of the western frontier was an indispensable condition for the development of free political life in Poland.[59]

Attlee and Bevin would both have preferred to settle for the Eastern Neisse. Mikolajczyk, however, reported that the attitude of Stalin towards the Poles had been markedly friendlier; he had listened to grievances and showed readiness to redress them; he had even admitted that the Red Army had been 'a little grasping'. Stalin also judged that the result of the British general election showed that the people there were more preoccupied with internal post-war problems than with the war against Japan and the holding down of Germany.[60] The British Ambassador in Moscow, present at Potsdam, favoured acceptance of the line of the Western Neisse, because he felt confident the Polish government would be allowed by the Russians to occupy the whole of that area and there was much to be said for accepting the full claim as part of a general settlement, rather than to submit later to a *fait accompli* secured by unilateral Russian action.

By way of a fig-leaf, all parties agreed that the decision about the Western Neisse concerned only the temporary administration of the area; in theory, the cession of territory was left to the Peace Conference. It was apparent that the notion of treating Germany as a single economic unit was incompatible with the proposals upon which the conference finally agreed. Sir David Waley of the British Treasury tried to convince Secretary of State Byrnes that the system of exchanges he had in mind was inconsistent with the notion of treating Germany as a single economic unit. 'I said that the peasant in Brandenberg who sells his potatoes to Berlin has to be paid by receiving boots and shoes from Berlin and cannot be paid by Russia receiving steel plant. I pointed out that if a line is drawn across the middle of Europe, so that there is a frontier with Russia on the one side and the Western Powers on the other, this has an importance far transcending reparations.'[61]

When Molotov asked the new Foreign Secretary how soon the conference would end, Bevin replied jovially that it would end as soon as Molotov agreed to all his proposals. Unabashed, the Russian Foreign Minister replied that an equally speedy end could be secured if Mr Bevin agreed with his. As for the future, Molotov said, Russia should enjoy lasting peace and, asked for a definition of 'lasting', replied that he meant a peaceful life for two generations. If such a peace lasted until the end of the century, 'people would get out of the habit of settling their disputes by war and eternal peace would follow.'[62]

Explaining the results of the conference to Eden, Attlee remarked that he and Bevin wished to stand on the Eastern Neisse, 'but the Americans rather suddenly gave way'. The British delegation had therefore agreed to the Western Neisse after long meetings with the Poles, from whom they had extracted 'very specific' pledges about elections, facilities for the press and the repatriation of Polish forces. There had been a long wrangle about reparations at which the British had to concede a higher percentage of reparation deliveries than they would have liked. They had received satisfaction, on the other hand, in respect of the supply of food and materials to Western Germany, and in the decision to maintain the German economy at a reasonable level.

The new Prime Minister believed the conference had ended in a good atmosphere, and was careful to say that the Labour ministers had been building on the policy of Churchill and Eden.[63] Churchill remarks that Attlee and Bevin were forced to go to Potsdam without any serious preparation. This was true of Bevin, who had not expected to be Foreign Secretary, but scarcely so of Attlee, who had been present at the conference throughout and enjoyed access to all the papers of government. Although Churchill says that he would have faced a public break if necessary rather than allow anything to Poland beyond the Oder and Eastern Neisse, he half-concedes the point by saying that the real time to deal with such issues should have been when the fronts of the allies faced each other in the field, before the American and British armies had retreated westwards.[64]

In many important senses, the conference at Potsdam had failed. No basis for a European peace treaty was reached. No satisfactory settlement had been secured in respect of Poland. There was not even an approximate meeting of minds about the future of Germany. All the same, the issues were not quite so clear-cut at the time as it has been fashionable to suppose since. The urge to preserve as much as possible of the alliance remained strong. Churchill spoke from the Opposition front bench in mid-August almost as he had done after Yalta; and while he admitted that in most regions under Russia's influence the Communist forces had obtained dictatorial powers, he said this did not mean that 'the Communist system is everywhere being established, nor does it mean that Soviet Russia seeks to reduce all those independent states to provinces of the Soviet Union. Marshal Stalin is a very wise man, and I would set no limits to the immense contributions that he and his associates have to make to the future.'[65]

A high official in Washington had told the British that the State Department believed Britain to be a major American interest, politically, economically and sentimentally, and wanted Britain to be strong and prosperous. One of his counterparts in London said that Sir Alexander Cadogan would have been able to judge at Potsdam whether Truman and Byrnes shared this feeling towards Britain. On this crucial question, Cadogan noted in his compressed style:

> *Rather difficult to say. I don't think it was very obvious. The impression I got was that both the President and Mr Byrnes were rather on the 'mediation' tack.*
> *The President's slick and snappy manner (whether natural or assumed) is rather inclined to result in quick decisions about which he does not consult us and in which he appears to ignore our interests. But that may be due to inexperience, and he may improve in that respect.*[66]

After the conference, in place of the visit to Britain which Roosevelt had several times promised, Truman spent a few hours on board a British warship. 'I have got to lunch with the limey King when I get to Plymouth!' he wrote to his family.[67] However, the combination of the King's quiet charm and the hospitality of the Royal Navy seems to have produced a more favourable impression.

Attlee sent a telegram summarising the conference to his fellow Prime Ministers in the Dominions. It spoke of an atmosphere of goodwill and cordiality, combined with the utmost freedom and frankness of discussion. It had been evident, the message went on, that all three delegations had felt deeply their responsibility for the future of the world. The British ministers, Attlee said, had made it their prime concern to see that the new Poland would be independent, democratic and in free communication with the world at large. There was a good deal more to the same effect.[68] From Field Marshal Smuts, in distant Pretoria, came a counter-commentary based upon acute judgement and long experience. The enlarged Poland might prove to be only another Russian republic; with much of Eastern and South Eastern Europe falling within the Russian sphere of influence, and Japan extinguished, Russia would be aggrandised to such a commanding position that it would bring further dangers to the future of Europe and the world. The United States might return to the business of that hemisphere; and even if that were too sombre a picture, what would be the position of Britain in such a new pattern of power?

Potsdam opens up a depressing prospect. In fact the whole vision we have had of the future, with the United States of America and the British Commonwealth together leading the van of the human advance to a happier freer future for the whole world, may turn to frustration so far as the immediate future is concerned... I am in no sense anti-Russian but I do view with grave misgiving the unbalanced lopsided depressed Europe which seems now to be forming with grave danger to our best hopes for the future.

By heroic efforts the world has been saved from the horrors of Nazism, but other dangers are emerging to which Potsdam appears to turn a blind eye... The harm has already been done but I hope our further negotiations and settlements will be marked by a spirit of sober realism and not merely by an effort to reach an accord between present conflicting interests of [the] Allies and their partisans.[69]

Churchill proclaims as the theme of his last volume about the war: 'How the Great Democracies triumphed and so were able to resume the follies which had so nearly cost them their life.' But the democracies did not resume all those habits of pre-war days which he condemns. Learning much from the experience of the first war and its aftermath, they felt their way towards an effective form of collective defence. Despite an obvious and growing disparity of power, the United States and Great Britain contributed more to the process of containing Russia than any other countries over a span of nearly two generations. Whatever initial suspicions Truman may have felt of the British, he did indeed 'improve in that respect'. Within a few months, he was to preside when Churchill delivered his celebrated oration at Fulton, Missouri. There followed a long period during which the

West was said to have 'won the war and lost the peace'. That was always too simple by half. Almost fifty years after Potsdam, President Yeltsin told Parliament in London that Churchill had been right to regard the former Soviet Union as a communist aggressor, adding for good measure that the policy of quarantine adopted by the West had been proved right by time.[70]

Discussion

Presenting his paper, *Professor Dilks* drew particular attention to the importance of the atomic bomb as the 'unseen item' on the Potsdam agenda—the dog that didn't bark in the night. At Potsdam no one knew that the war in the Far East would end in August, and the American decision—backed by the British—not to share atomic secrets with the Soviet Union could be seen as an allegory of Great Power relations. *Dr Deighton* appreciated Professor Dilks' metaphors, and observed that Potsdam seemed a sort of diplomatic dance which marked the beginning of the Cold War while the real power lay with forces on the ground. *Professor Dilks* argued that this was only true because the war ended when it did. Cold War policies were determined by the Council for Foreign Ministers, not Potsdam.

Lord Bullock considered that Potsdam marked not just an end to war, but a new beginning: both President Truman and Ernest Bevin were newcomers to the scene. He stressed the 'unambiguous and indelible' impression made by Stalin on Bevin, who realised that the Russians would not form a constructive relationship even if they would not go to war. *Sir Frank Roberts* noted the extreme Soviet hostility to Bevin, whom they regarded as the worst kind of Trades Union leader, a 'man of the people' who read Marx and quoted him back at Molotov. Sir Frank agreed with *Lord Bullock* that Bevin was never charmed by the Russians, but argued that he tried hard to work with them until 1946. *Professor Dilks* also agreed in the importance of personalities at Potsdam: Churchill, in particular, was 'susceptible to flattery, not persistently but in bouts', and appreciated Stalin's skills as a negotiator, while resenting the refusal of Roosevelt and then Truman to visit the UK.

Dr Correlli Barnett asked Professor Rzheshevsky whether recently released Russian documents threw any light on Soviet motivation at Potsdam. *Professor Rzheshevsky* replied that the Soviet attitude was determined by certain factors: the termination of Lend-Lease; the atomic bomb, both because it heralded a cardinal change in the military balance, and because Stalin's exclusion by Truman affected his relationship with the President; and the innate contradictions between the communist and capitalist systems, which were thrown into relief after the war by the lack of a common enemy. *Dr Deighton* asked Professor Dilks whether the Russians got what they wanted out of Potsdam: he replied that if they did not, they made a good job of concealing what they wanted, and they were not known for keeping their aims secret.

In conclusion, *Professor Dilks* conceded the failures of Potsdam, but stressed that the delegates were grappling with vast uncertainties and doing their best to avoid a breakdown which would prejudice hopes for the new world organisation, the UN.

Notes and References

1 H Macmillan, *War Diaries: Mediterranean 1943-45* (London, 1984), p 612.
2 For a survey of the position see 'The Effect of our External Financial Position on our Foreign Policy', a paper by the Reconstruction Department of the Foreign Office, 30 March 1945, Public Record Office, London (henceforward PRO), FO 371/45694.
3 Earl of Avon, *The Eden Memoirs: The Reckoning* (London, 1965), p 525.
4 Avon, op cit, p 526.
5 W S Churchill, *The Second World War*, Vol 6 (Reprint Society edition, London, 1956), pp 363-7.
6 *Foreign Relations of the United States, The Conference of Berlin The Potsdam Conference), 1945* (2 vols, Washington, 1960); *The Tehran, Yalta and Potsdam Conferences* (the Russian transcripts of the plenary sessions, translated into English, Moscow, 1969); *Documents on British Policy Overseas*, Series I, Volume I, The *Conference at Potsdam, July-August 1945* (London, 1984) (henceforth *DBPO*).
7 Churchill, op cit, p 178; Avon, op cit, p 513.
8 *DBPO*, p 264.
9 Avon, op cit, p 529.
10 Viscount Halifax (Washington) to the Foreign Office, 21 April 1945, PRO FO 371/44556.
11 Churchill to Eden (San Francisco), 4 May 1945, PRO PREM 3/430/1.
12 Churchill to Truman, 6 and 11 May 1945, PRO PREM 3/ 430/1.
13 M Gilbert, *Never Despair: Winston S Churchill 1945-1965* (London, 1988), p 43.
14 Avon, op cit, p 37.
15 Truman to Churchill, 12 May 1945, PRO PREM 3/430/1.
16 Draft message of a telegram from Churchill to Truman, not sent, dated 17 May 1945, PRO PREM 3/430/1.
17 Churchill to Eden, 28 May 1945, covering a draft message from Churchill to Truman, same date, PRO Premier 3/430/1.
18 Stalin to Churchill, 30 May 1945, PRO PREM 3/430/1.
19 Churchill to Truman, 1 June 1945, PRO PREM 3/430/1.
20 Eden to Halifax (Washington), 30 June 1945, telegrams nos. 6792 and 6793 of 30 June 1945, PRO PREM 3/430/3.
21 Cadogan to Churchill, 2 July 1945, PRO PREM 3/430/3.
22 Eden to Churchill, 10 July 1945: *DBPO*, No 77.
23 Eden to Churchill, 12 July 1945, PRO FO 371/50866: *DBPO*, No 111.
24 Churchill to Halifax, 6 July 1945, *DBPO*, No 3. Lord Halifax's reply is printed ibid, No 21.
25 Churchill, op cit, p 488.
26 Lord Moran, *Winston Churchill: The Struggle for Survival, 1940-1965* (London, 1966), p 257.
27 Clark Kerr to Eden, 10 July 1945, PRO FO 371/47883: *DBPO*, No 78.

[28] C de Gaulle, *War Memoirs* (English edition, London, 1960), vol 3, p 199.

[29] R Jenkins, *Truman* (London, 1986), p 72.

[30] *Memoirs of Harry S Truman* (New York, 1955), vol 1, p 275.

[31] Eden to Churchill, 17 July 1945, *DBPO*, No 276.

[32] Attlee to Eden, 18 July 1945, *DBPO*, No 179.

[33] For an example, see M Djilas, *Conversations with Stalin* (London, 1962), p 115.

[34] Avon, op cit, p 485.

[35] Record of a private talk, drawn up by the interpreter Major Birse, 17 July 1945, and initialled by Churchill on the following day, PRO PREM 3/430/7: *DBPO*, No 173.

[36] R R James, *Anthony Eden* (London, 1986), p 307.

[37] Avon, op cit, pp 514-5.

[38] Moran, op cit, pp 278-9.

[39] Churchill, op cit, p 502.

[40] Note by Churchill of his conversation with Truman at luncheon, 18 July 1945, PRO PREM 3/430/8: *DBPO*, No 181.

[41] Jenkins, op cit, pp 72-3.

[42] Churchill, op cit, pp 533-4. His account, completed in 1951, was not published until 1954, long after much was known about Soviet penetration of the secret circles which had worked upon the atomic bomb.

[43] Record of a private talk between Churchill and Stalin at dinner, 18 July 1945, PRO PREM 3/430/8: cf *DBPO*, No 185.

[44] Moran, op cit, p 275-7.

[45] For a summary of British views on this subject as it developed, see the memoranda by P Dixon and F R Hoyer Millar to Eden, 18 & 20 July 1945, Eden's manuscript notes, 21 July, and further memoranda by Hoyer Millar of 21, 22 and 28 July 1945: all in PRO FO 934/2; *DBPO*, Nos 178.ii, 212 and 441.

[46] Sir J Anderson (Chancellor of the Exchequer) to Churchill, 18 July 1945 (two telegrams), PRO CAB 120/191: see *DBPO*, No 312.

[47] Minute by Hoyer Millar and manuscript note by Cadogan, 19 and 20 July 1945, PRO FO 934/4: *DBPO*, No 195.

[48] V G Lawford to P Dixon, 20 July 1945, PRO FO 934/5: *DBPO*, No 347.

[49] *DBPO*, No 258, pp 646-50.

[50] Moran, op cit, p 285.

[51] J Anderson to Sir W Monckton, 18 July 1945, PRO FO 934/1: *DBPO*, No 313.

[52] Churchill, op cit, pp 517-20.

[53] Churchill, op cit, p 516.

[54] *DBPO*, No 226, pp 534-8.

[55] Minutes by Cadogan, 23 July 1945, and Eden, 24 July, on a memorandum by D Allen of 22 July, PRO FO 934/2.

[56] Churchill, op cit, pp 527-31. For the records of the meetings of 24 July between Churchill, Eden, Bierut and others, and between Eden, Cadogan, Bierut and others late that night, see PRO FO 934/2: *DBPO*, Nos 257 and 267.

[57] Sir David Hunt, *On the Spot* (London, 1975), pp 49-50.

[58] Jenkins, op cit, p 73.

[59] Memorandum by the British delegation at Potsdam 'Polish western frontier and supplies from transfer to German territory'. 27 July 1945, PRO FO 934/2: *DBPO*, Enclosure in No 436.

60 *DBPO*, No 452. For the record of a meeting between Attlee, Bevin, Bierut, Mikolajczyk and others, 29 July 1945, see ibid, No 453 (PRO FO 943/2).

61 *DBPO*, No 485.

62 Record of conversation at a luncheon party given by Molotov at Potsdam, 31 July 1945, PRO FO 371/47883: *DBPO*, No 489.

63 Attlee to Eden, 1 August 1945, *DBPO*, No 527.

64 Churchill, op cit, pp 535-6.

65 C Eade (ed), *The War Speeches of the Rt Hon Winston S Churchill* (London, 1965), vol III, p 518.

66 Minute by Sir A Cadogan, 4 August 1945, on telegram from Mr Balfour (Washington) to the Foreign Office, 2 August, PRO FO 371/44574.

67 Jenkins, op cit, p 72.

68 Sir E Bridges to Sir E Machtig, covering the text of Attlee's message to the Dominion Prime Ministers, 1 August 1945, PRO PREM 3/430/13: *DBPO*, Nos 519-20.

69 Smuts to Attlee, 10 August 1945, PRO PREM 3/430/13.

70 Reprinted in *The Daily Telegraph*, London, 11 November 1992.

7 The Liberation of France and Restoration of Democratic Government

M R D FOOT

In the recently published Oxford Companion to the Second World War, Norman Davies has some sharp remarks about what 'Liberation' and 'Occupation' actually mean; did either the Nazi or the Soviet armies, for instance, in any sense 'liberate' Latvia?[1] On the whole, however, the French did feel, by the summer of 1944, that they wanted to be liberated; most of them by then had come to sympathize with their Resistance movements.

Most books about Resistance, alas, are bad or very bad. Let me invoke instead one of the rare jewels in this overcrowded pouch: Roderick Kedward's *In Search of the Maquis*.[2] In it, with usual skill, he shows how the peasantry of the south of France, much wooed by the Vichy régime headed by Marshal Philippe Pétain, came to turn against it and on the whole to support the maquisards, the youngsters who had run off to the hills instead of obeying the call for forced labour in the Third Reich. A complete turn-around in opinion has seldom been so carefully or so elegantly mapped.

Sauckel's insistence and Pétain's régime's stupidity knocked the props out from beneath Vichy; but what was to replace it? Pétain's deputy, Admiral J F Darlan, had happened to be in Algiers when the Allies arrived there in November 1942 and did a deal with Clark and Eisenhower[3] that appalled French Resistance (as well as shocking everybody left-of-centre in England). Was this the fate that was to await resisters in France when the Allies invaded the mainland?

Darlan's murder—by a young royalist who was an officer in SOE's local training section, using an SOE pistol[4]—but not, according to Sir Brooks Richards, who ought to know,[5] acting on SOE's orders—was swiftly avenged by the execution of the assassin, on the orders of General H H Giraud. Yet Giraud turned out not to have the weight of personality to outwit the junior, but much nimbler, de Gaulle; who by the end of 1943 had taken over the Free French Committee of National Liberation, which proclaimed itself a provisional government a few days before 'Neptune,' the assault phase of 'Overlord', the Normandy landings of 5/6 June 1944.

'Neptune' was a much closer-run thing than is commonly remembered: on its success the Liberation of France depended. Part of its eventual success derived from the aid given to it by Resistance, intensely secret at the time, and sedulously suppressed later by interested parties—staff college tutors, regular staff officers and

Clausewitzian historians. Five or six divisions' worth of resistance effort—the estimate is General Eisenhower's, and he, again, ought to have known—helped to turn the scale. 950 rail cuts by Resistance, for example, on the actual night of the landings played quite as significant a part as the more publicised air attacks. Rail and telephone traffic both became all but unavailable to the defending Germans, who lost control over their own rear areas. Innumerable, or at least unnumbered, small combats in central and south-west France accompanied the withdrawal to Germany of the garrisons there; and in the south-east Resistance played a vital role in support of the 'Dragoon' landings on the Riviera in mid-August (Arthur L Funk's *Hidden Ally*[6] has not yet made the impact it deserves on historians of war).

Endless arguments about whether 'Dragoon' should have been mounted at all often overlook its importance to the French: over half of General Patch's landing force consisted of French troops, taking part in the liberation of their own homeland, bearing American arms— provided on Roosevelt's orders for Giraud, and quietly taken over by the Gaullists.

Eisenhower was all for leaving Paris to be fed by his enemy as long as possible. When the Normandy front cracked in early August 1944, and the success of 'Dragoon' in mid-August unsettled the enemy further, Leclerc wrung leave from a reluctant Eisenhower and Patton to see what his French second armoured division could do. On 15 August, the day of the 'Dragoon' landings, but unaffected by them, the police came out on strike in Paris, joining earlier strikers, and the Paris rising followed—part a spontaneous uprising, part a bluff. De Gaulle may have had this rising in mind when he said once later to a friend, 'Resistance was simply a bluff that came off.'

When he reached Paris, late on 25 August, the same day as Leclerc, he was persuaded—with some trouble; the city was in a turmoil of delight—to visit the *Hotel de Ville*; where Georges Bidault, the head of the *Conseil National de la Résistance*, demanded that he proclaim the Republic. Internal and external resistance here stood face to face; external resistance carried the day. The General, stiff as ever, remarked that the republic had never ceased to exist; and stumped off to his old office in the Rue Saint-Dominique, where even the blotting-paper had not changed since 1940.

Next day the public took his side, as he processed down the Champs Elysées. There had been keen debate at the *Etat-Major des Forces Françaises de l'Intérieur*, the least competent headquarters with which I have ever had to deal, whether he would ride down the Champs Elysées on a white horse, a Bonapartist symbol, or on a black one, a Boulangist symbol: de Gaulle jumped easily between the horns of this dilemma and walked, with huge crowds on either side and behind him. He went on to a service in Notre Dame, riding in the car in which

Pétain had been acclaimed on the same journey in the previous April (can anyone write a monograph on who cheered both leaders?) Outside the cathedral there was a brief fusillade, caused perhaps by somebody's sten going off by accident, one of that bad gun's vices; he had been under much heavier fire at Verdun, and ignored it.

Roosevelt had long distrusted de Gaulle, as just another Boulanger: de Gaulle's manner indeed remained authoritarian, but he wholly opposed the authoritarian régime of Vichy, and had long determined to restore some improved version of the third republic. Pétain, who had proclaimed himself *Chef d'Etat*, was hustled out of France by the Germans late in August, and was held in house arrest at Sigmaringen castle in South Germany, the seat of the Roman Catholic branch of the Hohenzollerns; did any of the Germans who lodged him there know that that was the spot on which the Family had agreed to Bismarck's trick of a candidature for the throne of Spain, that triggered off the Franco-Prussian war and the founding of the Second Reich?

Meanwhile, how was liberated France being governed? The Americans had thought up a French version of the AMGOT that had served, rather oddly, in Italy—it had reintroduced the Mafia, which Mussolini had suppressed. De Gaulle had a better alternative. As the armies of 'Overlord' and 'Dragoon' advanced across France, they were accompanied by teams from the Gaullist *Missions Militaires de Liaison Administrative*. This is a fascinating point in politics: actual contact between political theory and political fact. The Gaullists had taken the trouble to read up how to seize power, in the works of the great modern expert on the subject, Trotsky. The leaders of the French communist party, who controlled a substantial slice of the active internal resisters, had been brought up to abominate Trotsky, and were not open to reasoned argument about his role in the seizure of power in Petrograd in 1917; they had none of them bothered even to glance at his advice to seize in every village the railway station and the telegraph office, if they existed, and all the horses; thus controlling the means of communication. The MMLA brought this up to date. Advancing quite close behind the leading infantry, in every village they entered they seized the telephone exchange, if there was one; the mairie and the post office, where ration cards were issued; and again, if there was one, the railway station. They thus controlled the state.

Michel Debré, a later prime minister, had toured France quietly during the previous twelve months, picking out in most departments which civil servant ought to become the Gaullist prefect;[7] Gaullist regional prefects had been fore-nominated also, as far back as January 1944; the machine of state continued, rather erratically, to revolve. The communists, having had no orders from Moscow to break it up, quietly conformed. The regional military delegates who had articulated the resistance were, equally quietly, marginalised. To celebrate the junction of internal and external resistance Bidault became Foreign

Minister, and Tixier, who had never known Occupation, Minister of the Interior.

In many of the remoter parts of France there was something close to anarchy, for a while; see for instance Emmanuel d'Astier's account of how his attempt to impose himself as a newly appointed minister was received by the peasantry of the Ardèche.[8] There was also in most villages and towns a local purge: girls who were known to have slept with Germans had their hair shaved off, if nothing worse (exactly as happened in Guernsey and Jersey);[9] and a fair number of private quarrels were settled out of hand. Figures vary widely; officially, just over 10,000 citizens were executed; I have seen an unofficial figure ten times as large, though I do not believe it.

Gradually, chaos resolved into order. There was a famine in Paris—food was even shorter in the first winter of 'Liberation' than it had been in the last winter of 'Occupation'.[10] The provisional government had put together the ghost of a parliament, called a consultative assembly, in November 1943. It resolved in October 1944 that henceforward women should have the vote—a long step forward for sexual equality, deriving from the leading part women had played in the resistance struggle.

If one anecdote be allowed, let it be of Lucie Aubrac, whose husband was arrested with Jean Moulin at Caluire in June 1943. She was already pregnant with her second child. She took off her wedding ring; went to see Barbie, out of whom she got no change at all; and applied instead to the Lyons head of the *Abwehr*, to whom she explained that she had been seduced by a prisoner he held, and wanted to avail herself of a provision in French law by which even a condemned man's mistress could marry him and bear a legitimate child. A date and place were arranged. Pistol in hand, she helped—when six months gone with child—to hold up the Gestapo van that carried her man, and went into labour on the Hudson that brought them safely to England.[11] After that sort of achievement, no one was going to refuse women the vote.

Voting for a constituent assembly was to be put off until October 1945, to make sure prisoners of war and forced labourers could get back from Germany to take part; as they did, leaving over 200,000 souls behind (see the monument at the eastern end of the Ile Notre Dame in Paris). The elections, when at last they took place, gave four seats in five to members from the left; a decisive repudiation of Vichy's conservatism.

There were also some show trials. Show trials have long been a familiar aspect of tyrannies; they are not unknown in politically milder climes. The Irish have never forgotten Casement; some of the English remember William Joyce and, more recently, Stephen Ward. A scholar of my own year at New College was killed after a show trial in Bulgaria in 1944.

Pétain himself was put on trial, and condemned to death; de Gaulle, acting head of state, had his old commander's sentence reduced to life imprisonment. Laval had a scandalously unfair trial, took cyanide after being condemned to death, and was brought round far enough to be led out and shot.[12] Robert Brasillach, who had denounced de Gaulle roundly by radio, was also tried and condemned to death. De Gaulle refused to reprieve him, with a delicate use of the conditional—'Il ne l'aurait voulu'. Any of us might have been unlucky enough to be in the same fix as Brasillach: pause a moment to think of it.

Discussion

Discussion centred on the role of the Resistance in the Liberation of France. *Sir Douglas Dodds Parker* stressed how crucial that role was, and that aspects of it still influenced French politics today. *Professor Bédarida* spoke of the vital issues affecting France before D-Day for Overlord: who would govern France? could the Communists seize power? The Resistance forces in the *Missions Militaire de Liaison Administrative* (MMLA) played an important part by following the Invasion forces and taking control of stations and telephone exchanges in each town. *Professor Foot* agreed, noting that the success of Operation Neptune had been assured by 5/6 divisions of Resistance fighters.
Sir Brooks Richards agreed on the importance of communications, particularly for de Gaulle and his followers, who would otherwise have been an 'heroic but exiled minority'. It was vital to be able to get people out of occupied France (*Professor Foot* interjected at this point that the man organising the escape flights turned out to be a double agent).
Dr Hanak asked whether Pétain's trial could really be classed as a 'show trial': *Professor Foot* answered that it should, because there was no question of his being acquitted.

Notes and References

[1] I C B Dear and M R D Foot (eds), *The Oxford Companion to the Second World War* (Oxford University Press, May 1995), pp 688-9.
[2] Oxford University Press, 1993.
[3] Published as long ago as 1953 by Arthur L Funk, with a couple of pages of introduction, in *Journal of Modern History*, xxv, pp 63-5. See also M R D Foot, *SOE in France* (HMSO, London, 1966), pp 220-1.
[4] Douglas Dodds-Parker, *Setting Europe Ablaze* (Windlesham, Surrey: Springwood, 1983), pp 115-16.
[5] Several conversations with him, circa 1980.
[6] Greenwood Press, 1992.

7 Conversation with him, 1981.
8 Emmanuel d'Astier, trans Humphrey Hare, *Seven Times Seven Days* (1958), pp 179-81.
9 See Madeleine Bunting, *The Model Occupation* (Harper-Collins 1995), pp 252-61.
10 See Antony Beevor and Artemis Cooper, *Paris after the Liberation* (London, Hamish Hamilton, 1994), pp 115-17.
11 See Lucie Aubrac, *Outwitting the Gestapo* (Lincoln, Neb, and London: University of Nebraska Press, 1993), passim.
12 See Peter Calvocoressi, Guy Wint and John Pritchard, *Total War* (revised 2nd edn, Viking 1989), p 329.

8 Italy: from Fascism to Democracy

CHRISTOPHER SETON-WATSON

Italy's transition from fascism to democracy started on 25 July 1943, when King Victor Emmanuel dismissed Mussolini, his prime minister since 1922, and had him interned. This event had been precipitated by military disaster: the Allied armies had invaded Sicily a fortnight before. There had been no popular uprising: rather it was a *coup d'état* carried out by the King, certain senior army officers, and dissident fascists, who saw the only salvation for Italy was Mussolini's removal. The King appointed as his successor General Pietro Badoglio, who formed a government of bureaucrats and technocrats. The Fascist Party was dissolved, and a large degree of press freedom allowed. But the democratic politicians who had ruled Italy before 1922, some of whom had been in touch with the King, were barred from public political activity. An armistice was secretly negotiated with the Allies, but plans for the capture of Rome by parachutists, simultaneously with the announcement of the armistice, broke down. On 9 September the King and government escaped to Brindisi, shortly to be occupied by the Allies, while the Germans took control of all Italy down to the current front line just south of Naples. On 12 September Mussolini was rescued by German parachutists, and subsequently set up a Fascist Social Republic, under German control, at Salo, on Lake Garda.

Italy was thus divided in two by the front line, which moved slowly northwards over the next eighteen months. For Italy it became a civil war. In October 1943 the Badoglio government declared war on Germany and was granted by the Allies the status of a co-belligerent. This was designed to give Italy a chance, in Churchill's words, to 'work her passage home', without modifying the legal status created by its unconditional surrender in the September armistice. Most of the Italian navy had joined the Allies in September, and by the end of 1943 small reconstituted units of the royal army were fighting alongside the British and Americans. Armed resistance to German occupation began almost at once, of a sporadic and uncoordinated character, and in 1944 it developed into a mass movement. The extent and importance of its military contribution is still a matter of controversy: but the importance of the part it played in the rebuilding of Italian democracy is incontrovertible.

With more than half the country occupied by the Germans, free political revival could only start in 'liberated' Italy, which became known as the Kingdom of the South. Progress was very slow, in part because of the physical obstacles created by war, in part because of the restrictions imposed by the Allies through the Allied Control Commission and AMGOT (Allied Military Government of Occupied

Territory). AMGOT's task was primarily to ensure order and stability behind the lines, and to ensure a secure base, lines of communication and supplies for the combatants. The first free political congress since 1922 was held at Bari in January 1944. Six parties participated: Communist (PCI), Socialist and Liberal, survivors from pre-fascist days; Christian Democrat (DC), a reincarnation of the pre-fascist Popular Party; the Party of Action (PdA), an outgrowth of the Justice and Liberty movement (with a liberal-socialist orientation), organised in exile in France; and Democratic Labour, close to the Liberals, hardly a party, more a loose group of anti-fascist personalities. The Congress drew up an anti-fascist programme of political and social reform, with the establishment of a republic as the first priority. They all refused to serve under Badoglio, he being an appointee of the King who had compromised himself in 1922 and right on until 1943 by supporting Mussolini, and had finally discredited himself by his ignominious flight to Brindisi. In February 1944 the King agreed to hand over his power to his son and heir, Umberto, as Lieutenant-General (ie regent) as soon as Rome was liberated. Till then, as the Allies, especially Churchill, were convinced that the maintenance of Badoglio in power was essential in the interests of victory, it seemed that all progress towards democracy was blocked.

This deadlock was dramatically resolved when on 27 March 1944 Palmiro Togliatti, general secretary of the Italian Communist Party (PCI), returned to Italy from Moscow after twenty years of exile. He at once agreed to accept office under Badoglio, so forcing the hand of the non-communist anti-fascists. This action accorded with Stalin's 'military imperative' which gave absolute priority to defeating Germany and meant postponing till the end of the war any revolutionary aspirations or activities which might weaken the alliance with Britain and the USA. But for Togliatti this move was also part of a long-term policy. From the first he emphasised in his speeches and writings the 'national character', as opposed to a narrowly class character, of the new Communist Party which the restoration of political freedom had made possible. The goal was a 'progressive democracy' (the exact character of which was left unclear), to be achieved by democratic methods, not a socialist revolution.

Meanwhile on 9 September 1943 a Committee of National Liberation (CNL) of the six anti-fascist parties had been set up in Rome, to operate underground under German occupation. Its chairman was Ivanoe Bonomi, leader of the Democratic Labour party, who had been prime minister in 1921-22. The committee was to be the political organ of resistance; and early in 1944 a Committee of National Liberation for Upper Italy (CLNAI) was formed clandestinely in Milan, to direct military operations in the occupied north. In April 1944 Badoglio formed a six-party government, including the PCI, the first major victory for the democratic forces. On 4 June Rome fell to the Allies, and a few days later Badoglio was replaced by Bonomi as prime minister. Victor Emmanuel retired in favour of his son, pending a referendum on a monarchy versus a republic.

The CLNAI viewed this compromise with suspicion, as a step back towards 1922. The Committee, and the military Resistance, were almost unanimously republican, and in general much more radical than their colleagues in the south. The general philosophy of the Resistance has been described as 'the purging of the shame of twenty years of fascist rule and the preparation of the ground for a regenerated, more socially equitable society'. Militarily the communists, organised in Garibaldi Brigades, were the dominant element; but there were also non-communist (and sometimes anti-communist) brigades. Politically it was the PdA which took the lead in working out post-victory plans: proclamation of a *de facto* government based on the CLNs; the appointment of prefects and mayors to take over the administration; and the formation of a police force from the partisans. The radicals of the south looked to the CLNAI to provide the 'wind from the north' which would unleash the forces of reform.

The attitude of the Allies towards the Resistance was cautious and suspicious, and at first it was not taken seriously. The first contacts with British and American intelligence were made in Switzerland in November 1943, and the first airdrop of arms and supplies took place on 23 December. At that time it was calculated that there were about 9,000 active resisters. But the movement grew rapidly during the spring and summer of 1944, and both the British Special Operations Executive (SOE) and the American Office of Strategic Services (OSS) began to show an active interest. On the one hand they welcomed small acts of sabotage and harassment, which would tie down German and Italian Republican forces, and the gathering of military intelligence. On the other hand they distrusted the political aims of the Resistance, and were well aware that the CLNAI regarded itself as a potential government which would take over northern Italy when German power collapsed. They were also disturbed by the PCI's leading role in the military formations. In August 1944 a conservative anti-fascist general, Raffaele Cadorna, was dropped into north Italy with the objective of establishing control over the military arm of the Resistance and bringing it under the authority of the Bonomi government. He had very limited success, owing to the opposition of both the PCI and the PdA. By the autumn of 1944 the Resistance numbered at least 80,000 and there was a big increase in airdrops. The climax was reached in September with the establishment of a Free Republic of Ossolo on the Swiss border in the far north-west. It survived only six weeks, and Allied assistance was given grudgingly.[1] On 22 August the local Resistance played an important part in the liberation of Florence, an action which greatly increased their prestige with the Allied forces and high command.

The winter of 1944-45 saw a bitter struggle for survival. In December a delegation of the CLNAI negotiated a series of protocols with Allied military representatives in Rome, whereby in return for desperately needed finance and increased arms and supplies, it undertook at the moment of Liberation to accept the authority of the Allied Command, hand over local power to AMGOT, and disband the partisan units. These protocols were complemented a few weeks later by an agreement between Bonomi and a representative of the CLNAI, whereby Bonomi recognised the latter as the organ of the anti-fascist forces in occupied Italy and agreed to delegate power to it. This in effect ruled out any immediate change in the political system or state structure at the moment of Liberation, and brought the Resistance under Allied control. But despite this curbing of its revolutionary potential, the Allied authorities continued to be fearful. It was decided that only a minimum quantity of arms should be dropped, for special individual tasks, and that the non-communist units should have preference over the communist. This caution was undoubtedly induced by contemporary events in Greece.

Meanwhile progress towards democracy in liberated Italy was very slow. The rate of progress became a source of considerable friction between Britain and the USA. In contrast with the British, the US army had fought the Italians only for a very brief period, in Tunisia and Sicily between November 1942 and July 1943. They did not therefore share the British insistence on maintaining the terms of the September armistice intact, as preparation for a punitive peace. Nor did Roosevelt share Churchill's monarchist prejudices or his contempt for Bonomi and other democratic survivors from the pre-fascist era.[2] In June 1944 (and again in November) Churchill vetoed the appointment as foreign minister of Carlo Sforza, who had established himself as a well respected leader of the anti-fascist exiles in the United States before his return to Italy in October 1943.[3]

Roosevelt was also much influenced by the need to cultivate the powerful American Italian lobby in a presidential election year. Churchill modified his views after a visit to Italy in August 1944, during which he met Bonomi and was greatly moved by the warm reception he received from Italian bystanders during his travels. A compromise between his and Roosevelt's views was reached in the Hyde Park Declaration of 26 September, which praised Italy's role in the struggle against the Nazis. An extension of Italian administrative independence was promised, as well as aid through UNRRA (United Nations Relief and Rehabilitation Administration) and other measures for the reconstruction of the shattered economy. The main burden fell on the USA as the British recognised that they had not got the resources to give Italy the assistance she needed. As a symbol of Italy's new status the title of Allied Control Commission was changed to Allied Commission, and diplomatic relations between Italy and the Allies were restored.

On 9 April 1945 the Allied forces launched the final offensive of the war in Italy. By 26 April the German armies had been destroyed south of the Po, and three days later the Act of Capitulation was signed at AFHQ in Caserta. Mussolini's Social Republic collapsed ignominiously. Meanwhile the insurrection so dreaded by the Allies started in Genoa on 23 April, and all the major cities of the north had been taken over by the CLNAI before the Allied armies arrived. Prefects and mayors had been appointed, and military tribunals set up to try fascist officials and collaborators with the Germans. Mussolini was captured on 27 April and summarily executed next day, and many other scores were privately settled. The total number of executions, with or without trial, has been estimated at 15,000. But it had previously been decided that members of the Republican forces should be treated as prisoners of war, and this is what occurred. There was no civil war. The CLNAI carried out its undertaking of December that the partisan formations should be disarmed and demobilised (though many arms were kept in hiding). The Greek experience of December 1944 was much in the minds of the PCI leaders, and Togliatti was able to convince his party that insurrection would be futile in the face of Allied military occupation. This was a bitter blow to the party militants, especially the factory workers for whom Stalin was a hero[4], and who were to hope for some years to come that revolution would come by Soviet invasion through Yugoslavia. But during May and June AMGOT took over power with unexpected ease and rapidity.[5]

On 19 June 1945 Ferruccio Parri, leader of the PdA with an outstanding Resistance record, was appointed Prime Minister. His cabinet was composed of the six anti-fascist parties, including elements from the CLNAI. But from the point of view of the Resistance, the Parri government was an almost total failure. One reason lay with Parri himself: he was a man of great integrity, but lacked the quality of political leadership (in striking contrast to de Gaulle, who was struggling with the same problems at the same time) and became overwhelmed by the complexity of his task. One cause of the Resistance's disillusionment was the abandonment of the process of purging (*epurazione*) of which it had had high hopes during the war. It was in fact Togliatti, as minister for justice, who decreed a general amnesty, as a result of which most of the fascists imprisoned during the Badoglio and Bonomi governments were released.

The main cause of Parri's weakness, however, was the disagreements within the coalition on the main lines of economic policy. The hard realities of the economic state of Italy made it essential to give first aid measures of reconstruction priority over reform. All were agreed on this: the Communist minister of finance declared that in present circumstances the revival of capitalism was the first need, and radical reforms must be postponed. The Liberal representatives, however, led by Luigi Einaudi, an economist with a world-wide reputation and governor of the Banca d'Italia, carried on a battle against all reform in principle, especially nationalisation of industry and excessive welfare legislation, and also criticised the government's inability to maintain law and order. At the end of November the Liberals withdrew from the government and Parri resigned.

Parri's successor was Alcide De Gasperi, secretary of the Christian Democratic party. He had been briefly imprisoned under fascism, and during the war worked as an assistant librarian in the Vatican. His appointment was welcome to the Allies, who immediately announced that the administration of all north Italy (except for a small area round Trieste, which was in dispute with the Yugoslavs) would be handed back on 31 December. De Gasperi retained Einaudi as his minister of finance, and the policy of capitalist restoration was continued. The CLNs were dissolved, most of the prefects and mayors appointed by the Resistance were replaced, and some ex-fascists reinstated.

De Gasperi's aim was to build a coalition of the democratic centre, which could secure the support of the mass of Italians who had acquiesced in fascism. In the short term he saw the need to maintain the coalition, realising the importance of obtaining all-party agreement during the drafting of the new constitution, and in particular for measures to safeguard the church's interests and for ratification of the peace treaty. He was determined to win the church's support for Christian Democracy, as the one and only Catholic party. There were strong influences in the Vatican, including Pope Pius XII himself, who distrusted the reforming tendencies of the DC's left wing and would have preferred a clerical-conservative party.

On 2 June 1946 a plebiscite was held on the question of monarchy versus republic, and a Constituent Assembly was elected. Less than a month before, Victor Emmanuel had abdicated in favour of his son Umberto. The result was 12.7 million (54 per cent) votes for the republic, 10.7 million (46 per cent) for the monarchy. It is questionable whether if Victor Emmanuel had abdicated in 1944, the monarchists might have won. The south voted overwhelmingly for the monarchy (80 per cent in Naples). The DC was split: its leaders, especially those who had participated in the Resistance, voted republican, but it has been estimated that three-quarters of its voters supported the monarchy. On 13 June Umberto flew into exile in Portugal. The vote has been described as the last triumph of Resistance ideals.

In the elections to the Constituent Assembly, conducted with the 'purest' form of proportional representation and with women voting for the first time, the DC won 35 per cent of the votes (207 seats), the Socialists 21 per cent (115 seats) and the PCI 19 per cent (104 seats). No other party polled more than 6 per cent. The PdA polled only 1.5 per cent, lingered on till the autumn, then dissolved itself. The DC had at that time only a very slender organisation, but the church mobilised all its strength in support, revealing its capacity to use the tools of democracy. The election signified the end of the political dominance of the liberal middle class élite, which had ruled Italy from unification till 1922. The age of mass democratic party politics had arrived in Italy.

The Constituent Assembly met on 25 June 1946. During the summer the international situation deteriorated, and the first signs of the Cold War began to affect Italy. But De Gasperi persevered with what he privately described as 'forced cohabitation'. These tactics were rewarded on 25 March 1947 when Article 7 on church-state relations was passed. This incorporated the concordat of 1929, and so confirmed the church's privileged position in society, especially in the fields of education, marriage law and morals (divorce remained illegal). Togliatti instructed his deputies, at the last moment, to vote (often very reluctantly) in favour. The PCI thus became directly responsible for the foundation of what its critics came to describe in the 1950s and 1960s as a 'clerical republic'.[6] Togliatti's decision was in accord with the policy which he had preached since 1944, of conciliation of the Catholic masses and avoidance of 'religious war'. Article 7 also meant that the church accepted the republican constitution and the DC's role in the future democracy, an objective that De Gasperi had always had in mind.

The peace treaty was signed in Paris on 10 February 1947 by Sforza, who had at last been given the foreign ministry a few days before. Despite appeals for leniency from the Italian government and many Allied authorities on the spot,[7] it was harshly punitive in character. Italy was required to renounce all claims to its former colonies, to accept frontier revisions in favour of France and Yugoslavia, and to submit to limitation of its armed forces.[8] The publication of these terms aroused bitterness throughout Italy, whose contribution to victory as a co-belligerent had been almost totally ignored. The handing over of most of the navy, which had fought beside the British and Americans since 1943, was especially resented, and for a time it seemed possible that it might scuttle its ships, as did the Germans at Scapa Flow in 1919. Most wounding of all was the preamble, which reminded Italy of its act of aggression on 10 June 1940, and imposed an obligation to guarantee the human rights of all its citizens. The treaty was nevertheless ratified by the Constituent Assembly on 25 July, with the PCI, by then in opposition, voting in its favour. (In fact the treaty turned out to be one of the shortest-lived in history: by the end of 1951 the military clauses had been allowed to lapse, and the clause on human rights was declared to be superfluous.)

On 13 May 1947 De Gasperi ejected the communists and socialists from the government. This followed soon after his visit to Washington, the first transatlantic journey of an Italian prime minister. His hope was to secure substantial economic aid, but he obtained little. Although the Americans welcomed the rupture with the Left, the allegation that they dictated it is now known to be false. But De Gasperi's action obviously reflected the growing strains of the Cold War. The proclamation of the Truman Doctrine in March was followed by the announcement of the Marshall Plan in June. Following instructions from Moscow, the PCI turned to militant tactics of protest in the factories and among the peasantry, often accompanied by violence. The contrast between this and the party's constructive behaviour in the Constituent Assembly led to accusations (often repeated in later years) of *doppiezza* (duplicity). The De Gasperi government played a full part in setting up the European Recovery Programme (ERP) for the implementation of the Marshall Plan, which the socialists and communists labelled as an act of American imperialism.

The constitution was approved by the Assembly in December 1947 and came into effect on 1 January 1948. Einaudi was elected as Italy's first president, and the continuation of his fiscal and economic policies began to show results: the lira was stabilised, inflation checked, and industrial production revived (in 1949 it overtook the level of 1939). The foundations of Italy's 'economic miracle' of the 1950s and 1960s had been laid.

Elections to the first republican parliament had been fixed for 19 April 1948. They took place under the shadow of the Czechoslovak communist coup in February. East-Central Europe had been progressively stalinized: would Italy be next? The US Government decided on massive intervention: aid poured in, and the American Italian community was mobilized. The DC fought the election in apocalyptic terms, as a battle between God and Satan. Catholic Action set up civic committees and mobilised 300,000 volunteers to promote the DC's cause. On the other side the Communist-Socialist Popular Front, which had hailed the Czech coup as a people's victory, denounced the DC as a tool of the USA, demanded rejection of the Marshall Plan and a foreign policy of non-alignment between East and West.

The results were an overwhelming victory for the DC, which polled 48.5 per cent of the votes and obtained an absolute majority in the Chamber of Deputies (a result never repeated since). The rank and file of the Popular Front, which had been confident of victory, were stunned, but accepted the result. The preparations for military intervention by the USA (the last Allied troops had been withdrawn on 31 December) and a British naval demonstration proved unnecessary. In retrospect it seems probable that some form of unwritten understanding had been reached between De Gasperi and Togliatti whereby Togliatti undertook to prevent unconstitutional action by his followers, while De Gasperi agreed not to suppress his party.[9] What was clear was that Italy was now firmly established in the Western camp. The transition from fascism to democracy had been completed.[10]

Discussion

Sir David Hunt argued that a punitive peace was inevitable. Italy's colonies were in any case already promised independence, or had been promised to other powers. In the circumstances of 1944-5, it was inconceivable that the Allies would have agreed to restore Italy's 1939 frontiers, and clear that her fleet must be scrapped. While conceding that Italian expectations were unrealistic, *Mr. Seton-Watson* maintained that the peace was harsh; the preamble was regarded as particularly humiliating.

In response to a question from *Sir Michael Howard* concerning CIA intervention in the elections, *Mr Seton-Watson* described it as 'massive', both in finance and propaganda: plans were laid for military intervention if the Popular Front were to win.

Notes and References

[1] Two other Free Republics, less publicised but probably of greater military significance, were set up in Carnia, in north-east Italy, and at Montefiorino, in the central Appenines.

[2] In 1927 Churchill publicly declared in Rome that had he been an Italian in 1922, he would have supported the Fascists.

[3] A possible explanation of Churchill's antagonism to Sforza may date from 1921, when Sforza was Italian Foreign Minister and Churchill was Colonial Secretary. At that time Sforza broke the Allied united front against Kemal Pasha by concluding an economic deal behind Britain's back. While passing through London in October 1943, Churchill extracted from Sforza a promise not to oppose the monarchy, a promise which he broke as soon as he arrived in Italy.

[4] They affectionately called him 'Il baffone' (Big Moustache).

[5] As a regimental officer in the British army in Italy at that time, I was genuinely apprehensive that I might be required to suppress an insurrection such as had occurred in Greece, and shall always feel grateful to Togliatti (and Stalin) for sparing me such an ordeal.

[6] This was an unjust accusation, for De Gasperi on many occasions stood up to Vatican pressure, was determined to prevent DC from becoming a wholly confessional party, and even after his overwhelming electoral victory in April 1948 maintained a coalition with minor 'lay' parties (Liberal, Republican and Social Democratic).

[7] Notably the Allied Commander-in-Chief, General Alexander, and Harold Macmillan, British representative on the Allied Commission.

[8] It was a 'British' treaty, drafted in the Foreign Office, though in consultation with the State Department. Churchill maintained his opposition to a 'lenient' peace at the Potsdam Conference in July 1945: when at the first plenary session Truman proposed the immediate admission of Italy to the United Nations, Churchill opposed him in an emotional speech which reminded the Conference

that Italy had stabbed Britain in the back in June 1940, and that the British had shed much blood fighting Italy in the following three years. See *DBPO*, Series I, Volume I, p 342.

[9] A conclusive confirmation of the PCI's 'constitutional' strategy came in July 1948, when a right-wing student shot and seriously wounded Togliatti. This provoked a general strike, massive demonstrations and a few insurrectionary episodes. But Togliatti and his colleagues urged calm, and the police rapidly restored order.

[10] De Gasperi remained in office until 1953. He was therefore the leading architect of the Italian democratic system, and also of Italy's rapid international rehabilitation. The discredit into which that system has recently fallen should not obscure the magnitude of De Gasperi's achievement.

Bibliography

Although I was serving in the British army in Italy throughout 1944-45, at that time I had virtually no knowledge of the events described in this paper. It is therefore a contribution by an historian, not a participant. It is based wholly on published sources. I list below six of the works in English on which I have mainly relied. They are all based on extensive archival research and take into account the monumental (and often polemical) Italian literature. Ginsborg's work contains a comprehensive bibliography. In the light of the current crisis of the Italian state, there will no doubt be fresh revisionist revelations, though interesting new details are emerging from the Moscow archives. Opinions will certainly continue to differ on the role of the Allies in the transition from fascism to democracy. Though the continuity in the structure of the Italian state and Italian society, which resulted from Allied policies, has had many negative effects and is the subject of renewed controversy today, my opinion would be that on balance the Allied contribution was positive.

David W Ellwood, *Italy 1943-1945* (Leicester University Press, 1985).
Paul Ginsborg, *A history of Contemporary Italy: Society and Politics 1943-1988* (Penguin Books, 1990).
John Lamberton Harper, *America and the Reconstruction of Italy 1945-1948* (Cambridge University Press), 1986.
C R S Harris, *Allied Military Administration of Italy 1943-1945* (HMSO, 1957).
Richard Lamb, *War in Italy 1943-1945: A Brutal Story* (John Murray, 1993).
James Edward Miller, *The United States and Italy 1940-1950: The Politics and Diplomacy of Stabilisation* (University of North Carolina Press, 1986).

9 The Liberation of Belgium, 1944-1945

MARTIN CONWAY

Introduction

The historiography of the Liberation long remained dominated by a particular perception of its historical significance with three key assumptions at its heart: firstly, attention was focused on Liberation as a decisive moment when an oppressive alien invader was replaced by a democratic government to a greater or lesser degree representative of the will of the nation. Secondly, the historiography concerned itself primarily with the key political, military and strategic decisions which determined the Liberation: the Allies, and to a lesser extent the political élites of the liberated countries, were at the centre of what was perceived essentially as a 'top down' process in which broader social and political forces played only a subsidiary role. Thirdly, attention was directed forward rather than backwards in time. The Liberation of Europe was analysed as a prelude to the subsequent international and domestic conflicts which characterised Cold War Europe during the 1950s and 1960s. Attention was focused at a national level on the political strategies of the European Communist parties which were seen as having been determined by this wider international conflict.

This perception of the Liberation and the particular agenda of issues which it defined has proved remarkably durable, but not surprisingly has gradually been undermined by new trends in historical research, of which the most important are three in number. Firstly, the demise of the Soviet Union and the subsequent marginalization or dissolution of European communist parties has hastened a reassessment of the phenomenon of European communism. Individual communist parties are no longer regarded as having been primarily vehicles of an international communist ideology or still less as tools of Soviet-directed influence, but as the products of distinct national circumstances. Though the reality of Soviet involvement in the direction and financing of these parties remains beyond question, such influence is increasingly seen as only one—and frequently one of the less important—factors which determined the history of these parties. Instead, the national context in which they operated and the constraints and opportunities this provided for their development is seen as the dominant influence on European communist parties.

This 'nationalisation' of the history of European communism has gone hand in hand with a second historiographical trend which since the mid-1980s has brought to the fore the internal European origins of the Cold War polarisation of politics. If for a long time it appeared natural to present the Cold War as a conflict which was imposed on post-war European politics from outside, obliging political forces to choose between support for Soviet-directed communism or American-led liberal democracy, work in recent years has stressed the internal European dynamics of the early Cold War. The international conflict between the Soviet Union and the United States mirrored and to some extent drew strength from the polarisation of domestic politics which took place in western Europe during the 1940s and which led the governments of western Europe to encourage the United States to commit itself both politically and militarily to the defence of the states of western Europe against perceived Soviet expansionism and internal communist subversion.

Thirdly, and most importantly, the last twenty years have witnessed a revolution in historiographical perspectives of the history of Europe during the years of Second World War. The tendency to perceive these years as a 'parenthesis' in the political history of Europe has been replaced by a recognition that the outbreak of war and the subsequent occupation of much of Europe by the Axis forces in no sense served to freeze the political process. Instead it accelerated and in many cases exacerbated the conflicts of the previous years, bringing to a head the socio-economic tensions of the previous decade as well as posing with a particular clarity the political choice between liberal democracy, the anti-democratic right and communism.

The cumulative impact of these historiographical trends has undoubtedly been to enrich historical perceptions of the period of the Liberation. At its most basic level, it has also served to increase its importance of the period of Liberation, which is seen now as a key element in a longer historical process with its roots in the pre-war history of Europe. Liberation was the culmination of the acute socio-economic and political conflicts which had dominated most European countries during the inter-war years and which contributed in no small measure to the Second World War.

The historiography of the Liberation of Belgium reflects these wider trends. The rapid liberation of all but a small corner of the country during the first days of September 1944 and the re-establishment during the subsequent winter of the pre-war political order has long attracted the attention of those historians concerned with the modern history of Belgium. It was, however, only in the 1970s that works began to appear which sought to go beyond the military and diplomatic history of the period.[1]

Subsequently, other aspects of the Liberation period have been explored.[2] There remains, however, no general study of the period of the Liberation and many aspects of the subject still await scholarly attention. This paper does not seek to fill this gap. Instead, by focusing on a particular aspect of the liberation—the re-establishment of the pre-war parliamentary régime—it is intended to provide a brief introduction to the forces which were of importance in determining the history of the Liberation period from September 1944 to the summer of 1945.[3]

The question why the manifold changes wrought by the war years should nevertheless have resulted in the return of the pre-war political order in Belgium is one which has long been debated by historians. The post-war régime was in certain important respects markedly different from that of the 1930s. The Communist Party, which increased its vote from 5.4% in 1939 to 12.7 % in the first post-war elections of February 1946, established itself incontestably—if not durably—as a major political force.[4] Conversely, the pre-war anti-democratic parties, the Flemish Nationalists of the *Vlaams Nationaal Verbond* and the Rexist movement led by Léon Degrelle disappeared from the political stage as a consequence of their collaboration with German forces during the Occupation.[5]

Moreover, though the three traditional political families—Catholics, Socialists and Liberals—remained the dominant political forces (winning almost 85% of the vote in the elections of February 1946), all underwent considerable internal reform which in the case of the Catholics and the Socialists resulted not only in a change of name but also in the adoption of modified internal structures. Substantial measures of political and socio-economic reform were also introduced. In December 1944 the first large-scale compulsory system of social security was introduced and, most importantly, in the elections of February 1946 women were allowed to vote for the first time.[6]

The enfranchisement of the female majority of the population can hardly be dismissed as a change of limited importance. Nevertheless, the dominant perception of the post-Liberation period remains the limited scale of the political and socio-economic reforms enacted after the war. The constitution remained substantially unchanged, the state was still based on the centralised structure introduced in 1831, the capitalist economic system remained in place (there were for example no measures of nationalisation) and the hierarchy of class, linguistic and ideological divisions symbolised by the threefold Catholic, Socialist and Liberal 'pillars' of Belgian society remained the dominant reality of political life.

It has been argued that this continuity was to some extent an artificial outcome brought about by the 'accidental' conjuncture of internal events with wider European diplomatic and military developments. Thus, a Cold War perspective of the Liberation (expressed notably by Churchill in his declaration to the House of Commons in December 1944 in the aftermath of the Resistance demonstrations outside parliament)[7] has assumed that Belgium was only 'saved' from a communist-inspired revolt by the prompt action of the Allied authorities. What might be termed this 'Greek' perspective of the

Liberation has found its natural converse in the belief that, had it not been for the intimidating presence of the Allied military authorities and the strength which this gave to the forces of the Belgian *ancien régime*, Belgium would indeed have undergone wide-ranging changes in the immediate post-Liberation period.

The belief that the Liberation of Europe constituted a moment of failed revolution—a twentieth-century equivalent of 1848, when, in A J P Taylor's famous phrase, European history was supposed to change direction but failed to do so[8]—is of course one which extends far beyond the frontiers of Belgium.[9] It is, however, an interpretation which has a particular resonance in the Belgian case. The post-war crises of the unitary Belgian state and the tortuous devolution of power to the Flemish and Walloon regions has quite naturally led many to see 1944 as a 'lost opportunity' when the Belgian nation-state could have brought about the reforms necessary to have enabled it to survive into the late-twentieth century. Instead, the failure to do so doomed both Belgian state and nation to a long and painful process of dissolution.

An Artificial Outcome?

For historians to speak of an artificial outcome is obviously to beg questions about what constitutes a 'natural' process of historical change. Nevertheless, this interpretation has an evident plausibility. In many respects, the momentum for radical change in Belgium in 1944-1945 seemed overwhelming. Almost uniquely in northern Europe, the structures of the state, of national identity and of political authority appeared to have been gravely undermined by the war years. The chaos wrought by the Occupation horrified those who returned to the country in the immediate aftermath of the Liberation. Allied bombing had damaged buildings and railways, the system of food rationing—crucial in a country which depended substantially on imports of foodstuffs—was close to collapse while the economy had been exhausted by German demands, shortages of raw materials and the deportation of large numbers of workers to the Reich.[10]

The tripartite Catholic-Socialist-Liberal government headed by Hubert Pierlot which returned from London in the baggage train of the Allies was ill-equipped to resolve these manifold problems. National and local government, the police and the *Gendarmerie* had all been weakened by the policy of the German Military Administration of appointing large numbers of its Rexist and Flemish Nationalist collaborationist allies to positions of responsibility.[11] The government's most serious difficulties were, however, political in nature. The bitter dispute which developed between King Léopold III and the government in the summer of 1940 had seriously weakened the latter's authority. While the King believed that the surrender to the German armies on 28 May 1940 marked the end of Belgian involvement in the war and sought to reach an accommodation with the Third Reich, his ministers wished to continue the war alongside the Allies and made their way somewhat belatedly from Vichy France to London in the autumn of 1940, widely regarded—and not just by supporters of the King—as traitors who fled the country in its hour of need.[12]

A reconciliation between King and government never took place. Although the ministers who left in 1940 gradually recovered some popularity, few in Belgium believed that they could or should remain in office after the Liberation. The Allies toyed with imposing their own military administration but in May 1944 decided to lend their support to Pierlot and his colleagues, hoping that they would make way gracefully in the aftermath of the Occupation for a new government composed of political figures who had remained in Belgium during the war. When the pre-war parliament assembled on 20 September, however, no such new government emerged and the Pierlot government, enlarged by a small number of new ministers, was obliged to continue reluctantly in office.[13]

At the back of everybody's minds remained the unresolved question of the King. Léopold III had been deported by the German authorities to the Reich in June 1944 and in his absence his brother, Prince Charles, was appointed as Regent in September 1944. The real difficulty, however, concerned the King's wartime actions. He had visited Hitler at Berchtesgaden in November 1940, and even before the war had made little secret of his desire to see political reforms introduced which would have increased the powers of the executive at the expense of the parliament and the political parties. Despite the popularity of his decision to remain in the country to share the sufferings of his people, his position had subsequently been undermined by his attempts to negotiate with the German authorities and by his decision while in detention in the Palace of Laeken to remarry in 1941 the nanny of his children.[14] Opinions as to his future role were greatly divided: while for many—especially Catholics and the Flemish rural population—the 'prisoner of Laeken' remained a patriotic hero, he was widely regarded, notably in the industrial heartlands of Wallonia, as a symbol of collaboration with the German authorities and of anti-democratic political reform.[15]

The King's absence postponed the confrontation of this problem but the government nevertheless had little success in winning the esteem of its compatriots. Criticism of ministers and their policies was universal. As the problems of food provisioning and industrial production went from bad to worse, they were accused of irresolution and incompetence. Above all, there was a general conviction that their wartime absence in London prevented them from understanding the mood of the population. The war had forged a strong if ill-defined desire for political and social change to which Pierlot and his colleagues—wedded to the mentalities of the pre-war era—seemed unable to respond.[16]

The Allies were aware of the volatility of the situation. The reports of the British military and political authorities and of the American ambassador paint a gloomy picture of a government staggering from crisis to crisis and presenting an overwhelming impression of feebleness.[17] Worrying comparisons with Greece frequently came to the mind of British observers and, though prompt action by the British military authorities resolved the direct challenge by certain Resistance groups to the Pierlot government in November 1944, they remained for a long time conscious of the extreme precariousness of the political régime in Belgium. As late as April 1945, the British military commander, General Erskine, warned his superiors of the prospect of a Communist-inspired uprising, commenting that the Belgian government would be unable to respond to such a challenge without the assistance of British military forces.[18]

How then was it possible to avert the collapse of the Pierlot régime and the introduction of radical reforms, or even the possibility of the descent of the country into a bloody Greek-style Civil War? Much, it is clear, rested on a series of circumstantial or 'accidental' factors which had the combined consequence of hindering change and enabling the pre-war régime slowly to recover its authority by the summer of 1945. This process was a complex one but, for the purposes of this analysis, six such factors would seem to be of particular importance.

The first of these was undoubtedly the remarkably speedy and almost uneventful Liberation of the country. Despite the momentum which the Allied advance had gained when it reached the frontiers of Belgium on 1 September, few—least of all the collaborationist allies of the Germans—expected the German armies to withdraw so speedily from the country. Mons was liberated on 2 September and Verviers, the last substantial centre of population, was occupied by Allied troops on 9 September.[19] Only a small area of the northern Limburg bordering the Netherlands remained under German control. This rapid and largely unchallenged Liberation had several consequences. In the first place it prevented the emergence of any prolonged power vacuum in which popular passions could have risen and events taken a more dramatic turn. For most Belgians, the experience of Liberation was a passive one. German retreat after small-scale skirmishes was followed shortly afterwards by the arrival of British, American or Canadian tanks. The role of the population was to watch, cheer and embrace those who had liberated them.

Secondly, the rapid Liberation prevented Resistance groups from mobilising in a manner which could have challenged the re-establishment of the Pierlot government's authority. Though the

Resistance did indeed achieve certain major feats during the Liberation (most notably of course the crucial capture of the port of Antwerp),[20] their scope for action was limited. German convoys were ambushed, road blocks were established and collaborationists were pursued and arrested but formal power evaded them. Even in rural areas such as the Ardennes, the absence of official representatives was short-lived and the arrival of the Allies was closely followed both by the arrival of the representatives of the Belgian government-in-exile and by the re-emergence of the pre-war local authorities who assumed responsibility for public affairs.[21] Thus, even when Resistance groups sought to play a more political role (and relatively few of them did), the space to assume such a role was forestalled by the circumstances of the Liberation.

The second factor which was of decisive importance in the maintenance of the political status quo was the challenge to the Pierlot government by the predominantly left-wing Resistance groups in the *Front de l'Indépendance* in November 1944. The Pierlot government, highly conscious of its own vulnerability and nervous of the armed power of the Resistance, ordered all Resistance groups to hand over their weapons. Many—notably the army-officer dominated *Armée Secrète*—agreed to do so, but the main communist-influenced grouping, the *Partisans Armés*, refused. The Communist ministers who had entered the government in September 1944 resigned, and in a highly charged political atmosphere the *Front de l'Indépendance* (to which the *Partisans* were affiliated) organised a mass demonstration outside parliament on 25 November. At least 15,000 attended, their anger focused on the government's manifold perceived failings since the Liberation. As the *Gendarmerie* (itself a target of popular hostility because of its substantial pro-German recruitment during the Occupation) sought to hold back the demonstrators, scuffles broke out and a grenade was thrown injuring several demonstrators. The violence was unintended but its political impact was enormous. Pierlot accused the *Front* of seeking to bring about a *coup d'état* and wild rumours circulated of a mobilisation of partisan units in Walloon industrial cities. In the event, nothing happened. Neither the Communists nor the *Front de l'Indépendance* wished to challenge the government directly and the British military authorities intervened decisively to insist upon the demobilisation of all Resistance groups.[22]

The confrontation had long-term consequences for the political situation. Though the *Front* energetically tried to present Pierlot as a British puppet and as 'l'homme qui a mitraillé le maquis',[23] Socialist suspicions of communist intentions were reinforced, giving the Right the opportunity to denounce communist conspiracies. Right-wing Catholic papers such as *L'Avenir du Luxembourg* stressed the need to maintain law and order, not hesitating to equate communist 'demagoguery' with the actions of the pro-German Rexists during the Occupation.[24] Above all, the confrontation bought the Pierlot régime a much needed breathing space. With attention focused on the Communists, the Pierlot régime was able to extract special powers from a reluctant parliament on 28 November and won some measure of popular support for its strong stance against the Resistance, which already by the time of the demonstration had lost some of its initial public esteem.[25]

The third factor which undoubtedly worked to inhibit change was the continuation of the war. The Liberation of September 1944 did not mark the end of Belgium's involvement. German rockets fell on Belgian cities and the country remained in the front line of Allied attempts to cross the Rhine and penetrate into the Netherlands and western Germany. The proximity of the conflict was abruptly reinforced by von Rundstedt's offensive in the Belgian Ardennes in mid-December 1944. The German armies re-occupied (or, in the words of their collaborationist allies, 'liberated') eastern areas of the Belgian province of Luxembourg and, though these returned after a few weeks to Allied control, the unexpected German offensive not surprisingly led all political groupings to stress the need to concentrate on the immediate military priorities.[26] Once again the Pierlot régime benefited from these events, enabling it to present its opponents as playing into the hands of the Germans.

More generally, the continuation of the war throughout the winter of 1944-45 acted as a brake on forces for political and social change. Sacrifices imposed on the population—and especially on the industrial working class—were justified by the need to maximise the war effort while strikers, notably in the coal mines, were accused, even by their union leaders, of having become tools of Nazi *agents provocateurs*.[27] The war also provided a justification for the postponement of measures of political and social reform. New elections could not be held until the war was at an end (they eventually took place in February 1946) and no major reforms, it was argued, could be introduced without a fresh mandate from the electorate.

The pursuit and prosecution of those who had collaborated with the German authorities during the Occupation was a prominent feature of Belgian political life in the months after the Liberation and in retrospect can be seen as having had the unintended effect of assisting the return of the pre-war political order. Hostility towards those who had assisted the Nazi forces politically, militarily or economically was at its peak in the immediate aftermath of the Liberation and remained to the fore throughout the subsequent winter, gaining new strength in May 1945 when the final German collapse led to the revelation of the sufferings endured by Belgian prisoners in Germany. The failure of the Pierlot government to act rapidly to prosecute many thousands of suspected collaborators who were in detention awaiting trial was a major source of bitterness against the regime.[28] The public demanded not merely revenge for their wartime sufferings but the public symbolism of a system of justice which would investigate thoroughly all those—including those in positions of influence—who had assisted the German authorities.

This was a process with considerable potential political consequences. As the government was well aware, to prosecute all those who had worked with the Germans would be to open to public debate the policy of *de facto* accommodation and compromise followed throughout the Occupation by much of the civil service, the judiciary and the economic élite.[29] To demand the full investigation of collaboration (rather than merely prosecuting those who had donned German uniforms or mouthed Nazi propaganda slogans) was therefore to question the existing political and social order, especially in the economic sector where demands for the prosecution of those employers who had benefited from German orders were inextricably linked with demands for nationalisation and some form of worker control.

Despite its radical potential, the demand for a thorough purge gradually became a divisive political issue which served to weaken calls for more general political and social change. Demands by some Resistance groups for a rapid and bloody purge, as well as the death sentences passed on some unfortunates who had served the German forces in very modest positions led some, especially in Catholic ranks, to call for greater leniency and discrimination in prosecution, prompting in turn accusations from the political left that some Catholic politicians were acting as apologists for collaboration.[30] The *épuration* thus rapidly became entangled in partisan political disputes and was exploited by the government to its advantage. When the Socialist Achille Van Acker finally replaced Pierlot as prime minister in February 1945, his government promised to 'frapper vite et fort' against those accused of collaboration. New measures were indeed introduced and trials held of the Flemish Nationalist and Rexist leaders who had worked with the German authorities. Little was done, however, to investigate the more sensitive areas of public life. The *secrétaires-généraux* who had directed the government ministries during the Occupation, the heads of the police and the judiciary were not threatened and the major economic enterprises remained untouched, though a number of prominent economic collaborators were prosecuted.[31] The post-war prosecutions had become not a challenge to the pre-war order but the manifestation of its continued power.

The inauguration of a new government in February 1945 was a fifth factor which had the effect of consolidating the existing political order. By the time of its fall, there was no doubt that the Pierlot government was exhausted. The short-term boost it had received from its confrontation with the *Front de l'Indépendance* had given way to a renewed chorus of disapproval at its failure to feed and heat the population or to offer effective political leadership.[32] Eventually, the Socialist Party decided to bring the government down by demanding a reshuffle of the key portfolios. Pierlot rejected their request and Socialist ministers withdrew from the government obliging Pierlot to resign.[33]

The task of forming a new government did not initially seem an easy one. The Catholic Party refused to participate in any government which included the Communists, while the Socialists insisted that the inclusion of the Communists was a condition of their participation. Briefly, it seemed as though a 'Popular Front' government of Socialists, Liberals , Communists and left-wing Catholics might be formed but, faced with the possibility of exclusion from office, the Catholics reluctantly agreed to participate in a new government of national unity. The new prime minister was the Flemish Socialist Achille Van Acker. As Minister of Labour in the previous government and one of the few leading politicians to have remained in Belgium during the war, he seemed almost the only political figure who possessed the abilities and the energy necessary to confront the country's problems. His appointment was broadly welcomed and in his first speech to parliament, Van Acker promised to resolve the pressing problems of food and fuel shortages, declaring unambivalently: 'Le pays veut être gouverné et il le sera'.[34]

Initially the new government appeared more radical. Spaak, firmly established at the Ministry of Foreign Affairs, was the sole survivor from the London government while Van Acker was only the second Socialist prime minister of Belgium. Key posts were in the hands of younger figures, such as the Flemish Catholic Gaston Eyskens who became Minister of Finance, and there were three Communist ministers.[35] The reality, however, proved to be less dramatic. From the outset, Van Acker made clear that his principal objective was to resolve the economic problems and this pushed him remorselessly in a more conservative direction. Large-scale purges of industrialists who had worked with the German authorities were ruled out by the need to maximise production and the government took special powers to enable it to mobilise under quasi-military terms key sectors of the workforce. Above all, the emphasis on the 'bataille du charbon' obliged Van Acker to confront the waves of strikes which continued to disrupt production in the coalfields of Wallonia. A wage freeze was imposed (accompanied by promises to stabilise prices) and Van Acker insisted that strikes were unacceptable at a time of national emergency. No major social reforms were introduced but were again postponed until after new elections.[36]

The Van Acker government, far from challenging the structure of Belgian politics and society, became engaged in the defence of the status quo. From May 1945 its day-to-day existence was, moreover, threatened by the intense political controversy surrounding the future position of the King. The release of Léopold III from German detention in early May had an immediate impact on the political situation in Belgium. The issue which had haunted many minds since the Liberation—namely, the desirability of the King resuming his constitutional position—suddenly became the dominant political issue, releasing a tide of passions which submerged all other concerns. Many Catholics, especially in Flanders, celebrated the King's release, obliging even those Catholic politicians who secretly harboured reservations regarding the King's pre-war and wartime actions to demand his return to the throne. Others, most notably the Socialist Party and other left-wing groups, opposed equally unambiguously the King's resumption of his powers, portraying him as an advocate of pro-German collaboration and the agent of a renascent neo-fascism.[37]

The *question royale* became a further factor which worked to hinder political and social change. As with the controversy surrounding the prosecution of those who had worked with the German authorities, it was a dispute which threw into question much of the Belgian established order. The King's *de facto* accommodation with the Germans was no different from the way in which much of the Belgian élite had acted, while the intense cult of the monarchy which had developed in Belgium during the inter-war years had made the King a central symbol of the Belgian nation-state. The manner in which the *question royale* developed during the summer of 1945 and after served largely to reinforce the existing social and political fault-lines. Van Acker travelled to meet the King soon after his release but agreement on the conditions for his return proved impossible to achieve. The King remained determined to resume his constitutional position and in August 1945 the Catholic ministers resigned from the government. Henceforth, the Catholic Party, encouraged by Cardinal Van Roey and the majority of his fellow bishops, made the King's cause their own while the governmental parties opposed his return and supported the continuation of the regency of Prince Charles.[38]

The *question royale* bedevilled the subsequent post-war history of Belgium, reaching a peak in the summer of 1950 when, after a bitterly contested referendum, a Catholic government invited Léopold III to return to the throne, prompting a general strike in Wallonia and, after much tense negotiation, a compromise solution whereby Léopold abdicated in favour of his son, Baudouin.[39] The dispute divided the country along traditional lines. Flemish-Walloon tensions were reinforced while the political alignment of the Catholic Party against a Socialist-Liberal alliance marked a return to the clerical-anticlerical disputes of the late-nineteenth century. Above all, attention was distracted from other political issues. Questions of social and political reform were displaced by a dispute which, despite its considerable symbolic importance, was of little real consequence. Rather like the Dreyfus Affair in 1890s France, it was a controversy focused on the past rather than the future and one which, as a group of socialist intellectuals noted with regret, symbolised the failure of the country to escape from 'ce climat malsain de liquidation de la guerre'.[40]

The dispute surrounding the King undoubtedly had the unintended outcome of hindering more wide-ranging processes of change. It was one of a constellation of factors, the combined impact of which undoubtedly helps to explain the process whereby the apparently highly volatile situation in Belgium in the immediate aftermath of the Liberation in fact resulted in the reconstitution of an only slightly modified version of the pre-war social and political order.

This 'accidental' interpretation of the Liberation period is not, however, in itself a sufficient explanation. Placing the emphasis on the radicalisation of Belgian politics brought about by the war years presents only half the story. The war, in Belgium as elsewhere in western Europe, served not only as a challenge to the existing social and political order but also in significant respects to reinforce it. Given the challenges faced by the liberal parliamentary régimes of much of western Europe during the 1930s, it might even be argued that the real significance of the war lay in the opportunity it provided for a conservative reconsolidation of the social and political status quo. This is an aspect of the war years which has long been neglected but which in recent years has begun somewhat tentatively to emerge from the work of a number of historians. As Richard Vinen and others have noted,[41] it is misleading to suggest that the war years had exclusively served to benefit the left. Though the anti-democratic right was discredited, the immediate post-war years in western Europe saw a renaissance in the fortunes of a conservative parliamentary right.

Such an interpretation can certainly be applied to the case of Belgium. The resurgence of the political right symbolised by the post-war success of the Catholic *Parti Social Chrétien-Christelijke Volkspartij*[42] (PSC-CVP) demonstrates that the war served as a prelude not so much to a failed revolution in the immediate aftermath of the liberation but to the consolidation of a predominantly conservative post-war democratic regime. Much historical research regarding this wider socio-political history of the war years remains to be undertaken. Nevertheless, it is possible to identify somewhat tentatively a number of themes.

The Real Reasons for Stability?

Central to the conservative impact of the war years was the manner in which they reinforced the power of a number of the established institutions of Belgian society. Though the King and the political elite were in different ways marginalized during the war, the circumstances of the German Occupation accorded the civil service, the judiciary, the Catholic Church and the leading industrialists an unprecedented pre-eminence in national life. The *Wehrmacht* officials of the

Militärverwaltung in Brussels sought to impose a system of indirect rule on Belgium, devolving responsibility for many issues to the established institutions of Belgian society. This policy was not without its difficulties. The efforts by the German officials to favour the cause of Flemish nationalism as well as their pursuit of policies dictated by Berlin such as the deportation of the Jews and the introduction of labour conscription frequently imperilled this *de facto* system of power-sharing with the Belgian élite. Nevertheless, it was a relationship which survived throughout the Occupation and which in retrospect can be seen to have done much to reinforce the formal and informal power of the established élites of Belgian society.[43]

The industrialists who negotiated collectively with the German authorities via the so-called *Comité Galopin*, the *secrétaires-généraux* who headed the central ministries, the judiciary and Cardinal Van Roey and his fellow Catholic bishops all acquired an importance in national life which in many respects reversed the process over the previous half century towards a more democratic political and social structure. Hierarchies of authority were reinforced and, though the explosion of popular energies at the Liberation momentarily challenged their position, the more durable legacy of the war was the prominent place which these 'notables' occupied in Belgian politics and society until the upheavals of the 1960s.

Nor was it merely the social order which was reinforced by the experience of the war. The nation and the constitution also emerged strengthened from the years of German Occupation. War perhaps always serves to increase patriotism, but this banal observation took on a particular importance in the Belgian context. During the inter-war years, the Belgian nation sought largely unsuccessfully to adapt to the twin processes of gradual social and linguistic liberation which shifted power away from a predominantly francophone bourgeoisie towards the industrial working class of Wallonia and the more rural population of Flanders. The political consequence was the emergence for the first time of a substantial movement of Flemish nationalism as well as the first stirrings of a Walloon regionalist sentiment hostile both to the centralised state and to the threat posed by the more numerous Flemish.

These processes could not be halted by the war years, but the German Occupation did have the consequence—albeit transient—of strengthening centrifugal at the expense of centripetal forces. Flemish nationalism was gravely damaged by the war years. The collaborationist policy pursued during the Occupation by the main Flemish nationalist political grouping, the *VNV*, deprived the cause of its political credibility and many of its most articulate spokesmen. At the same time, the war led many Flemish to rediscover the emotional ties which bound them to the Belgian nation and, though the subsequent purge of Flemish Nationalists accused of collaboration did much to rekindle feelings that the Flemish people were the victims of an unsympathetic Belgian state, the war did foster the emergence of a younger generation of Flemish politicians and opinion-leaders who sought to articulate a more 'positive' Flemish identity within a bilingual and democratic Belgian nation-state.[44]

In Wallonia, the effect of the war years on national loyalties was rather different. The spectacle of Flemish collaboration with the German authorities had done much to sharpen apprehensions of Flemish dominance and in the immediate aftermath of the war there was an upsurge in Walloon regionalist sentiment symbolised by the *Congrès National Wallon* held at Liège in October 1945 which called stridently, if not entirely coherently, for greater autonomy for Wallonia.[45] This laid the basis for the subsequent development of Walloon regionalism as a political force but at least in the short term it was of less significance than the optimism created by the war years—in both Wallonia and Flanders—that a new *compromis des Belges* was possible. The war imparted a new vividness and emotional strength to the Belgian nation-state and the post-Liberation press was notable for its tone of newly-discovered patriotism. It was the supposed common character of the Belgian people which was most prominently on display with frequent reference to the common sense, sturdy individualism and energy for hard work which allegedly typified the Belgian nation.[46]

Emphasis on the Belgian national character transcended political divisions and contributed to the belief that the co-existence of the nation's diverse elements was both possible and desirable. The constitution was a central symbol of this revivified Belgian patriotism: in the aftermath of the Liberation, figures from left and right combined in celebrating the traditions of freedom symbolised by the constitution of 1831. It seemed to express the long struggle of the Belgian peoples to free themselves from many variants of foreign oppression and, as the main francophone newspaper, *Le Soir,* declared in February 1945, its principles of free expression and parliamentary responsibility provided the best basis for the country's political life.[47] Unlike France, there was no aspiration for large-scale constitutional change. The authoritarian ideas of the Flemish Nationalists and Rexists had perished in the sufferings of the war years and, as one younger political figure subsequently observed, in the celebratory atmosphere of the Liberation it was difficult to voice any criticism—however modest—of the parliamentary régime.[48]

This new-found enthusiasm for parliamentary politics was a central element of the post-Liberation years. In Belgium, as in much of western Europe, the parliamentary régime had been widely criticised during the 1930s as outdated, corrupt and inefficient.[49] After the war, however, it was the virtues of the parliamentary system which were celebrated. A sovereign parliament became the symbol of a true democracy and when the Pierlot government finally fell in February 1945 there was much pleasure in the press that this had occurred by means of an open debate in parliament, rather than as a consequence of the backstage manoeuvrings of the political parties.[50]

Post-war enthusiasm for the parliamentary regime was not merely sentimental. It was also rooted in material conditions. A crucial factor in the political stabilization achieved after the war was that it was built upon a partial amelioration of the socio-economic grievances which during the 1930s had contributed much to the weakening of the political system. This was most obviously so in the case of the industrial working class. As a number of recent studies have shown, many—though certainly not all—employers came to favour during the war a system of collective bargaining with representative trade union leaders which, it was hoped, would provide the basis for a more stable form of labour relations. This was first evident during the *Conférence Nationale du Travail* held in September 1944 which granted substantial wage increases to many workers and laid the basis for the subsequent legal recognition of the rights of trade union representatives. In addition, the war opened the way to a significant expansion in the social security system. Clandestine meetings between employer and trade union representatives in Belgium during the war culminated in the signing of a 'social pact' in April 1944 which, though it had no official status, encouraged the post-Liberation government to press forward with the introduction of a new compulsory system of invalidity and unemployment insurance which was introduced by the Minister of Labour, Achille Van Acker, by a decree of 28 December 1944.[51]

Neither the move towards collective bargaining nor the social security measures were sufficient to bring social harmony. Many employers opposed the formal recognition of trade unions in the workplace while the demands of workers for improved conditions and greater industrial democracy ensured that strikes remained frequent until the early-1950s.[52] Nevertheless, the changes introduced after the war did mark a move away from the confrontational atmosphere of the social conflicts of the inter-war years and helped to foster a more positive image of the state as an arbiter in industrial disputes and guarantor of social justice.

The post-war years also saw a significant decline in the grievances of the commercial lower middle class and of the agricultural population. Both had been central to the electoral success of the anti-democratic Flemish Nationalists and Rexists during the 1930s and their improved economic position was significant in ensuring the marginalization of the anti-democratic right in post-war Belgium. This was especially so in the case of the rural population. Low agricultural prices, rural indebtedness and government regulations had forged an embittered mentality among many of Belgium's agricultural producers during the inter-war years. The German Occupation, however, brought about a reversal in their fortunes. The short-comings of the food rationing system gave rise to a vast black market and, though it is impossible to generalise, it is clear that many farmers enriched themselves considerably during the war years. Rationing and food shortages persisted into the post-war years and opportunities for fraud remained. The attempts by the Van Acker government to enforce official prices provoked violent demonstrations in southern Belgium in May 1945 but the black market remained a lucrative source of income for many farmers.[53]

The importance of the black market highlights the extent to which the war, far from forging a new radical political mentality, in many respects had the effect of 'depoliticising' the population. The normal structures of political engagement—elections, parliament, political associations and a free press—were suspended for the duration of the war years and their absence distanced people from the political process, encouraging a more individualist mentality. The pursuit of sufficient food was the overriding concern of many people, forcing them to transgress the law by participating in the black market. For others, the law became an irrelevance. The young who evaded labour conscription measures by adopting a clandestine life were drawn into a world where resistance often bordered on petty criminality or banditry. Some revelled in the opportunities which the war provided for personal enrichment by denouncing their compatriots to the German authorities or by speculating in food or other essential commodities.[54]

The post-war legacy of this fraying of the normal structures of daily life was considerable. Crime levels remained high, the black market continued to flourish and among the young the experiences of the war years encouraged a rejection of the constraints of law and of social conventions.[55] The political impact of these developments is more difficult to assess. In some respects, the war forged a more liberated and less reverential society. In other ways, however, it fostered a new individualism, the long-term political impact of which was more conservative than radical in nature. The intense material sufferings of the winter of 1944-1945, with shortages of food and fuel as well as the dangers of German rocket attacks and concern for family members still trapped as prisoners-of-war or conscripted workers within the Reich ensured that for most Belgians their personal interests and those of their families remained dominant.[56] 'L'individualisme alimentaire', as *La Revue Nouvelle* aptly described it, fostered a withdrawal into self-interest which was also reflected in the surge in devotion to the Virgin Mary, a comfort and solace in dangerous times.[57]

Above all, the sufferings of the war years and their aftermath prompted a desire for a return to 'normality'. 'Le Belge moyen', so commentators concurred, sought an end to the disruptions of daily routine and the vexations of self-appointed Resistance leaders, preferring instead a re-establishment of the structures of law and order.[58] The validity of such generalisations is open to question. Observers, especially those anxious to minimise the need for social and political reforms, found in the population what they wished to find. But it would be wrong to dismiss such comments entirely. War did not merely radicalise the population; it also created a more conservative mentality which matched the significantly older, less industrialised and more female demographic structure of the post-war population.[59]

Conclusion

The political stabilisation of Belgium between 1944 and 1945 was at first sight remarkable. Not only was the political order of the pre-war years re-established but, in comparison with neighbouring states, few measures of large-scale social and economic reform were introduced. Belgium, it seemed, remained obstinately locked in a structure which was to remain substantially unaltered until the wide-ranging transformations of the 1960s.

The explanation of this continuity must combine an emphasis on the undoubted importance of certain circumstantial factors with a recognition of the ways in which the war years also served to strengthen the social and political status quo. It is difficult to underestimate the importance of 'accidental' factors such as the rapid liberation of the country, the subsequent continuation of the war, the replacement of the discredited Pierlot régime by the more dynamic Van Acker government and the reinforcement of traditional political cleavages brought about by the dispute surrounding the King. But for this fortuitous constellation of circumstances, it would seem unlikely that the pre-war élite would have been able to reimpose its control so rapidly and so effectively on the life of the country.

Broader influences were, however, also at work in favour of the re-establishment of the pre-war parliamentary régime. The war undermined anti-democratic ideologies of the right and simultaneously provoked a new enthusiasm for the values symbolised by the 1831 Constitution. The socio-economic changes wrought by the war alleviated—though they certainly did not remove—the class antagonisms which had threatened the régime during the 1930s while the disruptions of the war years and the subsequent material difficulties fostered a mood of conservative individualism which helped to define the character of the post-war political order.

The return of pre-war political forces resulted in the marginalization of those calling for substantial change. The *Front de l'Indépendance* never recovered from the confrontation with the government in November 1944. The *Etats-Généraux de la Résistance* which it organised in February 1945 was widely regarded as demonstrating its domination by the Communists and by mid-1945 it had ceased to exercise much political influence.[60] The Communist Party re-entered government with the formation of the Van Acker administration in February 1945 but its attempt to radicalise the government from within while simultaneously posing as the advocate of the demands of the working class proved unsuccessful.[61] Above all, the Communists lacked potential political allies. The fusion of the Communist-influenced trade union grouping, the *Comités de Lutte Syndicale*, with the Socialist-dominated *Fédération Générale du Travail de Belgique-Algemeen Belgisch Vakverbond* merely resulted in the subjugation of the Communist organisation to the reformist objectives of the Socialist leadership.[62]

As early as November 1944, the Socialist Party had chosen to support the Pierlot government against the Communist-influenced Resistance groups and this policy of *de facto* support for the established political order continued to dominate Socialist strategy. Paul-Henri Spaak and other leading figures hoped for a pan-confessional Labour Party on the British model which would include Catholics and Communists, while some Socialist intellectuals—notably those associated with the review *Cahiers Socialistes*—advocated a new socialism which would avoid both Communist 'totalitarianism' and opportunist reformism.[63] These forces for reform were, however, repulsed. Under the presidency of Max Buset, the Socialist Party remained loyal to its quasi-Marxist heritage, symbolised by the decision to retain the 1894 *Déclaration de Quaregnon* as the doctrinal basis of the party, while in practice participating in governments of national unity and seeking to erode the popular base of their traditional Catholic opponents.[64]

The forces for change proved similarly ineffective in Catholic ranks. The War had led to an upsurge in support for Christian Democratic ideas reflected in the creation of a new dissident Catholic grouping, the *Union Démocratique Belge*, and in the emergence of a number of Catholic periodicals, such as *La Revue Nouvelle*, which advocated new forms of Catholic political engagement.[65] Such innovations were not without consequences. The post-war Catholic Party—the PSC-CV—not only had a new name but its initial statement of principles declared its ambition to break away from the defence of Catholic confessional interests in favour of a new openness to believers and non-believers alike. Such hopes were, however, short-lived. Condemned by Cardinal Van Roey as a source of dissension in Catholic ranks, the *Union Démocratique Belge* rapidly disappeared while the PSC-CVP soon became engaged in the clerical-anticlerical struggles provoked by the controversy surrounding the future of Léopold III.[66]

The Liberation was a time of social and political release from the intolerable constraints imposed by the Nazi occupation. Euphoria proved, however, to be an insubstantial basis upon which to build political and social change. The vision offered by the Liberation of a new, more democratic and pluralist Belgian society was short-lived. Within a few months the exaltation of September 1944 had given way to a tense, defensive mentality in which considerations of political, social and personal self-interest had largely supplanted plans for fundamental reform. Far from having proved to be a decisive turning-point, the period of the Liberation served ultimately to reveal the resilience of the existing social and political order.

Discussion

Dr Schöpflin referred to the ethnic differentiation in Belgium: the Flemish were interested in compromise and regionalism, and wanted to find an identity within, but not against Belgium: the failure of this strategy led to the growth of Walloon regionalism and a new Flemish identity in the late 1940s. *Dr Conway* agreed that the lack of any tangible devolution to Flanders put a time bomb under Belgium, although the Flemish question did not really become a live issue until the 1960s. Meanwhile, Belgium benefited from stability.

Notes and References

[1] See Geoffrey Warner's pioneering 1978 article which, exploiting for the first time the British official papers for this period, analysed the crisis of November 1944, demonstrating categorically that the violent clashes between Resistance groups and the police outside parliament should be seen as a product of much wider domestic political conflicts rather than a failed Communist *coup d'état*: G Warner, 'Allies, Government and Resistance: The Belgian Political Crisis of November 1944', *Transactions of the Royal Historical Society* XXVIII (1978), pp 45-60.

[2] See José Gotovitch's magisterial doctoral thesis, which analysed the strategy of the Belgian Communist Party at the moment of Liberation, while Mark van den Wijngaert has traced the gradual reconstruction of the Catholic Party as a major political force: J Gotovitch, *Du rouge au tricolore: Les communistes belges de 1939 a 1944* (Brussels, 1992); M van den Wijngaert, *Onstaam en stichting van de CVP-PSC: De lange weg naar het kerstprogramme* (Brussels and Amsterdam, 1976). See also J Gérard-Libois and J Gotovitch, 'Léopold III: le non-retour', *Courrier hebdomadaire du CRISP* Nos 1010 and 1020-21 (1983); L Huyse and S Dhondt, *La répression des collaborations 1942-1952. Un passé toujours présent* (Brussels, 1993); E Witte, JC Burgelman and P Stouthuysen (eds), *Tussen restauratie en vernieuwing* (Brussels, 1990); D Luyten, *Het korporatisme in België 1886-1944* (Brussels, 1995); P Pasture, 'The April 1944 "Social Pact" in Belgium and its Significance for the Post-War Welfare State', *Journal of Contemporary History* XXVIII (1993), pp 695-714.

[3] Any attempt to define when the Liberation period ended will necessarily be arbitrary. However, for the purposes of this paper I have defined it as having come to an end in the summer of 1945 when the liberation of King Léopold III by Allied troops brought to the fore the so-called *question royale*. This dispute concerning whether Léopold III should return to the throne dominated post-war

Belgian politics and, though its origins clearly lay in the history of the preceding years, any extended consideration of it would clearly be beyond the scope of this article.

4   E Witte and J Craeybeckx, *La Belgique politique de 1830 à nos jours* (Brussels, 1987), p 157.

5   B De Wever, *Greep naar de macht: Vlaams nationalisme en nieuwe orde. Het VNV 1933-1945* (Tielt and Gent, 1994); M Conway, *Collaboration in Belgium: Leon Degrelle and the Rexist Movement 1940-1944* (New Haven and London, 1993).

6   G Vanthemsche, *La Sécurité Sociale* (Brussels, 1994), pp 64-74.

7   *TheTimes,* 9 December 1944, p 6, 'Parliament'. Churchill spoke of 'a *Putsch* organized...in order to throw out the government of M Pierlot'.

8   A J P Taylor, *The Course of German History* (London, 1945), p 68.

9   See for example T Judt (ed), *Resistance and Revolution in Mediterranean Europe* (London and New York, 1989), p 7.

10 J Rens, 'Impressions de mon voyage en Belgique du 16 septembre au 20 octobre 1944' in *Centre de recherches et d'études historiques de la seconde guerre mondiale* (Henceforth CREHSGM), Brussels, PR 5, Doc 387.

11 E Verhoeyen, *La Belgique occupée. De l'an 40 à la libération* (Brussels, 1994), pp 53-117.

12 J Stengers, *Léopold III et le gouvernement: les deux politiques belges de 1940* (Paris-Gembloux, 1980).

13 L Huyse and S Dhondt, *La répression des collaborations,* pp. 281-83; G Eyskens, *De memoires* (Tielt, 1993), p. 128.

14 J Gotovitch, 'L'opinion et le Roi, 1940-1944', *Res Publica* XX (1978), 55-98.

15 J Rens, 'Impressions de mon voyage', p 12, CREHSGM, PR 5, Doc 387.

16 J Rens, ibid, p 15; *La Revue Nouvelle* 1 February 1945, pp 26-7, 'La situation politique'.

17 See for example Belgium and Luxembourg 19 December 1944, PRO, FO 123/581; P Lagrou, 'US Politics of Stabilization in Liberated Europe. The View from the American Embassy in Brussels, 1944-1946', *European History Quarterly,* forthcoming.

18 Erskine to SHAEF April 1945 and Foreign Office to Chargé d'Affaires Brussels 5 May 1945, PRO, FO 123/582.

19 J Wynants, *Verviers libéré* (Verviers, 1984).

20 V Marquet, 'La sauvegarde du port d'Anvers', *Cahiers d'histoire de la seconde guerre mondiale* XIII (1990), pp 149-217.

21 J Wynants, *Verviers libéré,* pp 25 and 56-7; Y Bourdon et al, *La poche de Mons* (Ottignies-Louvain la Neuve, 1994).

22 G Warner, 'Allies, Government and Resistance', *Transactions of the Royal Historical Society* XXVIII (1978), 45-60; Gotovitch, *Du rouge au tricolore,* pp 429-38; G Eyskens, *De memoires,* p 129.

23 eg *Front* 14 January 1945, p 6, 'Comment "ils" ont traité les Soldats du Front Intérieur' and 21 January 1945, p 1, 'Blague dans le coin'.

24 *L'Avenir du Luxembourg* 21-22 November 1944, p 1, 'La leçon du dimanche' and 27-28 November 1944, p 1, 'De quoi s'agit-il?'

25 Gotovitch, *Du rouge au tricolore,* pp 438-41; Belgium and Luxembourg 19 December 1944, PRO, FO 123/581; *L'Avenir du Luxembourg* 29-30 November 1944, p 1, 'L'inévitable malaise'; *La Revue Nouvelle,* 1 February 1945, pp 59-62, 'Le mois politique'.

26 eg *Le Peuple* 28 December 1944, p 1, 'Le Parti Socialiste belge...' and 31 December 1944-1 January 1945, p 1, 'Au Bureau du Parti Socialiste Belge'.

27 *Le Soir,* 31 January 1945, p 2, 'Les grèves dans les mines' and 20 April 1945, pp 1-2, 'Un grave avertissement'.

28 J Wynants, *Verviers libéré,* p 87; J Rens, 'Impressions de mon voyage', pp 10-11, CREHSGM, PR 5, Doc 387; G Eyskens, *De memoires,* pp 153-54; Belgium and Luxembourg 19 December 1944, PRO, FO 123/581.

29 M Van den Wijngaert, *Het beleid van het comité van de secretarissen-generaal in België tijdens de Duitse bezetting* (Brussels, 1975); D Luyten, 'De "opdracht" van de regering aan het Galopin-Komitee op 15 mei 1940', *Bijdragen tot de geschiedenis van de tweede wereldoorlog* XVI (1994), 163-71.

30 *Le Soir,* 10 February 1945, p 2, 'Une lettre pastorale de Mgr. Van Roey': *Le Peuple,* 19 February 1945, p 2, 'Le Conseil National du PSB...'

31 *Le Soir,* 16 February 1945, p 1, 'Le Cabinet Van Acker devant le Parlement'; L Huyse and S. Dhondt, *La répression des collaborations,* pp 288-97.

32 Aveling to Eden, 3 February 1945, PRO, FO 123/581; *Front* 4 February 1945, pp 1-2, 'Le pays en a assez!'; *Le Soir,* 6 February 1945, p 1, 'D'une semaine à l'autre'.

33 *Le Soir,* 3 Feb. 1945, p 1, 'Les ministres socialistes...' and 8 February 1945, pp 1-2, 'Le débat sur la politque du gouvernement'.

34 *Le Soir,* 9 February 1945, p 1, 'Gouvernement d'union nationale...?', 13 February 1945, p 1, 'M Van Acker a constitué...' and 16 February 1945, p 1, 'Le Cabinet Van Acker...'; G Eyskens, *De memoires,* pp 137-43; Knatchbull-Hugessen to Eden, 15 February 1945, PRO, FO 123/582.

35 *Ibid.*

36 *Le Soir,* 4 April 1945, pp 1-2, 'D'une semaine à l'autre', 17 April 1945, p.2, 'M Van Acker parle a Liege', and 20 April 1945, pp 1-2, 'Un grave avertissement'.

37 *Le Courier de l'Escaut,* 12 May 1945, p 1, 'Chronique locale'; *Front* 3 June 1945, p 1, 'De Du Bus de Warnaffe à Léopold III'; *La Revue Nouvelle* July 1945, pp 47-53, 'Chronique politique'; A Molitor, *Souvenirs* (Paris-Gembloux, 1984), pp 209-12.

38 J Gérard-Libois and J Gotovitch, 'Léopold III: le non-retour', *Courrier hebdomadaire du CRISP* No. 1010 (1983).

39 P Theunissen, 1950, *le dénouement de la question royale* (Brussels, 1986).

40 *Cahiers socialistes,* July-August 1945, pp 40-43, 'Au delà de la question royale'.

41 R Vinen, 'The *Parti Républicain de la Liberté* and the Reconstruction of French Conservatism, 1944-1951', *French History* VII (1993), pp 183-204.

42 M Conway, 'Belgium' in T Buchanan and M Conway (eds.), *Political Catholicism in Europe 1918-1960s* (Oxford, 1995).

43 E Verhoeyen, *La Belgique Occupée,* pp. 53-211; J Gérard-Libois and J Gotovitch, *L'an 40* (Brussels, 1971), pp 167-99.

44 G Eyskens, *De memoires,* pp 132-33; *La Revue Nouvelle* 15 March 1945, pp 258-65, 'Le mouvement des idées en Flandre'; *La Cité Nouvelle* 1 March 1945, p 1, 'La pensée politique flamande...'.

45 J Lothe, 'Le mouvement wallon: divisions, fluctuations et prélude à la mutuation' in H Hasquin (Ed.) *La Wallonie. Le Pays et les hommes* (Brussels, 1980) II, 319-32; *La Revue Nouvelle* 15 November 1945, pp 484-90, 'A la rcherche de l'opinion wallonne'.

46 eg *L'Avenir du Luxembourg,* 15-16 November 1944, p 1, 'Etranges échos des principes totalitaires'; V Larock, *La Grande Cause* (Gent, no date), pp 20-23.

47 *Le Soir,* 6 February 1945, p 1, 'D'une semaine à l'autre'.

48 A Molitor, *Souvenirs,* p 202.

49 eg M Conway, 'Building the Christian City: Catholics and Politics in Inter-War Francophone Belgium', *Past and Present* No 128 (August 1990), pp 117-51; D Luyten, 'Politiek corporatisme en de crisis van de liberale ideologie (1920-1944)', *Belgisch Tijdschrift voorNieuwste Geschiedenis* XXIV (1993), pp 175-80.

50 eg *Le Soir*, 4-5 Feb. 1945, p 1, 'La situation politique' and 6 February 1945, p 1, 'D'une semaine à l'autre'.

51 G Vanthemsche, *La Sécurité Sociale*, pp 43-74; P Pasture, 'The April 1944 "Social Pact" in Belgium', *Journal of Contemporary History* XXVIII (1993), 695-700; D Luyten, *Het korporatisme in België 1886-1944*.

52 P Pasture, op cit, 700-10.

53 *L'Avenir du Luxembourg*, 3-4 December 1944, p 2, 'Marché noir et répression' and 25-26 May 1945, p 1, 'Graves incidents...'; *Le Soir*, 24 February 1945, p 2, 'Le revitaillement'.

54 J Rens, 'Impressions de mon voyage', pp 7-10 and 23-28.

55 *Le Soir*, 15 Feb. 1945, p 2, 'La police judiciaire...' and 10 March 1945, p 1, 'Une déclaration de M Van Acker'; *Le Courrier de l'Escaut* 15 April 1945, p 1, 'Chronique locale'.

56 *Le Soir*, 31 January 1945, p 1, 'Les Belges endurent des souffrances terribles'; *The Times*, 5 April 1945, p 5, 'What Belgium Lacks'.

57 *La Revue Nouvelle*, 1 Feb. 1945, pp 63 and 66, 'Le mois politique'; *L'Avenir du Luxembourg* 9-10 Dec 1944, p. 1, 'Le Luxembourg à Marie'; *Le Courrier de l'Escaut* 15 Feb 1945, p 1, 'Mandemant de carême'.

58 *L'Avenir du Luxembourg*, 21-22 Nov 1944, p. 1, 'La leçon du dimanche'; Belgium and Luxembourg 19 Dec 1944, PRO, FO 123/581; *Le Soir*, 10 Feb 1945, 'Une lettre pastorale de Mgr. Van Roey'.

59 For example, the number of people aged 20 to 35 in the population numbered 1,810,249 in 1947 (21% of the total population) compared with 2,095,595 (26% of the total population) in 1930. The population of Wallonia fell by 61,392 between 1930 and 1947 while the population of Flanders increased by 386,250. The percentage of economically active people in the population fell from 46.35% in 1930 to 41.62%in 1947: *Recensement général de la population, de l'industrie et du commerce au 31 décembre 1947* I, 172, V, 11 and VII, 15 (Brussels, 1949, 1951 and 1953).

60 *Front*, 25 Feb. 1945, p. 1, 'Le premier congrès national du FI' and 5 August 1945, p 7, 'Le bilan des activités du FI'; *La Cité Nouvelle* 20 Feb 1945, p 1, 'Le Congrès du Front de l'Indépendence'.

61 Knatchbull-Hugessen to Eden, 21 April 1945 and Minute by Aveling, 28 April 1945, PRO, FO 123/582.

62 I Vansweevelt, 'Poglingen tot progressieve frontvorming in de vakbeweging tijdens de bevrijdingsperiode (1944-1947)' in E Witte *et al. Tussen restauratie en vernieuwing*, pp 149-66; J Gotovitch, *Du rouge au tricolore*, pp 455-56.

63 *Le Soir*, 4 Apr 1945, p 2, 'Une manifestation socialiste à Gand'; *Cahiers Socialistes* Nov. 1944, pp 3-37, 'Manifeste aux Hommes de bonne volonté'.

64 *Cahiers Socialistes*, July-August 1945, pp 43-44, 'La vie politique'; *La Revue Nouvelle* 15 Sept 1945, pp 244-49, 'Situation du socialisme belge'; L Huyse and S Dhondt, *La répression des collaborations*, pp. 292-94.

65 J C Willame, 'L'Union Démocratique Belge', *Courrier hebdomadaire du CRISP* No 743-44 (1976); A Molitor, *Souvenirs*, pp 191-216.

66 *Principes et tendances du Parti Social Chrétien* (Brussels, [1946]); M Conway, 'Belgium' in T Buchanan and M Conway (eds), *Political Catholicism in Europe*.

10 The Synthesis of the Political Order and the Resistance Movement in the Netherlands in 1945[1]

PETER ROMIJN

Restoration and Renewal

In a radio address on June 27 1945, Queen Wilhelmina introduced the new Dutch prime minister to her people. His name was professor Willem Schermerhorn and he was relatively new to politics; before the war he had been chairman of the anti-National Socialist organisation 'Unity Through Democracy'. In 1940, the German authorities had interned him along with a number of other prominent Dutchmen. After his release in 1944, Schermerhorn had been involved in preparations for the establishment of a progressive popular party, intended to provide a new political alternative to the polarised society of the Netherlands. By Liberation day, Schermerhorn's star had risen to such heights that he and the Social Democrat leader Willem Drees received a royal order to form a 'national government of restoration and renewal'. Newly-appointed Dutch prime ministers normally present their governments' plans to the States General, but as the Germans had disbanded parliament in 1940 and it did not reconvene immediately after the Liberation, Schermerhorn presented the main points of his policy over the airwaves. He appealed to the Dutch people for confidence, invoking the language of armed resistance against the Nazis: 'are you prepared [to regard] this government as the Dutch people's central Assault Squad?'[2]

The prime minister added that the enemy would not be truly defeated until the democratic order in the Netherlands regenerated itself. This could only be achieved if restoration and renewal went hand in hand. The main question was whether, in the next ten to fifteen years, the necessary political stability could be created to allow restoration and renewal. It was certain that it would first be necessary to find acceptable solutions to a number of pressing problems. To survive as a nation, it was not enough to repair the extensive material damage done by war: it was equally imperative to restore parliamentary democracy and the constitutional state. At the same time, it was felt that the political and social order needed drastic reform, but politically, innovation was not just a logical consequence of restoration—the two objectives might also clash. 'Renewal' was a slogan rather than a set of well-formulated proposals for reform, and the political form it should take was a controversial issue.

Equally controversial was how to tackle the purge of public institutions and government apparatus. The most drastic proposals argued for the dismantling of not only the National Socialist order, but also the pre-war order. A third issue, which underlay the first two, was the role the Resistance movement would play in politics after the liberation. This was important because influential segments of this pluriform movement believed they represented the political will of the Dutch people.

Politics during the Occupation

It was inconceivable that Dutch politics after the Liberation would pick up exactly where it had left off on May 10, 1940. Despite German oppression, political life had carried on, though in a very different way. The Queen and her government had taken refuge in London in May 1940. The government assumed that the Germans would exercise authority over the Netherlands for the duration of the war in accordance with international law, but this belief was soon dispelled by the extremely ideological and expansionist character of the German Occupation. The Germans tried to advance their own political goals, installing a civil administrative body, the *Reichskommissariat*, which made a radical break with the parliamentary democratic order. Parliament, the Provincial States and the local councils were all forced to cease operation in 1940. Administrative bodies were gradually nazified and turned into instruments to serve the occupiers. The Germans intended to use Dutch production potential in their own war economy. In the long run, the 'Germanic brother people' in the Netherlands was to be incorporated into Hitler's Third Reich. One of the extreme goals of the Nazi racial doctrine, the segregation and deportation of Jews, was also applied to the Netherlands; the end result was genocide.

After only a few months of occupation, it became clear that the German occupiers and the Dutch Nazi party NSB, headed by Anton Mussert, were usurping the role of the Dutch government. There were different reactions to this. In the Netherlands, as elsewhere in Europe, there arose an opportunist movement which was willing to accept German hegemony in Europe in order to make a new start. But as the Occupation became more repressive, turning into tyranny and terror, resistance grew. It began hesitantly, but with time became massive. The Dutch government-in-exile started to identify with this 'home front' and tried to gain its loyalty. At the same time, the leadership in London became more critical of the civil servants who had stayed behind in occupied territory. When the ministers left for London, they had transferred control over their departments to their permanent secretaries, who were instructed to remain at their posts as long as this was in the people's interest. Many civil servants found themselves in an extremely difficult position: in order to prevent nazification, they had to remain in office; but they had to make so many concessions to keep their jobs that from 1941 onwards, they came into conflict with the rising Resistance movement, which held the opinion that leading civil servants should step down to avoid complicity in the repression.

The situation in the occupied Netherlands produced four political spheres of influence, with sometimes overlapping and sometimes conflicting goals: the occupiers and their collaborators who had usurped power; the civil service, hoping against all odds to hold on to as much power as possible; the government-in-exile, which wanted to regain power; and the resistance movement, which wanted to remove the enemy from power. The precariousness of this situation was explained by K J Frederiks, permanent secretary of the Internal Affairs Ministry and one of the most important civil servants in occupied territory. As he wrote in 1945, he had to wage a four-front war: against the Germans, against the NSB, against his government in London and against the resistance movement.[3] Once the enemy had been defeated, the next challenge would be to create some form of consensus among all patriotic forces, which would make possible a joint approach to post-war problems. But how should such the consensus be created? This question dominated political debate both in occupied territory and among the London exiles. A key concept in this debate was 'renewal'.

The concept of renewal was born from a reassessment of pre-war society, a realization of its shortcomings, and the bankruptcy of the old order resulting from the defeat of 1940. Dutch society was deeply polarised, segregated along religious and political lines. Contemporary critics felt that this institutional division had prevented the country from effectively combating the causes and consequences of the economic and social crisis of the 1930s. The German Occupation dealt a heavy blow to the old order. The opportunist movement, which was dominant in the summer of 1940, thought it could use the German occupation to realize its own goals. The most important political formation to sprout from this movement was the Dutch Union ('*Nederlandse Unie*'), which in 1940 grew into a mass movement aimed at national revival. The Union called for breaking down the barriers between the various denominations and between capital and labour: it wanted the state to shape its socio-economic responsibilities in a corporatist fashion. The Dutch Union was controversial—and was to remain so until long after the war— because it worked in consultation with the occupiers. However, when it became apparent in 1941 that the Union's leaders were not prepared to take part in unconditional political collaboration, the *Reichskommissar* banned the Union.

Criticism of the pre-war order also played an important role in the political discourse of the Resistance movement. One issue raised was whether the failure of the pre-war system was responsible for driving so many people to National Socialism. It was agreed that the new, post-war Netherlands must set a new course. These discussions also reverberated in London. The appealing, but vague notion of 'renewal' became an article of faith for all those involved in preparing for post-war politics. It alternately covered constitutional reform, political regrouping, moral rearmament, socialization of the means of production and the introduction of a welfare state—or a mixture of all these.

Problems in the Transitional Period

One of the main policy issues facing the government in London was constitutional reform. The government became deeply divided as to whether it should decide on this matter *before* the Liberation, and hence without consulting Parliament. Queen Wilhelmina was strongly opposed to a return of pre-Occupation political divisions. She and several of her advisers believed that the political system had to be revitalized by drastically strengthening the executive power at the expense of the representative bodies: a royal administration would end all divisions and spearhead a strong restoration policy. The Queen intended to involve Resistance members, whom she considered a 'new nobility'. Critics of these plans argued that the war must be won in order to reestablish constitutional law, not to discard it.

The socialist internal affairs minister, J A W Burger, gave the discussion a new impetus by advocating a compromise, which he called 'synthesis': he proposed to retain all representative bodies elected before the war and to placate the Resistance movement by filing any vacancies with leading Resistance figures. Burger's scheme was an elaboration of what had already been going on ever since the liberation of the Netherlands became a realistic prospect. In consultation with the Allied liberators, the government-in-exile was striving to discipline and subordinate the resistance movement. At the time of the Normandy invasion, an attempt had been made to coordinate Resistance operations nationwide. On government orders, the Grand Advisory Commission of the Resistance Movement (GAC) was formed in occupied territory.

It was soon apparent that there were profound differences of opinion about the role of the Resistance movement after the war. The political centre within the GAC advised 'London' by courier that they saw restoration of the constitutional order as the ultimate goal of the Resistance movement. The activist wing, however, announced that it wished to be involved in the post-war restoration policy, to help build a 'better and purer' nation. This wing consisted of a mixture of radical left and orangist *homines novi*, who were divided by politics but united in their claim of political influence for the Resistance. This corresponded exactly with what Queen Wilhelmina wanted: after all, she saw the Resistance movement as a pillar of the will to renewal. After the liberation of the southern part of the Netherlands in the autumn of 1944, she reconstructed her government incorporating progressive Catholics and technocrats who had been involved in the Resistance movement.

The prime minister-in-exile, P S Gerbrandy, refused to go along with the Queen's drastic plans. The government decided that a state of political emergency would remain in force for some time after the Liberation: there would be an Emergency Parliament, with only limited powers, and the government would steer the normalization of the political process, culminating in the election of new representative bodies. Once this had been accomplished—probably in the course of 1946—final decisions could be made on constitutional reform.

When Schermerhorn and his team of ministers accepted the responsibilities of government, their basic premise was 'synthesis'. It is interesting to note, however, that their policies were immediately aimed at preventing the Resistance movement from cherishing any unfounded illusions. Schermerhorn and his deputy prime minister Drees felt that the largest problem with the Resistance movement in Europe was how to 'direct it, that is to say, to send it to bed, politically speaking'.[4] In the last stages of the occupation, Drees chaired various consultative bodies of the resistance movement and of the political parties, thereby managing to discipline the Resistance movement and secure their cooperation. He had been partly responsible for getting the Resistance movement, including the armed resistance, to accept the authority of the government in London and for dissuading them from political adventurism. After the Liberation, he wanted to consolidate this discipline at all costs.

Political Synthesis

In his radio address of June 1945, Schermerhorn warned the Resistance movement in flattering but clear terms against seeking an independent political role: 'political life is shaped by forces other than those that play a role in the selection of personality and character, courage and steadfastness, that has made itself felt in the resistance movement.'[5] His government's assignment was to guarantee the continuity of the constitution and simultaneously to effect the necessary 'change'. Again the key word was 'synthesis',[6] a concept viewed more widely in the liberated Netherlands than in London. Leading politicians also referred to the need for 'an integration between the Resistance movement and the "loyalists"'.[7] In this case, the proposed synthesis ran along the same lines as what became known in France as the 'sword-and-shield-theory'. Cooperation with the occupying forces had been the shield with which the population was protected, while the Resistance had been the sword with which to fight the enemy. Therefore, it was believed, it should be possible to reconcile the opposing parties soon after the Liberation. Fighting with sword and shield, however, demands coordination of the limbs, and as it turned out, this had been sorely lacking between the resistance movement and the loyalists—both in France and the Netherlands.

This also put the spotlight on the problems surrounding the purge. During the Occupation, the civil service had become the focus of a double crisis of confidence: one between the government-in-exile and the civil servants that had remained loyal to it; and another between the same civil servants and the Resistance movement, who insisted on a thorough purge, according to 'absolute standards of right and wrong'. They wanted to remove from the civil service all Nazis, but also all those civil servants who had been too lenient towards the occupying forces. In the resistance fighters' minds, these weaklings had proven their inadequacy and had to be replaced by courageous, unselfish people who had proven themselves in the resistance.

The government, too, was in favour of a strict purge, but admitted that the civil servants had been in an extremely difficult position. The normalization and reconstruction process was likely to be greatly delayed by too drastic a purge. In order to prevent this, the then internal affairs minister, L J M Beel, opted for the development of a set of procedures which left the final decision about dismissal or disciplinary measures in the hands of the minister himself. In other words, he opted for a purge by internal disciplinary action instead of judgement by an independent, judicial body. This meant that the purge as implemented restored the government's confidence in its civil service, but did not entirely solve the crisis of confidence between civil servants and Resistance fighters—something that remained a latent source of controversy for quite some time.

The government-in-exile in London had decided that, until parliament could convene, the Resistance movement would be allowed to influence government policy by way of its Grand Advisory Commission, but those who had hoped for a more important role were disappointed. The main policy lines had been set by the political parties in May and June of 1945 and laid down in the June 1945 coalition agreement.[8] Decisions had also been taken on the composition of an Emergency Parliament with limited powers which would convene until the 1946 elections. According to a decree issued on 2 August 1945, the composition of the Emergency Parliament would be the same as on 10 May, 1945, except for members that had since resigned, died, or whose membership had been revoked on the grounds of their behaviour during the occupation.[9] The same applied to government institutions at regional and local level. The purging commission was instructed to remove only those members of parliament who had been National Socialists or who had compromised themselves through collaboration with the occupiers.

In applying the 'synthesis concept', the government passed over the demands of the GAC, who had also wanted to settle a score with

144

politicians who had not been actively involved in the Resistance, but were now standing in line to take up their old positions; they were known as the 'politicians in air-raid shelters'.[10] Out of a total of 150 parliamentary seats, there were 40 vacancies. It had also been determined in advance that each political party would keep the number of seats it had before the war; any vacancies were to be filled by party members. Only the NSB vacancies were allotted to some non-party figures from the Resistance movement. The Grand Advisory Commission appealed to the government for more room for former Resistance fighters, but the Schermerhorn government was intent on keeping strict control over the whole process. In a cabinet meeting, Minister Beel stated that the Resistance movement had been 'somewhat spoiled' by the government in London.[11]

The new government regarded the advisory bodies of the Resistance movement as a necessary link in political demobilization. Schermerhorn somewhat smugly called them 'a safety valve', while the former Resistance newspaper *Het Parool* bitterly labelled them 'a dummy'.[12] Those who believed the former Resistance movement should have independent political influence could let off steam in the advisory bodies without ever constituting a real threat. As it turned out in the summer of 1945, however, they were in any case a minority within the Resistance movement, whose protests against a government policy of *faits accomplis* were not very effective. This was partly due to the fact that the most prominent figures in the Resistance movement had shifted their priorities. The Resistance movement was in principle just as pluriform as Dutch society as a whole. Every political and denominational movement had participated in the Resistance (as well as in the collaboration). This experience gave new impetus to national cohesion, a sentiment also expressed in how political leaders referred to the occupation—for example, Schermerhorn's reference to the government as the 'Central Assault Squad'. This cohesion also led many prominent Resistance figures to return to their pre-war political 'roots'. Since democracy had been reinstated, they reasoned, that was the appropriate realm for debate and decision-making.

Before long, any trace of the former substantial political clout of the Resistance movement had disappeared. Even at grass-roots level, it quickly lost its power. Immediately after the liberation, the Military Authority had called on local Resistance fighters to take over administrative duties, including giving advice concerning the purge. The government in the summer of 1945 decided to give absolute priority to a return to normal political relations. This included a quick demobilization of the Military Authority and the Resistance movement. So, at this level too, the former Resistance movement quickly lost any influence it had on the government. Many deserving members of the Resistance stayed in important positions, but they did so in a private capacity rather than as representatives of the former Resistance movement.

Conclusion

April 1946 saw the first post-war elections. The results were a disappointment to the Labour Party, led by Schermerhorn. The new progressive movement obtained nearly the same number of seats as the pre-war Social Democrats and as a result, the old party system remained in place. Nevertheless, the election provided the basis for over ten years of cooperation between the Roman Catholic and Socialist peoples' parties. Reflections on the shortcomings of the pre-war system, together with the experiences of war and occupation inspired the politics of restoration which would turn out to be one of the main foundations of the post-war welfare state.[13] The hotly debated institutional renewal may have never materialized, but Dutch politics proved itself capable of effecting a synthesis between the old system and the need for change. This synthesis has not always been uncontroversial—for example the permanent debate as to the role of the Dutch Union in 1940-1941. On the other hand, it has proved workable and sufficiently stable. The Resistance movement was successfully demobilized, but the political system offered sufficient scope for former Resistance fighters to develop their talents in the social structure, by way of political parties, administrative bodies, government institutions or the business world. The Grand Advisory Commission decided its usefulness had ended when the first elected parliament convened. From then on, all that remained of the Resistance movement were social ties, reunion groups and so forth. The synthesis, therefore, was successful and laid the foundation for the effective politics of reconstruction and moderate renewal.

Discussion

Discussion centred on the role of the Resistance. *Dr Riste* drew comparison between the return from exile of the Dutch and Belgian governments: the Belgian government returning 'at Allied bayonets', the Dutch seemingly stronger and more stable but quickly disappearing. *Dr Romijn* pointed out that when the Dutch government returned they were arrested by the Resistance for not showing proper identification. The Resistance now had to change the motto of their movement from 'sabotage' to 'protection', to achieve a synthesis between the pre-war 'legal' authorities and the 'illegal' Resistance leaders, not all of whom were capable of holding down responsible posts. *Dr Romijn* also agreed with *Dr Hulas*'s contention that purges were an important political instrument in the return to legality in the liberated countries.

Notes and References

1 This paper is based upon a chapter in my book Snel, streng en rechtvaardig. Politiek beleid inzake de bestraffing en reclassering van 'foute' Nederlanders, 1945-1955 (Swift, Severe and Fair Justice. The Problem of Collaboration and Collaborators in Post-War Dutch Politics, 1945-1955) (Houten, 1989).

2 Assault Squads were small armed groups of the Dutch resistance, employed to liberate prisoners, seize ration cards, cover sabotage action etc. For the text of the radio-speech by Schermerhorn on 27 June 1945 see Keessings' Historisch Archief, 1 July 1945, pp 6345-49.

3 K J Frederiks, Op de bres, 1940-1945. Overzicht van de werkzaamheden aan het departement van binnenlandse zaken gedurende de oorlogsjaren. (On the Battlements. A survey of the work done by the Ministry of the Interior during the Occupation) (Den Haag, 1945), p 15.

4 Report of the Parliamentary Commission of Inquiry on Government Policy 1940-1945, vol V, part A, p 859.

5 Radio broadcast by Schermerhorn of June 27 (see note 2).

6 Parliamentary Commission of Inquiry, op cit, p 858.

7 L N Deckers in: Verslag van Handelingen van de Tweede Kamer (Acts of Parliament, Second Chamber), vol 1945, October 11 1945, p 79.

8 Parliamentary Commission of Inquiry, p 881 and see WH Sandberg, Witboek van de Grote Advies Commissie van de Illegaliteit (White papers of the Great Advisory Commission of the Resistance Movement) (Amsterdam, 1950), pp 248-50.

9 Wetsbesluit (Decree) no F 131 of August 2 1945.

10 An editorial in the former resistance paper Trouw ('Faithful') of June 19 1945.

11 Cabinet Minutes, July 3, Algemeen Rijks Archief (General State Archives), The Hague.

12 F J F M Duynstee and J Bosmans, Het kabinet Schermerhorn-Drees 1945-1946 (The Schermerhorn-Drees Government 1945-1955) (Assen, 1977).

13 On the long-term social effects of the occupation see JCH Blom, 'The Second World War and Dutch Society: Continuity and Change' in A C Duke and C A Tanse (eds), Britain and the Netherlands. Papers delivered to the sixth Anglo-Dutch Historical Conference (Den Haag, 1972).

11 The Liberation of Norway

OLAV RISTE

Early Plans

The complete Liberation of Norway from German occupation was the overall aim for everything that the Norwegian Government in exile and the Resistance at home undertook from the very beginning. During the first two years of the war, however, Liberation was not something which could be planned for, at least not in the proper sense. To the extent that Allied military operations on Norwegian territory were envisaged, they were conceived partly as morale boosters for the Allied cause, and partly to show the Soviet ally that the western powers' conduct of the war was not entirely defensive. Also, the Norwegian government needed time to establish a forward-looking relationship with the Allied great powers on the one hand, and with the Resistance leadership at home on the other.[1]

Gradually, during 1942 and 1943, that triangular relationship began to take shape. An initial and very important prerequisite was the establishment, in February 1942, of a Norwegian unified Defence High Command with the primary task of planning for the Liberation. Those plans and preparations had to cover many different aspects. Given Norway's limited manpower resources, it was evident that any military operation for the liberation of Norway would have to be mainly an Allied effort. Norway's contribution, as envisaged by the Defence High Command, would have two main components: first, the Norwegian secret Military Organisation inside the country, which was then estimated at a strength of about thirty thousand men. Sufficiently trained and equipped, these home forces could perform valuable tasks by creating confusion behind the German lines after an Allied landing had taken place. They could also play an important part in maintaining law and order in areas recently liberated. The second component was the Norwegian forces in Britain, reorganized to form liaison staffs attached to all the different staffs and units of the Allied liberation forces, so as to ensure adequate concern for Norwegian interests and satisfactory relations between the allied forces and the civilian population.

In the matter of 'civil affairs', Norway was the first of the allied countries to open negotiations with the British about an agreement covering questions of administration and jurisdiction during Liberation operations. These negotiations in May 1943 led to a preliminary agreement between Norway and Britain on the principles to be followed—an agreement that came to serve as a model for allied agreements with other occupied countries.[2] In the aftermath of this agreement arose the first and only really serious conflict between the government and the leadership of the civilian Resistance movement. Disturbed by rumours of allied plans to install military rule in liberated areas which had been under German occupation, and distrustful of the government's ability to safeguard the sovereign interests of the people in occupied Norway in the face of such plans, Resistance leaders insisted that the administrative system in the period of transition from war to peace should be of their own making rather than a product imported from London. The end result was a compromise, but with the government being the conciliator. Throughout the war, in fact, the government sought to accommodate its policies to the views of the Resistance leadership, sometimes leaning over backwards, but the policy differences were never such as to threaten the fundamental harmony of views and interests between Norway in exile and the home front.

The draft Anglo-Norwegian 'civil affairs' agreement, having survived internal Norwegian skirmishes, got caught up in the autumn of 1943 in disputes between Britain, the Soviet Union and the United States about their respective roles in the planning and execution of the Liberation of Europe. While the British wanted the European Advisory Commission as a joint forum for such problems, and wished to submit the Norwegian Agreement for discussion in that forum as proof of their willingness to take the Russians into their counsel, the Americans objected on the grounds that it would allow too much civilian and political interference in what they saw as essentially military problems.[3]

In addition to this, the Russians were by the end of 1943 casting a steadily bigger shadow over planning for the Liberation of Norway. Repeated indications that Finland was about to withdraw from the war raised the prospect of the Red Army in hot pursuit of the Germans on the Arctic front near Norwegian territory. So far the Norwegian government had had every reason to think that Norway was designated as an area of British operational responsibility. Assumptions about tacit Soviet approval of such an arrangement were largely based on Stalin's statements to Foreign Secretary Eden in December 1941, when Stalin had expressed understanding for possible British desires for naval bases in Norway.[4] When the Norwegian Foreign Minister in the winter of 1944 raised this issue with the British Foreign Office, their answer was to confirm that Norway was assumed to be a British operational sphere, and that there was a great power 'understanding' to this effect. Specific written assurances could not, however, be given.

Rankin C

At the same time the Allied 'Rankin' plans for the Liberation of Europe, as revealed to the Norwegians in the autumn of 1943, appeared highly inadequate and unsatisfactory from the Norwegian point of view. The fact was that since the abandonment of the 'Jupiter' plans Norway had been rapidly becoming a strategic backwater in terms of the allied liberation plans for Europe.[5] In spite of what Churchill had maintained, the Allied staffs could not see Norway as a stepping-stone on the road to the final defeat of Germany, and the liberation of Norway was becoming in military terms a diversion from the main campaign. In the Allied planning organs there was therefore a natural tendency to reduce to a minimum the resources to be spent in such a peripheral theatre. As a result, Norway would have to expect a delay of at least six weeks after a German capitulation before a small Allied force of one British division, one American regiment, plus the Norwegian forces, would arrive to take over control in Norway. Moreover, this small force would be concentrated in South Norway, leaving Northern Norway as practically a no-man's land.

The Norwegian government remonstrated sharply against the inadequate provisions of the plans, both with the British government and with the allied military authorities, partly through Scottish Command which was SHAEF's agent as regards the Liberation of Norway. Weeks passed, however, and in the meantime the prospect of units of the Red Army becoming the first Allied soldiers on Norwegian soil forced the Norwegian government to reconsider its relations with the Soviet Union on an independent basis. The Allied failure to allocate troops for the reconquest of Northern Norway, combined with the lack of concern shown by the British Foreign Office at the prospect of Northern Norway becoming a military vacuum within easy reach of Soviet armed forces, led the Norwegian Government in the spring of 1944 to initiate closer cooperation with the Soviet Union. Besides suggesting the possible transfer of Norwegian forces trained in Sweden to the Northern Russian front for active duty with the Red Army, the Norwegian Foreign Minister, after seeing British attempts to gain Russian approval of the Anglo-Norwegian civil affairs agreement come to nothing, decided to approach the Soviet government about a separate civil affairs agreement in the event that Soviet troops might participate in the liberation of Norway.

In this the Norwegian Government acted against the advice of the British Foreign Office, which feared that such an approach might constitute a virtual invitation to Soviet forces to take part in Liberation operations on Norwegian territory.[6] In the opinion of the Norwegian government, however, the prospect of Russian forces operating in Norway without any agreement regulating their relations with the Norwegian civilian population or Norwegian authorities seemed the more dangerous alternative. The Soviet government, not surprisingly, greatly welcomed the Norwegian approaches, and an agreement, on terms identical with those agreed with the British and American governments, was signed on 16 May 1944.

The Liberation of Northern Norway

It remained to be seen what plans the Russians had as regards Northern Norway. Norwegian initiatives during the summer, for follow-up agreements about such matters as sending a Norwegian military mission to Russia, received no answer. In the meantime, SHAEF had revised its plans to the extent of agreeing to provide at least some forces in the event of the Germans evacuating Northern Norway in order to concentrate their forces elsewhere. In September 1944, after several months of discussions, the western allies finally made up their minds to approach the Soviet Union in regard to eventual coordination of western and Russian plans for the liberation of Northern Norway. The Russian General Staff, however, responded curtly that they had no such plans and that any coordination was therefore out of the question.[7] By that time Finland had withdrawn from the war, and on 7 October Russian forces opened their offensive against the German troops in Northern Russia and Northern Finland. A few days later, during Churchill's visit to Moscow, the Russians finally revealed that their forces were about to enter Northern Norway. Shortly afterwards an improvised token Norwegian force was sent from Britain to Northern Russia, for participation in the liberation of Northern Norway at Russian invitation.

In a curious interlude, the minimal size of this token force became the subject of correspondence between Stalin and Churchill, following a casual remark by Churchill in Moscow to the effect that he would be delighted to assist in the Russian operations in the North. Churchill, who had obviously lost all interest in Norway since the failure of his 'Jupiter' plan, here presented the minimal size of the force as the result of a Norwegian decision.[8] In fact, the Norwegian government throughout the winter made several efforts to persuade the Allies to let larger Norwegian forces go to Northern Norway, possibly assisted by forces of the western allies. The British War Office and Chiefs of Staff, however, refused to commit themselves to a course of action the consequences of which they could not clearly foresee, despite warnings from the British Foreign Office about the likely repercussions on Norwegian attitudes to the western allies, and despite Eisenhower's willingness to assist with logistic support.

There were of course many good reasons for the reluctance of the western allies to get involved in Northern Norway. As far as can be ascertained from internal British and American sources, neither the Foreign Office nor the State Department seemed to believe that the Russians had any ulterior, expansionist aims in Northern Norway that would bring the Russians into conflict with Norwegian sovereignty. With this view the Norwegian government was more or less in agreement, but this conclusion inevitably had a large measure of built-in uncertainty about it. Besides, Russia's aims in the North might suddenly change. This latter point was dramatically demonstrated when in November 1944, during Foreign Minister Trygve Lie's otherwise very friendly and cooperative talks with the Russians in Moscow, Molotov suddenly in the early hours one morning demanded a revision of the Spitsbergen Treaty and the transfer to the Soviet Union of a small island midway between Spitsbergen and Northern Norway.[9]

The crux of the matter was therefore how to insure against unforeseen or unpredictable developments which might endanger Norwegian sovereignty in the North. Here the position of the western Allies throughout was to stay away from the area altogether, and thus to avoid provoking the Russians and giving them even the slightest excuse for entrenching themselves on Norwegian territory. In spite of lingering suspicions that this policy was partly determined by the allied shortage of forces, in particular forces trained to operate in northern latitudes, and partly by a general lack of concern with Norwegian affairs, the Norwegian government had no choice but to acquiesce in this policy. Their suspicions were reinforced, however, when in the spring of 1945 the allies showed themselves uncooperative also in the matter of sending Norwegian forces and supplies to Northern Norway—even after strong indications that the Russians themselves would have welcomed a stronger Norwegian presence in the North. There is no question that the Norwegians felt let down by their western Allies over this issue.

No Western Forces

A potentially more serious blow to relations between Norway and the western Allies, however, was the lack of adequate allied preparations for the Liberation of the whole of Norway. By the end of 1944, although intelligence suggested the presence of between three hundred and four hundred thousand German troops on Norwegian territory— and no one could be sure that they would quietly pack their bags and leave—Allied preparedness to deal with any situation that might arise in Norway had not improved from the spring of 1944: quite the contrary, since the only division specially trained to operate in Norway had in the autumn been transferred to the continent. Thus General Thorne of Scottish Command, designated commander of the Allied land forces Norway, was forced to rely almost exclusively on the Norwegian forces abroad, plus the home forces of the secret Military Organisation in Norway.

Strong Norwegian pressure to alter this state of affairs was to no avail. For some time in 1944 even the British Foreign Office turned a deaf ear to Norwegian requests, and monotonously advised the Chiefs of Staff and SHAEF that their plans for Norway should be framed on strategic grounds only, with no consideration of political factors. Just before Christmas 1944, however, Foreign Secretary Eden took a personal interest in the matter, and had Sir Orme Sargent, the Permanent Under Secretary, write a letter to the Chiefs of Staff which began by saying that 'My Secretary of State is becoming somewhat exercised by the prospects of the situation that may arise in Norway about the time of the German surrender or collapse'. It went on to describe the trouble that so many Germans could cause 'in a mountainous country of under three million inhabitants which will be desperately short of food'.[10]

The letter further stated that 'the Norwegian government are in duty bound to satisfy themselves in the near future that they will have adequate means of controlling the Germans in Norway and maintaining law and order, and it seems to us quite improper to keep them in the dark or mislead them as to the extent and timing of the help we shall be able to give them'. The Foreign Secretary therefore wished the Chiefs of Staff to re-examine the whole matter, and if this should show that it would be impossible for the western allies to 'earmark and prepare an adequate force to go into Norway immediately upon the German collapse, Mr Eden may feel that the Norwegian government must be frankly informed that we are unlikely to be able to provide adequate forces at short notice, in order that they may consider the situation and make up their minds whether to ask the Swedish government for help and what other plans they can make to deal with it'.

Staff re-examinations of the problem, however, provided no solution. General Eisenhower, when asked for his advice, strongly advised against informing the Norwegian government of the present state of the preparations. He would not object to the Norwegian government approaching the Swedes about assistance, but this would have to be done without informing the Swedes about the Allied plans for the Liberation of Norway. At the beginning of February Christopher Warner, head of the Northern Department of the Foreign Office, put on paper his fears that the political consequences of the time-lag between a German capitulation and the entry of Allied forces into Norway 'may be really serious. The population in Norway, who have always rather underestimated the achievements of the western allies during the war, will react very badly if they have a bad time during the time-lag, with lasting effects upon their outlook towards this country, which may affect Norway's attitude to close cooperation and mutual security arrangements after the war.'[11]

Warner's comments were passed on to the Foreign Office's liaison officer to the Chiefs of Staff, but he thought further appeals to the military would be useless. His advice was that in the final hour the Norwegian King and Prime Minister Nygaardsvold might attempt an impassioned appeal to Churchill for immediate action. An appeal to Churchill was in fact attempted, at a lunch which the King of Norway gave for Churchill and Eden on 5 April. But Churchill's replies provided no encouragement, although he seemed to view with favour the prospect of Swedish assistance to Norway.

Swedes to the Rescue?

In fact, from the autumn of 1944 the Norwegian government had already taken a series of initiatives which amounted to a transfer to Sweden of the centre of gravity for Norwegian preparations for the liberation of the home territory. Through the winter of 1944/45 the Norwegian army trained in Sweden provided the mainstay for the reinforcement of Norwegian troops in Northern Norway. Norwegian troops from Sweden were also beginning to seem the only possible way of introducing Norwegian forces into Norway after a German capitulation, without the four to six-week time-lag foreseen for Allied forces from Britain. Even with regard to supplying and in general preparing the home forces for their tasks during the Liberation, Sweden was beginning to seem a more promising avenue than the direct route across the North Sea from Britain.

From the middle of February the Norwegians were no longer alone in fearing that the German army in Norway might refuse to surrender. On 18 February 1945 the British Joint Intelligence Committee completed a study of the situation that might arise if the Russians had taken Berlin and the Western Allies controlled the Ruhr area, whereas large German forces remained in outlying areas such as Norway and Denmark. They thought it not improbable that the Germans in such a case might try to hold out in those areas for as long as possible, clinging to the hope that fissures within the Grand Alliance would open possibilities for negotiations about more favourable armistice terms. The planning staff concluded from this that new plans were needed to meet the eventuality of a liberation of Norway against armed German resistance. After reviewing the possibilities they settled on an assault over land from Sweden as the best alternative—preferably with the assistance of the Swedish army to the extent of four of the six divisions deemed necessary.[12]

The planning staff next asked the Combined Chiefs of Staff to instruct Eisenhower's headquarters to prepare a plan for such an operation, and on 10 April such an order was in fact sent to SHAEF. This development did not come as a surprise to Eisenhower: Already on 14 April he reported to his superiors that operations against Berlin were no longer his top priority. More important were operations to 'clean up' the two areas where the enemy might offer prolonged resistance—Norway, and Southern Germany. On the following day Field-Marshal Montgomery was ordered to redirect his offensive towards Northern Germany, in preparation for a possible assault on Denmark. In a message to Moscow he explained that the supply situation for his Northern Army Group was becoming difficult due to the rapid advance, and besides he had to prepare for operations against possible German 'redoubts' in Austria and Norway.[13]

On 25 April SHAEF submitted an outline plan for the Liberation of Norway against armed German resistance. This envisaged a three-pronged offensive over land from Swedish territory against Oslo, Trondheim, and Narvik. Swedish cooperation would be necessary, and Swedish assistance with troops would be useful, particularly in the North. Staff talks with the Swedes would therefore be necessary.[14] An official request to the Swedish government for such talks was made on 30 April, and accepted on condition that the Allied mission would come in civilian clothes. This was now about to be overtaken by events. The Allied mission was kept in readiness at SHAEF during the armistice negotiations at Rheims, but was finally stood down in the evening of 7 May.

Internal Affairs

If the tasks for the civilian side of Resistance, as the end of the war approached, appeared less dramatic than the challenges for the military, the multitude and size of the problems to be faced was nevertheless considerable. From early on it had been clear that when the war was over, it was no use thinking that Norway could just tear out the pages of its history covering the war, file them in the historian's archives, and resume on the basis of status quo as of March 1940. After a break of five years, normal political and administrative processes could not be re-started at the press of a button. To begin from the top, the question of the postwar government until regular elections could be held could not be solved simply by the return of exiled Ministers. Their relationship to the people under Occupation had inevitably changed, and the Home Front leaders to whom the people were looking for guidance would not simply vanish into thin air on the day of the Liberation. Opinions were also divided about a recall of the Storting. Its role in the negotiations with the Germans in the summer of 1940 had not been a glorious one, and its authority was based on the elections of 1936, which now seemed a hundred years ago.

Similar problems arose at the local government level. Most pre-war county governors, town mayors and councillors had been dismissed by the Occupation régime as hostile to the 'New Order'. Not all of them had subsequently conducted themselves during the Occupation in such a way as to earn the public confidence needed during the difficult transition to normalcy. Often new men would have to be found, and their functions would have to be regulated, but by whom: the Government abroad, or the Resistance leadership at home? By what principles should they be selected and their powers defined: on the democratic basis for which the war had been fought, or with primary regard for authority and efficiency given the extraordinary circumstances?

Last, but not least, the war criminals, traitors and other collaborators would have to be dealt with in an efficient but orderly and just fashion. Popular sentiment after five years of repression was not inclined to tolerate any excessive leniency in the settlement with the collaborators. It was essential to Norway's tradition of democratic justice, however, that the due processes of law should be observed and that no 'night of the long knives' should be allowed to blemish the record of Norwegian post-war democracy.

Such were the problems to which the Government in London and the civilian Resistance leaders turned their attention as the Liberation approached. There were some disagreements, and often prolonged debates by secret courier mail, later supplemented by occasional conferences on neutral soil in Sweden, or even in London. Slowly a complete blueprint for the transition from war to peace evolved.

'Worst Case' Scenarios

In the last winter of the war, uncertainty as to how the war would end in Norway was widespread, and by the early spring of 1945 the Norwegian government and the Home Front leadership both feared that the German occupation might end in catastrophe for Norway. There were good reasons for this fear. The Germans still had about 350,000 *Wehrmacht* soldiers—more than one for every ten Norwegians—well equipped and trained, in the fortified country. The Allies would have no sizable forces to spare before Nazi Germany had been ultimately crushed—and what would happen in the meantime? Would the Nazis in Berlin flee to *Festung Norwegen* and make their last stand there? Or, even if the *Wehrmacht* in Germany capitulated, would the undefeated army in Norway follow suit? Knowledge of widespread German preparations to demolish bridges, roads, ports, hydro-electric stations and telephone exchanges, accompanied by reports of what had actually happened during German withdrawals in the North, underlined the seriousness of the situation. Moreover, even if the *Wehrmacht* in Norway accepted a general capitulation by the German High Command, what would 'Reichskommissar' Terboven and the SS do? Thousands of Norwegians were at the mercy of the Germans in prison camps all over the country.

Faced with such possibilities the Government and the Resistance leaders had to do what could be done to prepare for the worst. The Home Front leadership worked out plans for a national strike to counter an increasing terror, or a situation where the lives of the Norwegian prisoners were endangered. Also, the Norwegian government tried to persuade the Swedes to mobilize and to stand ready to intervene, together with the Norwegian 'police troops', in case the German army in Norway tried to prolong the war. A Swedish mobilization would exert additional pressure on the Germans by demonstrating the futility of a last stand in Norway. Norwegian 'police troops' had been trained in Sweden, and by the spring of 1945 about 13,000 of them were ready as light infantry forces to play their part in the liberation of their country. The roughly 40,000 men of the military Resistance were also prepared to do their part. Even so there was little that the Norwegian forces could do on their own.

The transition from war to peace

To Norwegians at home and abroad the strain of waiting was nearly unbearable during the last days of the war. All over occupied Norway people gathered around 'illegal' radios to follow the end of World War II: Hitler's suicide on 30 April; the surrender of the German forces in the Netherlands, North-western Germany and Denmark on 5 May; and the unconditional surrender on all fronts declared by Dönitz, Hitler's successor, on 7 May. This included Norway, but would the German Commander-in-Chief in Norway, General Böhme, obey his orders?

It must have been a bitter decision. As he himself said, the Germans in Norway were 'undefeated and in possession of their full strength'. On 7 May he had given the troops orders to be on their guard and keep their formations, but not to start any demolitions. Although he still hoped for better conditions for his army than the unconditional surrender imposed elsewhere, he finally accepted the defeat. Through Milorg Eisenhower had sent directives to Böhme telling him how to establish radio contact with SHAEF, Supreme Headquarters Allied Expeditionary Force. This had been done to give Böhme an opportunity to inform the Allies that he was ready for the arrival of the announced military mission, but he waited until the morning of 8 May to do so. In the meantime, the Home Front leadership had been in contact with the German headquarters at Lillehammer concerning the role of Milorg. Would the *Wehrmacht* accept the Home Forces when they now appeared on the scene, or would a peaceful capitulation be endangered by German irritation over this 'civilian army'? Through a *Wehrmacht* officer, who considered it his duty to work for a peaceful surrender, contact with Böhme was established during the night of 7/8 May. After a dramatic series of telephone talks, the *Wehrmacht* was at last convinced that the appearance of Milorg would be a guarantee for law and order, and that it meant no danger to the German troops.

In a curious interlude, in the early afternoon of 8 May an Allied military aircraft landed at Oslo airport and created some confusion. The whole visit turned out to be a private trip by some Allied officers and journalists, who had flown up from Denmark to see how things were going in Norway. Finally, the real Allied armistice commission under the British Brigadier Hilton arrived with a handful of officers, the only Allied 'troops' in Norway at the time, and made contact with the German headquarters. The capitulation that followed was more peaceful than the most optimistic forecasts. The *Wehrmacht* forces were told to withdraw from all fortifications and assemble in certain areas, and to hand in their arms. German discipline did not fail: in a few days they had carried out their orders, although at the time no one could have forced them to do so. Actually, there were hardly any serious or violent incidents during the Liberation of Norway. A few die-hard Nazis, German and Norwegian, committed suicide, 'Reichskommissar' Terboven among them. Other SS and *Gestapo* officers tried to pass for ordinary *Wehrmacht* soldiers, having changed their uniforms, but most of those were later identified.

The lack of serious incidents also facilitated the peaceful transition from Allied to civilian Norwegian authority in the country. Always subject to the overall authority of the SHAEF Mission to Norway, in the person of General Sir Andrew Thorne as Allied Land Commander Norway and Mission Chief, from 7 to 14 May the Resistance Leadership were in control, as duly authorised by the Government in exile. They then handed over to a delegation of Norwegian Cabinet members, which had arrived the previous day together with Crown Prince Olav and General Thorne. The rest of the Government arrived on 31 May, accompanied by elements of the diplomatic corps and personnel from the Ministries. By then General Thorne judged the situation secure enough to set 7 June—five years to the day after he had had to leave the country for Britain and exile—as the date for the King's return and for the formal handing over of civilian administrative authority to the Norwegians.[15]

At the national level, on 14 June the returned Government in exile tendered their resignation. The old Storting was summoned for a brief session so that the constitutional requirement of parliamentary approval of the new government would be observed. It had been widely expected that the Head of the Resistance Leadership, Supreme Court President Paal Berg, would form a national government. But opposition from various political quarters made him give up the attempt, whereupon the chairman of the Labour Party formed an all-party coalition government. Only two members of the exile government, the Ministers of Foreign Affairs and of Defence, were included. 14 October was set as the date for a general election, and in the meantime all the parties joined together to complete a common election platform. Thus, in addition to their separate party programmes for the election, all the parties through that common programme made a joint pledge to carry on into the postwar years the national unity established during the war. Having gained absolute majority in the election the Labour Party could then form a single-party government.

At local government level, where Nazi penetration had gone deeper, persons with impeccable credentials, nominated by the Resistance

Leadership but appointed by the Government, were charged with overseeing the transfer of power, assisted by selected members of the pre-war local councils. Thus the stage could be set for local elections later in the autumn.

The singularly undramatic manner in which the Liberation of Norway was achieved was due to a number of different factors. The discipline of the military resistance, and the self-discipline of the German military, were of crucial importance during the first week after the armistice. The mixture of firmness and diplomatic finesse with which General Thorne handled his command was another vital contribution. On a deeper level, however, the peaceful transition from war and occupation to peace and normalcy was primarily due to the national unity forged during the last two years of the war between the people of Norway, the Resistance Leadership, and the King and his government in exile.

Discussion

Dr Salmon pointed out that for Sweden to allow Norwegian troops to train in Sweden was a very 'unneutral act'. *Sir Michael Howard* added that the origins of this arrangement lay in the 'Health Camps' set up in 1943 for the purposes of physical training for Norwegian troops; when the Swedish government saw which way the war was going, however, they decided to allow Norway to borrow arms, and to use some of them before the liberation.

Professor Bédarida asked why the government in Norway was not held responsible by the people for events during the war, unlike in some countries (eg France, Belgium). *Dr Riste* thought that it might be because the government had both constitutional authority and the confidence of the Allies.

Notes and References

1 For a full treatment of the Norwegian Government's relations with the Allied great powers and with the Resistance see O Riste, *'London-regjeringa': Norge i krigsalliansen 1940-1945*, vols 1-2, Oslo 1973-1978. (One-volume paperback edition 1995.)

2 The best study of the thorny problem of civil affairs in the countries to be liberated, seen from the British side, is FSV Donnison, *Civil Affairs and Military Government: Central Organization and Planning* (HMSO, 1961).

3 American views are reflected in HL Coles and AK Weinberg, *Civil Affairs: Soldiers become Governors* (Washington DC, 1964: in the series, *US Army in World War II: Special Studies*).

4 For the Stalin-Eden conversations in December 1941, see PRO, CAB 66/20, WP(42)8, 5 January 1942.

5   *[Cf the papers on Operation Jupiter by H P Willmott and Einar Grannes in Patrick Salmon (ed), Britain and Norway in the Second World War (HMSO, 1995), pp 97-118.]*

6   PRO, FO 371/40358, U 1190/5/74; U 1368/5/74; U 1575/5/74.

7   PRO, FO 371/43251, N 5345-6/1739/30. CAB 88/29, CCS628/3 with annexes.

8   See in particular PRO, PREM 3/328/8 'Crofter'.

9   The most recent treatment of this incident is S G Holtsmark, *A Soviet Grab for the High North? The USSR, Svalbard, and Northern Norway 1920-1953* (Oslo, 1993: No 7/1993 in the monograph series *Forsvarsstudier,* published by the Norwegian Institute for Defence Studies).

10   PRO, CAB 80/89, COS(44)1047(O).

11   PRO, FO 371/47506, N1714/158/30.

12   PRO, CAB 79/28, JIC(45)55.

13   A D Chandler, Jr (ed), *The Papers of D D Eisenhower: The War Years,* Vol. IV, (London, 1970), pp 2609-12, 2632-3, 2640, 2652.

14   Johns Hopkins University, Eisenhower Mss, Box 52: 'Secret to CCS 25 April 1945'.

15   PRO, FO 371/47511, N6468/158/30.

12 Soviet Policy in Eastern Europe 1944-45: Liberation or Occupation? Documents and Commentary

OLEG A RZHESHEVSKY

The Soviet troops' advance acquired new military-political features in 1944. First, the Red Army crossed the western border of the Soviet Union (the Romanian border on 27 March 1944 and the Polish border on 20 June 1944) and commenced the liberation of Eastern and Central European countries occupied and deprived of their independence by Germany. Second, the Red Army operations began to be coordinated with the actions of the Western Allies who, landing in Normandy in June 1944, opened the long-awaited second front in Europe.

The first coordinated effort was the Red Army's Byelorussian operation of 23 June-28 August 1944, undertaken in agreement with the Allies to support the establishment of the second front. The Red Army mounted an offensive along a 1100 kilometre frontage, routed the German army group Centre, moved 600 kilometres to the west, entered Poland, and approached the borders of Eastern Prussia.

Restoration of the independence of European countries seized by Germany was one of the goals of the Great Patriotic War. In his speech on the radio on 3 July 1941 Iosif Stalin, Chairman of the USSR State Committee for Defence said: 'The goal of the nation-wide Patriotic War against Nazi oppressors is not only to liquidate the threat looming over our country, but also to help all nations of Europe who languish under the German yoke.'[1] In fact, the same goals were proclaimed by President Franklin Roosevelt and Prime Minister Winston Churchill in their Atlantic Charter signed on 14 August 1941, to which the USSR acceded, and later, on a global scale, in the Declaration of the United Nations signed by 26 states in Washington on 1 January 1942.[2]

The Soviet vision of liberated Europe was first delineated in Stalin's conversation with the British Foreign Secretary, Anthony Eden, during the December 1941 Moscow talks and in the secret protocol it was proposed to annex to the Anglo-Soviet treaty. The main objective of that document was the restoration of independence to the European countries occupied by the Nazis, and of the 1941 Soviet frontiers.[3]

Questions relating to the Liberation of European countries from Nazi domination were thoroughly discussed at the Moscow Conference of the Foreign Ministers of Britain, the USSR and the USA (19-30 October 1943), and were being considered by the European Advisory

Commission set up specially for this purpose, which started its work in January 1944 and conducted more than 100 official and unofficial sessions before its dissolution in November 1945. These questions were also the subject of careful examination by the heads of the governments of Great Britain, the USSR and the USA at the Teheran (1943), Yalta, and Potsdam (1945) conferences.

There were no essential points of difference between the Great Powers in matters pertaining to their mutual determination to liberate the countries captured by the aggressor. However, at each meeting, as was quite natural, discussion of the liberation of the occupied countries was directly or indirectly linked to their post-war organisation and political orientation.

To my mind, Churchill's visit to Moscow in October 1944 and his conversations with Stalin were of fundamental importance in this matter. As is known, in the course of these conversations Churchill proposed to delimit the spheres of influence in Europe between the USSR and Great Britain. It should be said that Stalin's agreement to take Churchill's proposal as a basis has hitherto been denied in Soviet official literature, but the Soviet record of the conversation now available, and printed below, does not substantiate Stalin's disagreement.[4]

Document[5]

Record of Conversation Between Comrade I V Stalin and Prime Minister W S Churchill

Secret   October 9, 1944, 10 p.m.

Present:
Mr Eden, Sir A Clark Kerr, and Major Birse on the British side;
Comrades Molotov and Pavlov on the Soviet side.

At the beginning of the conversation Churchill presents a signed portrait of himself to Comrade Stalin.
Comrade Stalin accepts the present and thanks Churchill.
Opening the conversation Churchill says that it is necessary to clear out a number of questions, and since this is easier to do in private conversations, he, Churchill came here to Moscow. Private conversations allow to define what this or that party wishes and find solutions to the questions of interest to both parties. Personal conversations will save both parties from telegraph correspondence. The most difficult problem is the problem of Poland. Both parties must try to come to an agreement on a common policy toward Poland. It is no good that both parties have their 'fighting cocks'.

162

Comrade Stalin remarks that it would be difficult to do without cocks. The cocks give the 'rise and shine' call for instance.

Churchill agrees with this remark. He says that the question of the Soviet-Polish frontier is settled. They might look at the map again.

Comrade Stalin says that if the question of the frontier on the basis of the Curzon Line is decided, the task is facilitated.

Churchill replies that such are the views of the British Government.

Comrade Stalin remarks that the Poles understand it differently.

Churchill replies that when all allies meet at the table of an armistice conference—it is easier for the Americans to solve questions at an armistice conference; in this case the President can take decisions himself, while in case of a peace conference the President has to consult the Senate—he, Churchill, will support the Russians' claim for the frontier line shown to him in Teheran. He, Churchill, will state that this frontier is fair and essential to guarantee the security and the future of Russia. He, Churchill, is positive that the Americans will support him. Should General Sosnkowski disagree, it would not be of great significance provided Great Britain and the United States consider this decision correct. The British tried for several months to drive General Sosnkowski out. As for General Bor-Komorowski, now the Germans will take care of him.

Comrade Stalin says that the Poles are presently left without a commander.

Churchill replies that they have one colourless man. He, Churchill, wants to ask Marshal Stalin a question. Would Marshal Stalin find it appropriate for the British to bring Mikolajczyk, Romer and Grabski to Moscow. They are at the moment on board a plane in Cairo, tied.[6] They could be brought to Moscow in 36 hours. Should this be done? The British would like to settle this question.

Comrade Stalin asks whether the Poles have an authority to settle the question with the Polish Committee for National Liberation.

Churchill replies he is certain that the Poles in London want to come to terms with the Polish Committee. But the British and Soviet sides could force them all to come to an agreement here in Moscow.

Comrade Stalin replies he does not object against Mikolajczyk, Romer and Grabski coming to Moscow. Let us make one more attempt, Comrade Stalin says. We shall have to connect Mikolajczyk, Romer and Grabski with the representatives of the Polish Committee for National Liberation. He, Comrade Stalin, asks Churchill to keep it in mind that the Polish Committee has an army now, and not a bad army at that, which makes a serious force.

Churchill says that a brave Polish corps fights in Italy on the side of the Allies. There are Polish troops in France as well. Polish combatants have many friends in Britain. The Poles are good and brave people. The trouble is their political leaders are irrational. The trouble is, where two Poles meet there is always a quarrel.

Comrade Stalin remarks that if a Pole is alone, he starts quarrelling with himself.

Churchill says that the four have more chances to unite the Poles. We can put pressure on them—the British, on their Poles, and the Russians, on theirs.

Comrade Stalin says, let both sides try to do that.

Churchill says he would like also to touch upon some questions related to armistice with the satellites whom Germany forced to enter the war but who did not distinguish themselves in the war. Some of these satellites are much disliked by the British, others, by the Russians. He, Churchill, suggests that Eden and Molotov discuss these matters should Marshal Stalin agree.

Comrade Stalin agrees.

Churchill says that the question of Hungary is very important. He, Churchill, hopes that the Soviet troops will soon be in Budapest.

Comrade Stalin replies this is quite possible.

Churchill says there are two countries of particular interest to Britain. First, Greece. He, Churchill, is not worried much about Roumania. Roumania, to a great extent, is the Russians' affair, and the agreement with Roumania proposed by the Soviet Government was acknowledged by the British Government as quite moderate and testifying to the great political wisdom of the Soviet Government. No doubt, this agreement will contribute to world peace. As for Greece however, the British Government has much interest in this country. The British Government hopes that Britain will be allowed to have the right of deciding vote in Greek affairs, the same as the Soviet Union in Roumania. Certainly, Britain and the Soviet Union will keep contact both in Greek and Roumanian affairs.

Comrade Stalin replies that he understands that Britain lost much because the Mediterranean routes were intercepted by the Germans. He, Comrade Stalin, understands that if the security of these routes is not safeguarded, Great Britain will suffer great damage. Greece is an important point to safeguard these routes. He, Comrade Stalin, agrees that Britain should have the right of deciding vote in Greece.

Churchill says he has prepared a table. It would be probably better to expound the idea expressed in the table in diplomatic language because the Americans, for instance, including the President, will be shocked by the division of Europe into spheres of influence.

Comrade Stalin says that, apropos, he would like to speak about Roosevelt. He, Comrade Stalin, received a message from Roosevelt in which Roosevelt says about his desire that Ambassador Harriman should be present as an observer at the conversations between Churchill and himself, Comrade Stalin. Second, the President asks to consider the decisions to be made in the course of the conversations as preliminary. He, Comrade Stalin, would like to ask Churchill what he thinks about the President's requests.

Churchill says he informed Roosevelt that he would welcome Harriman's presence at some meetings with Marshal Stalin. But he, Churchill, thinks this should not affect private conversations between Churchill and Stalin or Molotov and Eden. In any case, he, Churchill, will keep the President informed of all matters. But he, Churchill, must say that being an observer, Harriman is not in the same position as he, Churchill, and Marshal Stalin.

<u>Comrade Stalin</u> *replies he would like to note that he sent a reply to Roosevelt saying that he does not know what questions will be discussed with Churchill. He, Comrade Stalin, has an impression from the message that the President is alarmed. He, Comrade Stalin, must say that he does not like the message because the President demands too many rights for himself and leaves too few rights to Britain and the Soviet Union which are tied by the treaty of mutual assistance. There is no such treaty of mutual assistance between the United States and the Soviet Union. However, he, Comrade Stalin, does not object against Harriman attending an official meeting that will not be of private character; he, Comrade Stalin, thinks that Churchill and himself will decide when to invite Harriman.*

<u>Churchill</u> *says he would now touch upon the Dumbarton Oaks Conference. The President did not want this question to be discussed in Moscow, especially now, and preferred it to be decided at the meeting of the three. Of course, we should keep in mind, Churchill says, that the President thinks about the elections that will soon be held in the United States.*

<u>Churchill</u> *says it would be right to acknowledge that at first the British were inclined to accept the American point of view. But now the British see a greater measure of justice in the proposal of the other side. Indeed, suppose China demands from the British Empire to abandon Hong Kong and, when this question is discussed, Britain and China are asked to leave and close the door behind them while Russia and the United States discuss this question—Britain would hardly like it. On the other side, suppose Argentina has some conflict with the United States—the United States would hardly like it if the American representatives are to leave the conference room while China, Russia and Britain are making decisions about Argentina. Naturally, all that he, Churchill, says is not for the press. It would be most reasonable to wait for the meeting of the heads of the three governments. He, Churchill, thinks that Marshal Stalin will confirm, if need be, that this question was not discussed in Moscow.*

<u>Comrade Stalin</u> *says, smiling, that he will certainly do.*

<u>Churchill</u> *says he has prepared a rather dirty and rough document showing the delimitation of Soviet and British influence in Roumania, Greece, Yugoslavia, and Bulgaria. He has made this table to show how the British see this matter. The Americans will be shocked at seeing this document. But Marshal Stalin is a realist and he, Churchill, is not distinguished by sentimentality, while Eden is an absolutely wicked man. He, Churchill, did not show this document to the British Cabinet, but the British Cabinet usually consent to what he, Churchill, and Eden suggest. As for the Parliament, the Cabinet has a majority in the Parliament, and even if this document is shown to the Parliament, they will understand nothing in it.*[7]

<u>Comrade Stalin</u> *says that the 25% stipulated for Britain in Bulgaria does not harmonise with the other figures in the table. He, Comrade*

Stalin, thinks that amendments should be made, namely, to stipulate 90% for the Soviet Union in Bulgaria, and 10% for Britain.

Churchill says that the Bulgarians grossly offended the British. In the past war, they behaved badly in respect to the British by attacking Roumania. In this war, the Bulgarians were very cruel in respect to the Yugoslavs and Greeks. He, Churchill, cannot allow the Bulgarians to sit at the same table with the Allies after all this.

Comrade Stalin says that surely Bulgaria must be punished.

Eden says that the British are spectators in Roumania, but they would like to be a little more than spectators in Bulgaria.

Molotov asks whether the Turkish question pertains to this issue.

He, Churchill, has not touched upon the Turkish question, he only wants to show what the British have in mind. He, Churchill, is very glad at how near the both parties' points of view appear to be. He thinks they might meet again and settle this question finally.

Comrade Stalin says that since the question of Turkey arose, he must say that by the Montreux Convention Turkey has all rights to the Straits, while the Soviet Union has very few rights. By the Montreux Convention the Soviet Union has as many rights as the Japanese Emperor. He, Comrade Stalin, thinks it is necessary to discuss the revision of the Montreux Convention because it is in complete disagreement with the current situation.

Churchill says that by now Turkey has lost all rights to enter the war. She did not enter the war earlier because of fear of Germany as she did not have modern weapons. Besides, the Turks are not only unskilled in handling modern weapons, but they do not have sufficient numbers of trained troops.

Comrade Stalin observes that the Turks have concentrated 26 divisions in Thrace. It is unclear however against whom they have concentrated these divisions.

Churchill says that the Turks feared the Bulgarians because the Germans gave the Bulgarians the weapons they captured from the French. Turkey learned to fear Bulgaria in this war. Looking into the future he, Churchill, can say that the British policy does not consist in preventing Russia's access to warm seas and the great world oceans. On the contrary, the British believe that this objective makes an element of the Russian-British friendship. The policies of Disraeli and Curzon do not exist any longer. What changes, in the opinion of Marshal Stalin, should be introduced to the Montreux Convention?

Comrade Stalin replies that he cannot say what changes are needed and what to replace the Montreux Convention with, but he feels that the Convention does not correspond to the present-day situation and is spearheaded against Russia. He, Comrade Stalin, would like to ask Churchill whether he agrees in principle that the Convention should be changed. Indeed, how can such a big country as the Soviet Union live in apprehension that such a small country as Turkey can close the Straits and put in question our export, import, and defence? He, Comrade Stalin, does not want to impair Turkey's sovereignty, but such a situation when Turkey holds Soviet trade and shipping by the throat cannot be tolerated.

Churchill replies that in principle he shares this opinion of Marshal Stalin, but thinks that this question should be better fixed on paper a little later; otherwise Turkey might get frightened and imagine that she is demanded to cede Istanbul. Churchill is of the opinion that Russia should get access to the Mediterranean both for the naval and merchant ships. We hope, Churchill says, that we shall work on this problem with the Soviet Union amicably, but we would like to approach this problem in cautious steps so as not to frighten Turkey. Suppose the Soviet Union and Britain sit together to work out an armistice agreement, and the Russians ask the British to consent to the access to the Mediterranean by Soviet naval and merchant ships—he, Churchill, would say that Great Britain does not object.

Comrade Stalin says he is not pressing Churchill, but he would like to let him know that this problem stands before the Soviet Union. He, Comrade Stalin, would like Churchill to acknowledge that the statement of this problem is legitimate.

Churchill replies that he not only agrees with this in principle, but he also thinks that the Soviet Union should take the initiative, declare its opinion that the Convention should be changed, and inform the United States of the Soviet position in this matter. On its part, the British Government finds the Soviet claims justified in principle and morally grounded.

Churchill says that the approach to the Balkans as he has just explained it would prevent a civil war that might break out there because of different ideologies. He, Churchill, maintains that the Allies cannot allow the Balkan peoples to have a small civil war after the Allies finish the Great War. Strife in the Balkans ought to be prevented by the authority and power of the three Great Powers. We must tell the Balkan peoples, Churchill says, that these matters have been decided by the three Powers and that they should be guided by the advice of the three Great Powers. Britain is not going to impose a king upon Yugoslavia, Greece, or Italy, but at the same time Britain believes that the nations must have the right to a plebiscite in peace time. Whichever the nations choose eventually—the monarchy or other system—they must have an opportunity to express their will freely. He, Churchill, would like to ask Marshal Stalin whether he has objections against cooperation with a king if the king is elected by the people.

Comrade Stalin replies he has no objections.

Churchill says that the British hope that power in northern Italy will be exercised under the direction of the allied army. The British do not intend to replace the Italian king, but they do not want a civil war in Italy after or before the allied forces leave Italy. It is desirable, Churchill says, that the Soviet Government should contain the Italian communists' activity so that the Italian communists would not stir Italy and cause agitation in the country. Everything can be settled in a democratic way, but we, Churchill says, do not want disorders in

Italy, where the allied forces stay, because disorders can lead even to clashes with the troops. Roosevelt regards the Italians with favour; he, Churchill, does not like it though. The thing is there are many Italian voters in the State of New York.

Comrade Stalin says it is difficult for him to exert influence on the Italian communists because he does not know the national situation in Italy. Besides, there are no Soviet troops in Italy, in difference to Bulgaria where there are Soviet troops and where we can order the communists not to do this or that. If he, Comrade Stalin, starts advising Ercoli, Ercoli might tell him to go to hell because he, Comrade Stalin is absolutely ignorant of the national situation in Italy. It was quite differently when Ercoli was in Moscow and he could converse with him. He, Comrade Stalin, can only say that Ercoli is a wise man and he will not take adventuristic actions.

Churchill says, however it may be, let the Italian communists not disturb Italy.

Comrade Stalin says the figure for Bulgaria should be corrected.

Churchill replies that, after all, he does not care a damn about Bulgaria and that perhaps Eden and Molotov might discuss this matter between themselves... [8]

Commentary

At that time the concept of 'spheres of influence' meant nothing more than the 'right' of Great Britain and the Soviet Union to determine their relations and occupation policy in their national interests, in a form which was understood by the leaders of the two countries. Although no document on the division of the 'spheres of influence' was signed officially, the agreement reached was implemented to a great extent, as can be seen from the example of ensuing events in Greece where the communist forces were already predominant in 1944 but where, nevertheless, a Western type of political system was established by force of arms. It can be assumed that the achieved division of the 'spheres of influence' stimulated plans for the establishment of pro-Soviet systems in the East European countries, and reanimated the slogan of world revolution which in the 1930s had given way to the maintenance of national security in Soviet foreign and military policy.

In November 1944 Ivan Maisky, former Soviet Ambassador to Great Britain and then Deputy People's Commissar for Foreign Affairs, developed his own conception of the post-war order in Europe. His view was based on the premise that in thirty or fifty years' time the European continent would be socialist. In the transitional period, according to the document prepared by Maisky, the USSR would take an interest in the state systems of hostile countries 'as well as presently occupied by the enemy countries', which should be based 'on the principles of wide democracy in the spirit of the national front ideas'.

'There is ground to believe,' the document further stated, 'that these principles will be implemented quite fully without any pressure from the outside in such countries as Norway, Denmark, Holland, Belgium, France, and Czechoslovakia. Things are different with such countries as Germany, Italy, Japan, Hungary, Roumania, Finland, Bulgaria, Poland, Yugoslavia, Greece, and Albania; it is possible that to create truly democratic regimes there, it will be necessary to put to action various methods of intervention from the outside, ie, including that on the part of the USSR, the USA, and Britain.' In the chapter entitled 'Main Europe' it stated: 'The most advantageous situation for us would be the existence in Europe after the war of only one mighty continental Power—the USSR, and one mighty maritime Power—Britain.'

Maisky's approach to the problem of the Pacific theatre of military operations is worth mentioning as well: 'The USSR is not interested in unleashing a war with Japan, but it is very interested in the military crash of Japan. From the point of view of the USSR it would be more important to give the 'honour' of routing Japan to the British and the Americans. This would save us human and material losses and at the same time make the USA and Great Britain to cough up some of their human and material resources. In this way the imperialist ardour of the USA would be somewhat cooled in the post-war epoch... This would also be our revenge for the position of the British and the Americans in the question of the second front....'

At the same time, Maisky arrived at the conclusion that the greatest threat to peace and tranquillity might come from a premature revolution. 'If the first post-war period leads to the unleashing of proletarian revolution in Europe, the relations between the USSR on the one side, and the USA and Britain on the other will have to assume tense or even sharp character. If, however, a proletarian revolution does not take place in Europe in the nearest future, there are no grounds to expect that relations between the USSR on the one side, and the USA and Britain on the other will be bad.'[9] It is important to underline that the idea of the export of revolution was not mentioned by Maisky: in the documents of the People's Commissariat for Foreign Affairs relating to the post-war period the state security interests of the USSR occupy the primary place.

Another important document defining the policy of the USSR and Western Allies is the well-known 'Declaration on Liberated Europe' adopted at the Yalta conference of the Big Three, which reflected the desire to jointly build post-war Europe on democratic principles.[10] Where and when did the downhill slide begin and latent confrontation begin to grow into a 'cold war'?

Without doubt, contradictions between the USSR and Western Allies on the Polish question triggered the cold war. After the death of the

Polish Prime Minister Sikorski and the shooting of Polish prisoners of war in Katyn, which became known in 1943, Soviet relations with the Polish Government in exile, despite Churchill's efforts, became irreparably critical. The roots of conflict between the USSR and Poland lie deep in the past, and in the Civil War in the USSR (Pilsudski's army drive on Kiev and Tukhachevsky's counter-offensive on Warsaw in 1920), and the death of 40,000 Soviet prisoners of war in Poland; Poland's participation in the division of Czechoslovakia (1938), and her refusal to let Soviet troops pass through Polish territory in the event of German aggression (which was one of the reasons for the abortive British-French-Soviet negotiations in Moscow in 1939); and much more.

The Soviet Government therefore resolutely opposed the restoration of the former Polish régime, hostile to the USSR, and sought the transfer of power to friendly forces, which led to the aggravation of relations between the USSR and Western Allies. The USA took retaliatory action, discontinuing basic lend-lease supplies to the USSR unilaterally in May 1945; then came the atomic bomb and Churchill's speech in Fulton in the presence of President Truman (1946), and thus the slide into cold war became irreversible.

Everything that happened after the Second World War should be viewed in the context of the cold war, which brought the world to the brink of nuclear conflagration more than once. Many of the Soviet Union's policies and actions were by no means based upon imperialism or occupation. Between 1945 and 1948 the USSR, in common with the USA and Britain, greatly reduced its military forces (from 11.3 to 2.8 million), as well as military expenditure (by 65%). In September 1945 Soviet troops were withdrawn from Northern Norway; in November, from Czechoslovakia; in April 1946, from the Danish island of Bornholm; in May, from Manchuria and Northern Iran; in December 1947, from Bulgaria, and in late 1948, from Korea. Soviet army groups in Germany, Poland, and Roumania, as well as in Porkkala Udd in Finland and Port Arthur in China were reduced considerably.

It should be emphasised, however, that the goal of liberating Europe from Hitlerite tyranny was common to the Western Allies and the USSR, and this goal was achieved through the mutual efforts of the Great Powers and other countries of the anti-Hitler coalition, with active support from the Resistance movement. During the Second World War the Red Army liberated completely or partially 12 European and Asian countries at the cost of a million servicemen killed in action, of which more than 600,000 perished at the liberation of Poland. The armies of the Western Allies drove the Italian and German invaders from the territories of Eastern and Northern Africa and began the Liberation of Europe already in 1943; they made the decisive contribution to the defeat of Japan and the Liberation of Asian and Pacific countries occupied by the Japanese aggressors.

It is the duty of historians to hold on to the truth about those events and convey it to the younger generations.

Discussion

Presenting his paper, *Professor Rzheshevsky* expressed the view that the most difficult of all post-war problems was the determination of the political orientation of liberated countries in a way which would take account of the interests of the Great Powers. The Percentage Agreement formed the keystone for some time of Anglo-Soviet orientation in Europe, as the concept of 'spheres of influence' took into account each power's national interests at that time.

Sir Frank Roberts challenged the view that differences over Poland caused the slide into Cold War. He argued that differing views on economic factors (to which Bevin attached the highest importance) formed the breeding ground for the Cold War. *Sir Michael Howard* agreed that the Cold War emerged from differences over Germany, not Poland. *Professor Rzheshevsky* explained that Soviet policy was dominated by the need to eliminate the German military threat and the need to extract as much as possible from German resources: fear of a resurgent Germany and the prospect of another war necessitated the establishment of pro-Soviet governments in vulnerable territories. This was not straightforward imperialism, but a multifaceted policy.

Dr Hanak maintained that Stalin's policies were imperialist, and *Mr Cviic* agreed: otherwise, why was the Soviet Union interested in the former Italian colonies such as Tripolitania? *Professor Rzheshevsky* responded that all the Big Three were imperialist: if the Italian colonies were 'up for grabs', why should not the Soviet Union have one?

Dr Romijn referred to local arrangements made by SHAEF for the transitional administration of occupied territories, and asked whether the Soviet military authorities had made any similar arrangements. *Professor Rzheshevsky* replied that while administration at the highest level was dealt by the Control Commissions, the local Kommendatura provided effective links between military and civil authorities. He agreed, however, that where Soviet troops remained, the power lay with them. *Dr Deighton*, referring to Germany, pointed out that Soviet-Western cooperation worked well at lower levels: *Professor Rzheshevsky* agreed that military commanders, allies in the war, worked well together. The problems lay higher up, where politics were involved.

Notes and References

1 I Stalin, *O Velikoi Otechestvennoi voine Sovetskogo Soyuzal* (On the Great Patriotic War of the Soviet Union) (Moscow, 1952), p 16.

2   The Declaration was signed by the representatives of Great Britain, the USSR, the USA, China, Austria, Belgium, Canada, Costa Rica, Cuba, Czechoslovakia, the Dominican Republic, Greece, Guatemala, Haiti, Honduras, Italy, Luxembourg, the Netherlands, New Zealand, Nicaragua, Norway, Panama, Poland, El Salvador, South-African Union, and Yugoslavia. [*See Woodward, op cit, vol ii, pp 210-19.*]

3   Archives of the President of the Russian Federation (APRF), 45/1/279, pp 10-21. [*Cf Woodward, ibid, pp 220-54.*]

4   The 'official' interpretation read: 'During negotiations with Churchill the Soviet Government declined the British proposal on the "division of influence" between Britain and the USSR in Yugoslavia and other Balkan countries. Churchill's attempt to prove the opposite wise after the event in his memoirs contradicts the truth.' (*Istoria vneshnei politiki SSSR. 1917-1980* (History of the Foreign Policy of the USSR), 2 vols, Vol 1: 1917-1945, Moscow, 1980), pp 459-60. In his earlier works the present author also followed this interpretation. Cf Woodward, op cit, vol iii, pp 150-3.

5   The translation which follows has been supplied by Professor Rzheshevsky and is reproduced verbatim.

6   [*The Polish Ministers were in London, where Mr Churchill sent the following message at 11.20 pm on 9 October: 'Marshal Stalin agreed at our conversations tonight that Polish Prime Minister, Foreign Secretary and M. Grabski should come to Moscow at once to join in conversations during our visit. Weather permitting party should leave night of October 9th/October 10th for Cairo, and come on immediately by shortest route to Moscow.' (C 13868/8/55. FO 371 39413) They left London on 10 October.*]

7   The delimitation proposed by Churchill appeared as follows. Roumania: Russia - 90%, others - 10%; Greece: Britain (in agreement with the USA) - 90%, Russia - 10%; Yugoslavia: 50:50%; Hungary: 50:50%; Bulgaria: Russia - 75%, others - 25%. (Martin Gilbert, *Winston S Churchill*, vol VII: *Road to Victory. 1941-1945* (London, 1986), p 993).

8   APRF, 45/1/282, pp 3-16.

9   Archives of the Foreign Policy of the Russian Federation, 06/6/168/16, p 26ff. For more details see A M Filitov, '*V Komissiyakh Narkomindela...*' (In the Commissions of the People's Commissariat for Foreign Affairs) in the book, *Vtoraya mirovaya voina. Aktualnye problemy* (The Second World War. Topical Issues), Moscow, 1995, pp 54-71.

10   [*The Declaration on Liberated Europe was issued as Article V of the Report of the Yalta Conference (Cmd 6598 of 1945), printed in BFSP, vol 151, pp 221-9.*]

13 Two Armies — Two Occupations: Hungary 1944-1945

PETER SIPOS

I The German Occupation

Until 19 March 1944, Hungary enjoyed a unique position in German-occupied Europe. Apart from the neutral states, it was the only country where no foreign troops were stationed. The forces of the anti-fascist coalition were still fighting hundreds of kilometres from the Hungarian frontiers in all directions. For a long time Hungary's ally, Germany, saw no reason to station troops there, or to occupy the country explicitly, as for all practical purposes the Hungarian leadership satisfied two major German demands: the country's communications network secured the *Wehrmacht*'s passage toward the southern wing of the Eastern front; and Hungarian industry, mining and agriculture were integrated into German war economy. In 1943 the Hungarian military contribution decreased in comparison to former years, but no major significance was attached to this in Berlin. For Hitler, it was far more important to try and extend the policy of *Endlösung* into Hungary, though for the time being he settled for the 'Jewish Laws', urging the Hungarians through diplomatic channels to follow the German model in policy towards the Jews.

Before 1943 not one German document even referred to Hungary's occupation. The German Führer and Chancellor was well aware that nothing could happen in Hungary without the agreement of the Regent, Miklós Horthy. By 1943, however, he also knew that Horthy was not the same loyal ally of earlier years. He decided, therefore, to instil a new element into the Horthy-Hitler relationship: to keep Horthy in the Axis by force, and above all to make him dismiss the Miklós Kállay government, which was gradually building relations with the Anglo-Americans, and replace it with a new, completely reliable government fully loyal to Germany. The occupation was first introduced in September 1943 with Plan Margarethe: the realization of this plan formed the centre of gravity of pressure. When Horthy met Hitler at Klessheim on 18 March 1944 he refused to consent formally to the occupation, but undertook to remain in office and to continue functioning as Regent.

On 19 March 1944 the *Wehrmacht* occupied Hungary without any resistance. The situation was well described by an anecdote: 'A diplomat asked one of the German generals how long it would take him to occupy Hungary. The answer: 24 hours. And if they resist? In that case 12 hours would be sufficient. How come? There would be no welcome speeches.'

Horthy vetoed the Germans' first choice as Prime Minister, Béla Imrédy, the leader of the fascist Hungarian Rejuvenation Party, and opted for Döme Sztójay, Hungary's ambassador in Berlin. He wished to appoint an acting bureaucratic government led by the general-diplomat. However, he gave up his plan in response to German threats and on 23 March approved a political government which met all constitutional criteria. The government's traditional oath expressed legal continuity. The behaviour of the Hungarian public administrative apparatus and armed forces was determined by the fact that the Regent's approval of various developments expressed unambiguously the Regent's confidence in the government.

This solution was exceedingly advantageous for the Germans. Hitler told the Romanian leader, Marshal Antonescu at their 23 May meeting at Klessheim: 'The advantage that the existence of such a government...gives is, that the Hungarians keep on operating their own public administration in the country and there is no need for Germany as an occupying power to set up a completely new administrative apparatus, which of course it would be unable to do even as far as the staff is concerned. It is also important for the Hungarian economy to go on functioning'.[1]

According to another German source, Germany's policy of occupation was:

not to deal with the questions of economy and public administration and to intervene only where resistance is met. Economy must be the least disturbed. They consciously acted in a different manner than in Italy, where before the re-installation of the (fascist) government a situation was quickly created which suited German demands. In order to gain points of departure as far as the method to be followed was concerned, they studied the methods that worked in Denmark in 1940.[2]

The German leadership was fully satisfied with the timing and the results of the occupation, witnessed by the fact that in early May 1944 they withdrew all combat-ready forces from Hungary. They were replaced by units which were in the process of organization and/or training, numbering 40-50,000 men. German interests and demands were safeguarded by a small occupational apparatus. The political and general control was in the hands of SS *Standartenführer* Edmund Veesenmayer. Veesenmayer's credentials—initialled personally by Hitler—spelled out that he had a dual function. The less important one was the traditional task of a diplomat, and he received a far greater scope of authority by acting as 'the plenipotentiary of the Greater German Reich in Hungary'. Among his duties was that 'the full administration of the country be carried out by the government under his control with the aim of exploiting all the resources of the country, primarily the economic sources for the purposes of the common war effort...[he] was responsible for all developments of Hungarian politics and received all his instructions from the Reich foreign minister.'[3] Veesenmayer also controlled the activities of all Hungarian civil government authorities in accordance with German interests, through a staff of about 20.

SS *Reichsführer* Himmler appointed a high-ranking SS and police leader in the person of SS *Obergruppenführer* Otto von Winkelmann, who directed the activities of the Gestapo and the SD in Hungary with his staff of 25. All in all roughly 500-600 people came under his supervision. Adolf Eichmann coordinated the deportation of Hungarian Jewry with about 200 men.

General Hans von Greiffenberg, the previous military attaché, was appointed general plenipotentiary in Hungary from 24 April 1944. In this capacity he was not only commander of the occupying armies, but also kept contact with the leadership of the Hungarian army, appointing German liaison officers to the Ministry of Defence, the various branches of the Staff and the larger military units, who directly supervised the army. General Fütterer, formerly German air attaché, as the commanding general of the German air force in Hungary was in charge of the full Hungarian air force, including land installations and anti-aircraft artillery.

The system of Occupation relied completely on the Hungarian state apparatus. The Germans were satisfied with personnel changes in top positions, the *Gleichschaltung* of political life (some ministers, palatine heads, top military and police chiefs were replaced), and were thus able to operate the Hungarian state apparatus according to their own needs. Out of 41 palatine heads, 29 were changed, plus Budapest's Lord Mayor, two-thirds of the mayors of all Hungarian towns, the leadership of the Hungarian National Bank, those in charge of broadcasting and the editorship of government papers, who were replaced mostly with men from the Hungarian Rejuvenation Party and the Hungarian National Socialist party. Close to 200 associations were banned, others were placed under new leadership. The Press was brought into line: several hundred papers and journals were banned. On the model of German book burning, the works of a number of Hungarian writers, poets and scholars were sent to the paper mill.

Thus Hitler managed to realize his basic political objectives in Hungary with minimal effort. He prevented Hungary from leaving the war, cleansed anti-Axis factors from political life, secured increased Hungarian participation in the war and achieved the deportation and annihilation of the great majority of Hungarian Jews.

Even in the autumn of 1944 the German leadership had enough reserves in Hungary to continue their tactics of 'minimal effort—maximum results'. On 15 October the Regent made an attempt to put into effect an armistice agreement and to actually 'jump out' of the war. His plan, which was carried out amateurishly both in the political and in the military sense, ended up in failure. Horthy was made to resign by military force, but the Germans were still not compelled to use their own resources to administer that part of the country still under their sovereignty (roughly 2/3). They had at their disposal Ferenc Szálasi, a retired staff major, the leader of a fascist organization called Arrow Cross Party-Hungarist Movement, who assumed power on 16-17 October without a hitch and continued the war on the side of the Axis Powers.

II Occupation and/or Liberation

In September 1944 the Soviet Army reached Hungarian territory. The aim of Soviet policy—which was harmonized with the British and the American Allies—was to secure, under the Regent's leadership, Hungary's secession from the war and from the German alliance. From the beginning of October an Hungarian armistice delegation sent by Miklós Horthy was negotiating in Moscow. There, a preliminary armistice agreement was signed which, however, was not put into effect because of the events of 15 October.

Even then, Soviet policy aimed at avoiding the introduction of a military régime over the occupied territories. Moscow was thinking in terms of a government which would include Hungarian politicians and generals, such as those who were members of the armistice delegation or went over to territories under Soviet jurisdiction. The Soviet leadership took the policy of recognizing Horthy's position so seriously that the leadership of the Second Ukrainian Front banned several Communist papers published in the occupied territories— because of their vehemently anti-Horthy contents.

However, by the end of October it became apparent that the majority of the Hungarian armed forces could not change sides because of the Germans' and the Szálasi government's forceful counter measures. The Soviet leadership's evaluation of the situation was that those few Hungarian politicians and generals who were in Moscow, or who changed sides after 15 October, were in an isolated position and did not have any significant politico-military support behind them. In the meantime Soviet troops had occupied nearly one-third of Hungary's territory. The Soviet leadership now had to act, and lacking any kind of central Hungarian government took steps to administer the territories under its control. On 27 October the Soviet Union's State Defence Committee commissioned the war council of the Second Ukrainian Front to organize and supervise civil public administration.

Following the arrival of the Soviet troops military commands were organized in the towns and the more significant villages. In smaller villages so called 'camp commands' were set up, which were constantly on the move following the forward progress of the front. These commands acted primarily in the interests of the fighting units, maintaining order among the civilian population, and furthermore they facilitated the restoration of normal life and production. Their operations began with a briefing and announcement of things to be done.

The Soviet military authorities endeavoured to set the former Hungarian state apparatus in motion throughout the liberated areas. They insisted on maintaining the old administrative system for several reasons, partly because the direct interests of the war demanded the highest degree of order possible in the hinterland, and they thought to achieve this by relying on the old apparatus rather than experimenting with new forms. The Soviet units did not set up a military authority to control the population, but commissioned the leaders of the old state offices, who remained in their places, to resurrect the civil administration and continue their work. Most of those who remained took advantage of this opportunity.

Where the former leaders had escaped, the Soviet command commissioned the remaining deputies or other higher officials, of both senior and junior rank, to govern the town, village or territorial unit. Only if the Soviet units in charge could not find a suitable person did they turn to a Communist who had become politically active, mostly as soon as the Soviets had arrived, or perhaps to intellectual groups or priests. With those who did not escape but stayed at their posts it was usually possible to begin the work of starting a new life.

In the territories west of the river Danube, state machinery did not collapse to the same extent and escape to the West was not so chaotic and resembling a migration. In the South-Eastern part of the Trans-Danubian region this might have been due to the unexpected and rapid appearance of the units of the Third Ukrainian Front, which—strange as this may sound—left no time for the evacuation of state apparatus and the escape of the officials. Not only a significant part of the public supply administration, but in many places even the police or the gendarmerie were unable to leave. In other parts of the Trans-Danubian region even the 'honourable country' was left virtually untouched, and there was little Hungarian territory to which one could escape without difficulty and danger. Leaving the country made people think, especially those who left their homes as a result of fascist propaganda: the rumours according to which the 'reds' were said to be vilifying or deporting *everyone* to Siberia were turning out to be false.

At the end of October and beginning of November the Soviet leadership strove to take Budapest and set up a government in the political centre of the country. However, this plan could not be realized because of military reasons too complex to be set out in this paper. The capital was taken on 13 February 1945 by units of the Second Ukrainian Front, after nearly two months' siege.

The prolonged fighting forced the Soviet government to set up a Hungarian anti-fascist, democratic leadership composed of all anti-German elements found in the occupied territories. It was a characteristic of Moscow's policy that in view of the position of its Allies it took painstaking care to avoid the impression that communists, proclaiming the dictatorship of the proletariat, arrived hard on the heels of the Red Army. For this reason they did not allow all communists to return home immediately, or a Hungarian government to be set up with a communist leadership or majority. Of course the Soviet government discussed with the communists what should happen and how. Stalin himself participated at the Moscow negotiations. He decided personally that rather than setting up a National Liberation Committee on the French model, a Provisional National Assembly and a Provisional Government should be established.

The composition of the government formed on 23 December was decided in Moscow: three colonel-generals of the Horthy army became members of the government, one of them, Béla Miklós, as Prime Minister; Count Géza Teleki, the late Prime Minister, Pál Teleki's son, was given a post, with the Communists and the Social Democrats having two, and the Peasant Party one, representative in the government.

After the formation of the government negotiations were renewed on the armistice agreement, which was signed on 20 January 1945 in Moscow. With this development a new phase began in the Soviet occupation policy. According to the Armistice agreement an Allied Control Commission was established under the presidency of Marshal K J Voroshilov, who arrived at the seat of the Provisional Government, Debrecen, on 23 February 1945.

The choice of Voroshilov is not unimportant. Right up to the beginning of World War II he was at the top of the Soviet military hierarchy and was one of Stalin's close confidants. Stalin held him responsible—not quite without reason—for the first terrible failures of the Red Army and Voroshilov lost favour. His mission to Hungary was a sort of elegant exile and at the same time a kind of purgatory. The general had to prove his eagerness to work, which he did by his rather aggressive and heavy-handed activity as proconsul. On the other hand, exactly because he was not just a nobody, from time to time he allowed himself the luxury of being expansive and flexible, though not of course to the detriment of primary Soviet interests like the economy.

The ACC's scope of authority—in the inner relations of Soviet organs—did not extend to the theatre of operations (50-100 kilometres inside the front line), or to the army groups engaged in fighting in Hungarian territory, the command of the Second and Third Ukrainian Front and their units. The ACC devoted its activity primarily to the exploitation of economic resources, partly in order to supply the army, partly to secure reparations. The situation is well illustrated by a memorandum sent by the Ministry of Public Supply to the ACC:

It is common knowledge, that the country's whole area was a theatre of war, which had been economically exploited by the German army, which under the pretext of preservation carried off as much of the country's agricultural products and animals as the transport vehicles at its disposal allowed. After the liberation the huge Russian army used the larger economic and commercial reserves for its own alimentation purposes, or took them as war booty, or as services rendered under article 11 of the Armistice agreement. [4]

The commanders at various levels of the Red Army reserved as war booty all kinds of economic and communications installations, money reserves in banks, granaries, factories, schools and hospital buildings. This activity was a violation of the armistice agreement, since according to article 7 only German military property could be taken as war booty, that is, explicitly armaments and other war material.

Nor did the agreement oblige the Hungarian government to cater for the Soviet army. This was the agreement's 'most sensitive, most loosely worded article which allowed for a variety of interpretations'. [5] The provision in the text for the supply of the Allied/Soviet High Command was interpreted by the Soviet side to mean an obligation to supply the army stationed in Hungary, that is about 1-1.5 million men in the summer of 1945. The Hungarian government had to supply— with the exception of military equipment—everything an army might have needed, ranging from foodstuffs and clothing to pharmaceuticals; including also, according to the schedule of Soviet requirements for the second half of 1945, 52 tons of sweets for non-smokers, not to mention 25,000 buckets with zinc coating. The inclusion in reparation payments of the significant expense of supplying the Red Army was decisively rebutted by the Soviet authorities.

Beside the demands made by the ACC, a very serious burden was imposed on the capital's districts by the arbitrary requisitioning of local Soviet commanders, of which no account was ever kept. According to the April 1945 report of the armistice division of the Hungarian Foreign Ministry, 'the Hungarian authorities have no idea what plants and stocks they have at their disposal in the field of agriculture, commerce and industry. The warehouses, factories, plants and public institutions are all guarded by Soviets, they keep everything locked and they take—without any plan—whatever they want. Thus there is no security of public ownership or production anymore.'[6]

Beside economic hardship the civilian population, especially at the end of 1944 and the first months of 1945, were particularly hard hit by the untrammelled rampage of some of the Soviet soldiers, particularly the numerous deserters, who leaving their units grouped into gangs, leading to a complete lack of personal safety. According to a letter written in February 1945 by Mátyás Rákosi, the First Secretary of the Communist Party 'the cases of mass rape of women, the lootings, etc. recur at the liberation of each territory, thus the last time in Budapest'.[7] Hundreds of thousands of civilians caught in the streets were deported to the Soviet Union for labour. Tens of thousands of people with German names were also carried away at that time.

At the end of hostilities the issue of reparations gained increasing prominence. During the talks lasting from February to June the Hungarian side asked for the reduction of the sum levied for 1945, and that the Soviets should reduce by half the dismantling of factories that was going on at an accelerated pace. These requests were left unanswered, just like the one asking the Soviets to refrain from using 1938 prices. The Soviets also refused to include the cost of transport and packing, and furthermore insisted on a 5% penalty on late delivery. A colleague of Voroshilov's stated that the Hungarian delegates were mistaken to think that they were in a position to bargain as in trade negotiations. Reparations were determined by different principles: the Hungarians must give what was demanded and when it was demanded. The reparations agreement was signed for six years (1945-51) on 15 June.

The 300 million dollar reparation payment ($200 million for the Soviet Union, $50 million each for Yugoslavia and Czechoslovakia) was not too great in comparison with pre-war Hungarian economic capacity, and annual payments were to be only 5% of the national income. However, in 1945 the national income reached only roughly 58% of the 1938 level. Because of this and the extremely detrimental prices determined for the value of reparation shipments, and taking into account the costs of Occupation, the burden might have reached 27% of the national income.

The Soviet Occupation authorities kept Hungarian domestic politics under their control too, yet in this field they showed greater moderation than in the sphere of economy. Of course there was a close confidential relationship between the Soviet leadership of the ACC and the leaders of the Communist Party: this is shown by the fact that the ACC commissioners kept an eye on the work of the Hungarian Communist Party's local organizations. If they were dissatisfied, they reported it to the party headquarters, which took the necessary measures. Some ACC divisions turned to the officials of the HCP for advice and recommendation in affairs deemed to be sensitive.

Naturally, the leaders of the ACC were well informed about domestic political relations. Thus, when on 26 October Voroshilov and ambassador Pushkin, the Marshal's political adviser, made a 'guess' about the possible outcome of the parliamentary elections, they predicted an absolute majority for the Smallholders, 15-18% each for the two labour parties, 7-10% for the Peasant party and 4-5% for the rest of the parties.[9] It was no coincidence that Voroshilov would have liked the coalition parties to make a preliminary arrangement on dividing the mandates between them, and to enter the elections on a common list. The Smallholders would then have received 47.5%, the Hungarian Communist Party and the Social Democrats 20% each, while the Peasant party would have obtained 12.5%, meaning that the Smallholders absolute majority could have been avoided. With the assistance of the British government common list elections were finally averted. The British representatives in Budapest declared that otherwise London would not accept the democratic nature of the elections, and would not receive Hungary's diplomatic representative.

If we compare the German and the Russian policies of Occupation, we find that in 1944-45 the Germans used Hungary exclusively as a hinterland of the front line, looking upon it as on theatre of war. Accordingly they strove for maximum exploitation of the resources of the ever-shrinking parts of the country under their control, and to make material goods and services which surpassed their requirements unusable for the advancing Soviet army. Hence the policy of paralyzation and evacuations, since at this late stage of the war they could have had no further interests as far as Hungary was concerned.

In the Soviet approach we find a mixture of immediate war objectives and the more long-term aspects of empire building. These collided with each other from time to time, since atrocities, both organized and spontaneous, weakened the influence of the Communist party which was the beneficiary from the perspective of more long-term objectives. Soviet policy—taking into consideration its international obligations— did not grant the Communist party a monopolistic position, but allowed the rest of the democratic parties to operate as well. Furthermore it supported other objectives which coincided with the Hungarian national interests: the elimination of fascism, land reform and other democratic measures. In this sense the elements of the politics of Occupation intermingled with those of Liberation.

Discussion

Dr Schöpflin, who described vividly his own experiences hiding in a cellar in Budapest in 1945, stressed the importance of Hungarian oil, bauxite and agricultural products to Hitler, who complained that his generals did not understand the economic aspects of war. *Dr Sipos* explained that the wartime German-Hungarian economic relationship grew out of the clearing agreements of the 1930s, which were based on barter: during the war German demand inflated the Hungarian economy, and Hungary provided large credits to Germany; under Soviet occupation Hungary was treated as a kind of economic annex to Germany, and the forcible introduction of Red Army currency exacerbated the inflationary situation. *Mr Cviic* agreed that the Hungarian economy was stimulated, rather than exploited by German demand during the war, leading to catastrophic inflation later.

Notes and References

1 *Hitler hatvannyolc tárgyalása 1939-1944* (Hitler's Sixtyeight Talks) (Magveto, Bp, 1983), vol 2, p 273.
2 *Kriegstagebuch des Oberkommandos der Wehrmacht.* Studienausgabe, Bernard and Grefe (München, 1982), vol 7, p 197.
3 *A Wilhelmstrasse és Magyarország 1933-1944* (The Wilhelmstrasse and Hungary) (Kossuth 1968), p.789.
4 *Országos Levéltár* (OL), Hungarian State Archives, IV-482-501.094/1945.
5 OL XIX-A-83/1945, március 9.
6 OL XIX-A-83a/1945, május 4.
7 *Politikatörténeti Intézet Levéltára* (PIL), Archives of the Institute of Political History. 274/10/38/1945, február 19.
8 OL IV-536-1/1945, szeptember 10.
9 PIL 274/10/39/1945, október 26.

14 The Soviet Occupation of Poland, 1944-45

NORMAN DAVIES

In the generation which followed the Russian Revolution, Soviet troops invaded and occupied Poland, or parts of it, on four separate occasions. In 1918-19, they advanced into the Polish borders in the ranks of the Bolsheviks' Western Army, which captured Wilno and created the short-lived Soviet Republic of Lithuania-Byelorussia. In 1920, they had been marching to spread the international revolution to Berlin, when they were heavily defeated on the Vistula by Marshal Pilsudski.[1] In September 1939, they came as partners of the Nazis with whom they held a joint parade at Brest-Litovsk before taking the eastern half of the country for themselves.[2] In 1944-45, they returned as the victors of Stalingrad, as members of the Grand Alliance and masters of the Eastern Front.[3]

People with long memories knew that Russian armies had overrun or marched through Poland on numerous earlier occasions: in 1914-17, 1863-4, 1830-31, 1813-15, 1799, 1794-5, 1792-3, 1768-72, 1756-63, 1747-8, 1733-5, 1710-21, 1655-67… Every Pole was taught how Peter the Great had wrecked the constitution of the old Polish Commonwealth: how Suvorov had massacred the inhabitants of Praga; how Catherine the Great had partitioned the Commonwealth with her fellow despots: how every patriotic attempt to restore Polish sovereignty had been crushed by Russian force.

The Russians, alas, learned different dates. They remembered only 1612, 1812 and 1941. They did not see Russia as the historic invader of Europe, but as the historic victim of European invasions.

Every analysis of the Soviet Occupation of 1944-5 must begin with a definition of 'Poland'. For Poland was a movable feast. Its frontiers were in doubt both in the East and the West. In legal terms, of course, there was no uncertainty. Poland's pre-war frontiers had been confirmed by international treaty, and could only be changed by consent of the signatories. The eastern frontier with the USSR was enshrined in the Treaty of Riga (1921). Yet Moscow was claiming that Poland's pre-war frontiers, like the pre-war Polish state, had ceased to exist. In April 1943, Stalin had withdrawn diplomatic recognition from the Polish Government in London; and at the Teheran Conference in the following November, he had extracted a secret undertaking from Churchill and Roosevelt to re-establish the Ribbentrop-Molotov Line of September 1939 to which diplomats would henceforth refer as the 'Curzon Line'. At Yalta in February 1945, 'the Big Three' gave their public blessing to Soviet views of Poland's eastern frontier. Poland's new western frontier along the Oder and Lusatian Neisse was imposed at Potsdam in July 1945. No general peace conference was convened to settle these matters by agreement.

In this light, the progress of the Soviet Occupation can be described in five distinct stages. As the victorious Soviet Army drove the retreating *Wehrmacht* westwards on the long road to Berlin, the political context of their operations was constantly changing:

In the **first phase** (4 January-20 July 1944), the Soviet Army occupied territory which still formed a legal part of the pre-war Polish Republic but which Moscow was treating as part of the Soviet Union. In that region, which included both Wilno and Lwów, the Soviet authorities acted without any reference to the Poles.

In the **second phase** (20 July 1944-17 January 1945), having crossed the River Bug, the Red Army entered the territory which Moscow had designated for the post-war Polish state. Using Lublin as a temporary capital, they introduced the nucleus of the future People's Republic. However, having advanced very rapidly to the Vistula—indeed, having established a bridgehead on the Vistula's western bank at Magnuszew—they made no attempt to move further into central Poland for six whole months, thereby denying assistance to the Warsaw Rising (1 August-2 October 1944).

In the **third phase** (12 January-28 June 1945), the Soviets first drove the *Wehrmacht* from central and western Poland, then completed the task of organising a Polish State. The ruins of Warsaw were captured in the first week of the winter offensive. Approval was obtained at Yalta for a Provisional Government of National Unity (TJRN) which was to replace the authority of the Polish Government in London. The last city designated for Poland—Breslau (Wroclaw)—was captured on 2 May. The TJRN took office on 28 June.

In the **fourth phase** (June-September 1945), the Soviet authorities continued to hold all the former German provinces pending implementation of the Potsdam decisions. After three months, Poland's so-called 'Recovered Territories' were handed over to the Warsaw regime, which was free thereafter to consolidate its hold throughout the country.

In the **final phase** (1945-47), the Soviets helped their Polish clients to eliminate all remaining opposition. A war between the communists and fighters of the former Underground continued for at least two years. Resistance in the mountainous Podhale region in the south, round Zakopane, was prolonged into the summer of 1946. In the south-eastern Bieszczady Mountains, the

Ukrainian Insurrectionary Army (UPA) held out against all comers until destroyed in the summer of 1947 by a joint operation of Soviet, Polish and Czechoslovak forces. Only then one could say that the Soviet occupation of Poland was truly complete.

Seen as a whole, the Red Army's operations in Poland may be characterised as three giant westward leaps, each followed by a prolonged period of consolidation. During the offensives, the main strategy was to surge forward incessantly in overwhelming numbers, 'with no operational pauses', leaving the German strong points to be eliminated later. Given the length of the front—450 miles at the longitude of Warsaw—the Soviets could always find space to manoeuvre, whilst the Germans could never find the means to construct adequate defences. Hitler's strategy of designating key sites, such as Poznan or Breslau, as fortresses to be defended to the last man, was mistaken. In theory at least, the *Wehrmacht*'s chances would have improved if it had withdrawn at an early stage to the line of the Oder, where a much shortened front was more defensible. The main puzzle, however, concerns Stalin's decision to hold the Front on the Vistula throughout the second half of 1944. One hypothesis stresses his nefarious political motives, another his desire to conquer the Balkans before moving into the German heartland through Vienna as well as to Berlin. The two explanations are not incompatible.

In the absence of the requisite documentation, no amount of speculation will solve the question of Stalin's exact calculations, but the Soviet leadership was facing an acute dilemma. The twin objectives of fighting the Germans all the way to Berlin and of organising a 'friendly' government in Poland were pulling in different directions. The Red Army could not afford to advance into Germany if its lines of communication were to be threatened by hostile Polish forces. (Stalin could not have forgotten the débâcle on the Vistula twenty-four years earlier.[4]) On the other hand, given memories of Soviet atrocities in 1939-41, there was little hope of assuaging Polish hostility without a clear commitment to the country's freedom and hence to the return of the Polish Government from London. In that case, all ambitions for a 'socialist Poland' would have to be abandoned. In other words, if Stalin were to press on for Berlin without first solving the Polish conundrum, he would be courting military disaster. Yet if he were to safeguard the Red Army by making concessions to the Poles, he was risking political failure. From the Kremlin's viewpoint, the most satisfactory solution was for all independent Polish forces to be eliminated before the decisive battle for Berlin was joined.

Operations on the German-Soviet Front caused immense damage and no small loss of life, but not the universal devastation which might have been expected. No Polish city suffered from military action to the same extent that Warsaw suffered from the aftermath of the Rising, when Hitler ordered Poland's capital to be razed. Wilno and Lwów survived essentially intact. Cracow was untouched. Generally speaking, the Front passed through very rapidly during each offensive, having stood inactive for long periods. There was less bombing of civilian targets than in September 1939; and the Germans did not establish any 'scorched earth zone' as they had done on the Dnieper. Prolonged fighting was largely confined to the flanks—to the Dukla Pass in August 1944, when the Soviets crossed the Carpathians to assist the Slovak Rising: to East Prussia, when they first entered German territory; and to the Pomeranian Wall. The siege of Breslau (Wroclaw) reduced the main city of Silesia to ruins but only after the Nazis had expelled all civilians. Danzig (Gdansk) was burned to ashes, but only after the Soviets had captured it.

One of the principal complications for the Soviet offensives in Poland, especially in the first half of 1944, lay in the presence of numerous bands of rival partisans. The largest formation, the Polish Home Army or 'AK', had been ordered to follow the guidelines of a strategy called *Operacja Burza* or 'Operation Tempest'. In its essentials, the plan ordered the AK to assist the Soviets in their military operations, to attack the *Wehrmacht* in the rear as soon as Soviet troops were engaged in any particular district, and then to take control of the liberated areas after the battle. Unfortunately for the Poles, Stalin's armies had no intention of leaving anything in the hands of independent Polish organisations. They made grateful use of Polish military assistance, but did not allow any other form of co-operation. What is more, the backwoods of eastern Poland were crawling with a variety of other underground organisations. Large numbers of Soviet partisans, parachuted behind the German lines, were operating to orders which took everywhere east of the 1939 frontier to be Soviet territory. The Ukrainian underground, in contrast, acted on the assumption that all the lands of 'western Ukraine' were rightfully theirs. When the extreme nationalist faction of the Ukrainian Insurrectionary Army (UPA-OUN) learned that the AK intended to assist the Soviet advance, they saw it as a sign of betrayal, launching a campaign of murderous reprisals against the Polish civilian population.

The crucial test came in Volhynia in February 1944, when the Red Army advanced into districts where the Home Army's 27th Infantry Division was stationed. At first, all went well. Prior to the attack in mid-March on German positions in the town of Kowel, Polish commanders made contact with their Soviet counterparts. They exchanged information with General Sergieyev, synchronised plans and received both a supply of arms and a promise of future comradeship. In due course, trapped from all sides, the Germans beat a hasty retreat, but then Soviet dispositions suddenly changed. Political officers of the NKVD refused to honour agreements made by their military colleagues, and Soviet partisans started to attack both the

AK and the self-defence units of Polish villages. Documents captured by the AK and forwarded to London showed that the Soviet partisans had received orders 'to exterminate all Polish underground organisations' and 'to execute their leaders'.[5]

In the second major battle in Volhynia, in April, the 27th Infantry Division was first promised the usual Soviet assistance, then abandoned. In a desperate five-day struggle on the River Turia, where it was encircled by *SS-Panzer Wiking* and bombed from the air, it received none of the expected ammunition and no operational support. One of its columns was able to escape across the Bug into central Poland, but the main body of survivors was trapped in no-man's land between the Soviet and German lines. In due course, they were surrounded and disarmed by Soviet patrols. The men were drafted into General Berling's First Polish Army fighting under Soviet command. The officers were arrested.[6] A pattern had been set. Similar events occurred in July in the Wilno region.

The Warsaw Rising formed the centrepiece of Poland's tragedy. Launched on 1 August 1944, it was designed to achieve what the similar Rising in Paris was to achieve a few weeks later—a co-ordinated assault on the German garrison by the local population and the advancing Allies, followed by the liberation of the capital city. The Home Army commander, General Bor-Komorowski, knew that timing was vital, and he waited till Soviet tanks had been sighted on Warsaw's eastern outskirts. He also knew, however, that the Varsovians were straining at the leash; and he thought that he could count on Anglo-American air support. The Red Army was broadcasting radio appeals to the citizens of Warsaw to take up arms, but it did not come to their aid. The German garrison reversed its retreat, and brought up heavy reinforcements including two of the nastiest formations of the *Waffen-SS* formed from the Dirlewanger and Kaminski Brigades. Two panzer divisions were able to recross the Vistula bridges, and to launch a counter-attack against the Soviets. In the city, savage street fighting persisted for 63 days. A quarter of a million Varsovians were killed, the cream of Poland's youth sacrificed. The largest body of committed support for a post-war democratic Poland was liquidated in one blow.[7]

The role of Berling's 1st Polish Army and of other Polish units under Soviet command was not insignificant. Originally formed in 1943 as the 'Kosciuszko Division', largely from ex-deportees and refugees in the USSR, Berling's force was entirely subordinated to communist political commissars, many of whom could speak no Polish. Blooded at Lenino, where it suffered heavy casualties, it was rapidly expanded to consist of five infantry divisions and one tank corps. It moved forward within the body of Rokossowski's 1st Byelorussian Front, until it reached the Vistula in the middle of the Warsaw Rising. Having defied Soviet orders not to render assistance to the insurgents, and losing many men in the process, it was withdrawn from the Front, and its commander dismissed. It reappeared in time to play its part in the siege of Berlin. The 2nd Polish Army came into being in 1944 as soon as local conscripts could be raised in central Poland. It fought in the ranks of Koniev's First Ukrainian Front. It, too, drove into Berlin, where it claimed to have captured the Brandenberg Gate.

Once the Warsaw Rising was crushed, the Polish Underground lost its capacity for concerted action. The Home Army, in effect, had been decapitated. It neither assisted nor resisted the great Soviet offensive of January 1945. After that, with the whole country occupied, it had little raison d'être: General Okulicki issued the order to disband. Meanwhile, the military wing of the Polish communist party, the People's Guard (GL) was free to flourish and to swell its ranks by recruitment. In the last weeks of the War, it took the offensive, not against the Germans (who had already been driven out) but against the few remaining anti-Communist formations that were still active. Chief among these was the 'National Armed Forces' (NSZ), a ferocious nationalist outfit which had never fully accepted the Home Army's authority.

By the summer of 1945, the dispersed and dispirited elements of the former Home Army were beginning to regret their disbandment. Although some 40,000 accepted the terms of an amnesty and laid down their arms, many others continued to oppose the new regime, and many returned to the fray when they found that the Amnesty had not put an end to the repressions. A clandestine army called 'Freedom and Independence' (WiN) fought on till the end of 1946. The exact numbers and circumstances of the Home Army soldiers who were killed or otherwise repressed in 1944-5 will never be known. A recent study by a British historian talks of 50,000 deportations.[8] What most western observers fail to realise is that non-communist members of the anti-Nazi Resistance were treated in the same category as Nazi war criminals. Indeed, they often ended up in the same cells.[9] Since the communists had captured quantities of the Gestapo's files and seals, it was a simple matter to forge evidence of the Home Army's alleged collaboration.[10] One of the arrested AK officers who was unusually fortunate in obtaining early release had been the commander of an AK unit in the Wilno Region. He was Jerzy Dzierzynski, nephew of the founder of the Cheka, parent of the NKVD.

Popular recollections of the Soviet occupation are in the nature of things partial and subjective, and must be treated with caution. On the other hand, they help to counterbalance the faceless narratives which are written by those who believe in 'historical forces' or who confine their observations to military movements and changes in political leadership. The view from ground level is not entirely irrelevant.

In my experience, Poles who witnessed the events of 1944-45 tend to stress three recurrent themes: reluctant admiration for the hardy Soviet soldiery; revulsion at the ubiquitous robbing and raping; and amazement that such an apparent rabble could ever have gained the upper hand against a well-fed and well-disciplined German adversary. To the question 'when you first saw a Soviet soldier, what did he look like?' Poles will repeat the same terms over and over again—*nedzarz* ('beggar' or 'tramp'), *nedzarz na koniku* (a beggar on a pony). Having rarely come into personal contact with the leading echelons of frontline troops, they describe dirty, drunk, ragged men in half a uniform, wearing someone else's boots, their trousers held up with string, their loot slung in a rough canvas sack over their shoulder. They talk of them eating scraps, sleeping rough, or tramping along with open shirts in ten or twenty degrees of frost. They also remark on the number of men with oriental features, usually defined by phrases such as *Kalmuk* or *hordy azjatyckie* , 'the hordes of Asia', and on the presence of women soldiers. To the question, 'what happened next?' they usually say 'they stole our watches' or 'they took the bicycles' or 'they drove off in our cart': and 'they were looking for girls' or 'they dragged the women outside'. One of the commonest stories features Russian women who supposedly dressed up in looted underwear, unable to distinguish between underslips and ballgowns. Yet Poles also comment frequently on the Soviet soldiery's kindness to children—a trait which stood out after six years of Nazi occupation.

To the question, 'how did they manage to win?' the reply usually gives some variant on the theme of numbers. Having seen their hospitals filled with countless German casualties, and their roads choked with the retreating*Wehrmacht*, Poles watching by the wayside were impressed above all by the endless flow of Soviet reinforcements. Column after column of trucks filled with fresh-faced young peasant boys headed towards the Front. They also comment on the speed and efficiency of Soviet political operations—on the 'security offices' set up in every small town, on the public meetings held to reassure the populace with slogans such as *POLSKA BeDZIE!* (There's going to be a Poland) or *Ziemia Chlopom !* (All Land to the Peasants).

The poet, Adam Zagajewski, was born in Lwów a few months after the Red Army's arrival in July 1944. Many years later, he would reconstruct a picture of the event from the torrent of broken images which he had heard from his family and friends:

> *Over meadows and fields, through towns, through woods,*
> *The armies march on, mounted and on foot.*
> *Horses walk, guns, walk, lads, lags and children walk.*
> *Lean whippets run; bedquilts shed their down.*
> *Sledges drive past, and detention wagons, and fine carriages.*

Ships sail by, and rafts and pontoons,
Whilst boats and steamboats sink like bark-built coracles.
Balloons fly overhead, and rockets and bombers.
Mortar shells whistle popular melodies
Above the screams of the flogged and men shouting orders...
Tanks roll by, and swords and daggers.
Katyusha rockets whine like speeding comets.
Fifes play, and leathern drums, and the creaking decks of ferries.
Here come the sons of the steppes,
Muslims, and convicts, and card players,
And lovers of Lord Byron. Suvorov limps along
Before fawning and dancing courtiers...
Stately camels step by, slowly and thoughtfully.

Russia is entering Poland,
Tearing through spiders' webs, and leaves, and the late summer
boughs:
Tearing up tendons, and frontiers, and treaties,
And bridges, and friendships, and bonds, and threads,
And washing lines, where the washing still hangs out to dry:
Tearing down our gateways and our grammar, our bandages, our
heartbeat,

Our future and our hopes....

Russia is entering my life.
Russia is entering my thoughts.
Russia is entering my verses.[11]

Marian Zielinski watched the arrival of the Soviet Army from his perch in the forest on a steep slope of the Beskid Mountains west of Krakow. Born in 1901 as the son of a poor rural schoolteacher, he held left-wing political views. He was a professional chemist and botanist, and had worked before the war as a director of the *Gymnasium* or 'grammar school' in Kety. He had spent most of the war years in Nazi concentration camps, notably in Dachau, Sachsenhausen and Mauthausen. Following his unexpected survival and release, he was hiding in January 1945 in the snowbound woods near his home, waiting to see the Soviet Army as it moved along the valley below:

> *The Germans had mined the dam at Porebka and the whole reservoir might have blown sky high. But somehow the local partisans got there in time to defuse it...*
> *The 'Russians' came through in clearly defined waves. The leading wave consisted of orderly first-class soldiers dressed in white snow suits and heavily armed. Some distance behind them, the second line was made up of shabby ranks of markedly inferior troops shuffling along in their felt boots, rifles slung on a string behind their backs. After them, there tramped a motley rabble of*

unfortunates trapped inside the Front and unable to flee. God knows who they were—deserters, men separated from their units, camp followers, women, stranded Germans who'd thrown away their uniforms, travellers and peasants caught up on the road. At the rear, there rolled the watertight cordon of the NKVD, driving all before them. They were instantly recognisable in their smart uniforms and fur collars, standing upright in their American jeeps, toting their sub-machine guns, and shooting all stragglers...[12]

When he returned home, Marian Zielinski was first told by a Soviet officer that 'the voice of the people' had elected him town Mayor. After three weeks he was abruptly arrested, charged with subversive activity, namely with interceding for the lives of innocent Germans. Tortured by three officers of the NKVD on the same table of the same police station where the Gestapo had tortured him in 1939, be was repeatedly pressed with the unanswerable question '*Pochemu Vy Zhyvyotye?*' (Why are you alive?) As the survivor of three SS concentration camps, he was obviously a traitor. He was the living embodiment of Poland's wartime history.

Janina Stankiewicz was a 16-year old girl when the Soviet 65th Army arrived in her village of Jezowo in Polish Pomerania on 16 February 1945. After a terrifying night of bombardment by 'Stalin's organs', the Germans withdrew and all fell quiet:

Three Russians appeared at our door, all wearing peaked caps with green bands (NKVD)... The Russians called us out: one of them had a long list of names which he read, amongst them was mine and my father's. They formed us into a column and we marched to [the nearest town] ten miles away. The soldiers would not speak to us. We were ordered into the cellars of the town's police station. Our group from Jezewo numbered about 50 people, but new groups were constantly arriving.

They would call us for interrogation at any time of the day or night. My interrogator kept asking me whether Mrs Regina W was a member of a German Woman's Organisation and if I said 'yes' I would be released. I explained that I did not know her and that during the German occupation had been busy shearing sheep. 'On German Farms?' 'Of course, there were no others during the war'.

After one week we were put into the local prison, and after two were marched to Chelmno. During this march our neighbour in Jezewo, Mr Francis Ostrowski, who was very sick, collapsed, and a Russian soldier finished him off with his rifle butt. Another soldier stopped a young woman, a passer-by carrying a milk churn. He knocked the churn out of her hands and made her join our column. She screamed that her two small children were waiting. The number of prisoners had to be maintained. Many good people gave us food and warm clothing on our continuous trek of 100 miles. In all there were about 500 people in our column and more than a dozen didn't make it.

After about a week, we were herded into cattletrucks in the railway station at Ilawa. Men were separated from women. I was parted from my father. Each truck held 40 prisoners. A hole had been cut in the floor to serve as a lavatory; and a couple of thin women managed to escape through it the first night. We travelled in darkness for many days and were fed on cabbage and dry bread. Eventually someone managed to make a hole in the wall and found that the station names were in Russian. We realised we were bound for Siberia.

Finally, we arrived in the vicinity of Czelabinsk. A camp named Rosa was ready to take us. It eventually filled up so as to contain 3600 inmates, Poles greatly outnumbering the Germans. People went on dying, particularly the Germans, whose spirits had been broken much more than ours. Our men worked in the nearby mine, women in the timber mill or on the railway line. A fulfilled work quota earned the prisoner 8 ounces of bread and a bowl of soup from the <u>bottom</u> of the cauldron. Diarrhoea was common and a few prisoners died every day. We worked from sunrise to sunset and women then had to help in the kitchen and chop wood.

During the summer the Russians grew noticeably gentler. One day, a Russian officer showed us our files. It appeared that three local communist sympathisers had denounced us all for being either German or German sympathisers. They were settling scores. However, we were going home.

I found my father in the corner of the truck—he was so ill that he didn't recognise me. When he did, we both cried deep into the night. Two more people died on the way back, but my father survived. Some young women in the next truck were raped by the soldiers returning from Germany. The guards did them a favour and allowed them to lock themselves in. They fixed a board on the outside saying 'Typhoid'.

I returned to Jezewo on October 28, my first day of real freedom. The man who denounced us was now a policeman. It did not stop our young men from beating him up so badly that he nearly died. There was no investigation and no repercussions.[13]

The view from the other side of the Front could be equally fraught. Alexander Solzhenitsyn arrived on the Vistula in August 1944 as an artillery officer of the 2nd Byelorussian Front. Anticipating the Soviet advance into East Prussia from the south, he remembered stories that his father had told of service in the Tsarist Army in exactly the same region thirty years before. He himself had only three weeks to serve before being arrested on a charge of slandering Stalin in a private letter. He would later recall his experiences in a long poem composed in the Gulag as *Prussian Nights:*

> *The conquerors of Europe swarm,*
> *Russians scurrying everywhere.*
> *In their trucks, they stuff their loot:*
> *Vacuum cleaners, wine and candles,*
> *skirts and picture frames and pipes,*
> *Brooches and medallions, blouses, buckles,*
> *Typewriters (not with Russian type) ...*
> *A moaning by the walls, half-muffled,*
> *The mother's wounded, still alive.*
> *The little daughter's on the mattress,*
> *Dead. How many have been on it?*
> *a platoon, a company perhaps ...*
> *It's all come down to simple phrases*
> *Do not forget. Do not forgive.*
> *Blood for blood. A tooth for a tooth.*
> *The mother begs, 'Tote mich, soldat' ...*[14]

Naturally, one cannot suggest that the Red Army brought misery to everyone. In places, it was cheered by the populace—which had never happened to the *Wehrmacht*. What is more, for certain groups and individuals, it brought unprecedented opportunity. Here, one would have to mention Poland's tiny coterie of Marxist and *marxisant* intellectuals, who had felt excluded from pre-war cultural circles, and who now believed fervently in the 'socialist dawn'. Among them were figures like Stefan Zolkiewiski, who immediately in 1945 launched the Marxist review *Kuznica*, and others, like Czeslaw Milosz or Leszek Kolakowski, who were destined in exile to become communism's most devastating critics.[15]

The political order established by the Soviet Occupation is often called 'the communist take-over',[16] but this is a misnomer. In October 1944, Stalin himself admitted that Poland was highly unsuited to the imposition of a Soviet-style system.[17] After all, he had ordered almost all the members of pre-war Polish Communist Party to be shot in the Purges only six years before. In 1944-5, the reconstituted Party (the Polish Workers' Party or PPR) simply did not have enough people to run anything. As a result, the Soviet political managers had to rely on a motley collection of disguised policemen and obscure collaborators, many with false names or 'revolutionary pseudonyms', who packed all the organisations that were created. What they engineered was not so much a communist takeover as a holding operation, a masterly piece of police-run political puppeteering.

At every stage, Moscow's clients were obliged to assent to policies and treaties which had been determined for them in advance. At the same time, they could carry out their assignments in the knowledge that all genuine politicians and parties would be obstructed from offering serious opposition. The so-called National Homeland Council (KRN), founded in December 1943 to usurp the powers of the underground Delegatura of the Polish Government, was entirely run from Moscow. Its 'President', Boleslaw Bierut, though presented as a 'non-party' figure, was a high-ranking NKVD officer, who would only reveal his true colours in 1948 when he emerged as Secretary-General of the next version of the Polish Communist Party, the PZPR.

Unbeknown to the populace, the members of the Polish Committee of National Liberation (PKWN or 'Lublin Committee'), the first Soviet-backed quasi-governmental body, were still in Moscow when its dubious manifesto was distributed on their behalf on 22 July 1944. It was flown in on 28 July when Lublin had been cleared of the Home Army. Its chairman, Edward Osobka-Morawski, was an unknown 'socialist' who had deserted the Polish Socialist Party. Its vice-chairman, Andrzej Witos, was the younger brother of the well known peasant leader and former premier, Wincenty Witos, who had refused to serve. Its activities were gilded by the co-option of assorted priests and princes. Communists directly controlled only three departments—security, defence and education.

Similar manipulations surrounded the formation of the Provisional Government of National Unity (TRJN) eleven months later. When Bierut explained to Churchill at Potsdam that there were very few Communists in the Polish 'Government', he was factually correct. He did not bother to explain that it was normal for Leninists to put state governments into a subservient role, always reserving real power for those who worked the system from behind the scenes. After all, Stalin's Soviet Union was not run by the 'Soviet Government' nor by the Soviet 'President' M K Kalinin.

An important step was taken in December 1944, when the Lublin Committee (PKWN) was recognised by the USSR as Poland's Provisional Government, thereby forcing the pace at Yalta. But its hands were completely tied. For example, by a secret agreement not published until 1954, it had transferred its jurisdiction over civilian crime to the organs of Soviet military justice. By its signature of a 'Polish-Soviet Treaty of Friendship and Co-operation' in April 1945, it preempted the decisions of the incoming TRJN, which was bound to a pre-determined programme completely subordinated to Soviet interests. Since Warsaw was in ruins, the TJRN was established in Lodz, which also housed the main Party schools for training the future communist cadres.

Much confusion was sown by the inimitable Leninist game of 'splitting' rival organisations. The Polish Peasant Movement (PSL), whose leader, Stanislaw Mikolajczyk, was the only minister of the Polish Government to return to Poland, found itself facing a spurious 'SL—Wola Ludu' (Peasant Movement of the People's Will), which enjoyed extensive official backing. The old socialists of the PPS were undermined by a 'reborn PPS' which was founded in Lublin in September 1944 under the protection of the PKWN. Even the Roman Catholic hierarchy found themselves in competition with a police-sponsored 'Polish National Catholic Church'. The former Roman Catholic charitable organisation PAX was replaced by a new organisation of the same name, dedicated to 'Catholic participation in progressive politics' and headed by the leader of the pre-war Fascist 'Falanga', Boleslaw Piasecki. Piasecki's miraculous conversion had taken place during his incarceration by the NKVD.[18]

Such popular support that the new authorities could muster was obtained by subterfuge. All truly communist policies on the Soviet model were carefully avoided. Indeed, no-one in authority breathed a word about 'Communism'. As a result, the political platforms of rival parties could be shamelessly raided. The PKWN declared itself for Land Reform (the policy of the PSL) and for the nationalisation of industry (the policy of PPS). Before 1948, there was no attempt to introduce collectivised agriculture or a Stalinist-type command economy. The massive programme of Reconstruction was something which any post-war government would have undertaken.

Despite the imposition of relative peace and stability in most parts of Poland, there was no sign in the course of 1945 of the 'free and unfettered elections' agreed at Yalta. A gerrymandered Referendum was to be staged in July 1946 as a sop to the growing unease of the Western Powers. When the Elections were finally held in 1947, they were shown to have been blatantly rigged, and the US Ambassador resigned his post in Warsaw in protest.[19] By then, it was too late.

The all-powerful security forces which ruled Poland in 1944-5 should not be seen as an arm of the new government. The Government was an arm of the security apparatus. In the early days of the occupation, all decisions were directly taken by the Soviet NKVD or by its dependent organisations in the front-line area, such as 'Smersh'. After July 1944, while reserving overall command, the NKVD delegated many of its powers to the nascent Polish apparatus to which many NKVD officers were seconded. Poland's post-war Ministry of Security under Stanislaw Radkiewicz, and the notorious Office of Public Security (UBP) under Jakub Berman both traced their origins to relevant agencies of the PKWN. The Political Departments of the emerging Polish armies were largely staffed by Soviet officers. The only body which maintained even a semblance of autonomy was the military wing of the PPR, the 'People's Guard (GL)' of 'General

Moczar' whose so-called 'Partisans' would surface between 1955 and 1968 as a powerful anti-Muscovite and anti-Semitic faction within the Polish Communist movement.

The success of these manipulations depended in large measure on systematic propaganda and censorship. The desired effect was obtained by stressing and even exaggerating the enormity of Nazi crimes, and by suppressing all information about Soviet actions. In April 1945, the release of the sensational item of misinformation that '4 million human beings of various nationalities' had been killed at Auschwitz was nicely timed to conceal the fact that several ex-Nazi camps were being recommissioned at that very time by the UBP. It also concealed the fact that the great majority of Auschwitz's victims had been Jews.[20] Support for the new régime was identified with 'Patriotism'. Any Polish citizen who dared to question these machinations was immediately denounced as 'unpatriotic', or a 'saboteur' of Reconstruction. When vice Premier Mikolajczyk protested to the Parliament about the misdeeds of the Censorship, his protest was neatly excised from the parliamentary record.[21]

The Polish Government in London was powerless to influence these events. After the break in diplomatic relations with the Soviet Union in April 1943 following revelations about the Katyn Massacres—that is Stalin's cold-blooded murder in 1940 of 26,000 Polish officer-prisoners[22]—it gradually lost the confidence of the Western Powers intent on giving Stalin absolute priority in Eastern Europe. It was not even informed about the decisions of the Teheran Conference, where Poland's future was secretly agreed in principle; and it was not represented either at Yalta or at Potsdam. Its leading members, headed by the socialist Premier, Tadeusz Arciszewski, and the forceful acting C-in-C, General Anders, were increasingly divided in their counsels. Although it enjoyed the participation of all of Poland's democratic parties, all of whom were opposed as much to the pre-war Sanacja regime as to the communists, it could not bring its democratic credentials to bear. Although it ran arguably the largest of the Allied resistance movements, it received minimal practical assistance. (The Polish Parachute Brigade in Britain was never flown to Poland, being diverted instead to Arnhem). Although the Polish Government represented the country for whose independence war was declared, its interests were systematically ignored. It lost its official standing in London on 28 June 1945 on the day that the Western Powers transferred their recognition to the Soviet-run Provisional Government of National Unity in Warsaw. Its one consolation lay in the fact that it was not expelled. It was allowed to stay in London in its private capacity as the 'Polish Government-in-Exile'.[23] Having guarded the flame of legitimacy for 45 years, it eventually handed over its insignia to President Lech Walesa in December 1990.

In Poland, the Polish Government's supporters suffered a much harsher fate. Having seen the country overrun by the Soviets, the underground leaders of Poland's five main democratic parties—socialists, peasants, nationalists, Christian Democrats and Democratic Unionists—decided to negotiate. After lengthy preliminaries, they received formal assurances not only of their safety during the proposed conference but of a plane to fly them to London for consultations. On 27-28 March, sixteen leading men, including the last C-in-C of the AK, Okulicki, and the last Delegate of the Polish Government, Jankowski, emerged from hiding and were taken under escort to Soviet HQ at Pruszków. There, they were arrested and flown, not to London but to Moscow. This was the moment, barely a month after Yalta, when Churchill, who knew only of their disappearance, confessed to Roosevelt that they had put their names to a 'bogus manifesto'. In the Lubyanka, the sixteen were tortured, and charged with all manner of imaginary 'illegal activities'. The obscene show trial, in which the Polish allies of the Western Powers were ritually humiliated by Stalin, was staged one week before the Polish Government in London was abandoned—lest anyone mistake the message. General Okulicki, unbroken, made a defiant, dignified speech. British and American diplomats watched from the gallery, convinced that their silence would save the defendants' lives.[24]

The details of the operation to ensnare Poland's democratic leaders have recently become known through documents from the former NKVD archives in Moscow. General Seriv, Beria's deputy, arrived in Warsaw in January under the name of 'Ivanov', accompanied by two regiments of Soviet interior Ministry troops. His 'Chekists' captured large numbers of AK personnel by 'filtering' refugees on the pontoon bridges thrown across the Vistula. Through their network of informers, and through interrogations in the prison camp at Rembertów (which was advertised as a detention centre for former Gestapo agents), they gradually established the whereabouts and intentions of the Polish leaders. Orders came direct from Beria. Bierut, having told Serov that the underground leaders deserved a trial, was kept in the dark. The Western Allies only learned of their fate on 3 May when, dining in San Francisco with the US Secretary of State, Stettinius, Molotov casually said: *'Oh yes, I forgot to tell you; the Red Army arrested them'.*[25]

One might have thought that the Soviet juggernaut would have left its main imprint on Polish society in the field of social levelling. In reality, after six years of Nazi occupation, there was little social levelling left to be done. The industrialists and landowners were already dispossessed, the bourgeoisie mutilated, the intelligentsia decimated. The principal transformations at the end of the war took place not in the social but in the ethnic sphere. The Soviet re-occupation completed the processes of 'ethnic cleansing' that had first been put into motion in 1939.

In eastern Poland, which in pre-war days had been inhabited by a majority of Ukrainian and Byelorussian peasants interspersed with large Polish and Jewish communities, ethnic segregation was already far advanced. 1-2 million Poles had been deported to Russia and Kazakhstan in 1940-41. The Jews had been murdered by the German *Einsatzgruppen*. From mid-1943, the Polish population of Volhynia and East Galicia had been subject to a persistent and systematic campaign of terror-cleansing perpetrated by underground Ukrainian nationalist bands, who claimed tens if not hundreds of thousands of victims.[26] After the war, when elements of the UPA took refuge in the Bieszczady Mountains, the entire region was laid waste and depopulated by the communist authorities.[27]

In western Poland, the German population was most at risk. The wholesale slaughters, mass rapes and wanton destruction which were inflicted on Silesia, Posnania, Pomerania and other parts of the former German East have been well recorded in official documents.[28] So too has the long programme of expelling all Germans from East of the Oder in consequence of the joint Allied decisions at Potsdam.[29] Much less known are the events which occurred in the twilight era in mid-1945 between the arrival of the Red Army and the full establishment of a regular Polish administration. During these months, there can be no doubt that the incoming communist security forces committed abuses and atrocities on the grand scale. Ex-Nazi camps were re-opened to be filled with totally innocent German civilians. Ex-Gestapo prisons were re-activated by the NKVD and the UBP in order to torture and to kill the inmates. A recent study centred on the district of Upper Silesia makes an estimate of 60-80,000 German dead from abuse and disease.[30]

The same author puts a controversial spin onto his research by arguing that the overwhelming majority of agents in the communist security service in 1945 were Jews (or rather ex-Jews). His chief informant and the central *dramatis persona* of his account is a certain Lola Potok, a woman now resident in California, who had survived Auschwitz before serving the UBP as a prison commandant in Gleiwitz (Gliwice).[31] Elsewhere, one can read about the adventures in 1945 of a group of so-called *francuzi* or 'Frenchmen', whom the UBP imported from France. These men, who had served in the underground communist cadres of the French Resistance, had been drawn from pre-war Polish migrants. They are sometimes mentioned in order to be contrasted with the predominantly Jewish elements supplied by the NKVD. It is not clear, however, whether this distinction is entirely justified.

Throughout Poland, these Jewish matters raised a series of issues which have rarely been honestly described. During the War, the Jewish and non-Jewish communities had been totally segregated by the Nazis: and the Holocaust had taken place in isolation. After the war, when Jews and non-Jews were free to mix again, each side traumatised by the most painful experiences, frictions flared. An estimated 150,000 Polish Jews had survived the war. And a large Jewish contingent entered Poland in the wake of the Red Army. There is no doubt that many of them, including many non-communists, made no secret of their gratitude to the Soviet regime for having saved them from Hitler. It could not have been otherwise. On the other hand, they were sympathising with a régime which was deporting, killing, looting and purging the defenceless Polish population without mercy.

What is more, the most disgraceful sections of the communist machine appeared to contain a wholly disproportionate number of Jews. The reasons for this are clear enough. According to the very best authority, Jakub Berman, a decision had been made by the Soviet comrades to exclude Jews from all Poland's post-war social and economic organisations. As a result, Jews were naturally channelled into other services, especially those which required a high degree of political reliability.[32] Also, since Soviet nationality law did not recognise Polish-born Jews as citizens of Poland if their birthplace lay east of the Curzon Line, entry into one of the communist-led organisations offered such people the easiest escape route from the Soviet Union. Nor were ex-Jewish chiefs likely to spurn Jewish recruits. Hence, it is conceivable not just that Jews held all the chief offices of the UBP in 1945, but also that they formed the largest single group amongst its agents. Clearly, more impartial research needs to be done. but one cannot put much reliance on Bierut's statement that only 1.7 percent of the UBP's 25,000 agents were Jewish.[33] The old Nazi fiction about 'Jewish Bolshevism' briefly seemed to be gaining substance. After all, at a time when the wartime Resistance was being mercilessly repressed, official training and protection was being offered to Zionist guerrillas. At a time when Catholic Poles were losing their ancestral homelands in the East, there was talk of forming an autonomous Jewish province in the West. It was a ready-made recipe for the intercommunal animosities which were to culminate in the pogrom perpetrated at Kielce on 5 July 1946. Until that point, the great majority of Poland's surviving Jews had little intention of emigrating.

Historians must be concerned, therefore, not to divorce particular incidents from the wider context. It is quite unacceptable, for example, for an ex-officer of the UB to publish a study of murders committed against Jews without reference to all the other acts of violence that were prevalent at the time. It may well be true that c1,500 Jewish citizens were killed in Poland in 1945-47. But is impossible to make an informed judgement about such a statistic if one does not also enquire into the overall number of killings.[34]

Thanks to the uncertainty about Poland's post-war frontiers, mass migrations began long before the fighting ceased. Conscious of the

Soviet atrocities of 1939-41, many Polish refugees fled the eastern provinces in fear of the advancing Red Army. Many of them were to find a new home in the Western provinces detached from Germany at Potsdam. As from June 1945, the Polish Repatriation Office (PUR) began to administer the transfers through official channels.

Poland's so-called 'Recovered Territories' in the West and the North comprised an area of 101,000 km. They encompassed Breslau, Stettin and Danzig as well as the southern half of East Prussia. In the period between their occupation by the Soviet Army and the creation of a dedicated Polish Ministry for the region in November, they were a veritable 'Wild West' of mayhem and lawlessness. German authority had collapsed, but had not been adequately replaced. The rural remnant of the German population was defenceless. The ruined shells of the towns and cities were largely empty. An estimated 40% of all buildings had been completely destroyed. Industrial capacity dropped to 30%. Soviet reparation gangs were dismantling everything that could be dismantled—machinery, power stations, even railway lines. Looters mingled in the ruins with the migrants and squatters who were taking up residence in deserted streets and villas. The agents of the UBP set up business in the former stations and prisons of the Gestapo. When Bierut's delegation dutifully appeared at Potsdam to press for the cession of the Territories to Poland, they were pressing for a step which, in practice, had long since been granted.

In Soviet parlance, the events of 1944-5 in Poland were officially called 'the Liberation'. Western commentators often followed the same fashion. The assumption was that the Red Army had liberated eastern Europe in the same way that the British and Americans had liberated western Europe. Reality was rather different. Of course, it is true that the Soviet advance freed the Poles from the horrors of German occupation. For the survivors of the Nazi camps and prisons, the Soviet troops were, quite literally, the saviours. It is also true that the harshest years of Stalinism were still to come. At the same time, they were the bearers of a new form of totalitarian oppression which began to persecute innocent citizens in large numbers from the very first day. Unlike neighbouring Czechoslovakia, where the legitimate regime was allowed to return from its wartime exile, Poland was never given the chance of restoring its independence and sovereignty. There was no general Liberation. Indeed, many Poles would have been surprised to hear that the war had ended:

> *Those who knew*
> *what this was all about*
> *must make way for those*
> *who know little, or less than a little,*
> *or simply nothing.*[35]

Discussion

Professor Davies spoke further of the strategic position in 1944: the advance of the Red Army on Berlin was greeted with relief by the Poles. Stalin could have let the Polish Underground take over the country in return for their support in his push to Berlin, but any such generous gesture was inhibited by the knowledge of Soviet behaviour towards the Poles in 1939-41. *Dr Deighton* asked about the Ukrainian Underground, which seemed almost a private affair independent of the war. *Professor Davies* said that in this area, Eastern Galicia/Western Ukraine—the rear areas of the Eastern Front—ethnic cleansing on racial grounds had been proceeding since 1940 in a climate of terror created by the Soviet occupation. Information on this flowed into London through Polish Underground channels.

Mr Cviic concluded that all Poland's tribulations had resulted in a Poland which was more viable, stable and strong than at any time this century: *Professor Davies* agreed.

Notes and References

[1]   On the events of 1919-20 see Norman Davies, *White Eagle, Red Star: the Polish-Soviet War of 1919-20* (London, 1972). Soviet propagandists always held that the war was started by the Polish advance to Kiev in April-May 1920; and Russian nationalists still cling to the fiction, often claiming that the Poles had invaded 'Russia' or even 'the USSR' (which was not founded until 1922). In reality, the Kiev Campaign occurred in the middle of the Polish-Soviet War, and was undertaken by the Poles in alliance with the Ukrainian Directorate. At the time, Kiev was not in Soviet Russia, but was the capital of the independent republic of Ukraine, which was under attack from the Bolsheviks. The entry of Polish and Ukrainian forces into Kiev was warmly welcomed by the local population, but not by the Bolsheviks, who launched an international protest movement under the slogan 'Hands Off Russia'.

[2]   See K Sword (ed), *The Soviet Takeover of the Polish Eastern Provinces, 1939-41* (London, 1991); also Z S Siemaszko, *W sowieckim osaczeniu* (London, 1991).

[3]   For a general outline, see J Garlinski, *Poland During the Second World War, 1939-45* (London, 1985).

[4]   In August 1920, Stalin had been serving as the chief political commissar of the Soviets' south-western Front before Lwów, whilst Tukhachevsky led the five main Soviet armies of the Western Front against Warsaw. At the critical moment, the south-western Front had failed to move in support of Tukhachevsky's attack, thereby provoking charges that Stalin was responsible for the Red Army's defeat. Trotsky claimed that his orders had been disobeyed: in due course, Stalin faced a Party enquiry into his activities. It was not the sort of experience which he forgot. Seventeen years later, when Stalin had Tukhachevsky and his associates shot in the Purges, the principal defendants at his show trial had all served as army commanders on the Western Front in 1920. The officers headed by Voroshilov, who signed their death warrants, had all served with Stalin on the south-western Front. See Norman Davies, *White Eagle, Red Star*, op cit. It is interesting to note that in the 1990s ex-Soviet

historians in Russia have returned to the idea that Stalin (but not Marshal Pilsudski) was responsible for the Red Army's defeat.

5 *Documents on Polish-Soviet Relations, 1939-45* (Sikorski Institute, London, 1967), No. 81: quote by Sword, op cit, p 147.

6 Sword, ibid.

7 On the Warsaw Rising, see: Jan Ciechanowski, *The Warsaw Rising* (Cambridge, 1974); Janusz K Zawodny, *Nothing But Honour: the Story of the Warsaw Uprising 1944* (Hoover Institution, Stanford, 1977); Joanna K Hanson, *The Civilian Population and the Warsaw Uprising* (Cambridge University Press, 1982).

8 Some estimates reach six figures. In one single round-up, in Lwów, 3-8 January 1945, 12,300 people were arrested: see Sword, op cit, p 164, with references.

9 K Moczarski, *Conversations with an Executioner* (London, 1974). Moczarski, an AK soldier, was cast into the same cell as Juergen Stroop, the SS officer who had suppressed the Warsaw Ghetto Rising. The record of their conversations in the months prior to Stroop's hanging provides a rare insight into the realities of Eastern Europe in 1945.

10 When the future Solidarity activist, Jacek Kuron, was imprisoned in 1965, he found himself in prison in the company of an ex-Gestapo clerk who had been kept alive for twenty years because he was an expert in such forgeries. See J Kuron, *Wiara I wina: do it od komunizmu* (Warsaw, 1990), pp 324-5.

11 Adam Zagajewski, 'Rosja Wchodzi do Polski' (Russia Enters Poland), *Zeszyty Literackie*, (Paris, 1986), 'Nowe Wiersze', pp 10-11: trans. Norman Davies.

12 Marian Zielinski, from a reconstructed conversation. Prof. Zielinksi was the author's late father-in-law.

13 Janina Stankiewicz, from an account distributed in London by a Polish officer of the RAF whose mother had died in this particular deportation and who had great difficulty trying to explain to their British comrades that Poland had not been liberated.

14 Alexander Solzhenitsyn, *Prussian Nights: A Narrative Poem*, edited and translated by R Conquest (London, 1977), pp 33, 41-3.

15 Czeslaw Milosz (b 1917), poet and Nobel Prize Winner for Literature (1981), author of *The Captive Mind* (New York, 1953): Leszek Kolakowski (b 1927), philosopher, author of *The Main Currents of Marxism* (London, 1978), 3 vols.

16 An up-to-date account may be found in Krystyna Kersten, *The Establishment of Communist Rule in Poland, 1943-48* (Berkeley, 1991). See also Norman Davies, 'Poland', in M McCauley (ed), *Communist Power in Europe, 1944-49* (London, 1977), pp 39-57.

17 Talking to Stanislaw Mikolajczyk in Moscow in October 1944, Stalin likened the imposition of Communist to 'putting a saddle on a cow'. He actually used the famous metaphor in relation to Germany, and to apply his words to Poland is a common misquotation. It is clear from the context, however, that the underlying sentiment was applicable. I am obliged to Oliver Freeman for this clarification.

18 Lucjan Blit, *The Eastern Pretender: Boleslaw Piasecki, his life and times* (London, 1965); also Andrzej Micewski, *Wspolrzadzic czy nie klamac* (Paris, 1978).

19 Arthur Bliss Lane, *I saw Poland betrayed* (New York, 1947); A Bergman, *Faked Elections in Poland* (London, 1947); F Wilk, 'Lista czlonków PSL zamordowanych 1944-64', *Zeszyty Historyczne*, vi (Paris, 1964).

[20] A systematic discussion of Jewish and non-Jewish deaths at Auschwitz was successfully avoided until the fall of Poland's Communist regime, when an overall estimate of 1.2-1.5 millions came to be generally accepted. See F Piper, *Ilu ludzi zginelo w KL-Auschwitz?* (Oswiecim, 1992). The previous figure of 'Four Million' could not possibly have been accommodated either within the 'Six Million' victims of the Holocaust or within Poland's total war deaths.

[21] See Stanislaw Mikolajczyk, *The Rape of Poland: the pattern of Soviet domination* (London, 1948).

[22] Following President Gorbachev's admission of Soviet guilt in 1990, the latest studies of the Katyn massacres include: Allen Paul, *Katyn: the Untold Story of Stalin's Polish Massacre* (New York), 1991; Philip Bell, 'The Katyn Graves Revealed', in *John Bull and the Bear: British Public Opinion, Foreign Policy and the USSR, 1941-45* (London, 1990), pp 109-27; Nicholas Bethell, 'The Cold Killers of Kalinin', *The Observer*, 6 October 1991; and Vladimir Abarinov, *The Murderers of Katyn* (translated from the Russian, New York, 1993). [*The number of Poles killed at Katyn has been the subject of discussion since the massacre was first revealed: it seems likely that the total figure was at least 15,000.*]

[23] Edward, Count Reczynski, *In Allied London* (London, 1963).

[24] See Z Stypulkowski, *Invitation to Moscow* (New York, 1962). The proceedings of the show trial were published by the USSR People's Commissariat of Justice as *Trial of the Organisers, Leaders and Members of the Polish Diversionist Organisations...June 18-21 1945* (Moscow-London, 1945).

[25] Andrzej Chmielarz (Military Historical Institute, Warsaw), 'Kombinacja Rozmowy' (The Conversational Variant) in *Gazeta wyborcza*, 24 March 1995. The 'Conversational Variant' was General Serov's codename for the operation.

[26] Ks B Wincenty Urban, *Droga krzyzowa arcydiocezju lwowskiej, 1939-45* (Wroclaw, 1983); M Terlecki, *The Ethnic Cleansing of Poles in Volhynia and East Galicia* (Toronto, 1983); R Torzecki, *Polacy I Ukraincy: sprawa ukrainska w czasie II wojny swiatowej na terenie II Rzeczypospolitej* (Warsaw, 1993); W Poliszczuk, *Gorza prawda: zbrodniczosc OUN-IPA* (Toronto, 1994).

[27] For partial accounts of the so-called 'Operation Vistula', see J Gerhard, *luny w Bieszczadach* (Warsaw, 1968); also B Szczesniak, W Szopa, *Droga do nikad: dzialalnosc OUN I ich likwidacji w Polsce* (Warsaw, 1973).

[28] German documents.

[29] Alfred De Zayas, *Nemesis at Potsdam: the Anglo-Americans and the Expulsions of the Germans: Background, Execution, Consequences* (revised edn, London, 1979).

[30] John Sack, *An Eye for an Eye: the untold story of Jewish revenge on Germans in 1945* (Basic Books, New York, 1993). Cf also *DBPO*, Series II, Volume V, No 26 and Volume VI, Nos 39 and 54.

[31] Sack, op cit.

[32] Jakob Berman, in Teresa Toranska, *Oni*.

[33] As cited by D J Goldhasgen in 'False Witness', a review of Sack, op cit, in *The New Republic*, 27 December 1993.

[34] Samuel Krakowski, in a paper read to the first Polish-Jewish Conference, Somerville College, Oxford, September 1984.

[35] Wislawa Szymborska, Stanzas from 'Koniec I Poczatek' (Beginning and End), to be published in English translation. Presented by Stanislaw Baranczak, in 'The Most Pressing Questions are Naive Ones', Conference on Contemporary Polish Literature, SSEES, University of London, 22-25 March 1993.

15 The Soviet Takeover in Romania, 1944-48

MAURICE PEARTON AND DENNIS DELETANT

The general facts about the Soviet takeover in Romania are known and have been recorded in existing literature.[1] Some significant material has emerged since 1989, however, which does not change the overall picture but does give a more detailed account of the steps taken by Stalin to transform Romania into a communist state.[2] This paper reviews those steps in the light of this new evidence.

The evidence supports the view that Soviet policies in Eastern Europe did not represent a series of *ad hoc* responses to the situation but followed a blueprint thought out in advance. Over and above their retributive and security aims, the Russians appear to have wanted to settle a long-standing feud once and for all by punishing the guilty and educating the volatile Romanian people in the higher, more serious, realities of Soviet life.[3] This last was a new element. In December 1941, Stalin had informed Anthony Eden that he expected the western frontier of the Soviet Union to be the frontier of 1941 (which included Bessarabia and northern Bukovina as part of the USSR), and that Romania should give special facilities for military bases to the Soviet Union. In short, he wanted from Britain what in August 1939 he had thought he had secured from Germany. By 1944, however, 'special facilities' were not enough. The principal reason for the change was, in a word, 'Transnistria'. From 1941-1944 that province, under proclaimed Romanian sovereignty, was a place of relative order, attractive to Russians and Ukrainians. Its existence provided damning evidence of the weakness of the Soviet system and of the ineffectiveness of twenty years' propaganda and coercion.

The decision at the Teheran Conference that Romania was to be liberated by the Red Army ensured that Stalin would be able to make his writ run wherever the Red Army advanced. The fundamental problem thereafter for the western Allies was what limits Stalin would observe, or could be persuaded to observe, on the freedom of action granted him at Teheran. The Allies, unlike Stalin, could not back their policies in Eastern Europe by military force. In 1944, the western Allies still had no clear picture of Stalin's objectives. The 'percentage agreement' was one effort to attain clarity.

From the autumn of 1943, Romania was trying to get out of the War on terms which would keep the Russians at arms' length but forestall any preemptive takeover by the Germans. As we know, it did break with the Axis, through the coup of 23 August 1944. At that date, the Red Army was already in Moldavia. When a week later it arrived in Bucharest, it found in place a genuine Romanian Government whose officers included the communist, Lucretiu Patrascanu, as Minister of

Justice ad interim. In this respect, the coup transformed the status of the Romanian Communist Party. It was henceforth officially tied into the future development of Romania, but not initially in a framework of Soviet devising.

Certain evidence now suggests that Patrascanu's participation in a bourgeois government was not in accordance with the original script. In September in Moscow for the Armistice negotiations, Patrascanu had an audience with Zhdanov. Although they had long been associated in the Comintern, Zhdanov addressed him as 'Mr' (i.e. not 'Comrade') and enquired sarcastically, 'What are you doing here ?' 'Well, we overturned the dictatorship and brought Romania onto the side of the Allies, and we've come to sign the armistice.' Zhdanov replied: ' You've done wrong, for you've upset all our plans.' These plans were for the Soviets to capture Bucharest, overthrow Antonescu, and to treat Romania as a conquered enemy, without the impediment of a Romanian government to deal with.[4] It is reasonable to suppose that Zhdanov was voicing Stalin's frustrations. Nevertheless, Patrascanu was *en poste* and the Communist Party— hitherto a small faction-ridden group with little or no effective resonance in Romania, its leadership divided between two main centres and constrained to respond to policies devised in Moscow reflecting Soviet political strategies rather than Romanian political conditions—was suddenly respectable. The problem for its members, and their Soviet masters, was to make it dominant.

Romania's external position immediately after the coup was that of an independent state waging war against its former allies on the side of its former enemies, with whom its relationships were covered by the Armistice Agreement signed in Moscow on 12 September 1944. Its drafting demonstrated the Soviet predominance conferred at Teheran.[5] It recognized Romania's complete reversal, particularly in its military implications (Articles 1-3) and secured the return of Bessarabia and northern Bukovina to the Soviet Union (Article 5). Stalin's initial territorial objectives were achieved, but for him 'security' implied not merely treaty guarantees but also the abrogation of the political power of those who had launched the invasion. Marxism-Leninism had already provided for their elimination as a class. The carrying through of a revolution depended internally on the creation of Communist agencies, using the presence of the Red Army as the ultimate deterrent to opposition, and externally on the Soviet Union's imposing its own policies for the settlement of Eastern Europe.[6] Both necessarily took time: the nullifying of both internal and external opposition was not completed till 1947—the one marked by the trial of opposition political leaders and the currency reform, the other by the conclusion of the Peace Treaty. The external issues have been well covered in the literature. This paper will concentrate on the internal developments.

Since the Soviet Union had a monopoly of its interpretation, the Armistice Agreement became the mechanism for the takeover of Romania. Articles 13 and 14 provided for the arrest of war criminals and the dissolution of 'Fascist-type' organizations. Article 18 established an Allied Control Commission, under the general direction and order of 'the Allied (Soviet) High Command, acting on behalf of the Allied Powers'. In practice, it functioned under statutes drawn up by the Russians, under which, until Potsdam, American and British officers were treated as delegations to the Commission, not structurally part of it. Hence rights formally granted to the Allies under the Armistice Agreement were defined and enforced by the Russians. Stalin, therefore, had two satisfactory instruments for pursuing his objectives in Romania: a Communist Party which was an acknowledged part of the country's political structure, and an agreement with his Allies giving the Red Army all the scope it needed.

The takeover of Romania resulted from the interaction between the two: while the fighting was still in progress, the Red Army, as any army, required order behind the front, but in Romania the only order acceptable to the Russians was that guaranteed by the RCP. The Party's role was to prevent the post-coup régime from establishing order on any other terms. That requirement implied, firstly, neutralizing the existing means of maintaining the social order, viz army, judiciary and police and redesigning them to the Soviet model; secondly, creating mass support, which the RCP totally lacked, and which would provide the new régime with the necessary theoretical legitimation. Both activities involved reliance on terror, and both could be relied upon to destroy any vestiges of support for the monarchy and for 'western' democracy.

In the caretaker government of General Sanatescu (23 August-2 November 1944), the majority of ministerial posts had gone to military officers, with only the Ministry of Justice being secured by the Communists in the person of Patrascanu. While several senior officers of the Intelligence Service, the SSI *(Serviciul Special de Informatii)*, were arrested in September 1944, the committee charged with screening the 600 personnel of the SSI employed nationally concluded, in a report of 20 October, that they could find only two officers against whom charges could be levelled and these were 'abusive behaviour and unseemly conduct'.[7] The personnel of the Ministry of the Interior and of the security police, the *Siguranta*, remained largely unchanged.[8] It was the failure to replace these figures that provided a pretext for the Communists to set about torpedoing the Sanatescu government. At the same time the Soviet authorities set about weakening Romania's army and police force.

On 2 October, the Soviet High Command demanded the reduction of the police force from 18,000 to 12,000. On 6 October, it forced the resignation of General Gheorge Mihail, the Chief of the Romanian

General Staff, because of his opposition to the Soviet order that all Romanian units should be disarmed, except for the twelve divisions fighting alongside the Russians. Mihail's successor, General Nicolae Radescu, consented under protest to the Soviet demand (26 October) that the Romanian army in the interior be reduced from 13 full-strength to 3 skeleton divisions with a total complement of 10,000, and that the numbers of frontier guards and gendarmerie be cut from 74,086 to 58,018. This process was continued over the next three years, leading to a fall in the strength of the Romanian Armed forces from 419,000 in May 1945 to 136,000 in December 1947.[9]

These actions by the Soviet authorities ensured that the Party could proceed without fundamental interference. Its first task was to broaden its bridgehead in government, which demanded admission to crucial ministries—Interior, Defence as well as Justice—and the creation of mass support, which could be used to demand radical political change. On 2 October, the Communist Party and the Social Democratic Party joined forces to form the National Democratic Front (NDF). Members of the Front threatened workers at major factories in Bucharest and elsewhere with arrest by the Soviet army if they refused to vote out the old works' committees and elect NDF representatives in their place. The new committees then took charge of the workers' canteens and rationing procedures and soon the NDF had much of industry in its grip, forcing workers to accede to its will under pain of withdrawing rations and special ration cards.

In industry and elsewhere, the threats were given weight by the 'Guards of Patriotic Defence', enlarged from the nucleus of armed workers who took charge of Antonescu after his arrest. Enlargement, in September 1944, was supervised by the Soviet Security Service, the NKVD, and placed under the command of Emil Bodnaras. It provided the ideal cover for the training of agents and thugs who were to be infiltrated into the police and security forces when the Communists gained access to the Ministry of the Interior. The 'Guards' were used to root out 'Fascists' and encourage recalcitrants to see the error of opposition. When necessary, they enjoyed the logistic cooperation of the Russian command. Their recruits included gaolbirds and former Legionnaires, whose intimidatory skills had, of course, been honed in the late 1930s.[10] On 15 January 1945 the Prime Minister, General Radescu, ordered the Guard's disbandment, but Georgescu and Bodnaras simply ignored the instruction. With the truncated Romanian army absent or disarmed, the Government had no countervailing power.

The Armistice Agreement had stipulated the dissolution of 'all pro-Hitler organizations (of a Fascist type)' (Art 15). This, widely drawn, was liberally interpreted. In early September, the Foreign Minister, Niculescu-Buzesti, and Starcea, the Marshal of the Palace (both leading figures in the coup of 23 August), called for the immediate establishment of a tribunal for the trial of war criminals and of pro-Germans holding responsible positions. Maniu raised legalistic objections and the proposal was dropped.[11]

Hence, what the proposers had feared came to pass: the liquidation of Fascism fell to the Russians and to their local minions. We should at this point recall that the war against the Axis still in progress was widely accepted as an 'anti-Fascist' crusade; that there were many in Romania who, in some sense or other, qualified as 'Fascist' and that the governments immediately after the coup appeared to be dilatory in dealing with them. An agitation to get rid of Fascists could count on some popular support. Events soon demonstrated that, in practice, 'Fascist' came to mean what the Communists said it was—and they could say it through 'spontaneous' demonstrations and a press which was rapidly being brought under control.[12]

On 8 October the NDF organized its first mass meeting in Bucharest, at which some 60,000 demonstrators called for the resignation of the Sanatescu government for having failed to remove 'Fascists' from public life. On the following day General Vinogradov, the head of the Soviet Military Mission, demanded that the government arrest forty-seven Romanians as war criminals, among them two cabinet ministers, General Gheorghe Potopeanu, the Minister of the National Economy who had served for a brief period as Military Governor of Transnistria, and General Ion Boiteanu, the Minister of Education. The slowness with which Sanatescu acted against Antonescu's officials merely provided grist to the mill of the Communist Party and Soviet authorities, who accused the Romanians of not respecting articles 14 and 15 of the Armistice. In their defence Romanian officials argued that the bureaucracy would not be able to function if large scale purges of the kind demanded by the Russians were implemented.[13] Confirmation of the Communists' charges came from an American OSS (Office of Strategic Services) report of February 1945 which stated that during the first six weeks after the August coup the Sanatescu government dismissed only eight Romanian officials.[14]

Demonstrations also focused on specific political figures whom the Communists wanted removed, such as the new Minister of the Interior, Nicolae Penescu, a National Peasant who was vehemently anti-Soviet. Mass demonstrations were organized to shout 'Down with Penescu'. At the end of November the NDF seized upon a suburban brawl as a pretext for demanding his resignation. A group of drunken Romanian soldiers shot dead two trade unionists, for whom the NDF organized a huge funeral. The Communist press raged about 'Hitlerist Fascist bullets from automatic rifles of the Fifth Column supported by leaders of the National Peasant Party.' The Peasant Party ministers and their National Liberal colleagues withdrew from the cabinet of Sanatescu whom they felt was too tolerant of Communist harassment. On 2 December, the King asked General

Nicolae Radescu, formerly Chief of the General Staff and a non-party figure, to form a cabinet.[15]

Radescu received strong backing from King Michael, who on 4 December warned Andrei Vishinsky, the Soviet Deputy Foreign Minister, that the Communists' activities threatened to throw the country into anarchy. Among these was an unremitting press campaign in the party newspaper Scanteia condemning the Romanians' alleged failure to fulfil the principal conditions of the armistice. Scanteia reprinted (6 December 1944) Soviet charges that the Romanian Government had systematically shirked from honouring its direct debt and had openly supported the administration which sabotaged the Armistice Convention. The leaders of the so-called 'historical parties' in Romania, the National Peasant and National Liberal parties who were widely represented in the Sanatescu government, were responsible. The conclusion was ominous:

> *The Soviet Command in this part of the Soviet-German front is displaying the utmost patience which is being abused by those Romanian politicians who have transformed this region of the front into an area of intrigue which is undermining the mobilization of the forces of the Romanian people and basic order in the country...*[16]

The King told Vishinsky that if the Soviet Union continued to support the Communists in this way he would find himself forced to abdicate and leave the country. Vishinsky was said to have been surprised by the King's boldness and denied any Soviet responsibility. In the government reshuffle the Communist-dominated NDF had hoped to secure the Ministry of the Interior, but Radescu reserved the post for himself. Thereupon the Party leaders, Ana Pauker and Vasile Luca, refused even to discuss NDF participation in the new government, but under instructions from Vishinsky they backed down.[17] Radescu did, however, concede the position of Deputy Minister of the Interior to the Communists, appointing Teohari Georgescu, a member of the Party's Central Committee; his Communist colleagues in the cabinet were Patrascanu, Minister of Justice, and Gheorgiu-Dej, Minister of Communications and Public Works.

Vishinsky's decision throws some light on Soviet intentions at this time. His long-term mission was to prepare Romania for Sovietization, but the short-term priority was to conclude the war against Germany as quickly as possible. Instability in Romania would compromise that aim. Furthermore, the Romanian Communist Party was still not strong enough to take over the administration of the country where the bulk of the population was hostile to Communism; therefore, should the King abdicate, the Russians were likely to have to assume part of the administration themselves. Such a move would expose their motives to Britain and the United States. Consequently,

Vishinsky lowered the temperature in Romania. He left the country as he had come, without notice, on 8 December.[18]

For a brief period, NDF meetings and street demonstrations ceased, but communist penetration of institutions continued unabated. Teohari Georgescu installed his own men in nine of the sixteen prefectures in the provinces with strict orders to avoid government instructions and to do only his bidding. He also ignored an undertaking to Radescu to disband the 10,000-strong communist militia and introduced into the *Siguranta* agents trained in the 'Patriotic Guards'. The truce ended with the publication of the NDF New Year's appeal to the people in which they condemned the Radescu government for failing to fulfil the terms of the Armistice, and called for agrarian reform of all property exceeding an area of 50 hectares within six weeks.

It was soon evident that the RCP's moves were Soviet-orchestrated. In early January 1945, Ana Pauker and Gheorghiu-Dej returned from Moscow claiming that they had 'received Soviet approval for the bringing into power of a communist government'.[19] The actions of the NDF bore this claim out. The NDF attacked its National Liberal and National Peasant partners in the government, denouncing them as 'Fascists' who opposed the will of the people, and on 27 January demanded a new government, immediate agrarian reform, and the democratization of the army. When the Liberals and Peasants attempted to answer these charges, their newspapers ceased to appear owing to the refusal of the communist-controlled printing union to produce them. The communist press accused Radescu of sabotaging the armistice by allegedly failing to cleanse Romanian public life of 'Fascism' but omitted to point out that it had failed to put its own house in order in the case of those ministries headed by communists.

Teohari Georgescu sent an open letter to the press accusing Radescu of having hindered the 'decontamination' of the Ministry of the Interior, and the Prime Minister responded by publishing on 16 February three circulars, dated 13 and 28 December 1944 and 20 January 1945, calling on the commission charged with compiling the list of officials liable for dismissal to complete its task. Radescu was able to point out that the commission for purging the Ministry of the Interior, of which Teohari Georgescu himself was a member, had taken three months to examine 75 cases out of 300, and that following the General's intervention 137 cases had been dealt with in twelve days. In fact, under the Radescu government 780 officers (ie employees of the Interior ministry) out of an estimated 14,000 workforce, were purged.[20]

Aware of the power which Georgescu and Bodnaras were amassing, Radescu ordered the disbandment of the 'Patriotic Guards' on 15 January but the two Communists simply ignored his instruction. In the meantime the Deputy Prime Minister Petru Groza, a tool of the

Communists, was encouraging peasants to anticipate land reform by seizing the land of the large estate owners. An article in *Scanteia* of 13 February 1945 reported the expropriation of estates by peasants in the counties of Prahova and Dambovita. Two days later Radescu accused Groza at a cabinet meeting of preparing civil war. Both Radescu and King Michael feared that the Left was preparing a coup amidst reports that the Russians were sending to Bucharest NKVD troops.[21]

Any hopes that the Romanian people might have had from the Declaration on Liberated Europe, issued at the Yalta Conference, that 'sovereign rights and self-government' would be restored 'to those peoples who have been forcibly deprived of them' were soon dispelled. Organized thuggery was practised by the 'Patriotic Guards' in support of the NDF committees whose hold over several key factories in Bucharest was challenged by non-NDF workers. This particular campaign of Communist-inspired violence began at the ASAM defence works early in February and spread to the Official Gazette and Stella works where the NDF committees were thrown out. At the union elections at the ASAM shops only 14 of the 600 workers voted for the Communist candidates while 180 voted for the non-party list (the remainder abstained).

On 6 February sixty members of the 'Patriotic Guards' and two NKGB soldiers drove to the ASAM works, beat up those who had voted for the independent list, and took eleven of them away to the NKGB headquarters. On 19 February 3600 of the 5500 employees at the Malaxa steel and armament works in Bucharest signed a resolution calling for the resignation of the NDF committee headed by Vasile Mauriciu, a former Iron Guardist. Voting on the resolution on the following day was interrupted when the NDF committee called on railwaymen and tramway employees to defend them at the factory. Fighting broke out between the Malaxa workers and the outsiders during which several workers were killed and the Communist labour leader Gheorghe Apostol was wounded. After the affray all those whose identity cards showed that they had voted were arrested and taken to NDF branches.[22]

Travesty was added to injury. *Scanteia* accused Radescu of attempting to foment a civil war; its attacks were echoed by *Graiul Nou*, the Red Army newspaper in Romania, and *Pravda*. Anatoli Pavlov, the Soviet political representative on the Allied Control Commission, followed the script by advising the chief American on the Commission that unless the Radescu government 'rid itself of...Fascist elements...the people themselves can be expected to take necessary corrective action'.[23] Matters came to a head on 24 February. At the end of a large NDF demonstration, the crowd moved into the palace square in front of the Ministry of the Interior where Radescu had his office. Shots were fired and several people were killed. On orders from Radescu the

Romanian troops guarding the building fired into the air to disperse the crowd. The American historian Henry Roberts:

> *watched the procession and was in the crowd no more than fifty feet from the first shots. Yet at that time and since I have been unable to discover precisely what happened. I do know that government had kept Romanian troops off the streets that day to avoid inciting trouble. The crowd did move toward the Ministry of the Interior building, although it showed little signs of direction. The first shots were fired from a small piece and fromsomewhere in the crowd, but by whom and for what purpose I do not know.*[24]

What was clearly established later by a joint Romanian-Russian commission of doctors was that the bullets extracted from the victims were not of a calibre used by the Romanian army, but these findings came too late for Radescu. Unable to contain his anger at the provocation, the Prime Minister broadcast to the nation denouncing the Communist leaders, Ana Pauker and Vasile Luca, as 'hyenas' and 'foreigners without God or country', a reference to their non-Romanian origins and their atheism. The Russians now intervened. The Soviet Deputy Foreign Minister Vyshinsky arrived unexpectedly in Bucharest on 27 February and went straight to the Palace to demand that Radescu be replaced. King Michael hesitated and told the Russian that constitutional procedures had to be respected. On the following afternnon Vyshinsky returned and demanded to know what action the King had taken. When Michael again announced that he was consulting political leaders, the Deputy Minister shouted his dissatisfaction and gave the King until six that evening to announce Radescu's dismissal. The King was intimidated into consenting.

King Michael turned to the British and American representatives for help and advice, but despite the lodging of Western protests in Bucharest and Moscow at Vyshinski's behaviour, the Deputy Foreign Minister continued to force the pace. Military pressure was added to political. On 28 February Colonel-General Ivan Susaikov, the Deputy-Commander of the Southern Group of Armies, replaced Lt-Gen V Vinogradov as Deputy Chairman of the Allied Control Commission.[25] Without consulting his British and American colleagues, he ordered some Romanian units stationed in and around Bucharest to the front and disbanded others. Their place was taken by Soviet tanks and troops who occupied the Prefecture of Police, the Central Post Office, and the Romanian General Staff Headquarters. Two Romanian bomber groups and two fighter squadrons based on the capital were disbanded, and the rest of the Romanian air force was grounded. Hundreds of plain clothes and uniformed police were dismissed and Soviet troops patrolled the streets of Bucharest, checking the documents of pedestrians and of drivers and their vehicles, and using this opportunity to commandeer even more Romanian vehicles.

On 1 March Vyshinski informed the King that Petru Groza, Radescu's deputy and a trusted nominee of the Russians 'was the Soviet choice'. Michael reluctantly gave Groza the go-ahead to form a government but the Liberals and Peasants refused to join a government controlled by the NDF. Groza's first cabinet was rejected by the King. On 5 March Vyshinski informed Michael that unless a Groza government was accepted he 'could not be responsible for the continuance of Romania as an independent state'.[26] Fearing a coup the King acquiesced on the following afternoon. Thereafter, the communist take-over of Romania proceeded rapidly.

Susaikov subsequently explained to the British and American representatives on the Control Commission (respectively Air Vice-Marshal Stevenson and Brigadier Schuyler) that the Groza government was indeed imposed by force, on the orders of Marshal Malinovsky who feared an uprising at the rear of his front. Susaikov had been sent to Bucharest to prevent a Romanian *volte-face* disarming Romanian troops and bringing in Groza.[27]

The new Groza government was dominated by the NDF, which held fourteen of the eighteen cabinet posts. Communists controlled the Ministries of the Interior, Justice, War, and the National Economy. Dissident Liberal and Peasants held the other four portfolios, the most notorious being King Carol's former Prime Minister Gheorghe Tatarescu, once an opponent and now a sycophant of the Soviet Union, who was made Deputy Prime Minister and Foreign Minister. Teohari Georgescu was elevated to the position of Minister of the Interior. Immediately after his appointment, he announced that 'in order to carry out its tasks...the Ministry of the Interior must rely on a powerful police apparatus that had been purged of all Fascist, collaborationist or compromised elements who had been perverted by anti-democratic and venal customs and practices'.[28] Of the 6,300 Ministry of the Interior personnel employed on 6 March 1945, 2,851 were placed on the reserve and 195 dismissed. In their place were brought in 'honest, democratic and capable elements'.[29]

The police, the *Siguranta*, the gendarmerie and the Corps of Detectives were reorganized, the latter body being given the special task of tracking down and arresting members of the Iron Guard who were still active.[30] Under the direction of an NKVD agent, Alexandru Nicolski, the Corps was to provide the nucleus of the *securitate*.[31] Georgescu's colleague, Emil Bodnaras, was promoted secretary general to the Prime Minister.

Bodnaras calls for special mention. On present evidence he was the crucial figure in all these developments. Successively organizer of the Patriotic Guards, Secretary General to Petru Groza as Prime Minister, and Minister of Defence, he was also an officer of the NKVD. All the various strands in the Communist take-over intersected in his office.

Within the Party he was directly involved in the decision to murder the former General Secretary, Stefan Foris, in February 1945, and he became a member of the Politburo in 1948.[32] Bodnaras, however, was not only pivotal but ambiguous; even now it is far from clear where his ultimate loyalties lay.[33]

On 7 March Groza announced that there would be a purge of 'Fascists' from public life and on 2 April the Party daily *Scanteia* declared that several hundred police and counter-espionage officers who were 'guilty of the disaster which had befallen the country' (communist jargon for the alliance with Germany) had been arrested. The arrests were carried out on 20 March. To complete Soviet control over the forces of repression, Groza signed an order on 27 April giving the Secretary General control of the Intelligence service, the SSI. The danger of any opposition to the Soviet and Communist presence by trained and armed forces was eliminated, and the new instruments for communizing Romanian society were in place.

Notes and References

[1]   See the Bibliography below.
[2]   Examples are G Buzatu, *Romania cu si fara Antonescu* (Iasi: Editura Moldova, 1991), where the Romanian diplomatic minute of the armistice negotiations held in Moscow in September 1944 is published (pp 259-71); Dinu C Giurescu, *Romania's Communist Takeover: The Radescu Government* (Boulder, Colorado: East European Monographs, 1994, based in part on primary and secondary Romanian material, and D Deletant, 'The *Securitate* and the Police State in Romania, 1948-64', *Intelligence and National Security*, vol 8, no 4 (October 1993), pp 1-25 which includes a brief account of Soviet penetration and manipulation of the Romanian security police after August 1944.
[3]   M Pearton, *Oil and the Romanian State* (London: Oxford University Press, 1971), p 265, note 5.
[4]   Reported by Patrascanu to Corneliu Coposu (secretary general of the Council of Ministers) on 14 September 1944, four days after the interview with Zhdanov. See 'Exilul Romanesc: Identitate si Constiinta istorica,' *Lupta*, no 232 (7 octombrie 1994), p 5.
[5]   Cmd 6585, *Conditions of an Armistice with Roumania*, Miscellaneous No.1 (1945), London: HMSO, 1945.
[6]   M Pearton, op cit, pp 265-67.
[7]   *Cartea Alba a Securitatii*, vol 1 (Bucharest: SRI, 1995), p 92. The officers arrested were Eugen Cristescu, the head of the SSI, Gheorghe Cristescu and Nicolae Trohani, both department heads, Florin Begnescu, an officer in the counterespionage section, and Eugen Haralamb.
[8]   The policing and public order duties were carried out by the Directorate General of the Police (to which the security police, the *Siguranta* was subordinated), the Corps of Detectives and the General Inspectorate of the Gendarmes. The latter were responsible for public order in rural districts. All three bodies came under the aegis of the Ministry of the Interior.
[9]   A Dutçu, 'Comisia Aliata de Control Destructureaza Armata Romana (3)', *Revista de Istorie Militara*, no 5, 1992, p 22.1. See Bibliography.

10   One of the advantages of a class theory of politics is that it legitimates casual murder. The 'Guards' victims, who were killed or later died of their injuries, have yet to be counted.

11   See the digest of OSS reports in FO to Minister Resident, Cairo, No 3251, 16 September 1944 (WO 201 1602).

12   The fate of *Viitorul*—the old National Liberal organ—is instructive. Between the Armistice and February 1945, publication was frequently suspended by order of the Control Commission, in consequence of its exposure of official communiqués claiming the liberation by Russian troops of towns already freed by Romanian units, and of its editorials attacking Communist leaders. Within the enterprise, from November a self-appointed Communist committee prevented printing of articles critical of the NDF. The workers capitulated, on the threatened withdrawal of their ration cards and possible deportation. The editor received death threats. Finally, the Control Commission ordered the paper's suppression, on 15 February, when all non-Communist journals were closed down. One of the charges was that the paper was printing suspicious abbreviations. They turned out to be the distinctions of Air Vice Marshal Stevenson, head of the British Military Mission, his 'CBE, DSO, MC' being interpreted as a coded message.

13   The same argument was invoked forty-five years later by former Communists in Romania in defending the retention of the Ceausescu bureaucracy after the revolution of 1989.

14   Paul D Quinlan, *Clash Over Romania. British and American Policies towards Romania: 1938-1947* (Los Angeles: American Romanian Academy, 1977), p 116, note 58.

15   Radescu had won the Order of Michael the Brave, the highest Romanian military decoration, during the First World War and in November 1941 had been interned on Antonescu's orders for writing a defiant letter to Baron Killinger, Hitler's envoy, in reply to disparaging remarks made by the Baron about Romania.

16   'In Bucuresçti acum 50 ani', *Magazin Istoric*, vol 28, no 12 (December 1994), pp 49-50.

17   Dinu C Giurescu, *Romania's Communist Takeover: The Radescu Government* (Boulder, Colorado: East European Monographs), 1994, p 135.

18   Ibid, p 137.

19   Quinlan, op cit, p 120.

20   *Cartea Alba a Securitatii*, vol 1 (Bucharest: SRI, 1995), pp 12, 92. The number of police officers remained virtually the same until the reorganization of the police according to the Soviet model in August 1948.

21   Ibid, p 121.

22   A broadsheet issued by the workers at the Malaxa factory on 23 February read: 'We protest most strongly at the terror tactics which irresponsible persons from outside the factory are employing at the Malaxa works in support of the committee of dishonourable agitators which has been kept in place against the workers' will. We protest at the violence of the armed mercenaries who were brought in by lorries under the direction of Gheorghiu-Dej, who has come to impose the will of a disparate minority which has even shot its own supporters. We denounce the hooligans who wish to halt with gun fire the free expression of the workers' will. We demand the arrest of the armed bands of NDF supporters, who have been brought in from outside and have no place amongst us. We demand the arrest of Gheorghiu-Dej and the other Trotskyist agitators. We want free elections and a secret ballot. We want trade unions

based on professions and not politically manipulated hordes. We demand that the government ensure freedom and the secret ballot, and prevent the terror practised against us by irresponsible criminals. We want work and order. We want peace. Down with the terror in the trade unions !'

23   *Cartea Alba a Securitatii,* op cit, p 122.

24   H L Roberts, *Rumania. Political Problems of an Agrarian State,* (New Haven: Yale University Press, 1951), p 263, note 29.

25   The nominal Chairman, Marshal Rodion Malinovsky, as Commander of the Second Ukrainian Front, was preoccupied with hostilities in Hungary and Czechoslovakia.

26   Quinlan, op cit, p 128.

27   Susaikov gave this explanation at the end of October 1945, asking Stevenson and Schuyler whether they would have done otherwise. They agreed that they would not, but thought that it was a pity that this had not been explained before (H Hanak, 'The Politics of Impotence: The British Observe Romania, 6 March 1945 to 30 December 1947', *Romanii in istoria universala, vol III/1,* ed I Agrigoroaie, Gh Buzatu, and V Cristian, Iasçi, 1988, p 433). Soviet sensitivity to disorder behind their lines had been conveyed to Schuyler at the time by A. Pavlov, the Soviet Political Representative. At a meeting of the Allied Control Commission on 14 February 1945, Pavlov had told Schuyler that 'no disorder can be permitted to occur in the rear of the Soviet armies...nor can any Fascist activities within the state of Romania be permitted (D Giurescu, op cit, p 67). Soviet unease about the possibility of a Romanian uprising had been fuelled by the infiltration of German agents and German-held Romanian prisoners of war into Romanian units in order to instigate mutinies. Roland Gunne, an SD officer from Transylvania, had wormed his way onto the staff of the Romanian Fourth Army which was fighting in Hungary. The commander of the Fourth Army was General Gheorghe Avramescu who, before the 23 August *coup* , had fought against the Russians in the Crimea and whose son-in-law was reputed to be a member of the Iron Guard. Avramescu's anti-Russian sentiments made him a prime candidate for German manipulation and Gunne allegedly persuaded the General to defect with his forces to the German side in the event of a successful German counter-offensive. P Biddiscombe, 'Prodding the Russian Bear: pro-German Resistance in Romania, 1944-5', *European History Quarterly,* vol 23, no 2 (April 1993), pp 205-12. On 3 March 1945 Avramescu was arrested in Budapest on the orders of Marshal Malinovsky. Avramescu's fate is unclear. According to the Soviet Red Cross, he was killed in a German air attack on Budapest on 3 March. No mention was ever made by the Soviet authorities of his arrest. His wife and daughter were arrested on the same day. The daughter committed suicide three days later, and Avramescu's wife spent eleven years in Soviet labour camps before being allowed to return to Romania. J Urwich-Ferry, *Fara Paşçaport prin URSS* (In the USSR without a Passport) (Munich: Iskra, 1977), vol II, pp 51-7.

28   *Cartea Alba a Securitatii,* op cit, vol 1, p 92.

29   Ibid. In June 1946 Georgescu reported that the numbers of Ministry of Interior personnel had risen to 8,500, of whom only 4,084 had been employed before 23 August 1944.

30   Ibid, vol 1, p 13.

31   The number of officers in the Corps of Detectives was, according to the available documents, halved from 221 in March 1945 to 101 in January 1947. Enrolled in the Corps after March 1945 were a number of Romanian-speaking Soviet agents, most of whom, like Nicolski, had been captured by the

Romanian authorities and had been released from jail after 23 August. Among these agents were Andrei Gluvakov, Vladimir Gribici, Misa Protopopov, Vanea Didenko, Iasçka Alexeev, Mihail Postanski (Posteuca), Misa Petruc, Alexandru Sisman and Pyotr Gonciaruc: P Stefanescu, *Istoria Serviciilor Secrete Romanesti* (Bucharest: Divers Press, 1994), p 163. A serialized biography of Nicolski was published in the Romanian weekly *Cuvintul* (April and May 1992) by Marius Oprea. In October 1944 he joined the police and after the imposition of the Groza government was named head of the Corps of detectives. On 17 April 1947 he was appointed Inspector General of the security police and when the *securitate* was established on 30 August 1948, he was named as one of the two deputy directors. For further details see Dennis Deletant, 'The *Securitate* and the Police State in Romania, 1948-64,' *Intelligence and National Security,* vol 8, no 4 (October 1993), pp 13-14.

[32] The decision to remove Stefan Foris as General Secretary of the Party was made in April 1944 in circumstances which are still not entirely clear, for the mists of politically-engineered distortion still linger over the matter. According to the version propagated during the period of Gheoghiu-Dej's supremacy within the Party, a meeting was held on 4 April in the hospital of the Tirgu-Jiu internment camp involving Dej, Emil Bodnaras, Constantin Parvulescu, Iosif Ranghet and Chivu Stoica at which Dej demanded the removal of Foris on the grounds that he was a police informer. In the course of time, Dej came to be portrayed in the Communist media as having been the architect of the decision to exclude Foris, for it served both as a stick with which to beat rivals such as Pauker who had allegedly questioned his removal when she arrived in Romania, and as a banner of Dej's defence of Romanian interests when the rift with Moscow occurred in the early 1960s. Yet the merit to be gained from Foris's removal depended on his being proved a 'traitor'. Without that proof his dismissal and, more importantly, his murder had no justification. Barely three years after Dej's death, the accusation of being a 'traitor' made against Foris was dropped: in April 1968 Nicolae Ceausescu condemned Dej for the 'assassination' of Foris, who was considered 'innocent' of being an enemy agent. Nevertheless, Foris was still branded as guilty of 'grave shortcomings' in his work which had made his removal necessary.

Eduard Mezincescu, who had occasion later to discuss in detail the career of Emil Bodnaras with Serghei Nikonov (Sergiu Nicolau), appointed head of the SSI, the Intelligence Service, under Bodnaras in April 1945, learned from Nikonov that the replacement of Foris had been first discussed in the prison hospital at Tirgu-Jiu in June 1943. Dej's view was that Foris should simply be ousted. The idea of placing him in a safe house, to which he was taken by Bodnaras on 4 April 1944, was apparently an initiative of the latter. Foris was only detained for two or three months and was seen looking for work at the Party headquarters in August 1944. He was re-arrested early in 1945 when Dej and Bodnaras allegedly produced 'proof' that he was working for the *Siguranta* . Ana Pauker's son-in-law, Gheorghe Bratescu, concedes that while his mother-in-law was a party to the order to arrest Foris, she was not consulted about the decision to murder him, which, he alleges, was taken one evening at a secret meeting of Dej, Bodnaras, and George Pintilie (head of the body responsible for Party security). Indeed, after Pauker learned of Foris's death, she told Dej that Foris should have been put on trial. Dej replied that the Romanian courts were not competent to handle such a trial. Pauker then said that in that case he should have been handed over to the Soviets (D Deletant's interview with G Bratescu, 30 July 1994).

Dej's failure to consult Pauker over the decision to murder Foris lends weight to the view that Dej, supported by Bodnaras, anticipated opposition from Stalin's protégé. Foris is believed to have had Moscow's backing in autumn 1943 to conclude a deal with Antonescu which involved the sacrifice of the Communists in Romania. With plenty of examples of Soviet cynicism from the interwar period to point to, Dej and his interned colleagues decided to preempt this move by removing Foris and taking over the Party before the arrival of the Red Army and the Moscow bureau, which of course included Pauker. The murder of Foris may well have suited Stalin, for any public revelations about attempts to forge a deal with Antonescu, not to mention one made at the expense of the interned Communists, would have exposed them to charges of duplicity before the Romanian public, severely embarrassed the Gheorghiu-Dej faction in the Party, and damaged Stalin's relations with the western Allies.

[33] Born in northern Romania at Iaslovat on 10 February 1904 of Ukrainian-German parentage, Bodnaras studied law at Iasi university where, according to his official obituary, he first came into contact with Marxist groups. He then joined the officers' academy in Timisoara where he completed his training in 1927 (*Anale de istorie*, vol 22, 1976, no 1, p 189). His obituary says nothing about the following seven years until his arrest and his sentencing in 1934 to ten years hard labour. The gap has been filled from other sources. In 1927 he was posted to Craiova with the rank of lieutenant and later transferred to a barracks at Sadagura in northern Romania only thirty kilometres from the river Dniester and the border with the Soviet Union. From there he defected to the Soviet Union. Two questions arise at this point. Why should Bodnaras, with his Ukrainian background, be posted so close to the Soviet frontier ? Was he, perhaps, recruited by Romanian military intelligence and his defection planned ? Information from the KGB archives now provides answers to these questions. It reveals that it was as the military intelligence officer of the 12th artillery regiment based in Sadagura that Bodnaras was sent into the Soviet Union in 1931. He was turned, however, by the Soviets and was trained as an agent at school in the town of Astrakhan: G Iavorschi, 'Pentru cine a lucrat "inginerul Ceausçu" ?', *Magazin Istoric*, vol 28, no 9 (September 1994), p 18. Bodnaras's fluent German allowed him to be used on various espionage missions by the NKVD in Poland and the Baltic republics before being sent to Bulgaria in 1934. En route through Romania he was recognized at Ploiesti station, and tried for desertion and 'Communist activity', and sentenced to 10 years' imprisonment.

Why was he sent by his Soviet masters to Bulgaria by train through Romania, with all the risks of recognition that the journey entailed, when he could have travelled direct by boat from Odessa to Burgas? Was he sent deliberately by train in the hope that he would be caught by the Romanians as a Soviet spy and imprisoned with the Romanian Communists whom he could infiltrate on behalf of the NKVD ? Was he, in fact, a double agent? His mission from the Soviets may well have been to evaluate Gheorghiu-Dej because the latter, unlike other leading figures in the RCP, had not studied in the Soviet Union. Serghei Nikonov, the Soviet-trained head of the SSI (the Romanian Intelligence Service) from 1945 to 1954, expressed the conviction in a conversation in 1988 with Titu Simon, a former officer in Romanian military intelligence, that Bodnaras had been recruited in the 1920s by an officer in the SSI named Georgescu to penetrate the NKVD and that this was the purpose of his mission to the Soviet Union. In 1947 information was passed to Bodnaras by the

Russians that Georgescu had worked as a double agent, for both the Romanians and the Soviets, and Bodnaras gave orders for his immediate execution, before Nikonov could investigate the charges. The reason for Bodnaras's haste, Nikonov believed, was to prevent the emergence of any details of his recruitment by Georgescu. T Simon, *Pacepa: Quo Vadis?* (Bucharest: Odeon, 1992), pp 77-78).

According to the official obituary Bodnaras served his sentence at Doftana, Aiud, Galati and Brasov. In Doftana he formed a close friendship with Gheorghiu-Dej and became a member of the Communist Party. He was released from prison on 7 November 1942 at the suggestion of the SSI (the Romanian Intelligence Service) and was settled in the town of Braila near the mouth of the Danube in order to act as a channel for peace-feelers with the Soviet authorities following the defeat at Stalingrad. Using the cover of a commercial representative for a small company based in Braila and the name of 'engineer Ceausu', Bodnaras travelled freely, albeit under the surveillance of the *Siguranta*, and was a frequent visitor to Bucharest and to Tirgu-Jiu where, by suborning Colonel Serban Lioveanu, the commandant of the internment camp, he was able to consult Gheorghiu-Dej on several occasions. Drawing on secret Communist Party funds, Bodnaras bought weapons from German soldiers based in Romania in order to arm Communist detachments which he formed in Bucharest in the early summer of 1944. This activity did not escape the attention of the Gestapo who requested his arrest but Colonel Traian Borcescu, the head of counter-intelligence in the SSI, resisted on the grounds that Bodnaras 'could be of use in Romania's exit from the war': G Iavorschi, op cit, p 19.

Bibliography

Cartea Alba a Securitatii (Bucharest: SRI, 1995), vol 1.

E Barker, *British Policy in South-East Europe in the Second World War* (London: Macmillan, 1976).

R Bishop, E S Crayfield, *Russia astride the Balkans* (London: Evans Brothers, 1949).

G. Buzatu, *Romania cu si fara Antonescu* (Romania with and without Antonescu) (Iasi: Editura Moldova, 1991), pp 259-71.

I Chiper, F Constantiniu and A Pop, *Sovietizarea Romaniei. Preceptii anglo-americane* (The Sovietization of Romania. Anglo-American Perceptions) (Bucharest: Iconica, 1993).

W Deakin, E Barker and J Chadwick (eds), *British Political and Military Strategy in Central, Eastern and Southern Europe in 1944* (London: Macmillan, 1988).

D Deletant, 'Some considerations on the implementation of the Allied-Romanian Armistice Agreement of 12 September 1944: A Soviet-Romanian exchange of letters in Spring 1946', in I Agrigoroaie, Gh Buzatu and V Cristian (eds), *Romanii in istoria universala* (Iasi, 1988), vol III/I, pp 399-419.

D Deletant, 'The *Securitate* and the Police State in Romania, 1948-64,' *Intelligence and National Security*, vol 8, no 4 (October 1993), pp 1-25.

A. Dutu, 'Comisia Aliata de Control Destructureaza Armata Romana (3)', *Revista de Istorie Militara*, no 5, 1992, pp 20-30.

R Garson, 'Churchill's Spheres of Influence: Rumania and Bulgaria', *Survey*, vol 24, no 3 (Summer 1979), pp 143-58.

D C Giurescu, *Romania's Communist Takeover: The Radescu Government* (Boulder, Colorado: East European Monographs, 1994).

H Hanak, 'The Politics of Impotence: The British Observe Romania, 6 March 1945 to 30 December 1947' in I Agrigoroaie, Gh Buzatu and V Cristian (eds), *Romanii in istoria universala* (Iasi, 1988), vol III/I, pp 421-42.

K Hitchins, *Rumania, 1866-1947* (Oxford: Oxford University Press, 1994), pp 501-47.

G Ionescu, *Communism in Rumania, 1944-1962* (London: Oxford University Press, 1964), pp 94-160.

G Lundestad, *The American Non-Policy towards Eastern Europe, 1943-47* (Oslo: Universitetsförlaget, 1978), pp 225-56.

R H Markham, *Rumania under the Soviet Yoke* (Boston: Meador, 1949).

M Pearton, *Oil and the Romanian State* (London: Oxford University Press, 1971), pp 264-325.

I Porter, *Operation Autonomous. With SOE in Wartime Romania* (London: Chatto and Windus, 1989).

H Prost, *Destin de la Roumaine* (Paris: Éditions Berger-Levrault, 1954), pp 168-211.

P D Quinlan, *British and American Policies towards Romania: 1938-1947* (Los Angeles: American Romanian Academy of Arts and Sciences, 1977).

H L Roberts, *Rumania: Political Problems of an Agrarian State* (New Haven: Yale University Press, 1951), pp 242-331.

H Seton-Watson, *The East European Revolution* (3rd ed, London: Methuen, 1956), pp 167-317.

V Tarau, 'Campania electorala si rezultatul real al alegerilor din 19 noiembrie 1946 in judetele Cluj, Somes si Turda', in Sorin Mitu and Florin Gogaltan (eds), *Studii de Istorie a Transilvaniei* (Cluj: Asociatia Istoricilor din Transilvania si Banat, 1994), pp 204-12.

B Vago, 'Romania', in M McCauley (ed), *Communist Power in Europe, 1944-1949* (London: Macmillan in association with the School of Slavonic and East European Studies, University of London, 1977), pp 111-30.

R L Wolff, *The Balkans in Our Time* (Cambridge, Massachusetts: Harvard University Press, 1956), pp 278-92.

16 Bulgaria at the End of the Second World War 1944-1945

MALCOLM MACKINTOSH

From the point of view of the Allied Powers the situation of Bulgaria towards the end of the Second World War was to some extent an anomaly. Bulgaria had been for most of the twentieth century a close associate and sometimes an ally of Germany, but as a Slav nation had felt both gratitude to, and sympathy for Russia and the Russian people, especially in religion and culture. Bulgaria's own position in the Balkans and her territorial ambitions since her liberation from Ottoman rule by the Russians in 1878 tended to isolate her from her immediate neighbours: primarily Greece, Serbia (later Yugoslavia) and Romania. With the establishment of Soviet rule in Russia after 1917, Bulgarians and their rulers saw Germany as their main contact with the outside world in terms of power politics: though with some reluctance as Hitler came to power and dragged Europe into war in the 1930s. In 1939 Bulgaria initially sought neutrality, though Germany's early victories tempted her to satisfy her territorial claims against Yugoslavia and Greece in the wake of these German conquests. Bulgaria joined the German-dominated Axis Alliance in 1941, declared war against those two countries and against Britain, France and the United States, annexed Yugoslav Macedonia and northern Greece, and sent considerable forces to help Germany and Italy in the occupation of Serbia and other parts of the Yugoslav state. Bulgaria refused, however, to take part in Germany's war against the Soviet Union—partly because of the traditional pro-Russian sentiments of the Bulgarian people—and remained neutral in that conflict until the Soviet armies reached the Balkans in their counter-offensive against the Germans in the autumn of 1944.

During this period, however, Bulgaria played a significant part in the war in the Balkans. She had mobilised her full military strength of 450,000 men organised in 21 infantry divisions, 3 cavalry and 1 armoured brigade, nine of which were deployed in Yugoslavia and three in Greece. The remaining nine divisions were located inside Bulgaria: the normal strength of a Bulgarian division was about 12,000 to 13,000 men.[1] In Yugoslavia the main opponent of the Bulgarian Army of Occupation was Marshal Tito's Army of National Liberation to which Britain and the United States gave much support. Some resistance in Serbia came initially from non-communist units known as 'Chetniks', under the royalist General Draza Mihailovic but by 1944 a mutual fear of Tito's communist-dominated forces, by then expanding to a nation-wide resistance movement, led the Chetniks and the Bulgarian Army in Serbia to collaborate on an informal basis. Bulgarian forces saw relatively little action in Greece since the main partisan groups, communist-led or non-communist, were operating further to the south. But partly at the request of these two Allied governments, British and American air raids were carried out against targets in Bulgaria in 1944—though never on a large scale.

Of particular relevance to the events in Bulgaria at the end of the war in Europe in 1944-45 was the attitude of the population to the war and to the possibility of the emergence of a resistance movement against the policy of the Bulgarian government and its support for German war aims. The evidence suggests that much of the middle classes and the large agricultural labour force seem to have been indifferent to the war until 1944, and content with the restoration of Bulgaria's 'lost territories' in Yugoslavia and Greece; the peasants, in particular, had benefited economically from the peaceful occupation of the country by some 20,000 well-behaved German soldiers whose leaders used Bulgaria as a logistic and communications base rather than a battle zone.[2]

There was, on the whole, relatively little organised resistance to the alliance with Germany in any military sense inside Bulgaria. It is true that some stirrings of political opposition appeared after the Soviet-German war had been under way for about a year, primarily among members of the Bulgarian Communist Party, anxious to be active in support of the Soviet war effort. This Party was, at that time, small and unrepresentative, and its leaders realised that it would have to form some sort of alliance with other political groupings if resistance was to become a reality. Much of the first year was spent in discussions with selected leaders of opposition and anti-fascist organisations which eventually led to the creation of an alliance known as 'the Fatherland Front' (*Otechestven Front*).[3] The main figures in this alliance were Anton Yugov and Dobri Terpeshev for the Communists, Nikola Petkov for the Agrarian Party, and Dimiter Neykov for the Socialists. More significantly in operational terms, the Front included a group of pro-Western retired or reserve army officers who had formed an organisation called 'Zveno' (the Link). The most senior members were retired Colonels Kimon Georgiev and Damyan Velchev, along with Majors Vlado Stoichev and Kiril Stanchev. In fact, most of the Fatherland Front figures were well known to the authorities, who made little effort to break up their organisation or place them under arrest for their opposition to the war.

There were, however, some members of the Communist Party, who did try to put together a form of military resistance to the government's policies. Partly owing to lack of support among the population at home, the most important Bulgarian Communist-led partisan detachments were deployed and trained in Macedonia, then claimed by Bulgaria, but recognised by all the Allies—and by Marshal Tito's partisans—as Yugoslav territory. As the Bulgarian units grew in size and enjoyed British military aid through a military mission under the Special Operations Executive (SOE) led in 1944 by Major

Frank Thompson, the Yugoslavs pressed them to return to Bulgaria proper and raise the flag of revolt in their 'home country'. After some debate, the Bulgarian partisans agreed to leave Macedonia and entered Bulgaria in early May 1944—aiming for the mountains to the north and south-east of the capital, Sofia. Major Thompson accompanied the northern group which, unhappily, was surprised and routed on 23 May in the village of Batulya, near Vratsa in the Balkan mountains. Major Thompson, badly wounded, was taken prisoner, and tried and executed on 5 June 1944: one of the most tragic events in British attempts to help the Resistance movements in the Balkans during the Second World War.[4]

Meanwhile, in Bulgaria there were indications that the government realised that the war was about to enter a new and, perhaps, final stage with the victory of the Allies and the defeat of Bulgaria's partner, Germany. As the Red Army approached the Romanian frontier in April 1944, the Soviet Union launched a major diplomatic and propaganda campaign against Bulgaria and its collaboration with the Germans. Unless it broke with Germany and took other measures, declared Moscow Radio in April, Bulgaria could expect no sympathy from the Soviet Union, despite its neutrality in the Soviet-German war. Thoroughly discouraged by the turn of events, the pro-German government of Dobri Bozhilov resigned on 22 May, and a week later a new Premier, Ivan Bagrianov, formed a government with the task of paving the way for Bulgaria to leave the Axis, to make its peace with the Western Allies and repair relations with the Soviet Union. But before Bagrianov could put his plans into effect, there came news of the major Soviet victory at Iasi-Kishinev in Moldavia and the surrender of Romania to the Allies on 23 August: Bulgaria stood for the first time in the front line between the Russians and the Germans. Moreover we now know that it was at this point that Stalin decided to invade Bulgaria. On 22 August 1944 Marshal Zhukov was summoned back to General Headquarters in Moscow from the front, and on the following day Stalin told him to 'prepare for war with Bulgaria'.[5]

Bagrianov, in terms of diplomacy, acted swiftly. On 25 August he issued a statement emphasising Bulgaria's 'total neutrality' in the Soviet-German war. He ordered the disarming of all foreign (that is, German) troops on Bulgarian soil, formally asked Britain and America for their terms for the country's 'withdrawal from the war', and despatched an emissary to Cairo with authority to negotiate an armistice with them. But Bagrianov's pro-Allied moves provoked a quick reaction from the Germans. Bulgaria was too large a country and maintained too powerful an army—21 divisions—for the Germans to consider an invasion plan or indeed any military action which would bring Sofia back into line and destroy Bagrianov's attempts to desert the German alliance. Nevertheless there was one way in which the Germans could strengthen their general position in the Balkans, which was already weakened by the Yugoslav and Greek resistance efforts, and punish the Bulgarians for their imminent defection. They could act against the Bulgarian armies of occupation in Yugoslavia, clear Macedonia of doubtful elements and deprive the Bulgarians of their most experienced military force. On the same day that Bagrianov made his unrealistic speech about his intention to leave the war (25 August), the German High Command decided to attack the Bulgarian army in Serbia and Macedonia and drive it back in disorder to Bulgaria.[6]

The first German priority in this situation was to allay the Bulgarian government's suspicions while they prepared their attack. On 26 August, the senior German officer in Bulgaria, General Schneckerburger, informed Bagrianov that Hitler had decided to withdraw his forces from Bulgaria peacefully, in accordance with Bagrianov's wishes. Bagrianov, for his part, issued orders to the Bulgarian Army Corps occupying parts of Serbia to withdraw back to Bulgaria, and to regular army units deployed in eastern Bulgaria, including the crack 1st infantry division, to take up positions in the west of the country along the Bulgarian-Yugoslav frontier to cover the withdrawal. These orders, which were easily intercepted by the Germans, created the ideal conditions for a German attack. The Bulgarian commanders, in an act of 'collaboration' or incredible naivety, decided to hand over their divisional areas to the Chetniks, who thereupon attacked the retreating Bulgarian units. In the total confusion which followed, a senior Chetnik envoy arrived at each of the Bulgarian divisional headquarters, attributing these attacks to a 'misunderstanding', and inviting the Bulgarian commanders to discussions with the Chetniks about their unimpeded withdrawal. The Bulgarian commanders, either unsuspectingly or willingly co-operating with the Chetniks, assembled at a rendezvous, where they were promptly seized and handed over to the Germans as prisoners of war.

In this situation, and lacking orders from their commanders, the Bulgarian formations halted irresolutely. On 28 August, the Germans joined the Chetniks in an all-out attack on the leaderless Bulgarians, disarmed them and drove them in total disorder eastwards towards the Bulgarian border. Here and there determined or perceptive Bulgarian officers succeeded in rallying their men and returned to their homeland with their units more or less intact, but by the end of August 1944 there were no organised or armed Bulgarian units in Serbia—a characteristic example of German thoroughness in an emergency of this nature.

The next day, 29 August, was a day of shocks for the Bagrianov government and the Bulgarian people. The first stragglers from the Occupation Corps began to arrive in the capital, and their stories of what had happened spread like wildfire through the city, causing alarm and panic among its people. Then General Schneckerburger called on Bagrianov to tell him that new orders from Berlin required him to resist Bulgarian attempts to disarm his troops in Bulgaria, and to attack the Bulgarian Fifth Army occupying Macedonia—which he proceeded to do from his headquarters at Gorna Banya, just outside Sofia. The third shock for Bagrianov was an announcement from Moscow Radio that the Soviet Union did not and would not recognise Bulgaria's neutrality in the war: Russia's first public warning that it might declare war on Bulgaria and occupy the country by force. On 30 August, Bagrianov heard that his emissary in Cairo had been told by the Western Allies that Bulgaria's proposals for an armistice were unacceptable; and that to the north, the Red Army had reached the Bulgarian-Romanian frontier in the Dobruja and along the lower Danube. Bagrianov felt that the task for which he had been chosen was hopeless, and on 31 August 1944 he resigned.

Gradually the extent of the crisis was dawning on the political leaders in Bulgaria, who were also receiving reports of increased activity by the communist-led partisans in various parts of the country. The Bulgarians, however, still pinned some hopes on coming to terms with Britain and America, and on 2 September the Regents' appointed a new government of well-known 'liberals', led by a member of the Agrarian party, Konstantin Muraviev. Almost immediately the Soviet government announced that the new Cabinet and its policies were unacceptable, and accused Muraviev of giving even greater assistance to the German forces in Bulgaria than his predecessors had done. On 4 September Muraviev heard from Macedonia that, in addition to the continuing operations of the Yugoslav National Liberation forces of Macedonia, German troops had launched their offensive against the Fifth Army. Two of the three Bulgarian divisions there were broken up in disorder, and by the next day the road and rail link between Belgrade and Salonika was clear of Bulgarian troops. Only one division, the 15th, deployed in the far south-west of Macedonia near Lake Ohrid, remained intact; and of particular importance in the days ahead was the recall of the commander of this division, Major-General Ivan Marinov (who had the reputation of being a liberal-minded officer) to be Minister of War in the Muraviev Cabinet.

Muraviev now gave up all hope of obtaining an armistice from the Allies, and concentrated on trying to placate the Russians, whose Third Ukrainian Front under Marshal Tolbukhin was deployed in full strength along the Bulgarian-Romanian frontier. In a last desperate attempt, Muraviev announced on 5 September the dismissal of the Parliament which had voted to join the Axis, a total amnesty for all political prisoners, the immediate expulsion of all the remaining German troops (many were being pulled out anyway as the Germans had given up any hope of influencing the Muraviev government) and the withdrawal of all Bulgarian troops behind the frontiers of 1940. One early consequence of these measures was the exploitation of the amnesty by the partisans, some of whom emerged from their mountain strongholds and began for the first time to enter towns and villages and to settle old scores with local officials, police and gendarmerie.

That same evening the Soviet Union declared war on Bulgaria on the grounds of her continuing collaboration with Germany. Immediately Muraviev asked the Soviet Union for an armistice—a request which Moscow refused, for the Soviet Union did not want at this stage to deal with a Bulgarian government which was basically 'bourgeois', and seemed to be politically inclined towards the Western powers. Stalin wanted to see a Fatherland Front government established in Bulgaria, dominated by the Bulgarian Communist Party—the only participant in the anti-fascist alliance which had actually put partisans in the field. He therefore looked to the Fatherland Front, and particularly its Communist members, to seize power in Sofia before he would consider any armistice.

Key officials of the Fatherland Front who also wanted to seize Sofia and other important towns prior to the arrival of Soviet troops were faced by a number of dilemmas. Communist partisan groups moved close to the capital as well as Sliven, Plovdiv and Pleven and tried to contact local officials—but in many cases were rebuffed. Major units of the regular army were passing through these towns on their way to the western frontier in response to Bagrianov's original orders, and many of these formations were commanded by officers sympathetic to the German cause and saw no reason to switch their allegiance to the Fatherland Front. Law and order was breaking down as more and more deserters and refugees from the army in Yugoslavia flooded into the Sofia area disrupting communications and the lives of the ordinary people. The Fatherland Front called for a rising in Sofia on 6 September, but in the confusion and chaos this day came and went without action by the Front.

Two days later, at dawn on 8 September, the Red Army crossed the border from Romania into north-east Bulgaria, occupying without resistance most of that part of the country and taking 14,000 prisoners. Muraviev's reaction was once again to seek an armistice; and, to encourage Soviet acceptance, he declared war on Germany at 4 pm on that day. The leaders of the Fatherland Front, however, also realised that this was their last chance to seize power as a Resistance movement. The Communist Party renewed its appeal to the city authorities in Sofia and began to infiltrate partisans into its suburbs; but the decisive action was taken by the military group in the Front— 'Zveno'. Exploiting the contacts they had with the army and with the newly-appointed War Minister, General Ivan Marinov, who, although not a member of Zveno or the Fatherland Front, realised the way the situation was developing and threw his weight behind his former colleagues, Colonels Georgiev and Velchev.

General Marinov informed Zveno that the one Bulgarian armoured brigade, normally deployed south of Sofia at Samokov, was on its way to the capital under the original orders, and had reached the village of Vakarel that afternoon, a few kilometres from Sofia. Colonel Velchev realised at once what an opportunity this was for the Fatherland Front, and ordered one of his officers, retired Major Kiril Stanchev, to take command of the brigade and lead it into the capital. The plan worked without a hitch. Major Stanchev arrested the brigade commander, and in the small hours of the morning of 9 September he entered Sofia. By 6 am the city was fully under the control of Zveno and the Fatherland Front; its streets were already filling up with communist-led partisans who linked up with the troops of the armoured brigade. The Muraviev government collapsed, and the Premier and his Ministers were arrested as a new Fatherland Front government was formed with a senior Zveno leader, Colonel Kimon Georgiev, as Prime Minister. Now the Soviet government accepted the Bulgarian offer of an armistice; the Red Army continued its advance westwards through Bulgaria towards Sofia and the Yugoslav border.

On 15 September 1944 the Russians entered the capital unopposed and deployed their forces for the next stage of their campaign in the Balkans. This was to involve participation by the Third Ukrainian Front in an advance into north-eastern Yugoslavia, the liberation, with Yugoslav partisan forces, of Belgrade, and a link-up with the Second Ukrainian Front in southern and central Hungary on the road to Budapest and Vienna. One Army of the Third Ukrainian Front, the 37th, was detached by the Soviet High Command to act as the garrison of Bulgaria. With a strength of nine divisions and an armoured corps and supporting air and naval forces, this army, under the command of Colonel-General S S Biryuzov, remained in Bulgaria until the conclusion of the peace-treaty with the Allies in 1947.

The first Fatherland Front government under Kimon Georgiev appeared to be strongly balanced in favour of the military group Zveno which carried out the final coup in Sofia on 8/9 September. Colonel Damyan Velchev, now promoted Minister of War as a Major-General, appointed General Ivan Marinov as Commander-in-Chief, Majors Vlado Stoichev and Kiril Stanchev as Army commanders with the rank of General, and Professor Petko Stainov became Foreign Minister. However, the leading Communists, Anton Yugov and Dr Mincho Neychev, were given the key Ministries of the Interior and Justice respectively, while the other Ministries were divided between the Agrarians, the Socialists and the Independents. In addition the Communists and the Agrarians each had a Deputy Prime Minister: Dobri Terpeshev for the former and Nikola Petkov for the latter. However, behind this Cabinet stood a much more powerful organisation which really controlled the government of the country: the new National Committee of the 'Fatherland Front'. After the coup of 9 September—a date which became Bulgaria's National Day for the next 45 years—the Committee was re-formed, and the most important vacant places were given to Communists. Tsola Dragoicheva, an active member of the partisan movement, became chair of the new Committee; Dobri Terpeshev and Anton Yugov were members, as was Traicho Kostov, the General Secretary of the Communist Party who had spent most of the war in prison. The Committee quickly spread its authority throughout the country, setting up miniature reproductions of itself in every town and village. Local partisans dominated these regional committees which reported only to the National Committee in Sofia, not to the government, thus laying the foundations of total control of Bulgaria by its Communist Party which continued until the early 1990s.

Meanwhile, on the military front, the Soviet High Command ordered General Velchev at a Council of War on 18 September to mobilise the whole of the Bulgarian Army on the western frontier in order to re-enter Yugoslavia as the left flank of the Third Ukrainian Front on the advance towards Belgrade. The northern (Second) Army was placed under the command of General Kiril Stanchev, the central (First) Army under General Vlado Stoichev and the southern (Fourth) Army under a General Sirakov. The Bulgarians, under Soviet command this time, re-crossed the Yugoslav-Bulgarian frontier into Macedonia and Serbia, and in a month-long campaign cut the Germans' road and rail communications link between Belgrade and Salonika and occupied a number of towns in those two provinces. The Bulgarian Army then withdrew to Bulgaria itself, but soon found that the Russians expected them to continue to serve in the front line alongside the Soviet Army. On 17 November 1944 the Soviet High Command asked the Bulgarians to provide an army of 5 or 6 infantry divisions to join the Third Ukrainian Front, then fighting in southern Hungary. The Bulgarians immediately complied and at the end of February 1945 the 1st Bulgarian Army under the command of General Vlado Stoichev arrived in Hungary, taking up positions along the river Drava on the southern flank of the Soviet Front. The 1st Army participated in a number of battles, defensive and offensive, on this sector, until, at the end of the war, they had reached the foothills of the Austrian Alps.[8]

This was the military situation of the Bulgarian Army on VE Day. Meanwhile, at home in Bulgaria, the Allies established an Allied Control Commission in Sofia to supervise and direct the policies of an 'ex-enemy country' under the inter-Allied arrangements agreed at the Summit meetings held during the war between Churchill, Roosevelt and Stalin. In the spirit of what became known as the 'percentage agreement' between Churchill and Stalin reached informally in Moscow in October 1944, the Soviet Union dominated the Control Commission in Bulgaria. The Chairman was officially Marshal Tolbukhin, who very rarely appeared; day-to-day authority was exercised by General Biryuzov, who also, as already noted, commanded the garrison army in Bulgaria. A large and influential Soviet political and military staff took almost all the Commission's decisions on Bulgaria's internal and external policies, while the small British and American missions could do little more than enter protests against proposals of the Bulgarian government which increasingly originated with the Bulgarian Communist Party element in the 'Fatherland Front'.

As early as January 1945, one influential pro-Allied but non-Communist Bulgarian politician was placed under house arrest and was forced to seek the protection of the American Political Representative in the Control Commission in order to save his life. On 1/2 February 1945, the Bulgarian authorities tried and executed all 103 members of the wartime parliament, including those who had voted against joining the Axis in 1941. It is true that in the final months of the war in Europe the primary interest of the Soviet government and Armed Forces was the completion of the military campaign in the Balkans and the Danube valley. They seemed to take relatively little direct interest in the internal affairs of the Bulgarian state, and the 37th Army in Bulgaria concentrated on its occupation duties and its role in securing the frontiers of the country—especially towards Turkey and the Straits. Indeed, Soviet requests for a revision of the Montreux Convention on the freedom of passage through the Straits appeared diplomatically as early as February 1945—at the time of the Yalta Conference between the Allied leaders. This action was accompanied by a mobilisation of the 37th Army in eastern Bulgaria, possibly intended to intimidate the Turks—though without success. A detailed account of the policies of the Bulgarian authorities at this time is outside the scope of this paper; but there can be no doubt that before hostilities ceased in Europe in May 1945, the Bulgarian Communist Party was taking every opportunity, with or without direct Soviet political or military support, to prepare the ground within the country for its eventual assumption of total power in Bulgaria under the title of a 'People's Democracy'. When VE-Day arrived, the Bulgarian Party was probably a good deal further along that route than its opposite numbers in any comparable 'ex-enemy country' or member of the Western alliance in Europe.

Discussion

Presenting his paper, *Mr Mackintosh* explained that as a Slav nation Bulgaria was traditionally pro-Soviet and refused to help Germany against the Soviet Union, though playing a major pro-German role in the Balkans: hoping to play both ends against the middle, all they achieved was to be in everybody's bad books. The Soviet Union, however, was not really interested in the Bulgarian state. *Dr Crampton* agreed: Bulgarian communism had been well established since 1918, and Bulgaria had a relatively easy time under occupation. There was no real purge of the bourgeoisie: the communists did that later.

Notes and References

1 Major-General M M Minasyan: *Osvobozhdenie Narodov Yugo-Vostochnoi Evropy*, (The Liberation of the Nations of South-East Europe) (in Russian, Moscow, 1967), p 389.

2 W Deakin, E Barker and J Chadwick, *British Political and Military Strategy in Central, Eastern and Southern Europe in 1944* (Macmillan Press, London, 1988), p 239.

3 Tsola Dragoicheva: *Pobeda* (Victory) memoirs (in Bulgarian, Sofia), vol 3, pp 13-14.

4 M R D Foot, *Resistance* (London, 1976).

5 Marshal G K Zhukov, *Reminiscences and Recollections* (Moscow, 1989), p 596 (Russian edition).

6 In this section, I have relied on Tsola Dragoicheva's memoirs, *op cit*, and my personal papers and other unpublished material relating to my membership of the British Military Mission in the Allied Control Commission in Bulgaria 1944-1946.

7 A Regency Council had been appointed in Sofia after the death of King Boris in mysterious circumstances in August 1943.

8 Minasyan, *op cit*, pp 389 and 401.

17 The Campaign on the Eastern Front 1944-45 and its Political Aftermath: a British Perspective

MALCOLM MACKINTOSH

Introduction

The aim of this paper is to trace the final campaign waged by the Soviet Armed Forces on the Eastern Front in Europe in the Second World War from its opening phase in June 1944 to its victorious conclusion in May 1945 with the capture of Berlin and the destruction of the Nazi war machine. The paper then takes a look, from a British perspective, at political events in Eastern Europe after that victory, and tries to assess the motives and intentions of the Soviet government of that time, dominated as it was by Josef Stalin, as it planned for the future of Europe in the post-war era.

The first part will therefore deal with the success of Soviet arms, beginning with 'Operation Bagration' in June 1944 to the end of the war in Europe: an attempt at a straightforward account of the campaigns involved. The second part considers the way in which the military victory was used by the Soviet government to achieve not only defensive goals for the security of the Soviet Union, but also Great Power political and ideological aims. This second part will attempt to analyse these problems, based partially, at least, on the fact that Stalin, who wielded absolute power in Soviet policy-making, including in foreign affairs, lacked personal experience of the traditions and the realities of life in the countries he wished to dominate, particularly in Central and Eastern Europe.[1]

I The Military Campaign, 1944: 'Operation Bagration'

By mid-1944, the Soviet Armed Forces had reached a strategic battle-line following the successful campaigns of 1943-44 which stretched from the Arctic Ocean near Murmansk along the Soviet-Finnish frontier to Leningrad and the Baltic coast, southwards through a massive arc of territory west of Smolensk across the Dnieper river into Ukraine, the Carpathian mountains, north-eastern Romania to the Black Sea coast at the estuary of the Dniester river. The main target for the Soviet 1944 summer offensive, code-named 'Operation Bagration', was the German Army-Group Centre of fifty divisions, 1000 tanks and 1400 aircraft, whose headquarters was in Minsk in Belorussia. Army-Group Centre consisted of three all-arms armies, the 2nd, the 4th and the 9th, and one Panzer Army, the 3rd: in all some 1,200,000 men.[2] On its left flank lay Army-Group North, which covered the area south of Leningrad and the Baltic States, Estonia, Latvia and Lithuania. To the south of Army-Group Centre were Army-Group North-Ukraine, with the 1st and 4th Panzer Armies and the 1st Hungarian Army, and Army-Group South-Ukraine, comprising the 6th and 8th German Armies and the 3rd and 4th Romanian Armies, deployed mainly in north-east Romania and Bessarabia. In the far north, the Finnish Army garrisoned the Karelian Isthmus and Karelia up to the Arctic coast, supported in that area by the German 20th Mountain Army.[3]

The Soviet forces massed for the summer offensive were concentrated in the central sector, and included 2,400,000 men in the strategic arc from Velikie Luki in the north to Kovel in the south. Four Soviet 'Fronts', roughly the equivalent in numbers to German Army-Groups, were assembled against Army-Group Centre. The First Baltic Front, under Army-General I Kh Bagramyan, and composed of four armies, faced the northern flank of the German Army-Group. The Third Belorussian Front, commanded by Army-General I D Chernyakhovski, lay to the south of Bagramyan's men, opposite Vitebsk, also with four armies. To the south of him, the Second Belorussian Front, under Army-General G F Zakharov, deployed partly in reserve, had three armies, and faced Mogilev on the Dnieper river. Largest of all, and linking up with the Soviet armies in the Ukraine, was the First Belorussian Front, commanded by the distinguished veteran of Moscow, Stalingrad and Kursk, Marshal K K Rokossovski, with four armies and a cavalry-mechanised group for operations in the treacherous Pripyat marshes. Rokossovski's main target was the fortress of Bobruisk, on the middle reaches of the Dnieper river. These four Fronts were supported by the 1st, 2nd, 8th and 16th air armies, and had three times as much artillery and mortars and twice as many aircraft as were operational on the German side. 'Operation Bagration' against Army-Group Centre was co-ordinated by Marshal G K Zhukov and Marshal A M Vasilevski.[4]

The whole of the summer offensive of 1944 was executed according to a well-known Red Army strategic plan known as 'consecutive operations', attributed in Soviet military literature to military thinkers of the 1920s and 1930s such as M V Frunze, M N Tukhachevski and V K Triandafilov, under which each operation contributed to the success of the subsequent one by destroying strong-points and opening up vulnerable flanks. In 1944, the first offensive to be launched was that in the far north against the Finnish Army south and north of Lake Ladoga, the former carried out by the Leningrad Front under Army-General L A Govorov, from 9 to 20 June, when the fortress and port of Viborg fell to the Russians. The northern offensive, executed by the Karelian Front under Army-General K A Meretskov, took Petrozavodsk, the capital of Karelia. These operations led to the conclusion of an armistice between Finland and the Soviet Union on 19 September, and although Finnish troops later participated in fighting against the Germans, hostilities between Russia and Finland effectively ceased in the autumn.[5]

The successful conclusion of the Finnish campaign allowed the Soviet High Command (the *Stavka*) to turn to their main target, Army-Group Centre. The Belorussian offensive opened on 23 June 1944 with simultaneous assaults by the First Baltic, and the First, Second and Third Belorussian Fronts from Velikie Luki to the Pripyat marshes. The first tasks of the offensive were the elimination of the three great German bastions on this sector: Vitebsk in the north, Mogilev in the centre and Bobruisk in the south. Against these fortresses all the destructive power of the Red Army was unleashed: relentless air bombardment, massed heavy artillery fire, and barrages of 'katyusha' rockets. On 24 June the infantry went in. Fighting was bitter in the extreme, and casualties on both sides were appalling. But on 25 June, the 43rd Army of the First Baltic Front linked up with the 39th Army of the Third Belorussian Front west of Vitebsk, cutting off five divisions of the German 3rd Panzer Army, and on 27 June the fortress fell. Two armies of the Second Belorussian Front forced the Dnieper river and took Mogilev by storm on 28 June, though Russian casualties were so heavy that the Front was forced into the reserve temporarily to refit. To the south, Marshal Rokossovski carried out a brilliant operation on the First Belorussian Front. Moving over marshy ground and crossing countless small rivers and lakes, his advance cut off parts of two Panzer corps of the German 9th Army which were then subjected to a shattering aerial assault by the Soviet 16th air army. On 29 June the encircled German group disintegrated, and Rokossovski's troops entered Bobruisk, taking 24,000 prisoners.

From then on, the Russians pursued and the Germans retreated, giving hasty and sometimes ferocious battle as they went. General Bagramyan's armies crossed the Dvina river and captured Polotsk. The First and Third Belorussian Fronts, now operating in tandem, completed the encirclement of the greater part of the 4th German Army near Minsk: they swept across the historic river Berezina and, on 13 July, Minsk fell. On that day, according to the diary of the German General, Heinz Guderian, 'Army-Group Centre ceased to exist'.

The Russian advance westwards continued at an ever increasing pace. The First Baltic Front crossed the river Nieman into Lithuania and moved on to the East Prussian frontier which it reached in late August. Rokossovski and the First Belorussian Front attacked on a wide arc from Baranovichi in the north to Kovel in the south across the river Bug towards Brest-Litovsk and eventually Warsaw on 2 August. This was the period of the heroic but tragic Warsaw uprising when partisans in the capital rose under General Bor-Komarowski and held out for nine weeks against massive German opposition. The Soviet Army just across the river Vistula made no attempt, apparently mainly for political reasons, but with a military element, to help the rising, which was ruthlessly suppressed.

Rokossovski's Front was re-joined by a reinforced Second Belorussian Front which entered the line to the north and north-east of Warsaw. At the southern end of the Front, Rokossovski's troops forced the southern Bug river, and on 24 July, captured the Polish town of Lublin, where a Soviet-appointed Polish Committee was set up to administer liberated Polish territory. The three Belorussian Fronts halted along this line after their massive advance from the Smolensk area; and, in fulfilment of the 'consecutive operation' principle, other Fronts took up the offensive. In the north, the Second and Third Baltic Fronts launched offensives into Estonia and Latvia in July, and to the south, Soviet troops of the Second and Third Ukrainian Fronts—later to be joined by a newly formed Fourth Ukrainian Front under Army-General I E Petrov especially assigned to the Carpathian Mountain sector—opened up their offensives in the Ukraine. The Germans had concentrated 38 divisions here, with over 600,000 men and 1000 tanks against the First Ukrainian Front of Marshal I S Konev, who had five armies under his command. On 13 July, the First Ukrainian Front went into the attack. German strength—they had expected the main Russian 1944 offensive to be launched in the Ukraine—was so great that Konev's men could only advance slowly and with great casualties. The vital city of L'vov was captured on 27 July, along with an important bridgehead on the west bank of the Vistula, which the Russians retained in spite of vigorous German counter-attacks. The German Army-Group North-Ukraine thereupon withdrew in good order to the line of the Carpathian Mountains and awaited the next stage of the Soviet advance.

The subsequent 'consecutive operations' occurred further south, and led the Red Army from the Ukraine into the Balkans. They involved an offensive by the Second Ukrainian Front under Army-General R Ya Malinovski southwards into Romania and the Third Ukrainian Front, under Army-General F I Tolbukhin, advancing westwards from the Dniester river in an encircling movement against the 6th and 8th German Armies of Army-Group South-Ukraine and the 3rd and 4th Romanian Armies in Bessarabia and Moldavia. The attack began on 20 August, and broke through the lines held by the 8th German and the Romanian armies facing General Malinovski's troops, while Tolbukhin's struck westwards and linked up with the former on the River Prut, thus isolating the forces in a pocket around Kishinev.

At this point the situation changed radically, for on 23 August a coup d'état took place in the Romanian Royal Palace in Bucharest, and the pro-German régime of Ion Antonescu was overthrown by the young King of Romania, Mihai. A new Romanian government, acting on the King's direct orders, surrendered unconditionally to the Allies, including primarily the Russians. The two Romanian armies of Army-Group South-Ukraine laid down their arms; the whole of Romania south of the Carpathians lay open before the Russian advance. The Second Ukrainian Front occupied Bucharest unopposed on 30

August, while the Third Ukrainian Front eliminated the pocket held by the 6th German Army around Kishinev in fighting which was still fierce.

While the Second Ukrainian Front moved rapidly up the river Danube towards Yugoslavia and crossed the Carpathian Mountains into Hungarian-held Transylvania, the Third Ukrainian Front closed up to the Romanian-Bulgarian frontier and prepared to enter that country which, although it had not participated in the Soviet-German war, had joined the Axis in 1941 and sent troops to garrison Yugoslav and Greek territory during the war. On 5 September 1944 the Soviet Union declared war on Bulgaria and Soviet troops crossed the frontier three days later. A coup d'état took place in Sofia on 9 September, and Soviet troops occupied the country quickly—and without Bulgarian resistance. Soviet troops advanced from Bulgarian territory into northeast Yugoslavia, participated in the capture of Belgrade on 20 October 1944, and moved on into Hungary where, with the co-operation of the Second Ukrainian Front advancing from the east, they encircled Budapest, which fell eventually, after a long siege, on 13 February 1945.

The Final Campaign: the Capture of Berlin, 1945

At the beginning of 1945, the Eastern Front ran from Memel on the Baltic Sea along the East Prussian border to the river Vistula near Warsaw, from there across Poland and eastern Czechoslovakia to the Danube river near Budapest, and thence along Lake Balaton to Yugoslavia, where Marshal Tito's partisans were deployed. Eight Soviet Fronts, varying in strength from three to fourteen armies, gave the Russians an overwhelming superiority in men, artillery, mortars and tanks: eleven Guards Armies, five Shock Armies, six Tank Armies, one Cavalry-Mechanised Army and forty-five All-Arms armies were supported by thirteen air armies. On a rough calculation, the final Soviet assault on Germany was carried out by between $4\frac{1}{2}$ and 5 million men serving in the active army. On the German side, about $2\frac{1}{2}$ million men were deployed, organised in 170 German and 15 Hungarian divisions and 21 German and one Hungarian brigade.

The *Stavka* in Moscow selected four major break-through points at which to open the assault: along the Nieman river towards Königsberg; north of Warsaw in the direction of Danzig; south of Warsaw across the Vistula; and from the Sandomir bridgehead in southern Poland towards Silesia. The first offensive by the Third Belorussian Front towards Königsberg began on 13 January 1945, but fierce German resistance in defence of the Prussian heartland slowed down the Russian advance. At the end of January the Front had penetrated to the Baltic coast north and south of Königsberg, though the *Stavka* decided to postpone the storming of the city-fortress until later in the campaign.

North of Warsaw, Marshal Rokossovski, who had succeeded the less-successful General Zakharov in command of the Second Belorussian Front, struck north-west towards the Baltic Sea at Elbing, which he reached on 31 January, cutting off the 2nd and 4th German armies in East Prussia. This Front also crossed the lower Vistula river and marched on towards Pomerania and its important Baltic ports. The furthest advance in this January campaign was achieved by the First Belorussian Front, now commanded by Marshal Zhukov. His six armies (two of them Tank armies) first captured the city of Warsaw and then pushed westwards towards the Polish-German frontier and the river Oder, which they crossed in early February. Zhukov's advance was matched by that of the First Ukrainian Front of Marshal Konev operating in southern Poland. From the Sandomir bridgehead his armies, five All-Arms and two Tank, broke out westwards into German Silesia and also reached the Oder river near Oppeln and Goben. The line-up for the assault on Berlin was almost complete.

While the final preparations for this offensive were under way, General Chernyakhovski launched his major attack on Königsberg: so fierce was the opposition that his troops made little progress, and the General himself was killed by a shell fragment in February. He was succeeded in command by the Chief of the General Staff, Marshal A M Vasilevski, who completed the campaign by storming Königsberg on 9 April. In the Danube valley, the Second and Third Ukrainian Fronts resumed their offensives in March 1945: the Second advancing through northern Hungary and Slovakia, and the Third directly towards Vienna, which was captured on 13 April. The troops of the Fronts linked up with the American army near Linz in Austria, and approached Prague from the south at the end of the month. The war on the southern flank of the Third Reich came to an end with these operations in central Europe.

In the meantime, the Soviet forces along the rivers Oder and Neisse prepared to launch their offensive against Berlin. The *Stavka*'s plan envisaged a direct thrust by the First Belorussian Front under Marshal Zhukov across the Oder river to Berlin, moving in two parallel columns aiming at the north-east and the south-east of the city. The main problem was the penetration of the hilly and heavily-wooded area known as the 'Seelow Heights' protecting the capital. Marshal Konev's troops were to cross the river Neisse and advance simultaneously towards Potsdam and Dresden in order to assist in the encirclement of the Berlin area. Marshal Rokossovski was to cross the lower Oder, capture Stettin and advance westwards, ready to help Zhukov with his Front's left wing if necessary.

The great assault began at dawn on 16 April with a tremendous artillery and air bombardment. Resistance in the German armies was intense, and after 2-3 days the Red Army had advanced only two to five miles into the 'Seelow Heights' in the centre, and up to eight miles on Zhukov's left and right flanks. Marshal Konev's troops, operating against less heavy opposition, had pushed eight miles ahead on the first day, and he began to turn his armies northwards towards Berlin. Rokossovski, too, registered speedier success on his Front. Nevertheless, Zhukov's forces began to break up the defenders' positions: by 20 April he had broken through over 20 miles, and one of his armies, the legendary 'Stalingrad' 8th Guards Army, entered the capital's south-eastern suburbs. On 25 April Berlin was completely encircled and its garrison split into three parts. On the afternoon of 28 April, units of the 3rd Shock Army captured the Reichstag; Hitler committed suicide on the same day, and shortly after mid-day on 2 May 1945, the German garrison of Berlin ceased resistance. Russian troops had meanwhile linked up with American troops at Torgau on the river Elbe, and with British and Canadian troops near Wismar and Schwerin. The war in Europe was over.

II Victory in Europe: the Political Aftermath

At the end of the war in Europe in 1945 the goodwill of millions had been secured for the Soviet Union, thanks to the wartime achievements and sacrifices of the peoples of Russia and the efficiency with which the Soviet leaders had organised their vast country for total war. The Soviet conquest of Nazi Germany also increased the influence and prestige of Communist and pro-Soviet political Parties, particularly in France and Italy, where Party membership figures approached or passed the two-million mark. The attitude to the Soviet Union of many British people was summed up by the Secretary of the Labour party, Mr Morgan Phillips, in 1946 when he addressed a goodwill mission about to set off for the Soviet Union:

> It seems to me to be the most natural thing in the world that the peoples of Britain and Russia, now both governed by Socialist administrations, should wish to understand each other more thoroughly. Our approaches to the final objective may be different, but we hope and believe that we are both striving towards the realisation of the world of the common man.[6]

Moreover, much sympathy was felt in Britain at that time for the search by the Soviet government for a system of security along the country's vulnerable western frontier: many Western observers placed a great deal of faith in the treaties signed during and after the war between the Allies, such as the Teheran, Yalta and Potsdam agreements on the future of Europe in the aftermath of the common victory, although they also raised issues of potential conflict at the diplomatic level, such as the repatriation—sometimes forcible—of prisoners of war to the Soviet Union and the new state of Yugoslavia.

In practice, victory found the Soviet Armed Forces in occupation of large tracts of eastern and central Europe, allowing the Soviet government to take important military and political decisions on the future security of the Soviet heartland (which many people in the West understood) but also to decide unilaterally what kind of régimes should take power in the countries within the Soviet sphere. Indeed, the Soviet victories presented their leaders with political and ideological dilemmas. The Soviet leadership could have regarded them as removing the danger of aggression and lawlessness in international relations, and offering the opportunity to concentrate on the rehabilitation of war-torn Russia and the rebuilding of the Soviet economy. On the other hand, the Soviet leaders could interpret their position of tremendous strength as proof that the doctrines of Marxism-Leninism on world revolution were correct, that the Soviet army paved the way for the expansion of Communism throughout Europe, and that to shrink from turning Lenin's prophecies into history was little short of treachery.

The essential decisions were Stalin's: his was the sole and supreme authority in foreign and military policy-making, as well as in domestic, state security, ideological and economic matters. Even before the end of the war, Stalin's mind seems to have been made up. Soviet security certainly must be achieved; but his sense of ideological mission must also be upheld: the 'revolutionary situation' in Europe must be exploited. This meant, in practice, the establishment of totally loyal communist-governed states in all the countries reached by the Soviet army during the war, a process which would both protect the security of the Soviet Union and open the door to the expansion of communism as an ideology into Eastern Europe and beyond. How could this policy be achieved most successfully for the Soviet Union without taking unnecessary risks?

Much valuable and revealing research and analysis work has been done on Stalin's personality, background, his capacity to terrorise his colleagues, and his utter ruthlessness, based partly on his obsession with 'conspiracy theory' assessments of personalities and events.[7] One aspect of his thinking was undoubtedly his belief that the most effective way of imposing his will on a foreign country was through the use of military and state-security power: witness his famous letter to Marshal Tito on behalf of the Central Committee of the Soviet Communist Party in 1948:

> *The reason why there is now no Communist government in Paris or Rome is because in the circumstances of 1945 the Soviet Army was not able to reach French or Italian soil.*[8]

Stalin was not, however, reckless in action on foreign affairs. In the immediate post-war years he was conscious of the enormous military, political and economic power of the United States, especially its unilateral possession of the atomic bomb with operational experience of using it: though Stalin also knew that his scientists were working on the creation of a similar weapon for the Soviet Union.

It is against this background that Soviet policy towards Eastern Europe in the post-war period should be seen. The lynch-pin of this policy was the decision to impose communist or communist-dominated régimes on as many of the East European countries as possible, and Soviet attention was, not unnaturally, focused on Poland. Russia and Poland had an unhappy record of conflict. The flat plains of central Poland led directly, and without natural defences, to the flat plains of western Russia. But Poland was an Ally: the first country to be attacked militarily by Hitler, and in whose defence Britain and France had declared war on Germany in 1939. Many Poles had fought bravely in the Red Army after 1941: and the British had a special feeling of respect and admiration for the Poles, whose airmen had helped to defend London in 1940, whose troops had fought in North Africa, Italy and north-west Europe, and whose navy had played a major role in the war at sea. With the Americans sharing these views, the Russians had to move cautiously in imposing their will on Poland, at least in the initial stages of the process.

So important was the future relationship with Poland to Stalin that he debated the issue with the Polish Premier, General Sikorski, in Moscow in December 1941 when the Germans were at the gates of his capital.[9] As already noted, a pro-Soviet Communist Committee was set up by the Russians in the town of Lublin in July 1944, with powers to govern Polish territory liberated by the Russians. On 31 December 1944 the Lublin Committee declared itself to be the legal government of Poland, and on 5 January 1945 was so accepted by the Soviet government although the other Allies recognised the exiled government based in London. A month later, however, at the Yalta Conference in the Crimea, it was agreed by Stalin, Roosevelt and Churchill that the Lublin government 'should be reorganised on a broader democratic basis with the inclusion of democratic leaders from Poland itself and from Poles abroad'.[10] It seemed in the West that a three-Power agreement had been reached which would satisfy all parties.

The Yalta Conference, however, was hardly over before it became clear that the Soviet idea of reorganising the Lublin government on a broader democratic basis differed from that held by Britain and America. The Western Powers were thinking in terms of a new Polish government embracing all elements not hostile to Russia; the Russians of a slightly expanded Lublin government whose first priority would be obedience to the Soviet Union. Within a month of the Yalta agreement's signature, the Soviet authorities arrested the main leaders of the Polish home-based resistance movement, an act which ensured that they could not take part in the formation of a new government. They were later tried and imprisoned on charges of 'sabotaging the communications of the Red Army', and their leader, General Okulicki, died in prison.

In the Coalition government which was formed in Warsaw on 23 June 1945 from elements of the London and Lublin authorities, the Polish Communists secured the key Ministries of Public Security, Defence and Information. In May 1946, despite protests from the Western Powers based on the Yalta agreement, the Polish 'Workers' (Communist) Party set about destroying all other political parties, particularly the Peasant and Socialist parties. In February 1947, after a communist-organised general election, the Peasant Party was expelled from the Coalition government, and many of its prominent figures arrested. The Party's leader, Stanislaw Mikolajczyk, who had returned to Poland from London to try to make the Yalta agreement work, fled to the West, and the Party disintegrated. In March 1948 the Socialist Party agreed to merge with the Workers' Party, and disappeared as an independent political entity. There followed a big purge of Army officers who had served in the West, and by 1949 all non-Communist political activity in Poland had ceased. Poland became *de facto* a one-party state within the Soviet orbit.

For the reasons already suggested, Poland was to Stalin and the Soviet government a special case, and some care was exercised to allay certain Polish sensitivities: for example, the retention of traditional Polish military uniforms in the armed forces and the absence of a major ideological campaign against the Roman Catholic Church of which a huge majority of the people were devout members. However, the process of integrating other countries of Eastern Europe moved more speedily, especially in the smaller 'ex-enemy' states— first Romania and Bulgaria, then Hungary.

The Romanian Government had broken with Germany on 23 August 1944. The Yalta Conference agreed on 11 February 1945 that the three Allies would:

> act in concert in assisting the peoples liberated from the dominion of Nazi Germany and the peoples of the former Axis satellite states in Europe to create democratic institutions of their own choice.[11]

Sixteen days later, on 27 February 1945, the Soviet Deputy Foreign Minister (and former Stalinist purge judge), Andrei Vyshinski, arrived in Bucharest and, without informing his allies, gave the King an ultimatum to form a new government immediately according to a list of personalities approved by Moscow. On 6 March such a government

240

of Communists was indeed formed. In November 1946, a general election was held in which only the Communist-dominated coalition was allowed to put forward candidates, and the result was a foregone conclusion. The Romanian Peasant Party ceased to exist on 30 January 1947, and its leader was imprisoned. Romania officially became a 'People's Democracy' under a constitution modelled on that of the Soviet Union, on 13 April 1948.

The story in Bulgaria was similar. After the unopposed occupation of the country by the Red Army in September 1944, Bulgaria was governed by a coalition of Communists, Peasant and Republican Parties, with the former holding the key Ministry of the Interior. The Communist Party began their campaign against the other Parties early in 1945, first against the Peasant Party and later the Socialists, who refused to enter a totally Communist-run administration in December 1945. By this time, the internationally-famous Communist leader and former Head of the Comintern, Georgi Dimitrov, had arrived on Soviet orders to take over the Premiership. Under his direction the campaign intensified; the first target was the Bulgarian Army, many of whose senior officers had served in the resistance movement or commanded Bulgarian troops fighting alongside the Red Army in the Third Ukrainian Front. Most of these officers were dismissed and imprisoned. A general election was held on 27 October 1946, in which the Peasant Party recorded surprisingly good results, under the courageous leadership of Nikola Petkov, a staunch anti-Nazi during the war. In June 1947, Petkov was arrested and condemned to death in a farcical trial in which prosecution witnesses contradicted each other and the prepared indictment. Petkov was executed on 23 September 1947. The other political Parties were disbanded, and Bulgaria too became a 'People's Democracy' in 1948.

The turn of the third 'ex-enemy' country, Hungary, came a little later, delayed, perhaps, by Moscow's need to consolidate its gains further east, and the relative proximity of the country to the Western Allies in Austria. Although under Soviet military occupation, Hungary enjoyed the privilege of a free election in November 1945, in which the Communist Party polled only 17 per cent of the votes cast. The leader of the Smallholders' (Peasants) Party, Ferenc Nagy, formed a government which, however, was unacceptable to the Soviet Union. In the course of the next year the Hungarian Communist Party worked subversively but successfully to reduce the Smallholders' majority in Parliament: its Secretary-General, Bela Kovacs, was arrested in February 1947, and the party began to disintegrate. The Communists organised another election in 1948, which they won, according to their own statistics, by disqualifying half-a-million voters.[12] The Communists then formed their one-Party government, accepted the Stalin constitution, and Hungary became a 'People's Democracy' also in the same year.

Another country in central Europe which had been liberated by the Soviet Army in 1945 was Czechoslovakia. Until 1948, the Soviet Union treated Czechoslovakia in a different and more lenient way compared with its eastern neighbours. This may have been partly due to the widespread admiration of the Czech and Slovak peoples for the Russian people and the Soviet war effort: Czechoslovak troops fought in the Red Army and in the West, and an uprising against the Germans occurred in Slovakia in October 1944. The wartime London-based government under President Benes returned to Prague in 1945, and ruled the country as a genuine coalition administration. Benes surrendered Czechoslovakia's most eastern province, Ruthenia, to the Soviet Union in 1945, and the Soviet Army left the country shortly afterwards. By 1948, however, the virtually complete imposition of Stalinist rule on the other countries within the Soviet sphere—though this concept was never formally agreed by international treaty—and the growing tension between Moscow and Belgrade (see below) led the Soviet Union to bring Czechoslovakia into the same camp. Following a minor Parliamentary dispute in Prague, the Czechoslovak Communist Party organised a coup d'état intended to bring them to power. President Benes was threatened with civil war if he did not accede to the appointment of a Communist-led government: he capitulated on 25 February, resigned on 13 May, and Klement Gottwald, the Communist leader, took over the government of the country immediately. Czechoslovakia became a 'People's Democracy', and, as an epilogue to Czechoslovakia's attempt to maintain democracy, the man who had worked so hard for compromise all his political life, Eduard Benes, died on 3 September 1948.[13]

Potentially the most dangerous episode in Stalin's pursuit of his goals in East and Central Europe at this time was the dispute between the Soviet Union and Marshal Tito's Yugoslavia which came out into the open in 1948 with the expulsion of Yugoslavia from the Cominform, the Soviet-dominated international grouping of communist states formed in the previous year. The heart of the clash was partly the deeply-rooted reluctance of the South Slavs to subordinate their policies and priorities to any foreign power—even to the leader of world communism, the Soviet Union, particularly since most of the fighting in German and Italian-occupied Yugoslavia had been carried out by the Yugoslavs themselves, with Soviet participation only in the capture of Belgrade in October 1944. Yet the Russians expected Tito to accept all Soviet decisions and demands without question or hesitation, including unrestricted access to Yugoslav intelligence resources, authority to recruit Soviet agents among the local population, and freedom of movement for Soviet government officials throughout the country. When these and other economic and commercial demands were rejected in Belgrade, Stalin decided to bring about Yugoslavia's submission by threats if arguments failed.[14] The Soviet Union therefore rushed into an ill-considered attempt to browbeat the Yugoslav leadership into acceptance of satellite status. The Yugoslavs, initially bewildered by Stalin's action, nevertheless stood firm, and eventually won recognition of their right to independence—though not until after Stalin's death in 1953.

There remained one other country of Eastern Europe which had been engaged in hostilities against the Soviet Union in the period 1939-44, but which was treated very differently from the other 'ex-enemy' states: Finland. Although the Armistice terms of 1944 and the subsequent Peace Treaty of February 1947 imposed severe conditions on Finland in economic, foreign affairs and defence matters, as did the Soviet-Finnish Treaty of Friendship, Co-operation and Mutual Assistance of 6 April 1948, the Soviet government never attempted to impose a communist government on Finland. Nor did Moscow threaten reprisals when a coalition government which came to power in Helsinki in 1945 forced the resignation of the Communist Minister of the Interior, Yrjo Leino, after a Parliamentary vote of censure on him in May 1948. No action was taken by Moscow when a Social-Democrat-led government succeeded the Coalition in 1948, and was followed by the election of a joint Agrarian and Social Democrat administration in 1951.

It is tempting to speculate that the Soviet Union did not regard Finland, even the 'old enemy', as a strategic and military danger to Soviet security; and that if Finland was left to its own devices, its particularly close relationship with the Scandinavian countries, especially Sweden, could be encouraged in ways from which the Soviet Union might benefit economically and industrially. There are other factors which may have influenced Soviet decision-making: Finland's refusal to participate in the attack on Leningrad in 1941-42, and her *volte-face* from an anti-Soviet stance to the acceptable policies of the 'Paasikivi-Kekkonen Line' in the post-war years. For whatever reason, Finland emerged after a particularly difficult war without the Stalinist legacy of the other East European countries, and enjoyed post-war a period of self-rule and prosperity which compared favourably with most of its eastern neighbours.[15]

Conclusions

There can be little doubt of the genuine nature of the tremendous admiration felt and expressed by the overwhelming majority of the people of Britain for the sacrifices, the losses and the final victory of the Soviet people and their Armed Forces in the war on the Eastern Front from 1941 to 1945. A recently-published British study of these campaigns revealed, on the basis of Soviet analytical work, that in the operations covered in this presentation in 1944-45, 2,500,000 of the Soviet armed forces had been killed or were missing.[16] From the battle of Kursk in the summer of 1943 onwards, the strategic and professional military leadership of the Soviet Forces had been welded into a pattern of the highest quality, from the *Stavka* at the top, through the General Staff, the field and Front commanders and their staffs to the soldiers in the firing line, the airmen operating over the battle-field, and the sailors on the seas and on the coasts. The Soviet government had certainly developed and maintained in action in the most difficult circumstances a military machine which won the war in the east and contributed massively to the common victory over the aggressor.

Once victory had been achieved, the Soviet Government found itself in physical occupation of large areas of eastern and central Europe on whose future fundamental decisions had to be made. Certainly military and strategic factors were very high in their priorities, and every plan listed the need to protect the frontiers of the expanded Soviet state as its most important task. Some military thinking was also directed towards the possibilities of extending these frontiers and the offensive military actions which this might entail.[17] Then there were considerations of Russian and Soviet patriotism: should not the victory won entitle the state not only to assume 'Super-Power' status in the world, but also to incorporate foreign lands and economic resources into the Soviet Union as of right: goals which leaders of the country's Imperial past might have supported?

Certainly the ideological imperative of Marxism-Leninism demanded the use of Soviet power as created by the victory in Europe and in the Pacific in order to push ahead with the pursuit of classical communist goals, including the exploitation of a re-born 'revolutionary situation' in Europe to set up loyal and obedient communist régimes in the liberated areas and beyond. The evidence of this paper appears to suggest that elements of all these motives and intentions were present in Stalin's mind as he surveyed the fruits of victory in 1945. His instinctive urge seems to have been to select the straightforward military solution in order to change the situation in his favour wherever this could be used: this is what occurred in Poland, Romania, Bulgaria, Hungary, and later in Czechoslovakia. It failed in Yugoslavia, and was not pursued in Finland. Perhaps one realistic answer to this question is that Stalin was determined to impose absolute controls, political, military and economic, over the countries in Eastern and Central Europe which might, in other circumstances, have posed a threat to Soviet power: this would hardly be applicable to Finland. This aim, in the Soviet view, may have been achieved by 1948, after which a period of consolidation may have been planned. If thoughts of further expansion in Europe did occur to Stalin in the following years, the return of American power to the continent in the shape of the Marshall Plan and then NATO must, historically speaking, have provided an essential and effective deterrent to any significant programme of future action along these lines.

Discussion

Dr Hulas considered that the threat posed to the Soviet Union by Central Europe was exaggerated by Stalin, because of his paranoia. *Dr Correlli Barnett* disagreed, however: Stalin's view of a Central European threat was not unreasonable in view of events in the late 1930s, and the German advance had showed how vulnerable the area could be. *Professor Dilks* agreed: the change in the post-war period was that the weight on the 'threatening seesaw' belonged to the Soviet Union rather than Germany.

Professor Riste wondered why the Soviet Union did not fear and upsurge of revanchism or revolution in Finland, as an ally of Germany. He attributed this to the complete political *volte-face* in Find after the armistice, when Finns took a realistic view and realised they had to cooperate with the Soviet Union if they wished to retain their independence; *Professor Erickson* noted that Finland had not pushed its luck by advancing east when it could have done. *Mr Cviic* referred to Stalin's very sophisticated and rally underestimated understanding of national sensitivities and historical patterns; a point supported by *Sir D Hunt*, who reminded the Conference of Stalin's former role as Commissar for Nationalities.

Discussing the Slovak rising, *Professor Erickson* agreed that the rising of 1944 has been neglected by historians, but warned against any comparison with the Warsaw rising. The Russians had done their best to help the Slovaks, and were appalled at subsequent German reprisals: the episode had an important impact on Czech armies in the East.

Notes and References

1 For a portrait of Stalin, politically and personally, see Colonel-General D A Volkogonov, *Triumph i Tragedia* (Triumph and Tragedy), (Moscow, 1989), especially Book II, part 2.

2 For the military strengths of the opposing armies, see *50 let Vo-oruzhennykh Sil SSSR'* (Fifty Years of the Armed Forces of the USSR), (Moscow, 1968, Military Publishing House). See also Colonel Vladimir Yeliseyev: 'The Liberation of Belorussia', in *Military News Bulletin*, Moscow, No 5, May 1994.

3 Tomas Ries: *Cold War*, (Brassey's Defence Publishers, 1988), pp 149-150.

4 Yeliseyev, op cit, see also *Krasnaya Zvezda*, 1 June 1994, p 2.

5 Ries, op cit, pp 150-158.

6 Paul Winterton: *Inquest on an Ally* (The Cresset Press, London, 1948), p 213..

7 Volkogonov, op cit, Book II, part 2, passim.

8 Royal Institute of International Affairs: *The Soviet-Yugoslav Dispute* (1949) and *Documents, 1947-48* (1952).

9 John Erickson: *The Road to Stalingrad* (Weidenfeld and Nicolson, London, 1975), pp 294-96.

10 Text of the Yalta Agreement, 11 February 1945.

[11] Ibid.

[12] Winterton, op cit, p 66, quoting the Hungarian Premier Dinnyes' statement at a press conference.

[13] Hugh Seton-Watson, *From Lenin to Malenkov: the History of World Communism* (Frederick A Praeger, New York, 1966), pp 258-9.

[14] Royal Institute of International Affairs, *Documents 1947-48* and *1949-50*. See also *The Soviet-Yugoslav dispute, op cit,* and also Vladimir Dedijer, *Tito Speaks* (Belgrade, 1953).

[15] Seton-Watson, op cit, pp 301-3.

[16] John Erickson and David Dilks (eds), *Barbarossa* (Edinburgh University Press, 1994), pp 260-62.

[17] Colonel-General I S Glebov, 'Intrigi v General'nom Shtabe' (Intrigue in the General Staff), *Military-Historical Journal*, November 1993, p 38 (Moscow).

Index

Norway *cont.*
　　secret military
　　organisation 148, 152
　　Spitsbergen 152

Oder-Neisse Line *see* Poland
Overlord, Operation 1, 52
　　D-Day 105
　　'Neptune' 101-2, 105

Patch, Gen A M 7, 102
Patton, Gen G S 6-7, 102
Pauker, A 209-10, 217-19
Percentage agreement 90, 162-
　　8, 171-2, 204, 228
Persia 82, 87, 91
Pétain, Marshal P 101, 103,
　　105
Pierlot, H 120-1, 126
Poland 57, 59-60, 66-9, 78-9,
　　91-2, 96, 163-4, 169-70, 182-
　　203
　　armed forces 49, 163,
　　186-7
　　church 195
　　Cttee of National
　　Liberation (Lublin
　　Cttee) 66-7, 163, 194,
　　239-40
　　communists 188, 193,
　　201, 240
　　Curzon line/E frontier 58,
　　63, 67, 163, 183, 199
　　elections 195
　　expulsion of Germans 69
　　government in London
　　66-67, 183-4, 196, 239
　　Home Army (AK) 186,
　　188
　　Jews 196, 198-9
　　Kielce 199
　　National Armed Forces
　　(NSZ) 188
　　Oder-Neisse Line/W
　　frontier 58, 68, 92-5,
　　183, 199-200
　　Peasant Party 58, 195,
　　240
　　Provisional Govt of
　　National Unity 184, 194,
　　240
　　Polish-Soviet Treaty 194
　　security services 198-9

Ukrainian Insurrectionary
　　Army 185-6
Warsaw rising 61, 85,
　　184-5, 187-8, 233
Potsdam Conference 55-6, 69,
　　71, 77-98, 162, 196

Radescu, Gen N 207-9. 211
Refugees 70
Remagen 8, 10
Reparations 56, 71, 91, 180
Rhine
　　crossings 3, 6, 8, 12, 15
　　offensive 3
　　strategy 4
Ribbentrop-Molotov Pact 1939
　　58, 67
Roey, Cardinal van 122, 129,
　　134
Rokossovski, Marshal K 15-
　　30, 232-4, 236
Rome *see* Italy
Romania 58, 78, 91, 164-6,
　　204-20, 240
　　ACC 204, 211, 213
　　armistice 205-7
　　communists 205-7, 210,
　　217
　　coup d'état 234
　　Groza govt 213-14
　　monarchy 208, 211, 213
　　Radescu govt 207-13
　　security services 209,
　　213-14
Romer, T 163, 172
Roosevelt, FDR 10, 43, 55-
　　62, 64, 78-98, 164-5
　　death 81
　　de Gaulle 103
　　Italy 110
Runstedt, F-M G von 6, 8,
　　124
Russian revolution 3

Saar 7
Sanatescu 206, 208
San Francisco, Conference
　　1945 78
Sargent, Sir O G 92, 153
Schermerhorn, W 139, 143
Serbia 221, 228
　　Chetniks 221, 224
Sforza, C 110, 113

250

Printed in the United Kingdom for HMSO
Dd302105 4/96 C15 G3397 10170